# *USS* Pampanito

# USS Pampanito

*Killer-Angel*

GREGORY F. MICHNO

University of Oklahoma Press
Norman

## ALSO BY GREGORY F. MICHNO

*The Mystery of E Troop: Custer's Gray Horse Company at the Little Bighorn*
(Missoula, Mont., 1994)
*Lakota Noon: The Indian Narrative of Custer's Defeat* (Missoula, Mont., 1997)

Published with the assistance of the National Endowment for the Humanities, a federal agency which supports the study of such fields as history, philosophy, literature, and language.

**Library of Congress Cataloging-in-Publication Data**

Michno, Gregory, 1948–
    USS Pampanito : killer-angel / by Gregory F. Michno.
      p.    cm.
    Includes bibliographical references.
    ISBN 0–8061–3205–1 (cl. : alk. paper)
    1. World War, 1939–1945—Naval operations—Submarine.  2. World War,
1939–1945—Naval operations, American.  I. Title.
D783.5.P4M53  1999
940.54′51—dc21                                    99–30578
                                                      CIP

Text design by Gail Carter

The paper in this book meets the guidelines for permanence and durability of the Committee on Production Guidelines for Book Longevity of the Council on Library Resources, Inc. ∞

1  2  3  4  5  6  7  8  9  10

*For my father . . . and all the submariners still on patrol.*
*Sailor, rest your oar.*

# Contents

# *Illustrations*

## MAPS

# *Preface*

A large number of submarine stories have appeared since the end of World War II. Among them have been physical and operational descriptions, general studies of strategy and tactics, and exploits of individual submarines. The great majority of these books were written by commanders of the boats or upper-echelon officers. Generally, the commanders/authors were rightly proud of their accomplishments, and the stories of their submarines were expressed in superlatives. Each book seemed to compete with its predecessor for the top of the showcase.

The story of *Silversides* was one of the first of its genre. *Trigger* was one of the most long-lived and highest-scoring boats. *Wahoo* was America's most famous submarine. *Tang* sank the most ships on one patrol. *Tautog* sank the most ships. *Jack* was a premier tanker killer. *Flasher* sank the most tonnage. *Archerfish* sank the most tonnage on one patrol. *Batfish* sank the most Japanese submarines. *Harder* sank the most Japanese destroyers. *Barb* was the most tactically revolutionary and had the best single patrol. *Halibut* took the worst beating. Other prominent boats included *Rasher, Bowfin, Sculpin, Drum, Seawolf,* and on and on. They were all the most, best, and greatest in their own unique way.

What other possible superlatives can we offer with a history of the USS *Pampanito?* Surprisingly, there is one category in which *Pampanito* was unexcelled; she rescued more men at sea than any other American submarine. Perhaps more importantly in the long run, however, is the methodology and focus of the story. *Pampanito*'s chronicle is not told by the captain or the executive officer. Besides one taped interview with a commanding officer and a few junior officers' reminiscences, the great majority of recollections come directly from the enlisted men.

We will not dwell on the skipper in action, eye pressed against the periscope, beads of sweat forming on his brow and dripping, regular as a metronome, to the conning tower deck. The story is about the average seamen, the electricians, torpedomen, or motor machinists, and their experiences and thoughts about the men who led them, about their boat, their families, the war, and its impact on their lives. It is a story not always painted in romantic brush strokes, and as such, it parts ways with the majority of its predecessors. The chronicle is told by the average submariner with nothing to gain, lose, prove, or protect with the telling. The *Pampanito* story is the rule, not the exception.

My interest in submarines has been long-standing. My father served aboard *Pampanito* as a motor machinist's mate. As a child, I was often the unwilling beneficiary of his numerous sea tales—tales that seemed to grow after successive shots and beers. Occasionally he would haul me along with him on a visit to his old stomping grounds at the sub bases in Portsmouth, New Hampshire, or New London, Connecticut. He would show me around an old fleet boat and explain how a valve, gauge, or other piece of equipment worked.

In 1995, I visited the *Pampanito* with my own son. It is tied up at San Francisco's Fisherman's Wharf as a national historical landmark. As our footsteps echoed on the deck and we touched the cold metal pipes, gauges, and levers, my thoughts could not help but turn to the past.

A half-century earlier, she was alive with the sounds, sights, and smells of seventy or more men, fighting, living, and dying for a cause that today seems rather trite and misplaced in our nation's short collective memory. She is just a cold steel boat bobbing in a cold-water bay. But there is a story there. A story that can be a more fitting memorial to the boat and the men who served aboard her. And of my father, well, it turned out that he was not just telling me tall tales. I only wish that I had paid more attention when I had the chance.

# *Acknowledgments*

A great number of people have helped me with this project. I would like to thank my wife, Susan, for manuscript corrections and suggestions; the late Russ Booth of the National Maritime Museum in San Francisco for many of the crew's addresses; John D. Alden, submariner and author, for his constructive critique of the manuscript; Dr. Carl Boyd for his laudatory comments and suggestions; Kathleen Lloyd at the National Archives for the boat's muster rolls, patrol reports, and officer biographies; Katharine Swift, who worked in intelligence and code-breaking during World War II, for her sleuthing through today's declassified ULTRA and radio intelligence archives; John Taylor at the National Archives for helping me find the appropriate records groups; Clay and Joan Blair for advice and permission to use their taped interviews; and Jennifer King of the University of Wyoming's American Heritage Center for arranging receipt of those tapes. *Return from the River Kwai*, by Joan and Clay Blair, was very useful in reconstructing the stories of the Australian and British prisoners of war.

I would like to thank the Australian POWs who answered my inquiries and sent me letters or audio tapes of their experiences: Roy Cornford, Cliff Farlow, Bob Farrands, J. R. Hocking, Harold Martin, Ken Williams, and Don Wall.

Most of all I owe a debt of gratitude to the enlisted men and officers who shared their most intimate experiences with me. The contributors were, in alphabetical order, Norman Arcement, Ralph Attaway, Robert Bennett, Daniel Bialko, Jacques Bouchard, Duncan Brown, Hubert Brown, William Bruckart, Clarence Carmody, Harold Chinn, Fred Clarke, Walter Cordon, George Debo, Joseph Eichner, Donald Ferguson, William Grady, Ona Hawkins, Gordon Hopper, Frank Lederer, Renard Lombardi, Walter Madison, Lloyd MacVane, Clyde Markham, William McClaskey, William McCollum, Rob Roy McGregor, Charles McGuire, Frank Michno, George Moffett, Lawrence Noker, Paul Pappas, Walter Richter, Arnold Schade, Richard Sherlock, Wendell Smith, Edmund Stockslader, Spencer Stimler, Ted Swain, Albert Van Atta, Roger Walters, Earl Watkins, Clarence Williams, and Woodrow Weaver.

I have annotated my sources with the exception of the above submarine veterans. Their appearance, virtually on every page, dictated confining citations of their contributions to the bibliography.

I would like to thank all the former crew members that shared with me their pictures, mementos, and memories, and I sincerely apologize to any of them that I might have failed to list. I thank them for their written recollections, audio and video tapes, countless phone calls and letters. I thank them for letting me visit them with my tape recorder, notes, and endless questions. The anecdotes by and about fellow shipmates were told in a friendly spirit, with the intent of presenting the truth as they remembered it. On that rare occasion when it was requested that I not use a particular story, I have honored that request.

There were some who were unable to participate. Some were reluctant to share their personal experiences with a stranger, and a nonsubmariner at that. Others were unable to help simply because the physical and mental obstacles fifty years after the fact were just too difficult to overcome. Yet the spirit was still there. One veteran responded that he was unable to write very well. He was not in good shape. In fact, he was in a wheelchair. But when the need arose, he wrote, "I can still go like hell!" He asked me to please come over and talk to him.

This simple eloquence strikes a chord. We must get these old submariners' stories. They are too precious to let slide into oblivion after the last of them passes along on final patrol.

*USS* Pampanito

## CHAPTER ONE

# Construction and Launching

The Piscataqua River has its headwaters in the verdant foothills of New Hampshire's White Mountains. It is not a long river, as rivers go. Yet what it lacks in length, it makes up for in obstinacy, especially near its estuary, where it flows into the Atlantic. Along the tortuous lower course its swift and unpredictable currents could run from seven to eight knots on flood tide and ten to twelve knots on the ebb.[1]

On the south bank Portsmouth had grown, a naval port since Revolutionary days. It was there John Paul Jones claimed to be the first captain to hoist our new national emblem over a ship-of-war, and perhaps there he made his famous statement that he relished a fast ship, for he intended to place himself "in harm's way." The area has always been tied to the sea, from colonial commerce to modern war. On the north bank, in Kittery Point, Maine, across the creaky Memorial Drawbridge from Portsmouth, the naval shipyard took root.[2]

The nation's first government-built submarine was launched there in 1917. In the 1930s Portsmouth was the premier submarine yard in the country. Yet Portsmouth, her backup yards at Mare Island, California, and later the Cramp Shipbuilding Company of Philadelphia were hard pressed to meet the submarine construction necessary in a world at war. To stimulate design and construction competition, the government split annual contract awards with private shipyards, primarily the Electric Boat

Company of Groton, Connecticut, and its backup yard at Manitowoc, Wisconsin.[3]

The sailors arriving at Portsmouth during the spring of 1943 were treated to the spectacle of a shipyard running at full capacity. Twenty thousand employees worked around the clock on three shifts, seven days a week. The sounds of hammering, clanging steel, and shouting men and the sights of trucks, cranes, smoke, and the nighttime glow of welding torches left an impression that few would forget.

Taking shape in the ways and basins were several submarines in a long line of boats being laid down in near-alphabetical order at shipyards across the land. There were hull numbers 382, 383, and 384: *Picuda, Pampanito,* and *Parche,* the first two with their keels laid the same day of 15 March. The Navy Department wanted names of fighting game fish for its new undersea men-of-war, but names were limited, and the Bureau of Fisheries provided scores of names of less belligerent denizens of the deep.[4]

What is a pampanito? Technically it is *Tranchinotus rhodopus,* belonging to the group Pampanos and the family Carangidae. The word *pampanito* is Spanish, meaning a small species of pampano. The fish reaches a length of fifteen inches and inhabits the Pacific coast from the Gulf of California to Colombia, South America. It is a rapid swimmer, colored brown or black on top and silver below, with four or five black vertical crossbars. The fins range from bright yellow to maroon. Did it fight? Actually it was rather mild-mannered. Time would tell how its steel namesake would behave.

At the submarine base the sailors became students. A typical day consisted of four hours in the classroom and four hours of instruction on the boats. They spent exhausting days tearing down and putting together almost every piece of equipment on board. They dismantled and rebuilt the diesels, rewound motors and generators, charged and discharged batteries, tore apart torpedoes, studied them, and put them back together. Every Monday, exams were given, and anyone failing two of them was washed out and quietly returned to the surface fleet. The crowning test came when they were required to strap on a Momsen lung and ascend an escape rope to a buoy in a hundred-foot tower filled with 240,000 gallons of water. It was no lark. Two students had been killed there in the early 1930s, and both novice and instructor took the training very seriously.

Most succeeded, even though with a fair amount of trepidation and sweat. After twelve weeks the fit, the intelligent, and the perseverant were turned into the men necessary to run the subs.[5]

Some of the men arriving at Portsmouth that summer were not new to the navy. The man selected to be *Pampanito*'s executive officer was Lieutenant Commander Paul E. Summers. He was born in Lexington, Tennessee, on 4 September 1913, the middle child in a family of six boys and one girl. In 1932, Summers was appointed to the U.S. Naval Academy. He thought his small country-school background was a disadvantage in competing with the more cosmopolitan, liberal education of the city boys, and he had to take a correspondence course in math to help him pass the entrance exam.

"I had to work extra hard just to stay even," he said.

Summers played one year of football and four years of baseball, much of it as a starting pitcher, at the academy. He liked math, physics, and engineering but struggled with the subjects. He graduated in 1936, "somewhere below the middle of the class." While at the academy he once received a letter addressed to "Mechanical Pete" Summers. Back in Tennessee, he could always be found working on his old 1917 Ford, and his buddies gave him the nickname. His roommates saw the letter and also began calling him "Pete." Years later he would forever be informally known as "Pete" to his submarine crews.[6]

The cool sea breezes and sunny weather in Portsmouth in June of 1943 were a balm to Summers's taut nerves. In 1936 he had been assigned to the cruiser USS *Chicago* (CA 29), but life on a surface ship soon lost its glamour. Summers thought about going to aviation school, but his mother did not want him to, because she thought it was too dangerous. Instead, in 1939 he attended submarine school, and in 1940 he was assigned to USS *Stingray* (SS 186) as a lieutenant, junior grade.

The boat was based at Cavite Navy Yard in Manila Bay when the Japanese attacked on 8 December 1941. *Stingray* avoided the bombs that damaged *Seadragon* (SS 194) and destroyed *Sealion* (SS 195). On her first patrol, *Stingray* luckily swam right into the Japanese invasion force steaming into Lingayen Gulf, Luzon. However, with the boat plagued by leaks that were sending air bubbles to the surface, skipper Raymond S. Lamb would not attack. Summers watched Lamb, waiting for some

aggressive maneuvering, but, said Pete, "He sat there and he froze."
*Stingray* headed away from the enemy. The succeeding days were carbon
copies, with halfhearted approaches and no attacks. They headed back to
Manila.

Once safely in port, Summers and the executive officer, Hank Sturr,
went to see Captain John Wilkes and told him they were not going to sea
with Lamb anymore. The boat was inspected, but no serious problems
were found. Lamb was removed from command, and Raymond J. "Bud"
Moore took over.[7]

The change of skippers did not change *Stingray*'s luck a great deal.
During the next three patrols she sank only two ships and was almost lost
herself during a crash dive. Summers took credit for their salvation. As
*Stingray* plunged below with locked bow planes, he got the crew to blow
bow buoyancy and called for all back emergency. "That's the only thing
that saved us," he contended.

*Stingray*'s fifth patrol was between Truk and Bougainville. Again, Moore
had trouble, making five attacks but damaging only one freighter.
Summers manned the periscope. When they finally hit a ship, he wanted
to watch it go under, but Moore wouldn't let him, and Summers fumed.
He thought he heard the ship breaking up but was not allowed to confirm
the sinking. They never got credit for it. Moore, too, was relieved of
command, "at my own request," he explained.[8]

*Stingray*'s next skipper was Otis J. Earle, but it was the same story. He
told Summers that he was going to do better than Dudley W. "Mush"
Morton, the famous skipper of *Wahoo* (SS 238). But, said Summers in what
was becoming a familiar litany, "He got scared." Earle also let Summers
handle some attacks. Off the China coast they made a night surface attack.
Earle worried that they were getting in too close, but Summers held on,
and on 2 May 1943, *Stingray* finally sank and damaged two more ships.
Still, Summers said, Earle was the "scaredest man I've ever seen, except
for Ray Lamb." After four patrols, Earle was relieved of command.[9]

Summers had now made seven war patrols. Back in Pearl Harbor he
went to see Rear Admiral Charles A. Lockwood, Jr., commander of submarines, Pacific Fleet (ComSubPac), and "Uncle Charlie" gave him a
vacation. Summers headed for the States to be the exec for a new
submarine then being built, USS *Pampanito*.

In Portsmouth in June 1943 the cool Atlantic wind was a welcome change from the tropics, the variation of scenery was pleasant, and the routine was a little more relaxing. Circumstances boded well for Summers's future.

Enlisted men as well as officers were assembling in Portsmouth. Born on Armistice Day, 1919, Charles A. McGuire, Jr., enlisted in the navy at age eighteen. The Depression had been life's one all-encompassing reality, and when Charlie finished high school in Philadelphia, Pennsylvania, the twenty-one dollars per month starting pay in the navy was quite a draw. "It was more than I could get stealing or raising on my own," he said.

Over the next few years, Charlie saw more of the world than he could ever have imagined. He served on USS *Texas* (BB 35) and USS *Omaha* (CL 4) and was in San Juan, Puerto Rico, when Japan attacked Pearl Harbor. He wanted to fight, but the submarine service was the only branch seeing action at the time. He thought he could join up. Besides, submariners got a 50 percent pay increase. Although he had it pretty good in Puerto Rico—he was a yeoman and a courier and got to wear sharkskin suits and Panama hats—his commander couldn't talk him out of the transfer. "I wanted to fight them bastard Japs," he said.

After sub school in New London, Charlie was assigned to USS *Shad* (SS 235). But this did not get him into the Pacific against the Japanese. *Shad*, part of the six-boat Submarine Squadron 50, spent all of its time in the Atlantic. Back in New London, Charlie requested transfer to a submarine that would be going to the Pacific. He had put his time in, he was now a yeoman first class, and finally, in May 1943, he got assigned to a new boat, *Pampanito.* Charlie McGuire would finally get to fight the Japanese.

Twenty-three-year-old Frank Ben Michno was from an old Polish neighborhood in Detroit, Michigan. From his family of one sister and four brothers, all of the boys would serve in the armed forces. Fresh out of Wilbur Wright Trade School, Frank joined a Citizen's Military Training Camp. After two years, much of it spent at Michigan's Camp Custer, Frank had made staff sergeant in Company I of the Fifty-Second Infantry Reserves.

All was going well, and Michno might have decided to choose a career in the Regular Army if he hadn't met up with an old high school chum who bet him he couldn't make it in the navy. They both went to the recruiting office. His buddy washed out, but Michno enlisted for a six-year hitch in the navy.

After the 1941 course at the Naval Training Station in Great Lakes, Illinois, a large number of graduates were gathered in a hall to take a "test." They were told to hold their breath. Those who lasted more than one minute were selected. "Congratulations," an officer said. "You are now all submariners."

Michno served on submarines *S-11* and *S-14*, out of Panama. Guarding the Panama Canal, patrolling the Caribbean, tropical heat, and the poor physical plants of the S-boats made almost every "pigboater" dream of a transfer to a modern fleet submarine.

Liberty in Coco Solo could be dangerous. Michno drank in a tavern where two tough-looking locals were speaking in Spanish. He never understood the language very well, but he easily heard the phrase that ended with, "Goddamn American submariners." Not about to suffer such an affront, Frank stood up and snarled, "What the hell's wrong with an American submariner?" The next thing he remembered was waking up in the alley with a headache and some serious facial cuts and bruises. Although still thankful he had his life, he knew he had to get out of Panama.

Michno had two chances to go to new construction, but other shipmates had the same wish. Both times he drew straws and lost. The war was passing him by. Finally, in the spring of 1943 his orders came to report to Portsmouth. Michno would finally get off those damned old S-boats.

The Depression years were also hard on the Weaver family, then making a go of it along the Clear Fork of the Brazos near Nugent, Texas. Woodrow Wilson Weaver, one of twelve children, was born in 1918. Somehow, amidst farm chores and almost constant uprooting for greener fields, Woodrow managed to finish high school. He wanted to go to college, but the family had no money. On the radio he heard ominous tidings about a German named Hitler who was marching his troops across Europe. There were rumors of war and talk of passing a draft law. To beat the draft, Woodrow went to Houston and in August 1940 enlisted in the navy.

After training in San Diego, California, he was shipped to Pearl Harbor aboard the aircraft carrier USS *Saratoga* (CV 3)—an anonymous individual among thousands. When given his choice of service on battleships or destroyers, he chose destroyers, and for the next three years Weaver made his home aboard USS *Anderson* (DD 411), training as a torpedoman.

In Pearl Harbor, Woodrow was shocked to see the damage done by the Japanese. USS *Nevada* (BB 36) was aground near the harbor entrance, the bottom of the capsized USS *Oklahoma* (BB 37) poked the water surface like an iron turtle, the superstructure of USS *Arizona* (BB 39) pointed like a skeleton toward the sky, and USS *West Virginia* (BB 48) and USS *California* (BB 44) sat unmoving on the harbor bottom. Debris and oil floated depressingly on the placid water.

*Anderson* was busy from that day on, participating in the Battle of the Coral Sea, the Battle of Midway, and the Battle of the Santa Cruz Islands. Weaver witnessed the sinking of three carriers, USS *Lexington* (CV 2), USS *Yorktown* (CV 5), and USS *Hornet* (CV 8). In March 1943, *Anderson* returned to the States, and Weaver went to Newport, Rhode Island, for a refresher course in torpedo school. There he learned that the submarine force needed men. He volunteered. "I wasn't trying to be a hero," he explained. "It was the pay factor which appealed to me."

Weaver took an advancement exam, passed, made torpedoman first class, finished sub school, and was assigned to *Pampanito*. He reported to Portsmouth with a chance to soon start earning that 50 percent hazardous duty pay.

All spring and summer of 1943 the crew assembled in Portsmouth. Hubert N. Brown, born in 1922 in Bluefield, West Virginia, finished Great Lakes Naval Training Center and then attended torpedo school. With this specialty he could have chosen destroyers, aircraft, or submarines. Brown passed the aptitude tests with flying colors and chose submarines. After three months at the sub school in New London, Seaman First Class Brown was assigned to new construction. He arrived at Kittery Point in September.

Twenty-two-year-old Pennsylvanian Earl Watkins worked for a company with a defense contract, so he was draft-deferred until 1942. When his deferment was up, Watkins joined the Naval Reserve. He didn't want to go into the army and take a chance on losing an arm or a leg. When the opportunity came to get into the submarine service, he took it. "I'm either going to come back in one piece, or I'm not going to come back," he reasoned. Watkins went to machinist's school and diesel school, spending one year learning the mysteries of internal combustion engines. He figured he might have a future in the automotive field after the war. From machinist's school, Earl, then a motor machinist's mate second class, went on to sub school, then to *Pampanito*.

Gordon Hopper was born in 1922 in Olney, Illinois, son of the Reverend Lewis D. Hopper and Barbara Hopper. He was attending Illinois Wesleyan University when he quit school to enlist in December 1942.

"We were saturated with patriotism and anxious to defend our country," Hopper said. "I was so impatient to get involved that I left college in my senior year and entered the navy as a seaman second." Even boot camp at Great Lakes and sub school in New London "failed to extinguish my patriotic fire and willingness to enter combat." He was shipped by troop train to Miami, Florida, then bussed to Key West. There, Seaman Second Class Hopper rode the old sub *R-10*, practicing cat-and-mouse games with destroyers. He was sent back to Portsmouth in September, "delighted" to be assigned to *Pampanito*.

Born in Parkersburg, West Virginia, in 1920, Paul Pappas, Jr., graduated from high school with thoughts of joining the Army Air Force. His father, however, who ran a photography studio, thought he'd be safer in the navy. Paul honored his father's request, enlisted in 1941, and attended boot camp in Norfolk, Virginia. He went to electrician's school and then decided on submarines. He didn't care for the formality of the Regular Navy, and besides, he wanted the extra pay. After sub school, Pappas was sent to Panama, where he served on *S-13*. Finally working his way up from low man, he got his chance for new construction and reported to *Pampanito* for duty as an electrician's mate second class in September 1943.

Albert D. Van Atta, Jr., was born in Dayton, Ohio, and was a 1939 graduate of Patterson High School. He joined the Naval Reserve in 1942 and went to boot camp in Pensacola, Florida. There, in order to cover all the angles, he volunteered for sea duty, a firefighting crew, aviation mechanics, pilot training, and submarine service. The first opening was in sub school, and he took it.

Somewhat miffed at the fiction that the submarine service was an all-volunteer operation, Van Atta was "picked" to be a quartermaster. After a refresher course, the new rates were sent either to a relief crew, to a sub already in the Pacific, or to new construction. Van Atta drew the last.

The men gathering at the shipyard in Kittery, Maine, came from various backgrounds, yet they all shared common, unifying bonds. They were adventurous youths, hankering for a little fun and perhaps a little danger. Some were there to avoid being drafted into the army. They were mostly from the middle or lower classes. The hard times of the Depression made even the penurious pay of the armed forces seem lucrative, and the increased pay of a sub sailor was a significant drawing card. As one navy lieutenant commented, "It was not much, but we were all hungry in those days."[10]

Most of the men were volunteers, but there were enough exceptions to make this a very tentative rule. Even Commander Edward L. Beach, later the author of many books, including *Run Silent, Run Deep*, had been ordered into submarines against his will. He made the best of it. According to Admiral Lockwood, submariners were all alert, friendly, agreeable, eager, intelligent, interested in their shipmates, and gregarious yet respectful of another man's privacy. They were round pegs in very closely machined round holes.[11] Above all, they were patriotic. They might have been taken against their will, and they might have signed up for the mundane reason of making a few more dollars, but they still loved their country. In a time today when such a characteristic is sometimes viewed as an unsophisticated anachronism, the sailors of 1943 were positive they were fighting for a good cause and in a "good war."[12]

As the weeks turned into months, the sections of hull, machinery, and miles of pipes, tubes, cables, and wires were beginning to resemble a submarine. *Pampanito* was a *Balao*-class boat. The older S-boats had a test-depth of 200 feet, and successively newer classes, such as *Perch, Salmon, Sargo,* and *Tambor,* had test depths of 250 feet. The *Gato* class, precursor to *Balao,* was built for 300 feet. Even so, increasingly efficient antisubmarine weapons and tactics dictated stronger construction. The *Balaos* were given seven-eighths-inch high-tensile steel hulls. They could withstand water pressure of thirty-five thousand pounds per square inch, with a test depth of 400 feet. With a 50 percent safety factor built in, a *Balao* could probably go down to 600 feet. According to submarine commander Admiral I. J. "Pete" Galantin, the depth increase from 300 feet to 400 feet was the single most important improvement made in our submarines during the war.[13]

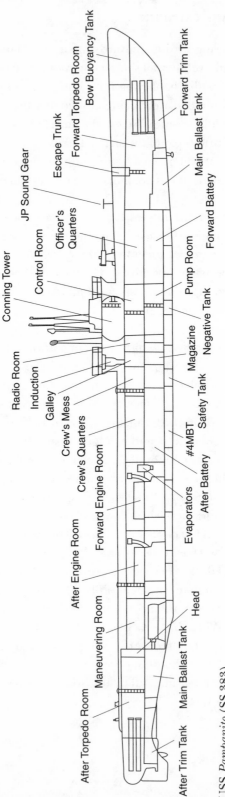

After Torpedo Room

Maneuvering Room

After Engine Room

Forward Engine Room

Crew's Quarters

Crew's Mess

Galley

Induction

Radio Room

Conning Tower

Control Room

JP Sound Gear

Escape Trunk

Forward Torpedo Room

Bow Buoyancy Tank

Forward Trim Tank

Main Ballast Tank

Forward Battery

Pump Room

Officer's Quarters

Negative Tank

Magazine

Safety Tank

#4MBT

After Battery

Evaporators

Head

Main Ballast Tank

After Trim Tank

USS *Pampanito* (SS 383)

The fleet boat was also strengthened by the shift from riveting to welding. Tests were carried out during the 1930s to determine which method was superior. Caissons built to represent pressure hull sections were lowered in 120 feet of water, and depth charges were exploded nearby. The riveted caissons popped their joints and sank, while the welded ones merely bent.[14] Welding, with no plate overlap, promised a 13 percent savings in materials, and it was an easier taught skill, which reduced labor costs. Neither method was foolproof. Rivets could pop loose, but welds could separate. Late in the war a few Liberty ships sank when their welded seams parted in heavy seas. Beginning with *Shark* and *Tarpon* in 1933, subs would have their hull sections welded.[15] Men looking out at the bustling nighttime shipyard could recall the eerie blue-white glows sparking and shimmering from scores of torches in the darkness.

Paul Pappas was awestruck by the work that went into constructing the boat, and he assumed that the designers, testers, and builders knew their business. He was unaware of the management and union conflicts, overtime and pay scale concerns, skilled labor shortages, and strikes. Seaman First Class Hubert Brown admitted he might have been a little naïve, but he figured the workmen knew what they were doing. Yeoman First Class Charles McGuire was not so sanguine. He had mixed feelings about the "yardbirds" and thought that some were hypocrites. They would say, "Okay boys, go out and sink one for me," but McGuire noticed that even before quitting time some of them dropped their tools and headed for the gates without finishing their work. "That was my life they were playing with," McGuire stated, and naturally he was concerned.[16]

On 12 July 1943, *Pampanito* was ready for launching. Although much internal work was still necessary, the outer hull was seaworthy enough to float her off and make room for the next submarine keel. In fact, there was a double launching from the construction basin, with *Picuda* and *Pampanito* being christened the same day.[17] Charles McGuire was at the bow, looking down as a spectacled lady, Violet Wolfenden, wife of Pennsylvania Congressman James Wolfenden, crashed the traditional champagne bottle against the hull. As the spectators cheered and the sparkling white wine trickled down into the red, white, and blue bunting, the flood gates to the basin were opened and the foaming waters of the

Piscataqua rushed in. Flags flapped smartly in the breeze. McGuire left his misgivings behind and felt pretty good about his new boat.

Frank Michno was not aboard for the ceremonies. The same day, in Saint Stephen's Church in Detroit, he was walking down the aisle with his wife. The bride, Marian H. Miedlar, was a neighborhood girl who had lived just two blocks away. The marriage was successfully launched, and within a few days the couple were packed and hurrying to Portsmouth.

Another launching of sorts was occurring in the Summers family. On a short leave from *Stingray* in the summer of 1942, Pete had visited his wife, Jane, and, as he explained it, had "laid the keel" for a new construction of his own. In March 1943, Summers returned to receive a promotion to lieutenant commander, in May he met his newborn son, and in June he was assigned to his new submarine.

The summer of 1943 was also a little more relaxed time for the officers. Pampanito's new skipper, Lieutenant Commander Charles B. Jackson, Jr., had arrived after serving aboard USS *Spearfish* (SS 190), an Electric Boat product commissioned in 1939. Paul and Jane Summers became close friends of Jackson and his wife, attending movies and parties together. In fact, some of the parties the Jacksons held became rather famous among a small circle of officers. One of them, Lieutenant William McClaskey, was a reserve officer who had enlisted in June 1941. He was assigned to USS *Swordfish* (SS 193), a Mare Island boat commissioned in 1939, and was present during the Japanese bombing of Cavite. Having made seven runs on *Swordfish*, McClaskey went to new construction, arriving just in time to attend a few of Jackson's parties. McClaskey remembered Jackson's "daiquiris" as a tall glass of rum with an ice cube. After a few of those, he needed help returning to the base. Far from his mind at the time was how his party-throwing, gregarious commanders would react under combat pressure.

In September 1943, while awaiting the finishing touches on their respective boats, the *Pampanito* crew played the *Parche* crew in a number of softball games. Gordon Hopper always saw *Parche*'s skipper, Lawson P. "Red" Ramage, actively participating in the games or cheering from the bench, while Jackson, said Hopper, "was nowhere to be seen." To most of the enlisted men, Jackson was something of a nonentity.

For weeks after the launching, *Pampanito* was still moored in the river with workmen scurrying about. Radio Technician Second Class George

E. Moffett developed a special affinity for the boat during these long summer days. Born in 1922 in Polo, Missouri, Moffett graduated from high school, worked for AT&T, and completed one year of college. When the Japanese struck Pearl Harbor, Moffett joined the navy. He recalled watching the submarine take shape: "I have always felt that those of us who were fortunate enough to be assigned to the new construction crew of a boat developed a special feeling for that boat. We were able to watch it being assembled piece by piece from the inanimate materials of which it was made—watch it take form and shape and to slowly develop a personality. Some boats were better than *Pampanito* in many respects, and some were worse, of this I am sure. All would at times develop idiosyncrasies, but in any case this was our boat, and we, the crew, were to live or die with her."

Twenty-three-year-old William C. Grady had been in the navy five years. He had served on the destroyer USS *Dunlap* (DD 384) and on USS *Pompano* (SS 181), and he had just finished six patrols on USS *Plunger* (SS 179) when he was assigned to *Pampanito*. When he got to Portsmouth two days after the launching, Grady discovered "wall-to-wall pipefitters, machinists, electricians, riggers, and so on, getting the boat ready for commissioning." Bill Grady and Frank Michno were assigned to the base machine shop to learn lathe operations. The course ran for two afternoons per week, and Grady noted that Michno took to the lathe well, for he "made two of the most beautiful screw jacks that I have ever seen."

Married men, such as Grady, Michno, Moffett, and Watkins, could rent quarters in town, and usually two couples would double up to split the rent, which was calculated according to rate. As a motor machinist's mate first class, Grady and his wife paid only twenty-seven dollars per month. Still, Grady complained, living on regular pay "was like being on welfare."

The yard was always a beehive of activity, and Paul Pappas was enjoying himself. He had worked in his father's photography studio since he was ten years old and knew almost nothing of any other trade. This learning experience was a thrill for him.

Edwin Kubacki was more savvy in the ways of the world. He had enlisted in Detroit in 1940. Like Grady, he had served on *Plunger* as a motor mac (motor machinist). A big, strapping fellow with sandy blond hair combed straight back, he was quite a character. In fact, according to Pappas, "If there was ever a discussion as to who could do more for you, the whores or the USO, Kubacki would be right in the middle of it."

A shipyard was generally a man's workplace, yet more women were getting construction jobs as the men went overseas. Two girls caught Kubacki's eye, and he turned on his charm but never got past first base. He was getting frustrated. What was worse were the taunts from his mates about how he kept striking out with the ladies.

"Striking out! You mean with 'Beast' and 'Scupper?'" Hell, Kubacki explained, he never wanted to go out with those broads. In fact, they were so ornery, noisy, and ugly, he thought he'd name his engines after them.

Sure enough, Kubacki had brass nameplates fashioned and installed on the sides of the two Fairbanks-Morse diesels in the forward engine room. Whereas Lieutenant Commander Frank D. Latta of USS *Narwhal* (SS 167), in a more reverent frame of mind, named his four engines "Matthew," "Mark," "Luke," and "John,"[18] Kubacki had a more typical submariner's sense of humor. "Beast" was self-explanatory, and "Scupper," at least in nautical terms, referred to the deck-level openings in a ship's side that allowed water to run off. Whatever analogy Kubacki had in mind, "Beast" and "Scupper" nameplates now adorned the two forward engines. It was all part of the *Pampanito*'s being tagged with the nickname "The Terrible *Pamp*," because, according to Pappas, they did "everything backwards or the hard way."

## CHAPTER TWO

# *Commissioning*

By November 1943, *Pampanito*'s engines were running smoothly, minor leaks were plugged, and all systems were found adequate. The yard would officially hand over the boat on 6 November. Most importantly to the crew, as sailors on an officially commissioned boat, they would start to draw submarine pay.

"Glory! Glory! Glory!" Bill Grady exclaimed about the long-awaited pay increase. He had it all calculated. Base pay was $126. Sea pay added $25. As a sub sailor he could add another $75. With $226 per month, Grady didn't feel like he was on welfare anymore.

A hall was rented in Portsmouth for the traditional commissioning celebration. Grady called it "a party to end all parties." Saturday night turned into early Sunday morning, and the celebration was still going strong. At 0100, Admiral Thomas Withers, Jr., commander of the Navy Yard, ordered everyone to break it up. A dozen persistent souls ended up at Grady's, but by 0300 almost everyone had "crapped out" on the floor. Sunrise meant hangovers for the majority and promises, generally unkept, never to do this again.

Time came for the first sea trials. *Pampanito* went down the Piscataqua and a dozen miles into the Atlantic. The dive would be handled slowly and carefully. The alarm sounded, the officer of the deck (OOD) pulled the lanyard on the hatch, and Quartermaster-striker Van Atta dogged it

Commissioning photo, 6 November 1943, Portsmouth, New Hampshire. Officers seated on floor, left to right: Harold Rahner, Francis Fives, William McClaskey, Charles Jackson, Paul Summers, James Heist, and Landon Davis. (Author's collection.)

down. He was excited and nervous. He checked the time for the dive: over one minute. Pretty slow, but they would do better.

Although some first-time submariners might have been blissfully ignorant of the danger, the great majority knew well the perils of diving. The motor macs listened intently as the diesels shut down and the batteries took over propulsion. They couldn't help but look up at the main induction and listen for that reassuring thump of the valves slamming shut, barring the cold, intruding sea.

Almost in the same location near the Isle of Shoals, just over four years earlier, USS *Squalus* (SS 192) was making what was thought to be just another trial dive. Her inductions, twin overhead pipes twenty-seven inches in diameter, supplied the prodigious amounts of fresh air needed to run the diesels. The pipes joined a larger tube that ran up through the superstructure and opened to the sky. Parallel to the main induction was a smaller tube that ran the length of the boat and supplied ventilation to all the compartments. When submerging, a hydraulic valve in the high induction would cover the air passages of both inductions and seal them from the sea.

In the control room of *Squalus* the men watched the indicator lights of the "Christmas tree" as, one by one, they changed from red to green, showing that all hull openings were closed. A blast of compressed air was blown into the sub to check for leaks. The barometer rose, indicating that the boat was airtight. Green board. Pressure in the boat.

It seemed like a perfect dive until the yeoman on the headphones heard frantic voices calling, "After engine room flooding!" "Forward engine room flooding!" The Christmas tree still glowed its safe green, yet tons of water poured through the open induction. *Squalus* sank into the mud 240 feet below. Eventually, thirty-three men who had managed to seal themselves off in the forward part of the boat were rescued by the successful use of an experimental diving bell. But twenty-six good men drowned.

When *Squalus* was refloated, the high induction valve was examined. When they tried to close it the first time, it didn't budge. When a little oil was applied to the hydraulic system, it snapped tightly shut, as it should have. A court of inquiry cleared the crew of any blame, and the sinking was attributed to a mechanical malfunction. To forestall future problems, strengthened bulkheads were to be installed between the forward and after engine rooms, and each room would have its own quick-closing, spring-driven inboard shutoff valves.[1] The disaster was not attributable to human error, but that was small comfort to other submarine crews.

The *Squalus* incident was just one of a striking number of submarine accidents. From 1900 to 1916, eleven submarines in the U.S., British, Italian, and French navies had battery explosions from excess hydrogen gas. In the 1920s, three S-boats were lost to collisions or open inductions. Even with the safety features installed after the *Squalus* disaster, there were no guarantees on submarines. In February 1943, USS *Jack* (SS 259) was making a trial run in Block Island Sound. A routine dive almost turned into another disaster when cascades of water began pouring out of her main induction. A red light showed an open valve, but no one noticed. The inboard flappers in the engine rooms were closed by hand, the water was stopped, and *Jack* managed to surface. Certainly there were mechanical malfunctions to worry about, but the sage submariner Admiral Lockwood always thought that "the submariner's greatest potential enemy is himself."[2]

While most of *Pampanito*'s crew were thankful that the equipment seemed to be operating properly, others with fleet boat experience were not so sanguine. Grady and Kubacki had made better dives on *Plunger*. They thought that Captain Jackson was too excitable and that he submerged with excessive down angles. Kubacki complained to the division commander. The commander thanked him and told him to return to his boat. He would look into the matter. He also contacted exec Paul Summers to let him know that there was dissension on his boat.

Back on board, most of the men attended their duties without complaint. Sea trials meant much concentration and hard work, and it was with relief that the men of *Pampanito* could head back to port at day's end. The best part, remembered Earl Watkins, was on that rare occasion when he was allowed up on deck, with the sun beginning to dip below the White Mountains in the west, to see his wife standing on the farthest sandy tip of Kittery Point, watching for him—watching and waiting as the wives of sailors have done from time immemorial.

*Pampanito* returned to the sea for more trial runs, spending several days at a time away from base. The weather turned steadily colder as the New

England winter closed in. With the sub running on the surface through howling northeasters, a number of men experienced their first bouts with seasickness and a biting cold that knifed through every thread of their clothing.

Robert Bennett, a twenty-three-year-old torpedoman third class from Mason City, Iowa, had never been so cold in his life. After graduating from high school and working for the S. S. Kresge Company for a few years, he joined the navy in Chicago and attended torpedo school with Hubert Brown. One year later, in August 1943, Bennett was in New London, where he finished sub school, got married, and was assigned to *Pampanito*.

Bennett recalled the shakedown cruises in the North Atlantic as "the coldest, most miserable time of my career." He stood watch, rotating among the helm, diving planes, and lookout. It seemed that when he was up on the periscope shears the weather was always at its worst. He tried to maintain his balance with one arm curled around the guard rail while trying to keep the binoculars from alternately pulling away from and slamming into his cheekbones.

Unable to see very far in the bad weather, and able to hear even less in the howling wind, Bennett was terrified that the diving alarm would sound without his knowledge. Just thinking of that hatch clanging shut and the decks going awash under icy blue fingers of water made his stomach queasy. He made Lieutenant McClaskey promise to pull on his pants leg to announce a dive. That made Bennett feel better, and it increased his admiration for McClaskey. He thought the lieutenant was "a great guy, and a favorite of the crew."

The poor weather made McClaskey discard his regulation navy clothing in exchange for cowboy boots and a heavy sheepskin overcoat. He was a big man, and the coat puffed out his bulk to such an extent that Bennett insisted he could feel pressure on his ears when McClaskey finally popped through the hatch like a cork from a champagne bottle.

Norman J. Arcement, born in 1922 in Cajun country in Raceland, Louisiana, joined the navy in November 1942. He went to electrician school in Minnesota and to sub school in New London, after which, as an electrician's mate third class, he was assigned to *Pampanito*. Arcement, called "Bud" by his mates, was proud that he "made the virgin dive on the *Pampanito*." Unfortunately, the weather was nothing like that of the

Mississippi River delta. "It was cold as a mother-in-law's heart," he maintained. Once, the water on the superstructure froze into a block of ice. "We couldn't dive," he said, "because the iceberg on top was holding us up."

Even down in the engine rooms the men were not free from the cold. "You have never experienced such discomfort as the engine room people had to live with during these trial runs," said Bill Grady. He, Frank Michno, and Motor Machinist's Mate Second Class Norbert A. Kaup, from Texas, were the throttlemen on battle stations. The temperature off the New Hampshire coast late in the fall was rarely above 20 degrees. "You can imagine," said Grady, "the gale that ran through the engine rooms through the main induction. We all wore winter clothing; heavy jackets, pants, aviator-style helmets, and even galoshes." When they dove, the outside air was cut off, the temperature quickly rose to about 100 degrees, and they had to strip off their foul-weather gear. Next, the surfacing alarm would sound, and, said Grady, "we were stripped down to our skivvies with a below freezing hurricane blowing through the engine rooms." Dressing and undressing in 20-degree or 100-degree temperatures was as constant as the cursing it caused. They would drag their weary bones into port, and the next day was a repeat performance. "But," Grady concluded, "we lived through it."

Unfortunately, returning to Portsmouth gave the crew little relief. The Piscataqua's current gave them fits. At maximum strength it ran from seven to twelve knots between flood tide and ebb tide, and the river could rise or drop as much as seven feet. Landmarks such as Pull-and-Be-Damned Point and the Horse Races underlined the need for caution. Channel buoys could disappear from sight at peak flow, and even the river pilots preferred to move ships up or down only at slack water.[3]

Bennett was on anchor detail with Torpedoman's Mate Second Class James H. Behney, a big Floridian who had transferred to the boat from the old *O-6* in early December. First, in order to tie up, they had to drop the frozen lines down in the torpedo room to thaw. Once squared away, they were still unable to have a peaceful night's sleep, for the current would inevitably drag them. Bennett hated to drop down from his top bunk to the cold linoleum in the middle of the night. Topside he would lie on the icy deck and shine a flashlight over the bow. With Behney hanging onto his legs, he would check the anchor's position, then they would inevitably work the windlass to adjust the chain to secure the boat. When Bennett returned to his bunk, it had lost whatever warmth it had, and he could only hope that the next inspection would prove that the current had been kinder to them.

On the first official day of winter, 21 December 1943, *Pampanito* set sail for New London, Connecticut. After rounding Cape Cod and passing Nantucket, Block Island, and Fisher's Island, she swung north into the wide mouth of the Thames River. Although easier to navigate than the Piscataqua, the Thames presented a few problems of its own with the low highway and railroad bridges that crossed it connecting New London and Groton. Submarines passing this spot generally flooded down until their decks were awash. This lowered their periscope shears enough to clear the underside of the structures and saved time, trouble, and traffic delays caused by the raising of the drawbridges.

This was not always a smooth operation, however. The previous December, USS *Harder* (SS 257) had attempted a routine transit under the bridge. There is also an ebb and flow of fresh and salt water in the Thames, and fresh water is about 3 percent lighter than salt water. The part of the river in which a sub filled its ballast tanks could make a difference in how far it had to flood down. That morning, *Harder* apparently had more of the Atlantic in her tanks than the Thames, for she ducked down too far under the bridge. The next moment there was water pouring in the main induction. All main ballasts were quickly blown, and she rose in time to prevent sinking. However, water spraying in the maneuvering room had short-circuited the controls. Somewhat embarrassed, *Harder*'s skipper, Lieutenant Commander Samuel D. Dealey, had to drop anchor and call for a tug to get a tow back to base.[4]

The first time up the Thames, Captain Jackson negotiated the bridges but couldn't nose *Pampanito* against the pier. The crew was getting restless to go on liberty. One docking attempt was at a bad angle, while another was too slow to breast the current, and the boat backed in and out repeatedly. It was embarrassing. "Smilin' Bob" Bennett was on anchor detail near Lieutenant McClaskey. When the lieutenant could take it no longer, he blurted out, "Let me have the damn thing. I'll get it in for you," then he quickly glanced at the bridge, hoping the skipper hadn't heard him.

Pete Summers thought that his past bad luck with commanding officers had returned to haunt him. Before *Pampanito* was launched, his relationship with Jackson had been smooth, for it was relatively easy to be friends at a cocktail party. During the first trial runs, however, the pressure of running a boat broke through the veneer of friendship. Summers saw a change in Jackson. Navy Yard officials rode with them to oversee operations, and Jackson did not handle the situation well.

About this time, Summers contracted measles and had to relinquish his position as exec for about two weeks. While he was hospitalized, he was replaced by Lieutenant Commander Fredric B. Clarke. Clarke, who had come off USS *Sawfish* (SS 276), was now the exec of USS *Pomfret* (SS 391), which had recently been launched and was being made seaworthy. While he had temporary duty on *Pampanito*, Clarke became acquainted with some of the men. In two short weeks he found that there was general dissatisfaction with Jackson and that "Pete had convinced the wardroom officers that he was the real power on board." Summers had been undercutting the authority of Jackson and had made it known that soon enough he would be taking over the boat.

Even with no Navy Yard officials looking over his shoulder, Jackson still appeared nervous at the helm. Summers was patronizing. "Poor old Charlie," he said, "started freezing up on the sub." Jackson seemed hesitant, unsure of himself, and unable to clearly think through a situation. Tension between the two men increased. Jackson knew of Summers's discontent. He reacted, according to Pete, by becoming more of a martinet. This inability even to dock the sub properly was a last straw.

Summers wondered if he was destined to sail again with a commander in whose abilities he had little confidence. In New London he paid a visit to the chief of staff to the commander of submarines, Atlantic Fleet (ComSubLant), George C. "Turkey Neck" Crawford. Summers told Crawford that they were leaving soon for Panama. He had been through some pretty "hairy" situations before with other commanders and could tell whether a man was going to cut it. Jackson, Summers said, "was not going to make it as a skipper." Crawford passed the warning along to Pearl Harbor.[5]

*Pampanito* conducted trials in Long Island Sound and Block Island Sound. The former is notoriously bad for trimming a submarine because it is shallow and has many rivers and streams pouring fresh water into it, causing unpredictable pockets of different water density. The latter is deeper, but to approach it the sub must traverse the Race, with its swirling currents and whirlpools.[6] Then again, to avoid this the sub could head out farther into the Atlantic and confront the heavy seas and howling winter winds. It seemed no matter where *Pampanito* went, she was hounded by bad weather, storms, and ice.

Al Van Atta would never forget the Atlantic winter. He stood bridge watch as long as he could, sick as a dog. When his relief showed up, he'd collapse in his bunk, wet gear still on, trying not to vomit. He thought he was going to die. After one solid week, he could take it no longer. Beyond the point of caring, Van Atta explained, "I got so sick I was afraid I was not going to die." The last time he dragged himself to his bunk for another night of misery, he managed to sleep for four or five hours. Suddenly a strange feeling made him sit bolt upright. The seasickness was gone, never to return. He could not explain it, but even while riding out some Pacific typhoons the following year, he never got seasick again.

Another victim of the seas, Hubert Brown, remained too nauseated even to change his clothes. At times he was detailed to chop ice off the bridge. When he got inside, he snuggled up next to one of several small electric heaters that graced the compartments. "I was never so cold in my life as on those Atlantic watches," he affirmed. "I couldn't wait to get to the heat of the Pacific."

A slight change in routine occurred when *Pampanito* was sent to Newport, Rhode Island. She had completed mock attacks, a six-day practice patrol, sound testing, test firing of the four-inch deck gun, and calibration of the pitometer (a device for measuring the submarine's speed) log. She had also been degaussed, which neutralized the ship's magnetic field in the hopes of giving her an edge against enemy magnetic mines or detection equipment. In Newport she conducted 20-mm gun training and fired exercise torpedoes. There, the men found another place to blow off some steam.

"The Terrible *Pamp*" invested the Ideal Club in downtown Newport. Paul Pappas had spent much of the day exploring the city when he decided to stop at the club to check up on his mates. He saw trouble. Perhaps forty or more crew members had taken over the club. Among them were two of his closest friends. Clarence "Mike" Carmody was a powerfully built, five-foot, ten-inch, 175-pound Irishman who had gotten his strength and physique from his job hauling ice and coal up and down thousands of tenement stairs in Brooklyn. He had transferred to *Pampanito* in November after serving for four patrols on *S-17*. Carmody was a great person to have as a friend and a shipmate, but his quick temper could sometimes be a liability. Pappas's partner in the maneuvering room was Electrician's Mate Third Class Walter H. Cordon. Cordon had enlisted in the navy when he was only seventeen and had just passed his eighteenth birthday two months before *Pampanito* was commissioned. He was the youngest sailor on board, and he was enjoying himself immensely.

The first thing the crew did was to throw out all the soldiers. They didn't particularly like the entertainers, so they booed them off the stage. Fireman Third Class Andrew L. Currier, a twenty-one-year-old from nearby Lawrence, Massachusetts, decided he could do a better job and got up on the stage to dance. He was soon followed by a half-dozen men in a bizarre chorus line accompanied by several obscene sea chanteys. Hubie Brown saw a shore patrolman standing by the door, arms folded across his chest. He thought to himself, "When's the bomb going to drop?" Brown decided he had better get out.

At first the waitresses didn't seem to mind the rowdy sailors. A stack of money was on the table, and beer was ordered by the case. Having chased out most of the regular customers, the sailors began to dance with the bar maids, or, failing in that, with each other. The waitresses put up with the shenanigans in exchange for the big tips. Then someone got his face slapped for being a little too handy. Next, big Ed Kubacki decided he would have to get all the waitresses initiated into the "ABA."

"What the hell is that?" they asked.

"Why, the Ass-Biters Association, of course," Ed explained. When a bar maid leaned over the table to wipe up a spilled drink, Kubacki placed his teeth on her protruding rear end. Table, waitress, and several drinks dumped over with a crash. Pappas decided it was time to go, and he headed for the door. One poor patron decided he had to defend the lady's honor, and Carmody let him have it. The rest of the tables went over, bottles were thrown, and fists were flying.

Pappas ducked into a drugstore across the street when he saw a paddy wagon slam to a halt in front of the club. Cordon was just coming out of the restroom and saw the shore patrol arresting anyone with the dolphin insignia on his sleeves. He quickly grabbed his coat off the hook, put it on, and slid into an empty booth in the back. When they got to him, he pretended he was alone. "Yeah, them goddamn submariners are always causing trouble," he agreed with the shore patrol.

Grady and Kubacki saw what was coming. When the melee began, they headed out the back door and found a restaurant to slip inside. They figured they were safe until a band of SPs came in and rounded them up simply because they wore the dolphins.

*Pampanito* was scheduled to sail early the following morning, but a slight delay ensued, since eleven men were missing. Commander Jackson exploded. The engineering officer, Lieutenant Landon L. "Jeff" Davis, Jr., was elected to get them back to the boat, pronto. At the hoosegow, Davis found his men in varying states of hangover, contrition, and belligerence. Kubacki, as the jailhouse lawyer, argued that the men knew their rights. They were jailed improperly, not because they did anything wrong, but because they were submariners. He tried to talk them into staying in jail until they received an apology. Normally a soft-spoken Virginia gentleman, Davis found himself taxed to the limit by these recalcitrant, obstreperous sailors. The arrangements had been made to get them all out of the brig, he explained as calmly as possible; now they would get their sorry asses back to the boat immediately or he would recommend a court-martial for the lot of them. *Pampanito,* a little late, headed to New London.

Despite all the sea trials, the run back to the Thames revealed a bother-some squeal in the propeller shafts. It was one more in a series of minor problems that seemed to plague them. More to the crew's liking was New Year's Eve liberty on the last Friday of December 1943, and, as in Newport, they overdid it. Two sailors went AWOL for a few days, and three more men disappeared for five days. One man was kicked off the boat for this indiscretion. A sixth sailor never came back. His accounts were closed out, and he was listed as a deserter. Kubacki, meanwhile, had dodged a bullet. After six days AWOL, he lost seventy-eight dollars in pay and was confined for twenty days, but because of a shortage of throttlemen with depth charge experience, he was kept aboard—at least for the time being.[7]

Were these sailors just overexuberant boys out to have a good time before being shipped to the war zone, or was there something more involved? Summers blamed Jackson. "He was too strict," he claimed. The crew was angry at him and morale was low. "In New London, one-third of the men tried to jump ship. We had to send patrols out to find them." And to top it off, Summers added, Jackson put the blame on him.[8]

One way to prevent men from jumping ship was to be at sea. On 9 January the persistent squeal in the propellers forced them to return to Portsmouth. They spent about three days in the yard for repairs. The men knew that their time stateside could now be counted in hours, and many spent the time writing last letters home.

One person who should have written home was Frank Michno. The New Year was not turning out happy for his family in Detroit. Some months previously, *Pompano* (SS 181) had sailed on her seventh war patrol. After sinking two Japanese cargo ships in September 1943, she was never heard from again. In mid-October she was reported as presumed lost. The sad tidings took time to be disseminated in the local newspapers. So it was that after Christmas, a customer of "Michno's Cafe" rushed in to the family's establishment as John Michno was tending bar. He told him the news: *Pampanito* was lost at sea with all hands. It was true, the man said, for he had read it in the paper. John and his wife, Katherine, were devastated. Their boy Frankie was dead. They passed the word to the Miedlar family, where Frank's wife, Marian, had just returned pending *Pampanito*'s sailing for the Pacific. Both families went into mourning. Finally someone wondered why there had been no standard military telegram sent to the next of kin, and where was that newspaper, anyway? When produced, it stated that *Pompano* had been sunk, not *Pampanito*. The Michno brothers, in no uncertain terms, warned that customer that if they ever saw him again they would take him out to the alley and fix him so that he could never even buy another newspaper.

With repairs of the propeller shafts completed, *Pampanito* left Portsmouth for a last stop at New London, where several more transfers were made. Across the gangway came Seaman Second Class Duncan Brown, a Connecticut native who had just come from the *S-48,* and George Ingram, African American, steward's mate first class from Philadelphia, who had been on the old *O-6.* A fast hunt was made for a signalman. Signalman First Class William S. Canty, from Illinois, had recently been assigned to USS *Porpoise* (SS 172), which had been withdrawn from combat, and he was looking forward to less stressful duty. He had just purchased a used car and was packing up for a drive when the shore patrol located him. They ordered him out of the auto and back to the base, doubletime. He'd been assigned to *Pampanito*. Canty protested. How much time did he have? Five minutes. He left his car, grabbed his gear, and was escorted to the boat. Canty felt that he had been shanghaied.[9]

*Pampanito* departed for the Panama Canal on 15 January 1944, and the crew was glad to place the icy winter astern. For much of the trip they traveled against the Gulf Stream. This current, a huge river in the ocean heading north along the eastern seaboard, is fifty miles wide and can reach a speed of several knots. *Pampanito* bucked it, but the current still knocked a few knots off her forward progress.[10]

Gordon Hopper, who spent much of his time as a topside lookout, found the weather growing pleasurably warmer every day they traveled south. Yet there was no relaxation of vigilance, for German U-boats still hunted the shoreline. Duncan Brown, a late arrival, missed the acclimatization that the North Atlantic sea trials would have afforded. He was seasick for the entire trip, with a torpedo for a bunkmate. Above him was the chain-fall, used for hauling torpedoes from their skids to the tubes. The chain dangled inches away from his head in the folded-down lower bunk. The spot was always reserved for new men so old salts could explain how dangerous it was. In fact, the torpedomen said with a straight face, the last guy who had that bunk had his head crushed when the entire pulley and chain came down on him. Duncan Brown lay there for five straight days, unable to do anything but roll his head from side to side. He only ate a few crackers and sipped a little water, and he never slept at all, contending with nausea and worried about that damn chain swaying above him like the sword of Damocles.

In the after engine room, Bill Grady spent the days teaching the new men about the Fairbanks-Morse engines. "Tex" Kaup was a veteran of USS *Halibut* (SS 232) and was familiar with them, but Michno, off the S-boats, only knew the Maschinenfabrik-Augsburg-Nürnberg engines, built by the Brooklyn Navy Yard and essentially copies of the engines that ran the German U-boats. Michno had to learn the finer points about overhauling "Grady's girls," the opposed-piston Fairbanks-Morses. Bill, like Kubacki in the forward engine room, had made nameplates for his own engines;

number three was "Miss Molly," named for an old girlfriend, and number four was "Miss Jean," named after his new wife.

Several times on the way down to Panama, *Pampanito* had troublesome, steep dives, much as Kubacki had complained about previously. At least one of them was initiated by the new fire controlman. William F. Yagemann hailed from Aurora, Illinois. He hoped to finish college at the University of Illinois but was on the verge of flunking. He wanted to get into aviation, but there was a long waiting list. When he saw a submarine recruiting film at a fraternity party, he said, "That's for me." Yagemann joined up in 1942 and enjoyed learning about the torpedo data computer (TDC). In January 1944, *Pampanito* had a vacancy for a fire controlman, and Yagemann came aboard.

Yagemann quickly formed an opinion about Captain Jackson. "He didn't cut the mustard. He panicked once on the way down to Panama." And Yagemann added: "Which I helped." Apparently Bill was on his first SD radar watch, and he did not know its idiosyncrasies. The SD radar was nondirectional. Bill saw a "pip" on the screen and called out, "Aircraft at two miles!" The "plane" was nothing but a pulse return from their own radar, but Jackson called for a crash dive, lost control, and went below three hundred feet. "It shook him up," said Yagemann. "He didn't react well."

Grady and his oilers took pride in keeping their engine room spotless, but after the last crash dive, he said, "We took such a down angle that the lubricating oil from the engine sumps spilled all over the fuel oil day tanks. I was really pissed off and told the oilers to forget it and let the inspecting officer see what the result of uncontrolled dives does to a neat and clean engine room." Summers did the inspecting. But, said Grady, "He did not say a word. He knew that the skipper was sitting on greased skids."

A potentially more serious drama occurred just two nights out of Panama. Although the weather was balmy and the seas were calm, danger still abounded. Coming through these very same waters just three months earlier was USS *Dorado* (SS 248), on her way to the Pacific for her first war patrol. When she did not arrive in Panama at her scheduled time, an air and sea search was immediately started. All that was found was floating debris and a large oil slick. An American PBM Mariner flying boat out of Guantanamo, Cuba, reported bombing a submarine on 12 October. Another possibility for her disappearance was a torpedo from a U-boat or one of the mines recently laid by *U-214*. Whatever the cause of her loss, the Caribbean closed over the *Dorado*, and she was never heard from again.

Now, almost in the same place, *Pampanito* cut along the surface of the nighttime waters. Charlie McGuire had just come down from lookout, and he stopped in the conning tower to watch the radar screen. After a few minutes he found himself mesmerized by the sweeping beam and the little green ridges of "grass" that appeared on the scope. Vaguely he heard an animated conversation occurring up on the bridge, then suddenly, Lieutenant Clifford C. Grommet's head poked down through the open hatch.

"Right full rudder! All ahead flank!" Grommet yelled. "Captain to the bridge!"

McGuire snapped out of his reverie. What the hell happened? It must be a torpedo, he thought. Grabbing the periscope to brace himself, he quickly figured that if he could survive the blast, he could get to the ladder and get out on deck. But then what would he do? He couldn't swim. McGuire waited for the explosion, but nothing happened. The bow had already cut the track of a torpedo wake. It had probably missed by only a matter of several yards. *Pampanito* continued its turn and dove. For the next fifteen minutes she played cat-and-mouse with an unseen adversary, and sub versus sub was no game to play. If she stayed on the surface, she would be a sitting duck. If she submerged, she couldn't get close enough for an attack. The sonar was not good enough to successfully fight an undersea duel. The scene was described as "two blindfolded men fighting in a pitch black cellar, each armed with a baseball bat." Then, from sonar came the announcement: "Sounds like a submarine surfacing." If it was, it turned tail and faded away. So did *Pampanito*. No one knew if they really had an encounter with a U-boat or a bout with a few overactive imaginations.[11]

While not quite as hazardous as playing tag with a U-boat, the transit of the Panama Canal was a highlight for the crew. Opened in 1914, the canal cut thousands of miles off the trip between the Atlantic and Pacific. Transit time takes about nine hours to cover forty-four miles. From the Caribbean Sea on 24 January, *Pampanito* crossed Limón Bay and penetrated the first of three pairs of locks at Gatún. After being raised about eighty feet, she sailed the calm waters of Gatún Lake. At the southern end, the canal continued to the Pedro Miguel and Miraflores

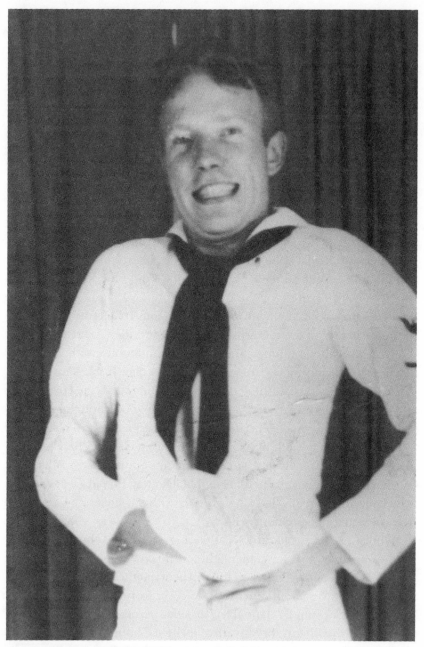

Charles McGuire in 1941. In his own words: "Gee, what a man. Weight about 160 soaking wet." (Photo courtesy of Charles McGuire.)

locks, which lowered her back to sea level. She finally tied up in Balboa, on the Pacific Ocean for the first time.[12]

Officers and men took the opportunity to explore the town. Charlie McGuire had entered a club jammed with submariners from several boats when he heard his name called. He was surprised to see Pete Summers and other officers at a table, motioning for "Red" to join them. They had never been on friendly terms. In fact, McGuire had more often than not described Summers as an "SOB." Now, suddenly, the exec bought him a beer and introduced him to the other officers as a terrific yeoman. McGuire didn't know what to think. He graciously accepted the drink, and after a minute of small talk he excused himself.

McGuire went down the street to another waterfront bar, where he met several men from USS *Golet* (SS 361), a Manitowoc boat also heading out for her first patrol. This time, McGuire was called by Lieutenant Commander James S. Clark, whom he had known when the latter had served aboard USS *Archerfish* (SS 311).

Clark, now *Golet*'s exec, asked, "'Red,' will you mind if I talk to your captain to try and get you on board the *Golet*?"

"I wouldn't mind," McGuire replied. "I'd sure like to be with you." They shook hands, and McGuire had his drink and moved on, somewhat surprised at all the attention he was getting. He never heard the result of the negotiations until a few weeks later, and in the meantime he went about his business of celebrating the last night in Panama.[13]

Among those returning to the boat early were Grady and Michno. Michno had cautioned Grady about the rough time that could be had in Panama. Michno related some of his S-boat experiences; being beat-up in an alley and partying with a "blue moon queen" who could love you one minute and deftly cut you up with a razor the next. Besides, he and Grady wanted nothing more to do with the other "gifts" that some of the Panamanian ladies might give them.

Balboa experiences extreme diurnal tidal fluctuations, with two complete cycles in a day; two highs and two lows. While the tides on the Caribbean side might vary three or four feet, the end-of-the-month spring tides off Balboa can rise and fall as much as eighteen to twenty feet.[14] When the crew left the boat about 1600, they could literally step off the submarine's deck to the pier. Rushing to get back to the ship

six hours later, they discovered that the submarine seemed to have disappeared. Actually, the tide had gone out, and *Pampanito* was about
eighteen feet below dock level, at the bottom of an almost vertical ladder.

George Moffett had volunteered for deck watch, while Duncan Brown
was ordered to remain aboard, thankful that he was not in the brig. When
they first pulled in to Panama, Brown, finally recovered from his
seasickness, hauled himself topside to blink at the first sun he had seen in
ten days. Lieutenant Commander Jackson noticed him and called him
over.

"What's your name, sailor," he asked, "and what are you doing on my
boat?"

"Seaman Second Class Duncan Brown," he replied. "I'm assigned to
the *Pampanito.*" Jackson had McGuire bring the sailing list.

"I already radioed New London that you failed to get on board,"
Jackson said. "You're officially AWOL."

Brown had been sick as a dog for a week, and they thought he had
deserted. Jackson told him to stay aboard until they could straighten out
the situation. That evening, Brown and Moffett watched as the drunken
sailors tried to get back aboard ship.

The first men found what appeared to be a drop-off into the darkness.
Wondering how far down it was, Kubacki found a ten-gallon milk can on
the pier and rolled it off into the void. The can sailed down, incredibly
finding its way directly through the open deck hatch above the after
battery. It hit with a tremendous crash next to several men playing acey-
deucey in the crew's mess, splattering milk all over them. Several inches
over, and *Pampanito* might have had her first war casualty.

Crewmen poured out onto the deck. Someone broke into the food
supplies, and the next moment, a food fight developed between dock and
deck, the air filled with flying apples and bananas.

Gordon Hopper saw a sailor speed down the ladder, hit the deck
running, and shoot right off the other side, splashing into the drink. They
were laughing so hard, it never occurred to them that someone might
drown.

Moffett watched incredulously as a sailor opened up a can of black
paint and poured it down the ladder. Inevitably, the next sailors unsteadily
grasped the ladder as they descended to the boat's deck, where they found

that black paint and white uniforms are incompatible. Now this group was spoiling for a fight.

Duncan Brown saw one man descend the ladder with a huge stalk of bananas over his shoulder. He waited for the man to tumble into the sea, yet incredibly the sailor walked down the near-vertical ladder, facing outward, as if he had been descending the stairs on his own front porch. The sailor crossed the deck and went down the hatch without picking up a spot of paint and without losing a banana.

The paint-covered sailors decided they would go for a swim and clean up. Jumping into the polluted water, thick with floating fuel oil, was no solution—but it was no deterrent, either. Radioman Third Class Ralph Herber decided that a swim was a good idea. Herber stripped down to his shorts and climbed to the top of the periscope shears. Moffett saw him debating with men on the dock, about eye-level with the shears, about whether it was possible to dive from there into the water without hitting the outer hull. Moffett remembered that the beam of the sub was about twenty-seven feet and quickly calculated that gravity would allow Herber to easily make the vertical distance, but that he would still have to add a fourteen-foot horizontal jump into the bargain. As Herber hung on the shears, the men took bets whether he could make it. Then he leaped. Moffett closed his eyes as Herber soared in an arc over the bridge and splashed safely into the drink, barely clearing the hull.

A few fractious crewmen found a sledge hammer and began knocking apart the wharf's planking, which roused the shore patrol. Summers, Jackson, and most of the officers were in town, and the OOD had disappeared. Moffett had to convince the SPs that everything was under control and that he would have all the crewmen calmed down in a jiffy. The SPs had no sooner left than the last of the sailors returned to the boat. They traversed the ladder and got paint-stained, and the fighting commenced again. Only the arrival of Jackson and Summers put an end to the fracas. Courts-martial and liberty bans were threatened if any such behavior were to occur again. Only Herber got a captain's mast, with a punishment of confinement to the boat. It was a night that Moffett never wanted to go through again.

Gordon Hopper said that Panama was the first foreign country that most of the men had ever visited. "Just about all hands ended up drunk and disorderly," and the liberty turned out to be "a disaster." When asked why he had participated in the ruckus, thrown bananas, and jumped into the water, Norm Arcement answered, "I think the thing that brought it on was called alcohol."

The next morning when the crew was making ready to sail, Duncan Brown was talking to the sailor who had strolled so nonchalantly down the ladder with the stalk of bananas. Brown asked if he remembered what he had done last night. "No," the sailor replied. When it was explained to him, he didn't believe it. The sub's deck, he said, was even with the dock. Although he still had a hangover, the man went topside for a look. By about 1000, the diurnal tide had already cycled through another rise during the night and was once again at its low point. "When he saw how high the dock was," said Brown, "his head followed up the ladder, his eyes rolled backwards, and he keeled over, passed out cold as a stone." *Pampanito* cast off her lines and headed for the Territory of Hawaii.

One pleasant surprise for those in the forward torpedo room was the addition of a fruit supply. Bob Bennett had secured the stalk of bananas and hung it in the escape hatch. Because fruit was always at a premium on long patrols, he used a little of his own money to buy a supply of canned peaches and a stabilized cream substitute. For days after leaving port, Bennett and a select group of torpedomen snacked on bananas, peaches, and cream. The news got around, and the officers wanted to know where the food was hidden and if they could share in the bounty. The officers' steward, George Ingram, called "Good Kid," by the crew, was sent in to negotiate. When Ingram promised he would pass along an officer's dessert at a later date, Bennett agreed to share his fruit with the wardroom. It was a typical sailor's compromise, but it set the stage for future trouble.

By now, everyone was becoming acclimated to the daily grind. Compensation was made for the Pacific waters. The ocean's dissolved mineral contents, combined with temperature and pressure, determine the density of the water. Sea water is saltier and heavier than fresh water, but all sea water does not have the same salt content. The Atlantic tends to be saltier than the Pacific, and the diving officer would have to make one set of calculations in the salty Caribbean and another in the Pacific.[15]

When calculating proper trim, one also had to consider the amount of fuel and water aboard, supplies, personnel transfers, torpedoes on- or off-loaded, or other equipment removed or installed. The trip through the canal, explained one sub commander, simply required being able "to correct the variable ballast by a factor equal to the specific gravity of urine." One needed to get a feel for diving, just as one did for flying a plane. Some could learn it instinctively, while others never could get the magic touch.[16]

Still another factor effecting trim was fuel and supply consumption while at sea. As fuel is consumed, the boat becomes heavier—contrary to what one might assume. To keep the weight as constant and evenly distributed as possible, seawater is admitted to the expansion tank, thence to the bottom of the fuel tank, as the fuel is burned. Fuel oil is lighter than water, floats upon it, and is drawn from the top of the fuel tank to a collection tank. A cubic foot of diesel oil weighs fifty-four pounds, while the same volume of water weighs about sixty-four pounds. A tank with a capacity of only one hundred cubic feet will be one thousand pounds heavier when filled with sea water than when filled with diesel oil.[17]

Learning to dive the boat, maneuver it, conduct an attack, and operate all the boat's systems was necessary for an officer to "qualify" in submarines. Crewmen were also busy trying to qualify. A sailor not only had to know the systems but also had to give an accompanied hands-on walk through the boat to demonstrate his practical knowledge. Succeeding in passing the "school of the boat," an officer would earn his gold twin dolphin pin and an enlisted man would gain his cloth twin dolphin patch, to be sewn on the right forearm just above the wrist.[18]

About one week into the trip to Hawaii, *Pampanito* submerged for what was to be another routine trim dive. She had long ago compensated for the Pacific salt water, and fuel and supply consumption had been calculated. Yet something went haywire. Gordon Hopper recalled that Captain Jackson, in order to help a couple of inexperienced men qualify, directed that they handle the bow and stern planes. Whatever happened, the daily trim dive was suddenly no longer routine. Paul Pappas awoke with his feet pressed against the bunk's horizontal bar. He explained: "My head was up, my feet were down, and I was almost standing." From his location on the port-side passageway in the crew's quarters near the showers, what he called the worst bunk in the sub, he could see right down the aisle into the crew's mess. At that moment, a salt shaker slid off one of the tables and hit the galley wall. Sounds of other loose items clanging and crashing to the deck snapped Pappas out of his bunk.

In the crew's mess, Chief Motor Machinist's Mate Clarence H. Smith barely held on to his breakfast plate. Smith, a man as large as Lieutenant McClaskey, was also a prodigious eater. Crewmen wondered how he ever got through a submarine hatch. In fact, more than once he was seen to polish off a dozen fried eggs and a loaf of bread at one sitting.

"On the way to Pearl, it was chow time," Smith said. He wasn't aware anything was wrong until he felt a tilt toward the bow and his breakfast attempted to escape from him. They were going down at a mighty steep angle. "The dishes and the chow went flying," he said. "The deck was slick, and we had to crawl on our hands and knees. We were out of control for awhile, and that's all there is to it."

Smith's sentiments were echoed by Electrician's Mate Third Class Walt Cordon, then standing in the control room, where, he believed, no one was in control. Cordon grabbed the plotting table to keep from falling. On the blow and vent manifold was Chief Torpedoman's Mate Harold J. "Turk" Rahner, chief of the boat (senior enlisted man). Rahner was an "old man" who had been in the service for two decades. Near Rahner was Melvin H. "Dinty" Moore, a chief motor mac and another old hand at this business.

In the center of the room was Captain Jackson—frozen. His feet were propped against the master gyroscope for balance. Cordon saw his lips moving, but no words came out. Was he praying? The depth gauge registered over four hundred feet and going down. Cordon looked at Rahner and Moore. They looked at him, then at Captain Jackson, who remained seemingly petrified. Would no one do anything? Was it a minute, or only seconds later that they acted? With a mutual, tacit agreement, Rahner and Moore rapidly worked the valves to send jets of high pressure air into the ballast tanks.

Accompanied by the sounds of rushing air and bubbling water, the sub leveled off and began to rise, only this time with an increasingly steep up-angle. Loose items resting against the forward bulkheads began their journey along the green linoleum decks to bang into the after bulkheads. Sleeping in the forward torpedo room, Bennett finally got dizzy enough to wake up. Said Bob: "I thought the sub was doing loops."

The twenty-three-year-old New York native Joseph Eichner, ship's cook third class, had enlisted in 1942, and *Pampanito* was his first boat. He was making breakfast in the galley when the sub started its roller coaster ride. "I had to hold on to the pot and pan rack with my left hand, while my right hand held on to a shelf. My left foot was placed on the front of the ovens, and the other foot was on the deck. We had a Worcestershire sauce bottle on the shelf that came tumbling down and smashed on the deck." Eichner thought it was Lieutenant Grommet who was in charge of the dive, for later, Joe said, "Grommet came into the galley and apologized to me for the mess that I had to clean up." Grommet never was one of the crew's favorites.

Gunner's Mate Second Class Anthony C. Hauptman, whom Red McGuire called one of the most savvy submariners he knew, and a talented artist to boot, commemorated the occasion. Tony got out his sketch pad and cartooned a porpoise-like *Pampanito* leaping in and out of the water all the way to Hawaii. Eichner remembered seeing one sketch with *Pampanito*'s stern out of the water, shooting torpedoes at airplanes in the sky.

Aboard a submarine, with more than seventy men living together in close proximity, one would think it impossible for any incident to occur without everyone knowing. Yet at any particular time, while not at battle stations or on watch, possibly one-third of the crew was fast asleep, and the rest of the men were confined to their separate compartments performing their duties. Not everyone remembered the bad dive. One man who did take note was Pete Summers.

## CHAPTER THREE

# To the Carolines

All hands were looking forward to landfall after two weeks and about four thousand miles at sea. *Pampanito* passed the thirteen-thousand-foot peak of Mauna Loa on the main island of Hawaii, far off on her beam, and on the morning of 14 February the lookouts sighted Diamond Head on Oahu. When the antitorpedo and boat nets opened, they continued up the loch and into Pearl Harbor.

Bob Bennett relished the moment. Although anchor detail was a little extra work, he could get out in the sun and fresh air sooner. "I could see the beautiful green mountains of Hawaii longer than the other guys," he said. As they passed by Hickham Field, a flight of B-26 Mitchell bombers flew overhead, tipping their wings in a salute.

As they swung east at the U.S. Naval Station Hospital with the dry docks to starboard and Ford Island to port, those topside still saw evidence of the Japanese attack over two years ago. It had been cleaned up quite a bit, but *Utah* was still being worked on and *Oklahoma* had been righted and was in Drydock No. 2. The realization finally struck Gordon Hopper that he would soon be seeing action. "For many of us, this would be our first war patrol," he said. "Unaware of what to expect, we were eager to make that first 'kill.'"

Before they could leave, there was more work to be done. The squeaking starboard propeller shaft, "fixed" once in Portsmouth, needed repair again. Workers rebored inboard bearings on both shafts and replaced the lignum vitae (tropical hardwood) bearings where the shaft penetrated the hull. Equipment was installed in both torpedo rooms for charging and ventilating the new Mark 18 electric torpedoes. Other installations included a baffle plate in the No. 1 main ballast tank (MBT) to decrease flooding time, a CUO radar detector (a "black box" used to search for enemy radar signals), identification friend or foe (IFF) radio equipment, and a variable-speed power trainer for the surface (SJ) radar mast.

American submarines of this period in the war were equipped with two types of radar. The low-frequency SD radar, for detecting aircraft, was omnidirectional and nonrotational. A plane flying at constant altitude would be detected, fade out, and be detected again as it passed through the beams of the antenna's rounded lobes. The target indicator was a five-inch cathode ray tube (CRT) with a nonlinear sweep, calibrated in miles. The early SDs were crude but useful. Submariners believed, however, that the Japanese could locate them on the basis of their emissions.

The SJ radar had a directional, high-gain antenna that sent a narrow, high-frequency beam to sweep the surface of the ocean to detect ships. It could rotate at variable speed or be trained manually. The beam from the solid reflector was narrow enough that the sub's roll would not affect detection range, but sea conditions could produce a visual clutter of "noise" out to a range of two thousand to four thousand yards, which made detection of small objects, such as mines or periscopes, almost impossible. Rain squalls interfered more with the high-frequency SJ than with the SD.

Target presentation for the SJ was shown on two screens. One was the plan position indicator (PPI), a nine-inch CRT with a sweeping beam circling like the hand of a clock. The other, the "A" scope, was a five-inch CRT with a single horizontal trace. Range was generated by moving a notch under the target and reading the range from a dial on the unit, much like an automobile odometer readout. More accurate readings could be obtained by "lobe-switching," moving a small obstruction through a double section of the waveguide in the antenna mast to create two pips on the "A" scope. When right on target, the two pulses would be super-imposed on each other. Lobe-switching would give very good bearing accuracy, within plus or minus one degree. However, while the antenna was manually operated, the PPI was nonfunctional except for a single intense line crossing the target. By 1944 the improved SJs could detect a battleship at twelve nautical miles or a submarine or low-flying bomber at five nautical miles.

On 23 February, *Pampanito* put to sea to test her new equipment and to test her officers. Newly arrived was Lieutenant Junior Grade William L. Bruckart. Born in Washington, D.C., in 1919, he had joined the Naval Reserves in 1937 and had won an appointment to the Naval Academy through a competitive exam but was disqualified for not having perfect eyesight. He graduated from the University of Kentucky in 1942 with a degree in metallurgical engineering, then went to Fire Control School at the Washington Navy Yard and radar schools at Bowdoin College and MIT. Bruckart volunteered for submarines and in 1943 was assigned to USS *Sailfish* (SS 192) as radar officer. On his first patrol they sank the light carrier *Chuyo*, the first of its kind to be sunk by submarines in the Pacific War. While *Sailfish* was being overhauled in San Francisco, Bruckart was assigned to *Pampanito* as the new radar officer.

Another new face was Seaman Second Class Walter H. Richter, a twenty-year-old from Hagen, North Dakota. He had won a few Golden Gloves championships and had turned to boxing professionally while still a senior in high school. He was inducted in May 1943 and was assigned to submarine duty. "They called it volunteering," Richter said. "Well, nobody ever asked me whether I wanted sub service, they just put me in it." He kept up his boxing in boot camp. "I was in great shape," he said. "They were all scared to put the gloves on with me."

Richter was sent to Hawaii to fit out submarines. There, he discovered a second "talent" that might be even more remunerative than boxing—gambling. In early September 1943, *Wahoo* had returned from her first abortive, dud-torpedo patrol in the Sea of Japan. While an angry Mush Morton took on a fresh load of supposedly "good" torpedoes, the sub received ten new men to replace those moving to relief crew or new construction. Richter helped load *Wahoo* for what would prove to be her last patrol. He also realized how easy it was to supplement his submariner's pay.

Walt borrowed two dollars from an electrician to get into a dice game. He laid the two dollars down and hit. He let the money ride and kept hitting. By the time he finished, no one would play him anymore. He returned to his buddy, and instead of paying back the two dollars, he gave the surprised electrician two hundred dollars while keeping eight hundred dollars of his own winnings.

Richter then got into a poker game in *Wahoo*'s mess. "I'll never forget it," Richter said. "It was high draw poker, and the chief motor mac opened the pot with aces over, and I had a straight flush to draw to." The chief drew and picked up another ace and a face card to give him a full house. Richter, in the slimmest of hopes, drew for an inside straight. "I caught the jack of hearts," he said. "It gave me a straight flush and I broke the chief."

Richter had honed his gambling skills to the point that he hardly ever lost. When assigned to *Pampanito*, he was ready to ply his trade with a fresh batch of sailors.[1]

While the crew trained, some of the tools of their trade remained troublesome. The Mark 10 torpedo ran deeper than set, and the newer Mark 14 was not tested adequately, for it either ran too deep or its magnetic exploder failed. With the war effort in high gear, torpedoes were being tested at almost every opportunity—a practice that should have been initiated before the war. Accompanied by USS *Litchfield* (DD 336), *Pampanito* went to Kahoolawe, where tests were conducted by firing at the little island's submerged cliffs.

The typical Mark 14 steam torpedo was about twenty-one inches in diameter and twenty-one feet long, weighed about one and one-half tons, and had an extreme range of nine thousand yards at thirty-one knots or forty-five hundred yards at forty-six knots. It packed about 500 pounds of TNT, and later, about 660 pounds of the more powerful torpex. Behind the explosive was the air flask with fuel and water. Steam for motive power was generated by forcing a spray of water through a combustion chamber of burning alcohol. In the afterbody were an oil tank, turbines, a depth engine, a gyroscope, an immersion mechanism, the starting lever, and a depth index. In the tail were the exhaust manifold and propellers. The torpedo was a projectile that, in theory, could dive, level off at a pre-selected depth, curve right or left, then streak to its target. It would explode either on contact or, if armed with a magnetic exploder, when it came within the magnetic field of a steel-hulled ship. It was a remarkable and complex weapon. All too often, however, it failed to work.

The original Mark 14, fitted with a Mark 6 magnetic exploder, cost about ten thousand dollars each, and few were expended in practice. The defects were not revealed until irate submarine skippers came home with reports of almost constant failure.

In a test conducted in Australia in the summer of 1942, James W. Coe in USS *Skipjack* (SS 184) fired his Mark 14s into a net, which showed that the torpedoes were running an average of eleven feet deeper than their settings. When these defects were corrected, it was discovered that the Mark 6 magnetic exploders were malfunctioning. Torpedoes ran right under a target's keel with no explosion, or exploded prematurely, dangerously close to the submarine. When Admiral Lockwood finally ordered the magnetic exploders inactivated in June 1943, the submarine force believed its worries were over. Yet now the Mark 14 even failed to explode when slamming hard into the side of a ship. Direct hits bent the firing pin so that it would not bury itself into the primer cap. The best shooting was rewarded with duds, while glancing blows produced occasional explosions. A modified firing pin finally produced satisfactory results. That was in September 1943, about twenty months since the war had begun.

Were the problems over? Not quite. In 1942, Westinghouse Company began producing an electric torpedo, the Mark 18, which was essentially a copy of a captured German model. Its chief feature was that it was wakeless; the battery-run propulsion system did not leave the bubble trail of the steam torpedo. It was slow, however, running about four thousand yards at twenty-nine knots. Cold water and low battery temperature made it run even slower, and some of the torpedoes sank or circled back at the submarine. Through the course of the war, U.S. submarines fired 14,277 torpedoes against Japanese targets for 4,794 hits, a 33.5 percent success rate. With all these problems, it is remarkable that they hit even one-third of the time.[2]

At Kahoolawe Cliffs in August 1943, USS *Muskellunge* (SS 262) fired three live torpedoes brought back from patrol by Mush Morton and *Wahoo*. The one resulting dud retrieved from fifty-five feet down was the first salvageable evidence that an exploder mechanism had crushed and failed. When *Pampanito* went to Kahoolawe in February 1944, the more optimistic men believed the torpedo problems had been eliminated.

Hubert Brown remembered that they were carrying a special load of sixteen fish specifically to test the explosive power of TNT versus torpex.

The newer torpex was a combination of standard TNT and RDX, which was made from an evaporated aqueous solution of ammonia and formaldehyde. Preliminary tests showed that torpex would provide an extra 50 percent wallop over conventional TNT. One by one the deadly fish went crashing into the cliffs. A few were duds, most exploded in a graphic demonstration of the greater power of torpex, and, just to make things interesting, one made a circular run.

Topside, Brown knew it was a Mark 14 steam torpedo, because he could see its bubbling wake go forward and then start to curve around in a big arc. Everyone on the bridge spotted it, too, and *Pampanito* quickly went to flank speed with hard rudder, avoiding the wild torpedo handily. Gordon Hopper watched the torpedo speed toward *Litchfield*. Clouds of black smoke belched from her stacks. She seemed to squat momentarily, then take off like a speedboat. The enlisted men topside thought it was hilarious; not so the officers. Obviously, the kinks were not yet ironed out of the American torpedoes, and although Captain Jackson had nothing to do with the ordnance supplied to him, nearly sinking *Litchfield* was another blemish on his efficiency record.[3]

Other obstacles that limited successful submarine operations early in the war included inadequate, unrealistic peacetime training, with an undue emphasis on remaining hidden. There was little training in night surface attacks or in wolf-pack tactics. Many submarine commanders were overcautious, placing survival above damaging the enemy. What was needed was aggressiveness, and captains who were unfit might have been more quickly replaced with younger men with a taste for battle.

The overprudent skippers were soon discovered, but the problem had no easy solution. Theories were advanced about what kind of man made the best skipper: the intelligent one who could solve complex problems; the dullard who wouldn't think but would charge right in; the athlete who had competed in organized sports; or even the peacetime misfit who was trying to redeem himself by building a winning record.

In truth, there were captains in all categories, some who could bring themselves to fight and some who could not. Some had confidence at first but tortured themselves with self-doubt when seemingly well-managed attacks brought only failure. Some lost confidence in their boats, in their crews, or in themselves.[4]

Admiral Lockwood was commendably concerned with saving the lives of his submariners, but this was war. Younger officers believed the policy of keeping the senior men in command was a mistake. Qualified executive officers with several war patrols under their belts chafed at the long wait before they could get their own boats.

To weed out the mediocre, Lockwood instituted a rigorous prepatrol training program, operated by Captain John H. "Babe" Brown. The ComSubPac director of training, Brown had some excellent former skippers working for him. They took charge of newly arriving boats and dealt out a brand of starkly realistic training, including War College–style board games ashore and tough indoctrinational sea operations.[5]

*Pampanito*'s first training run was supervised by Commander Lewis S. Parks, former skipper of *Pompano* and undoubtedly still mourning the loss of his former shipmates. Parks had the *Pampanito* crew make attack approaches against actual American convoys and set them against destroyers in antisubmarine warfare (ASW) practice. Parks then returned to Pearl and wrote up his personal assessment.

Perhaps because of Summers's complaints about Jackson, a second training patrol was scheduled. On board was Captain Frank W. "Mike" Fenno, who had made some notable runs on USS *Trout* (SS 202). When they went after another friendly convoy, Jackson, according to Summers, "froze" again. "It scared the hell out of Mike Fenno," Summers added, "which was pretty hard to do, because he was a tough son-of-a-gun." *Pampanito* made an approach on a tanker, and Jackson, Summers observed, was fooling around on the periscope and didn't know where it went. Fenno snapped, "You better do something, or I'm going to take over!" They eventually finished the exercise and returned to port. Fenno wrote his own assessment.

Little aware of what was occurring in the upper echelons, the crew prepared for patrol. On 6 March 1944, two days before sailing, a yeoman from ComSubPac hurried across the gangway and came aboard *Pampanito*. He handed Charlie McGuire orders to pass on to Lieutenant Commanders Jackson and Summers. They were orders, he confided, for Jackson's relief, orders to his new station, and orders for Summers to assume command.

McGuire was stunned. He made his way to the wardroom, where Jackson, Summers, and other officers were talking. McGuire excused himself as he entered, then explained what the messenger had said as he handed over the packets.

"Jackson got up and he was livid," McGuire said. "He just grabbed them and ran into his office." Summers sat unmoved, as if he were expecting it. McGuire never fully understood what happened. He figured that the younger Academy officers were taking over and that Pete had some influential friends in positions of importance. McGuire never thought that Jackson did anything wrong. "He was fine as a commanding officer," and, McGuire speculated, "I think he would have been a better one than Pete."

Summers sat calmly through the scene because he had already been to see Lew Parks. Parks had told him that both Parks and Mike Fenno concurred that Jackson needed some rest. Jackson was going to be sent to serve under Captain Charles B. "Swede" Momsen, who had been instrumental in developing the Momsen lung, the breathing apparatus used for diving or escaping from sunken submarines. Momsen, Parks said, "was going places," and they were sure he would have a position for Jackson. Summers, Parks told him, was to be the first exec ever to take over directly from his commanding officer.

After Jackson was removed, Summers met with his officers. "Listen," he said. "We're going out on patrol, and I'm not 'Pete' anymore. It may be a little difficult, but you're going to have to accept the fact that I'm your captain. I'm going to try to ignore any mistakes you've made along the line since I was Exec."

Summers appeared to be giving them all a fresh start. But why? Had they not done a good job previously? "The crew came around," Summers concluded. "There were no problems. They were happy and it was perfect." As was usually the case, however, the captain's assessment of the situation did not jibe with the crew's. It would have been news to many of them that everything was so perfect.

Al Van Atta thought that Jackson's quick disappearance was the result of some severe illness. "It seemed the whole affair was shrouded in mystery," he speculated, "And I remember wondering if Jackson knew something I didn't know." Lieutenant Bruckart said that an unspecified illness was the official reason given for Jackson's removal.

Seaman Second Class Jacques F. "Frenchie" Bouchard was more succinct. He was satisfied with Jackson. "Pete," he said, "was lousy."

For Charlie McGuire, everything was all right for less than two hours after Summers took over. Then the yeoman was summoned to the captain's quarters. "McGuire," he said, "I'm kicking you the hell off my boat. I want you to gather all your stuff," Summers ordered. "I'm sending you up to Squadron to do what they want with you. I'm recommending that they disqualify you from submarines and send you to some fast destroyer heading out for the southwest Pacific."

McGuire was in shock. Just a couple of weeks ago Summers introduced him as one of the best men in the navy. In silence, he loaded his gear. On the way out, he noticed a new yeoman already moving in. McGuire stopped to ask him what was going on. Summers saw them and told the replacement, "I don't want you to talk to this man. I don't want you to get any of his bad habits."

Summers followed McGuire topside. "Don't help that man with his bag," he called to the men on deck. "Let him carry it on his own." McGuire thought that the captain was quite a jerk as he walked away, puzzled and angry.

When he got to squadron headquarters, the commander questioned him and said that Summers had sworn that McGuire was not fit to be on submarines. Red still had no clue about what had happened.

"Do you have anyone around here that can speak for you?" the commander asked.

"No," he answered, "but *Golet* will be here in a few days, and the exec tried to get me aboard. Maybe that's what Pete is mad about. Maybe the guy talked to him, and Pete thought I was trying to get off his boat."

McGuire was ordered to the barracks. "Keep your nose clean until the *Golet* gets in," the commander said. "If the exec vouches for you, I'll let you go with him. If he doesn't, I will send you out on a tin can."

That was fair enough for McGuire. He hit the hay early, but about 0200 a chief was pushing on his shoulder, asking, "Are you McGuire from the *Pampanito?*"

"Yessir," he answered. "That is, I was on the *Pampanito,* but I'm not anymore."

"Captain Summers wants you down there immediately," the man said.

"I've been transferred," McGuire insisted.

"Now look," the chief poked him with a finger. "Don't give us any crap. He said you would." Meanwhile, two big Marines strode up. "You either come down on your own power, or I'll have these guys drag you down."

McGuire gathered his gear. On the gangway he met Gunner's Mate Second Class Tony Hauptman, who had served on *Shad* with him. Hauptman said that Summers had just gone to bed. He had an 0500 wake-up call, and McGuire was to take his gear below and wait in the crew's mess until then. At 0500, McGuire knocked at Summers's cabin and stuck his head in.

"Captain, this is McGuire. You sent for me?"

"Oh yes," Summers responded with an uncharacteristic grin. "I've decided to give you another chance. We're going to keep you aboard."

"Captain," McGuire protested, "I don't want another chance. I don't want to serve with you. You kicked me off and. . . ."

Summers cut him off with a growl. "You get your ass into that office and you get this boat ready. Make out the sailing list and get it ready for a war patrol. Now!" McGuire stomped off, cussing under his breath.

After a rush job with the sailing list, McGuire went topside to take the paperwork to the squadron office. Summers saw him leaving.

"Where are you going?" he called out. When McGuire explained, Summers said, "Oh no, you're not." He called to the OOD and a sentry on the pier: "If that man puts one foot off this sub and onto that dock, shoot him! That's an order." McGuire stood there in disbelief while the OOD took his paperwork from him. Fifteen minutes later the hawsers were thrown off, and *Pampanito* finally pulled out for her first patrol.

Later, McGuire learned what all the fuss was about. Apparently James Clark from *Golet* had asked Summers for McGuire. Pete was angry, thinking that McGuire had initiated the contact and was asking anyone he could find to get him off *Pampanito*. Pete blew his stack and told Clark to mind his own business and to stop trying to take his crew. Summers was so perturbed that he didn't want McGuire on *Golet*, but he didn't want him to stay on *Pampanito*, either. The incident that so abruptly changed his mind occurred within a few hours after McGuire was booted off. His replacement was a homosexual. An officer caught him in the crew's mess with a yard worker, in flagrante delicto, or, as McGuire put it, "practicing what homosexuals practice." He was booted off, and McGuire was hauled back aboard.

The episode was over, but it left McGuire feeling great consternation over his future with Captain Summers. "I'll never in my life figure that guy out," he said.[6]

On 15 March 1944, *Pampanito* departed Pearl Harbor escorted by *Patrol Craft 602.* That evening the escort was dismissed, and *Pampanito* proceeded independently to Johnston Island. She had recently been painted what Paul Pappas described as "our new war color." The first fleet boats were painted black, which was thought to be the best camouflage. Black was good for concealment in deep water, but it could be very obvious on the surface in tropical daylight or silhouetted against a yellow moon. Captains called for more moderate colors that ranged from gray to coffee to Mediterranean blue. *Seadragon,* running up and down the China coast in the early days of the war, was so long between proper overhauls that her paint wore down to the red lead undercoating, which made her as obvious as a crimson sore thumb. Experiments were tried with shades of blue paint, but by June 1944 light gray and dark gray were the standard colors. When *Pampanito* left in March, she wore a dusky dark gray on all her vertical surfaces.[7]

*Pampanito* stopped to top off fuel at Johnston Island, then pointed her bow for the Caroline Islands. By this stage of the war the Allies were firmly on the offensive. The defeats of 1942 were long past, and in 1943, Admiral Chester Nimitz's Central Pacific forces pushed their way back up the Solomon Island chain while General Douglas MacArthur's Southwest Pacific command struggled up the New Guinea coast. By February 1944, the Marshall Islands were captured, including Kwajalein, Eniwetok, and Majuro. The last was immediately prepared for submarines, with two tenders and a floating drydock moving into its fine lagoon, giving the Pearl Harbor boats a convenient forward base.

The Carolines, which stretched almost two thousand miles from east to west, consisted of about 550 coral islands, with Truk Atoll the most important in the east and the Palaus likewise in the west. By this time the once formidable Japanese base at Truk had been hit by devastating carrier plane raids and had been reduced to near impotence. Without letup, the western Carolines and the Marianas, north of the Carolines, were targeted. The operation in which *Pampanito* would participate would include strikes by the Fifth Fleet's fast carriers at Palau, Yap, and Woleai to destroy Japanese air potential before advances by both MacArthur and Nimitz. *Pampanito* would act as a lifeguard off the island of Yap, cruising the area in hopes of rescuing any aviators—called zoomies—that might have to ditch in the sea.[8]

On 19 March, *Pampanito* crossed the International Date Line, and the day jumped ahead to 20 March. Two days later she sighted her first unidentified plane, heading north at eight miles' distance. Strangely, it had not been picked up by radar. Summers dove the sub for about twenty minutes. When he returned for a look, all was clear. It was the first of thirty-four times this patrol that they were to be forced down by enemy planes.

On 23 March, two planes were picked up by the SD radar. The next afternoon, high periscope watch sighted a two-engine Japanese "Lily"-type bomber at nine miles and closing. Again, the radar did not detect it. *Pampanito* went down, this time for an hour and a half. Paul Pappas recorded in his diary that the plane "got a little closer than usual before being spotted." The arbitrary way the SD radar would either "see" or "miss" the planes was disturbing.[9]

The crew did receive a bit of good news on the radio the evening of 25 March. Bill Grady's wife, Jean, had given birth to their first child on 23 March. Both mother and daughter were doing fine. Grady was ecstatic—at least until he remembered promising his shipmates that if the baby was a girl he would get them all drunk. Now Bill would have to figure out how to live up to his word.

On 26 March, *Pampanito* experienced more of the equipment problems that would constantly plague her. Southeast of Guam another plane was sighted. When they submerged, they discovered that sea suction and discharge valves on the trim manifold were leaking badly, and they stayed down eight hours to grind and reseat the valves. Next, they found that number six torpedo tube had flooded. Surfacing that evening, Summers ordered the fish removed from the tube. The after body was flooded, and they pulled the gyro, steering, and depth mechanisms; cleaned them with oil; washed them in alcohol; dried them; baked them; and reinstalled them. In the twilight Summers decided to stop the boat. Tony Hauptman went over the side to inspect the outer torpedo tube door, but the door and gasket looked sound. The leak had to be somewhere inside the tube.

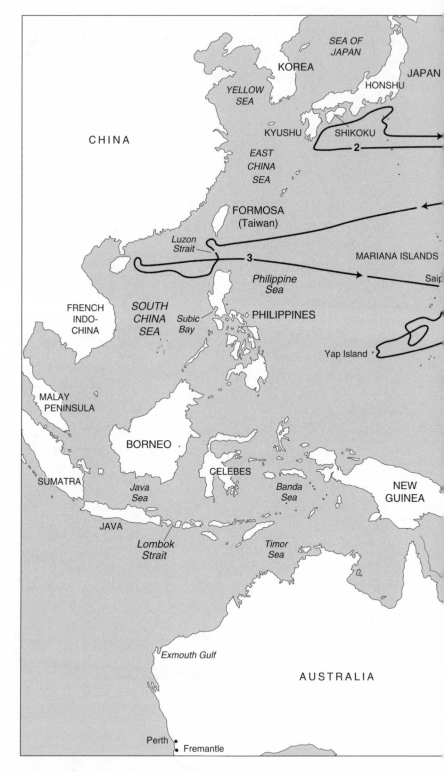

USS *Pampanito* patrol routes 1, 2, and 3

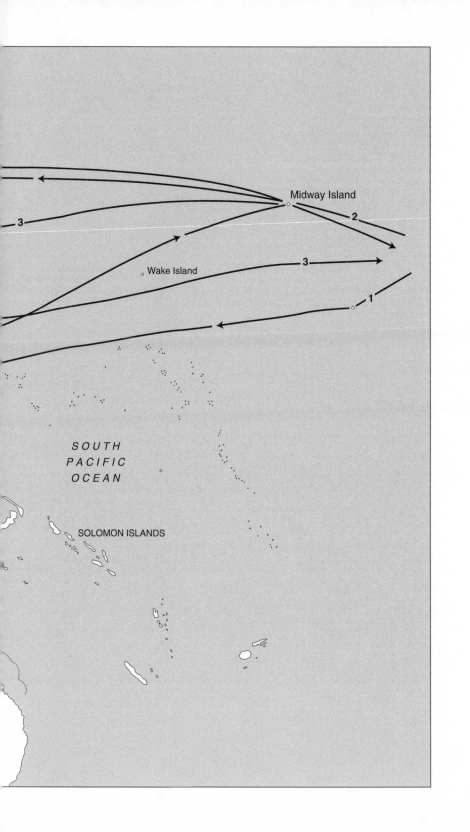

Midway Island

3

2

Wake Island

3

1

SOUTH
PACIFIC
OCEAN

SOLOMON ISLANDS

Meanwhile, George Moffett worked into the night to test and retune the SD radar. The events reinforced McGuire's belief that although the United States was supposedly wealthy and had the technology available to make high-quality products, it was too penurious to do so. A penny-pinching Congress, McGuire believed, "didn't give the sailors a decent product to fight with."

*Pampanito* reached its designated area on 27 March and spent the day on submerged patrol, slowly traveling west along the Saipan–Palau shipping route. The next evening, persistent leaking in number six tube forced another inspection. A 3/8-inch pipe plug was missing from the forward roller housing in a part of the tube that extended outside the pressure hull. Once again, Tony Hauptman prepared to go down into the void. However, at 2119 the retuned SD picked up a flight of five planes at six miles and closing. Quickly, Hauptman was recalled. On the bridge, Summers watched until the planes closed to four miles. Because of the fairly bright moonlight, he finally gave the order to dive.

Twenty minutes later they surfaced to try again. Entrance to the forward roller housing was down under the superstructure, in the maze of steel supports between the pressure hull and the topside deck, just aft of the chain locker, with direct access to the sea. Hauptman went in. Inside the forward torpedo room air pressure was built up so that when Hauptman removed the roller housing, water would not flood into the room. He removed the housing, and a brazed plug was installed in the hole. Back in the void, Hauptman held the housing in place while it was bolted in position from inside the torpedo tube. After an hour and a half, Hauptman returned for a well-deserved rest, and *Pampanito* again had service of all six forward tubes. Her equipment was functioning properly— at least for the time being.

While *Pampanito* was running on the surface early in the morning on 30 March, the radar brought two more plane contacts and two more dives. Shortly after the second dive a distant bomb explosion was heard. Had they been spotted? Summers held the boat down longer than usual, just in case. Before surfacing, however, a new and serious leak was discovered in the chief petty officers' quarters, this time in a joint of the hydraulic piping for the bow plane rigging. It was losing a considerable amount of oil. They stayed down while repairs were made with torch and silver-solder, which fixed the leak but fouled the air with smoke. Four hours later they surfaced and began taking a suction through the boat. It was 0837. Normally, by this time of the morning *Pampanito* would have had her batteries fully charged and be settled in for the day. Plane contacts and leaks had caused her to submerge before a full charge was taken. Now they had been up only two minutes when another plane contact was made: a two-engine bomber at five miles and closing. Down went the boat again. It would be an extremely long, hot, foul-air day.

While *Pampanito* had been jockeying for position south of Yap on 30 March, three of the four carrier groups of the Fifth Fleet had been pounding the Palau Islands. After blasting that target, the task force headed northeast to do the same to Yap. It was a large operation, and *Pampanito* was only a small part of it. Nine other submarines were directly involved. USS *Gar* (SS 206), USS *Blackfish* (SS 221), and USS *Bashaw* (SS 241) were stationed south of Palau, while USS *Archerfish* (SS 311), USS *Tunny* (SS 282), USS *Tullibee* (SS 284), and USS *Tang* (SS 306) were watching the northern quadrant. *Harder* had followed *Pampanito* from Pearl Harbor to Johnston Island, one day behind her. *Harder* was to perform lifeguard duty off Woleai.

Although it took care to swing south of possible Japanese search planes from Truk, the U.S. force was sighted the third day out of Majuro. The sighting, combined with increased U.S. radio traffic, convinced the Japanese to flee the area. The 63,000-ton battleship *Musashi*, the light cruiser *Oyodo*, and two destroyers headed north for Kure Naval Base. By pure luck, the group exited through a gap in the screen where *Tullibee* should have been. Only *Tunny*, on 29 March, managed to get in an attack, firing a salvo of six torpedoes. A destroyer spotted the sub and flashed a warning, and *Musashi* was able to evade all but one torpedo, which struck her bow and killed seven men but did little serious structural damage.

Where was *Tullibee*? On the night of 26 March, in a maelstrom of rain squalls, the lookouts caught sight of a fleeing convoy of four freighters and three escorts. Closing as near as he could, Commander Charles F. Brindupke fired two torpedoes at three thousand yards' range. A minute later, *Tullibee* was taken apart by a violent explosion caused by a circular run of one of her own torpedoes. Only a few survivors were blown off into the sea as the submarine sank almost immediately. The next day, the last survivor, Gunner's Mate C. W. Kuykendall, was picked up by a Japanese escort vessel.[10]

Perhaps this lifeguard duty was not such a "safe" type of patrol after all. Why was *Pampanito* assigned here? Admiral Lockwood generally sent the hottest ships to the hottest spots. The average boat went to a cooler area, where the skipper and crew could cut their teeth on an easier assignment.[11] *Harder* was considered a hot ship, however, and she was cooling her heels as a lifeguard off Woleai. The truth was, there were no "safe" patrol areas for a submarine. There was always the chance a Japanese convoy would blunder across *Pampanito*'s path, giving Summers an opportunity to prove his mettle.

The idea of acting as lifeguard for carrier raids was first tested in September 1943, and the first trial lifeguard mission was given to USS *Snook* (SS 279) in a carrier strike at Marcus Island. Although no planes were lost in that raid, one month later the program bore fruit. USS *Skate* (SS 305) was lifeguard for a carrier attack on Wake Island. *Skate* managed to pick up two airmen, but not before Lieutenant Junior Grade Willis E. Maxon III was mortally wounded by Japanese gunfire. Lockwood had to weigh Maxon's life. Should he have *Skate* proceed at top speed to Midway, or remain in the Wake area for the chance of picking up more fliers? *Skate* stayed. She eventually picked up four more downed aviators, although Maxon perished. From that time on there was an unbreakable bond between submariners and carrier pilots.[12]

Now *Pampanito* was bobbing in the gentle swells south of Yap, and her crew was thrilled to break the surface and throw open the hatches for some much needed fresh air. The last odors of the soldering torch were blown out, and the batteries were charged. It was 31 March, and the carrier strike would begin shortly after daylight. Unknown to them, *Gar* had been kept hopping the day before, 240 miles to the southwest, making six sweeps close in to the Palau beaches to rescue eight naval airmen.

At 0702, *Pampanito*'s tuned SD radar picked up a formation of planes at forty miles and closing. As the Dauntless dive bombers and Hellcat fighters from Rear Admiral John W. Reeves's Carrier Division Three roared in, one plane was seen diving in their direction. Although it may have been American, no plane diving on a submarine can be considered "friendly," and *Pampanito* went down again.

While she was underwater, the first strike of twenty-nine planes from USS *Enterprise* (CV 6) swept over Yap. The flight over the island found no ships or planes, but the dive bombers and fighters worked over two half-completed airfields. *Pampanito* was back on the surface at 0830 to see the first strike leaving and the second coming in. This group of twenty-five planes finished off the oil storage tanks, docks, warehouses, and radio station. *Pampanito* exchanged signals with one of the returning planes at 0947. No friendlies were down. With no targets remaining, a late morning third strike of forty planes was diverted to Ulithi Atoll. The last of those returning at 1240 sent "Thank you for standing by" to the submarine below. The raid was over. If Summers had hoped to pluck anyone from the sea, he would have to wait for another opportunity.[13]

With the day's excitement over, *Pampanito* closed Yap's south coast, patrolling on the surface. Tuning in the radio, the men were able to pick up Tokyo Rose. Tonight's broadcast, Pappas recorded in his diary, was directed "to the Yank fighting men in the southwest Pacific." The Americans, said Rose, were being outclassed and outfought by the Imperial Japanese Navy and Army, and they ought to give up their senseless struggle. "To hear them tell it," Pappas wrote, "the Japs are world beaters." The "Zero Hour" radio program was on the air—sixty minutes filled with "good old American swing recordings." Floating over the airwaves that evening were popular tunes such as Bing Crosby's "Poinciana," Tommy Dorsey's "I'll Be Seeing You," Dick Haymes's "Long Ago and Far Away," Harry James's "I'll Get By," Guy Lombardo's "It's Love-Love-Love," the Pied Pipers' "Mairzy Doats," and Frank Sinatra's "I Couldn't Sleep a Wink Last Night." "Morale," said Pappas, "was improved one hundred percent, and everyone had a good time." He speculated that if the taxpayers of Japan were paying for that program, they were sure taking a beating.[14]

At sunup on 1 April, *Pampanito* dove about ten miles southeast of Yap's Tomil Harbor and moved in to reconnoiter. There were no ships in the harbor, and they could see no visible damage except for one or two small columns of smoke, from the previous day's attacks, wafting lazily skyward on the breeze. It looked cool and refreshing on the beach. Had they known there were no operational Japanese planes ashore, they could have surfaced for a pleasant change of pace.

Photographer Paul Pappas rigged the ship's camera to the periscope and took various shots of the harbor. Pappas enjoyed the photographic work. The ship carried both a still camera and a movie camera, but private cameras, like diaries, were prohibited. Harold L. Chinn, a twenty-two-year-old fireman first class from Dayton, Kentucky, wondered how so many men secreted aboard supposedly forbidden items. "It was your ass if they caught you with a camera," he said. But, since most American servicemen were not concerned with regulations they saw as nonessential, both cameras and diaries were smuggled aboard and kept hidden away in sea bags and lockers.

The submarine slowly circled Yap. It had been another long, hot day. In fact, the torpedomen were beginning to complain about the heat. Although the forward and after torpedo rooms were usually the coolest compartments, temperatures there were approaching 100 degrees—generally a situation that only the enginemen had to contend with. What was wrong now? Even after surfacing at night, a cool air ventilation through the boat did not seem to help. The engines were running hot.

Properly functioning engines were essential on a submarine. Lacking the space of a surface ship, a submarine needed a small but powerful engine with a minimum of weight for the power produced. At first, gasoline engines were tried, but they were not safe in a submarine. The gasoline fumes were unhealthy even when the boat was running on the surface with open hatches, and they were dangerous because a mixture of gasoline vapor and air is highly explosive. Errant sparks could, and did, cause disastrous explosions.

The alternative was the diesel engine. It produced higher compression than a gasoline engine. Compression produces heat, and the great compression in a diesel produced enough heat to cause ignition. On the upward stroke of the piston the temperature reached one thousand degrees, and at that point a jet of fuel oil was injected which immediately burned and forced the piston back down with great energy. In a solid, airless injection, oil was forced into the cylinders at pressures as great as twenty thousand pounds per square inch. The injector was built to far greater specifications than in a gasoline engine, but its benefits were tremendous.

Diesels did not directly drive the propeller shafts in most of the fleet boats. Even on the surface they drove a generator, which could be used either to charge the battery or drive the electric motor. Motor speed was independent of diesel speed; the engine could always be kept at optimum, noncritical speed. Diesel-electric drive was also more reliable, because the operators could shut down one or more engines for repair while still running at a useful speed. Diesel-electric drive may have been the most important interwar American design innovation.[15]

In 1932 the Bureau of Engineering (BuEng) invited all U.S. diesel engine makers to bid on a new generation of lightweight engines suited for mass production. The most feasible bids came from the Winton Engine Corporation (later the Cleveland Diesel Engine Division of General Motors [GM]); the Fairbanks-Morse (FM) Company of Beloit, Wisconsin; and the Hooven, Owens, Rentschler (HOR) Company of Hamilton, Ohio.

The HOR engine at first excited interest because it offered more power in a smaller package than a GM or FM. Some of the first boats to get HOR engines were *Pompano, Salmon, Seal, Skipjack, Sargo, Saury, Spearfish, Seadragon,* and *Sealion.* However, initial optimism turned sour when it was found that brittle steel in the HOR diesels caused many breakdowns. Problems occurred with excessive cylinder-head wear, broken piston rods, ring troubles, carbon deposits, and engine block wear. To the dismay of many, the first twelve-boat squadron built at Electric Boat Company was fitted with HOR engines. As crews of HOR submarines were exposed to increasing breakdowns, they came up with more obvious salty nicknames for the disliked engines. Finally, Admiral Ernest J. King, commander in chief, U.S. Fleet, ordered the engines discontinued, and as the submarines came back to the States for their regular overhauls, they had their "whores" replaced by FMs or GM Wintons. In submariner's jargon, said Lieutenant Bruckart, the replacement process was called a "horectomy."

The GMs and FMs, similar to the large diesel-electric engines used in fast locomotives, came to be the most popular and reliable engines on the fleet boats. The GMs had sixteen conventional cylinders, but *Pampanito* was fitted out with four ten-cylinder, opposed-piston FMs. The two pistons in each cylinder were fired from a single injection chamber with crankshafts above and below. The FM used solid (airless) injection. The cylinders were small and needed less cooling water. Fresh water, rather than salt water from the sea, was circulated through a heat exchanger (radiator), thus eliminating saltwater crusting on the cooling surfaces. The fast-circulating fresh water was very efficient, and the engines usually ran at less than 500 degrees, compared with 750 to 1,000 degrees in other designs. Each engine was also rigged with a seawater system that circulated around the freshwater coolers, and the fresh water, in turn, circulated through the engine block.

The enginemen might have had the toughest job on board. Carmody said that at times it felt like 200 degrees. It was so humid that everything dripped with moisture. The air conditioners, which were installed mainly to keep the equipment running more efficiently and to cut down on electrical shorts, didn't help much in the engine rooms. Carmody lived in skivvies and sandals, contending constantly with prickly heat and foot fungus. They had to stand their watches in a terribly noisy environment where earplugs were almost mandatory, ready to make repairs that required brute strength on occasion. Yet, Earl Watkins liked the FMs, as did almost every engineman. He thought they were reliable, with no valves and fewer working parts.[16]

So why were *Pampanito*'s engines exceptionally hot? Watkins, as assistant oiler, would usually be in the bilges lubricating and cleaning the filters or running the evaporators so that fresh water was always available for the engines. And there was the trouble. Watkins added fresh water, but all the improvements built into the latest FM diesels could not overcome the misfortune of having a couple of broken circulating water pumps. Until they could be repaired, auxiliarymen scurried about the boat redirecting the air conditioning system to cool off the hottest compartments. With the torpedo rooms approaching 100 degrees, the engine rooms were intolerable at 120.

*Pampanito* circled Yap for the first four days in April. On the third, Summers pulled closer to Tomil Harbor for a good look. He spotted what appeared to be a small destroyer escort moored to the wharf, but he made no attack. In Japan, memorial day celebrations were proceeding for the Emperor Jimmu, and the cherry blossoms were beginning to bloom. But in the crowded submarine floating off the island of Yap, the heat and inactivity were stifling.

To pass away the endless hours, a marathon poker game was in progress. Walt Richter was raking in so much cash with sensational hands and bluffs

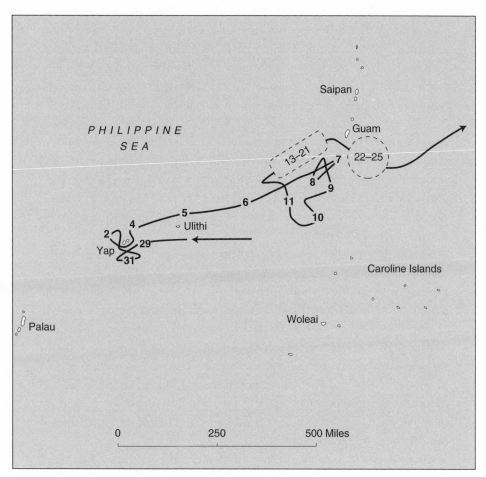

Detail of first patrol, 29 March–25 April 1944

that he was nicknamed "The Gambler." Some of the men were beginning to wonder just how much of Richter's winning streak was a result of good luck. The electricians were also winning big. The blond Texan Ralph W. Attaway, an electrician's mate first class, had spent some time on *S-44* and made the first six patrols on USS *Thresher* (SS 200). With his last full house he raked in enough chips to make his winnings top three hundred dollars. Grim faces stared at the cards as sweat dripped to the tabletop. Some men left the game angry, but there were always others to step in. Tempers grew short. Torpedoman's Mate First Class Robert J. Matheny lost money, and he was not particularly happy with the heat or the electricians. "Everything electrical is electrically full of shit," he bellowed while throwing in his hand.

But not all the electricians were serene, either. Electrician's Mate First Class Lawrence H. Langin was in an uproar because he was sure the batteries had been overcharged and hydrogen was building up in the boat. A check showed no unusual levels. Even the boat's pharmacist's mate, John B. O'Neill, had put himself on the sick list, where he had languished for days. Pappas recorded in his diary that at least the food was satisfactory. Sunday's supper included "good turkey and lemon pie," and on Monday, some "even better spaghetti." For the first time this patrol, the showers were turned on in the hopes of cooling down the men's temperatures and tempers.

Finally, late in the evening of 4 April, a dispatch from ComSubPac directed *Pampanito* to move south of Guam. It was good riddance to Yap. Hatches were briefly thrown open to draw air through the boat, and the night even seemed cooler than usual. Spirits brightened. Pappas recorded, "Everyone is hoping something shows up to offer a little excitement."[17]

Although it was not Summers's usual practice, on 5 April he brought *Pampanito* up for an uncharacteristic surface daylight patrol that seemed to perk everyone up. The record player was turned on, and men tapped their feet to some popular tunes. A Japanese broadcast was picked up telling of the dastardly American bombing of Yap Island, and it succeeded only in cheering up the crew.

Surface patrol was short-lived, however, for by sunup of 6 April, *Pampanito* went down for routine maintenance of her torpedoes and stayed down for the entire day. She had sixteen Mark 14 torpedoes in the forward torpedo room and eight Mark 18s in the after room, but would they ever be needed? The crew wanted action. Ever since they shifted areas, scuttlebutt was that they would soon find a convoy. In fact, the crew did not know it, but information had come from Pearl Harbor alerting *Pampanito* to an expected convoy southwest of Guam. Although these radio messages were to be kept under wraps, secrets were almost impossible to keep. Pappas wrote in his diary a few mundane facts, such as that they had run out of flashlight batteries, then added, "Rumors [are] we may pick up a convoy tomorrow."

Men thought about an upcoming attack and the possible depth chargings that might ensue. Many had never experienced either. Their only indoctrination came off Pearl Harbor during training, when a destroyer dropped several "ash cans" a few hundred yards away for their initiation ceremony.

Depth charge tests had been performed on submarines for many years. Tests were conducted in 1940 on *Tambor*-class submarines, which had the same 9/16-inch mild steel hulls as the *Gato* class. Charges were exploded from 340 yards away to as close as 100 yards. Damage ranged from broken bulbs to parted air lines to valve leaks and broken fuses. Yet depth charges proved less lethal than had been imagined, and surface ships increasingly had their three-hundred-pound charges replaced with six-hundred-pounders. By 1944 it was thought that a three-hundred-pound charge had to explode four to five yards away in order to break a pressure hull, but even at twice that distance it would probably disable the boat.

There were conflicting theories on minimizing depth charge damage. One school believed that a boat under excessive strain from great depths needed only a moderately close explosion to cave it in. The other school thought that submerging from two hundred feet to four hundred feet would only increase pressure a relatively minimal one hundred pounds per square inch, but that the chance of being hit with a lethal charge when doubling depth was reduced to one-eighth. There was no consensus, and skippers had to make their own decisions.[18]

What type of Japanese antisubmarine devices would *Pampanito* likely encounter? The underwater sound detector, a passive sonar or hydrophone, had an effective range of about one thousand yards, or less if the escort was making over eight knots. Since submarines generally fired torpedoes from beyond this range, hydrophones spoiled few attacks. They were more useful in tracking a sub after the attack, but currents and water temperature often disturbed their effectiveness.

Active sonar, which relied on underwater soundwave echoes, much as radar used microwave echoes, was more dependable than the hydrophone. Fortunately for the Americans, however, the Japanese equipment was substandard. Models used in 1944 had a practical range of twenty-two hundred yards in a vessel traveling at six knots. Increasing speed decreased its reliability, until at twenty knots it was useless.

High-frequency direction finding (HF-DF) was a method of locating ships by crossing bearings from their radio transmissions. Under optimum atmospheric conditions a skilled operator could pinpoint a bearing within a few degrees. More cross-bearings might narrow the target space down to twenty-five square miles. "Huff-duff" was used to great effect in the Atlantic, but as late as April 1944 the Japanese Maizuru Naval District reported that it had never located an American submarine using radio bearings.[19]

If *Pampanito* were to be found and depth-charged, it would most likely be as a result of giving away her own position during an attack. Almost every Japanese ship carried depth charges, from merchant ships to the smallest patrol craft. A fleet destroyer might carry only thirty, and a patrol craft thirty-six, while a *kaibokan,* a coast defense vessel resembling an American destroyer escort, might have up to three hundred. The standard depth charge was a 350-pounder, armed with 230 pounds of explosive. Severe damage could be achieved by an explosion within fifty or sixty feet, but the lethal radius apparently had to be within twenty feet.

The Japanese knew little about the correct use of radar and sonar in detecting submarines, and evidently they had little understanding of how sound was affected in relation to temperature layers. Another problem facing the Japanese was one of their own making. Japanese naval strategists assumed that Americans were too soft to endure the physical and mental rigors of submarine duty, and thus they never thought it necessary to fully develop their ASW tactics. Neither did the Japanese realize the depths to which American submarines could dive, and they habitually set their charges too shallow. One reason for this may have been that the deepest most of the Japanese submarines could dive was about 330 feet. As a result, Japanese ASW tactics called for setting charges from 150 to 200 feet. At first, American submarines merely had to dive below 250 feet to escape. Eventually the Japanese began using larger explosive charges and setting them deeper.

It has been said that the Japanese changed tactics because of an infamous leak in the otherwise "Silent Service." A public official who had either visited a front-line base or had access to a secret briefing in Pearl had gone back to the States and had informed the press that American submariners did not fear Japanese destroyers because their depth charges were not powerful enough and were set too shallow. This was believed to have led to the loss of ten submarines when the Japanese promptly made adjustments.[20]

Even when Japanese ASW forces made contact with a submarine, the escort skippers were loath to engage the sub. High command was torn between saving its destroyers for the big decisive fleet engagement on which it had based its war strategy and the need to use them as convoy escorts. The destroyer captains even argued that their ships incurred too much risk in stopping to attack a submarine. Therefore, Japanese destroyers tended to lay down charges just long enough to get a convoy safely past the point of attack and not stick around in a cat-and-mouse game with a submarine. Also, the limited number of depth charges available would dictate how many were dropped. One always had to save charges for a future encounter. In fact, the Japanese had lost escorts to the explosions of their own depth charges, and they were getting very frustrated about their inability to sink American submarines. Instead of blaming their own poor ASW weapons and tactics, the Japanese believed the Americans had developed some secret, special measures of evasion.[21]

Not knowing of the problems the Imperial Japanese Navy was having, many U.S. submarine captains still exercised caution. The skippers and the men knew only too well that since the war's beginning, a large number of submarines had been lost, and whether by poor fortune, by skilled Japanese attacks, or by accident, they were still gone, taking hundreds of sailors with them.[22]

So, after spending the day safely submerged for routine maintenance on her torpedoes, *Pampanito* finally surfaced at 1900 on 6 April. An hour later, a plane contact just after sunset drove her down again. By 2030 she was back up, entering a quadrant that the ComSubPac radio message indicated might be fertile waters for enemy shipping. The clock ticked past midnight. It was Good Friday.

Belaying his one-day experiment with surface patrolling, Summers took the boat back down at sunrise. He just could not seem to shake his old habits. "I've made some patrols before, and I've been through some pretty hairy times," Pete explained. "In fact it has got me so damn conservative because of these other skippers I've been associated with."

It was a lonely and frightening experience to command a submarine. There were no ships sailing in company, no visible support, no one else to take responsibility. The skipper had his boat and the lives of about eighty men on his conscience. Deep in enemy waters and thousands of miles from a friendly base, he had to devise his own tactics, weighing the chances of his boat against real or imagined enemy countermeasures. In the first year of the war, 30 percent of the skippers were relieved of command for lack of aggression. As the older men were phased out, younger officers took over. By 1943 the average commanding officer was thirty-two years old, and in 1945 there were a few twenty-six-year-old skippers. Pete Summers was thirty, and one of the first of the Naval Academy Class of 1936 to command his own boat. He had plenty of experience under his belt—perhaps too much.

This day he was not about to let the ghosts of his past commanders haunt his decisions. He had complained enough about their poor performances, and now he would show them all what he could do. At half past noon, sonar picked up the sound of echo-ranging, bearing 078. Two minutes later, smoke was spotted on the horizon. In expectation of the coming attack, Summers dove to three hundred feet, looking for a temperature gradient, a cool deflective layer that would confuse enemy detection attempts.

Water temperature affected the transmission of sound. Warm and cold layers would bend sound waves either up or down, much as light bends through a prism. A submarine right on or slightly under a gradient might be completely missed by the deflected sound waves.

A bathythermograph (BT) measured and recorded water temperatures at different depths. Developed by Woods Hole Oceanographic Institute in 1934, the BT was first tested for submarine use in 1942. It employed a stylus that traced a waving vertical line on a lampblacked card that visually recorded temperature changes during a dive. The BT could locate a "shadow zone" for a submarine to hide in, where it might maintain trim without pumping, blowing, or changing speed to maintain depth. The gradients could be ideal places to hide and float silently and effortlessly.[23]

On this day there was no temperature gradient, just a straight isotherm all the way down. "To hell with it," Pete cursed, as he took the boat back up to periscope depth. "I was full of piss and gin," he said later. He would get in his first attack as a new skipper come hell or high water.[24]

A Japanese convoy was steaming southwest, course 240, in an almost glassy calm sea about seventy miles southwest of Guam. It looked like it

might be heading for the Palaus, now that the American carriers had left
the area. At 1239 Summers held the periscope up, since they were still
much too far away for it to be spotted. There was one small coal-burning
ship putting out a lot of smoke. The exec, Jeff Davis, thumbed through the
Office of Naval Intelligence Manual and pointed to *Hokuyo Maru,* a
freighter of about forty-two hundred tons.[25] Summers concurred with his
identification. Another look showed one escort that appeared to be a
*Chidori*-class torpedo boat.[26] The bearing was 072. Summers ordered down
periscope, and *Pampanito* proceeded on a normal approach course. At
1252 Summers raised the scope again. The sea was still calm but disturbed
slightly with undulating three- to four-foot swells. Lack of a fresh breeze
meant the periscope-hiding, white-breaking curls were absent. Observations were to be cut to a minimum.

There was another small freighter in column astern of the leader, while
the *Chidori* remained on his port bow. There must have been something
of value in this small group, for it was making radical zigs at twelve knots
while keeping to a base course of about 240 degrees.

By 1326, Summers was pleased with the approach and the setup. He
conned *Pampanito* left to 110 degrees for a 75-degree starboard track on
the leading freighter. Suddenly, the *Chidori* began to swing right, crossing
over toward the sub from the port to starboard bow of the target freighter.
There was no serious problem yet, but a further periscope sweep revealed
a second mast approaching. It looked like another escort, this one astern
and to starboard of the second freighter in column.

Four minutes later, when Summers brought the periscope up, *Pampanito*
was pointing like a gun barrel at the leading freighter. The forward
torpedoes were set with zero gyro angles. There would be no course
adjustments needed, for they would streak straight and true to the target.
The torpedo run was to be fourteen hundred yards.

"All right, a final periscope look and we'll shoot," Pete announced. A
quick scope swing to the right revealed . . . wait! Something was wrong
with the scope. Summers pulled his head away as if to adjust his eyes, then
again pressed it against the eyepiece. His field of vision had gone completely
gray. In a flash he realized he was in high power and flipped the
magnification to low. The solid gray suddenly became the side of the
*Chidori,* rapidly reducing her own angle to zero and heading in fast.

Foam boiled at her bow. Her range was less than five hundred yards and closing.

"Take her deep!" Summers called out to Jeff Davis. "By golly damn, he's right there!" Without lowering the scope, Summers saw the leading freighter swing hard to port with smoke billowing from its stack. He watched until the water closed over his field of vision.

It happened so fast that the *Chidori* pounded over *Pampanito* without having her depth charges ready. Somewhere astern, one charge exploded, but not very close. The men chuckled a bit. If that's the best the Japanese had to offer, there was nothing to fear. Yet there was no point in firing now, with the setup changing so rapidly and the target heading away. Summers decided to continue on his course. He could run under the target and come up on the other side of the formation or possibly make an attack on the second ship in the column.

"Okay, we'll get under the other side," he told the team in the conning tower. He wondered why the escort was able to pick him up so quickly. He thought that his periscope exposure was minimal. Perhaps the sound man was very expert and was able to pick up the air noises while the torpedoes were being made ready, or maybe he was very good at echo-ranging. It was a disturbing predicament.

The lack of follow-up depth charges convinced Summers to belay the deep dive. He called for periscope depth. Listening intently on the JP hydrophone in the forward torpedo room, Radioman Third Class Roger Walters heard screws astern, moving in rapidly. He reported over the phone. No one in the conning tower, where they were engrossed in plotting another attack, seemed to react.

At 1345, Summers realized the improbability of running under a target that was making twelve knots and heading away from him. He popped the scope up for a quick look at the second freighter, now on his port quarter. In the forward torpedo room the drumming in Walters's headphones was deafening. He repeated his call: "High speed screws dead astern!" Finally there was a reaction. Summers swung the scope to see another escort's bow bearing down on him. Radioman First Class Mervin Hill, on the JK sound gear in the conning tower, heard the warning. For the second time he saw Summers neglect to lower the scope. The captain folded his arms across the handles and shouted, "Take her down. All ahead emergency!"

Roger Walters pulled his headphones off. There was no need for them now. Everyone in the boat could hear the swish, swish, swish of the escort's screws. On sound with Walters was Radioman Second Class William H. McCollum, a last-minute transfer from Submarine Division 201's relief crew. He had been on *S-28* in the Aleutians, and he was very familiar with the sound gear. He didn't know why no one in the conning tower had got the word the first time. He plainly heard the approaching screws and guessed it was a small, high-speed boat, probably a *Chidori*. "It ran right over us at periscope depth," he says.

Nearby, Bob Bennett heard the screws getting louder. "It's like being under a railroad trestle when a train goes by," he said. In the crew's mess, Charlie McGuire waited out the action. Having finished his turn at the helm, he sat at a table off the passageway and listened to the talker on the intercom. He heard the orders to open the outer torpedo tube doors and the standby to fire. The explosion startled him. "What the hell's that?" he said. "Did we fire already?" McGuire didn't believe it was a depth charge coming so soon after their own approach.

Paul Pappas waited out the attack in the after torpedo room. The first depth charge was a surprise. "It got everybody hepped up about it," he said. There was nothing to do but go deep and wait. Pappas helped the torpedomen rig the compartment for a depth charge attack "in nothing flat." He wondered how that son-of-a-gun had picked them up so fast. Three minutes later *Pampanito* was jolted by two depth charges, fairly close, but high and to starboard. "He really let us have two nice ones," Pappas recorded. He wished the boat was deeper. The explosions took his mind off trying to sink a Japanese ship.

Bennett listened to the escort speed by. Some seconds later he heard the telltale click of the hydrostatically activated bellows that armed the device to explode when it reached its preset depth. The click, said Pappas, "sets your hair on edge." A fraction of a second later came the whoomp! of the explosion, followed by the prolonged swish of the pressure wave forcing water through the superstructure. The second click . . . whoomp! followed, sending its advancing pressure wave in to resonate with the retreating initial turbulence. The boat rocked. Light bulbs rattled and swayed, and men looked instinctively up at the bulkheads.[27]

*Pampanito* continued her dive. It sounded like there were two escorts above. The crew heard the screws of one crossing over in one direction, followed by the second on another tangent. Walters picked up the fathometer pinging. The Japanese were ranging in. Bennett visualized what was going on above them. One escort was directly overhead, while the other stood off at a distance, pinging at an angle. "They're working two sides of a triangle," Bennett said, "trying to pinpoint us."

Fifteen minutes passed. The first few explosions didn't impress everyone in the after torpedo room. Bob Matheny, torpedoman in charge, was cooled off after losing his poker money and managed to joke about it with the electrician Pappas. The other torpedomen, Leonard Baron (first class), Lewis J. Agnello (third class), and Bernard Zalusky (third class), kept each other's spirits up by joking about the Japanese detection efforts. The fifth torpedoman, Frank J. Lederer (second class), was the only crewman who had not been born in the United States. Frank hailed from Graz, Austria, where he had been born on 11 November 1921, Armistice Day, but he was well accustomed to the American way of life—and American humor. "Everybody is kidding each other about how good that Jap sound man is," Pappas wrote, "and that his Captain ought to promote him." All the while they really hoped and prayed that he would lose them. In fact it was, Pappas recorded, "just the lull before the storm."

In the forward torpedo room the torpedomen were close to the sound men, and they got the action first-hand. One set of screws pulled away—but wait, here came the other, from astern again. Sound reported: "They're pinging. Switching to short scale. They're going to make a run."

"The target bears about 180," Bill McCollum called out.

"The target!" Woody Weaver snapped back. "We're the target!"

Van Atta was standing near Mervin Hill, who operated the high frequency sound gear from the conning tower. Hill gave the same warning, "They're starting another run," and removed his headphones to prevent ruptured eardrums. It was the signal for Van Atta to go "white knuckled."

About 1403–1405, Seaman Gordon Hopper in the forward torpedo room listened to the screws rumble overhead. He tilted his head slightly, following the noise as it trailed from stern to bow. He grabbed onto a bunk frame and held his breath—ten seconds . . . twenty seconds . . . thirty . . .

Ha! Hopper was delighted. The Japanese had passed directly overhead without knowing where they were.

Ka-boom! *Pampanito* was rocked by a tremendous detonation. It threw Hopper off his feet. He realized he had not considered the time it took for the depth charges to sink. Let's see, about ten feet per second, times . . . ka-boom! Another one rocked them. Bennett's locker blew open, plastic labels popped off the telephone jacks, gaskets on the torpedo tube doors were damaged and leaking, and the chainfall swung viciously over Duncan Brown's vacated bunk. To Hopper the sound of the exploding charges "defied description." Sea valves were spun open by the force of the exploding "cans." He watched, "horrified, as the massive air manifold over the torpedo tubes bent to a horseshoe shape." Hopper didn't know what to expect next. It had only been a few seconds, but he thought the attack would go on forever, and surely they would sink. While holding on, Hopper prayed that he might die bravely.

Woody Weaver took it a bit more in stride. It was his baptism of fire, and although the sub vibrated like a tuning fork, Weaver was too busy reseating valves and assessing damage to be frightened.

Ka-boom! In the maneuvering room, Electrician's Mate Third Class Donald I. Ferguson heard the clicks on the first charges, then lost track in the successive blows. The percussion stunned him. He saw stars. It was eerie, because the entire room was enveloped in fog. No, he blinked, it was not fog, but rather a year's accumulation of loose cork, paint chips, and dust, fluttering down to cloud his vision.

Bud Arcement was in the forward battery room and searched the staterooms for leaks. No one had a regular battle station in officer's country, and he had drawn the duty. He had on his headphones, mouthpiece, and extension cord. While he was on his hands and knees securing the forward battery-well hatch, a depth charge exploded and knocked a jacket off a hook and over his head. Everything went dark. He couldn't feel the jacket because of the headphones. He fumbled for his lantern. In the blackness he couldn't see and he couldn't hear. He thought he was dead.

Ka-boom! The fifth charge went off. Pappas thought all of them "came within a space of three to four seconds," with the last two being "right on the ball." Cork flew off the overheads. Light bulbs burst. Number seven main ballast tank began to leak, and splits appeared in sections of the main hydraulic system. The boat, wrote Pappas, was "shaking like a Model T Ford going over a dirt road."

In the after engine room the call to "rig for depth charge" galvanized the men. Everything was secured that could be, with one exception: the stop valve on the six-hundred-pound air inlet to the two-hundred-pound reducing station for the main engine was frozen open. Grady tugged on it, but it wouldn't budge. Normal procedure was to open it fully, then close it an eighth of a turn to facilitate closing in an emergency. Grady said, "What the hell," and ignored it. A charge exploded just above the bulkhead between the forward and after engine rooms. Suddenly six-hundred-pound pressurized air shot through the system, lifting the downstream relief valve. Grady ran over and spun the "frozen" stop valve to a closed position as if it had been greased. "Amazing how strong one is when in an emergency," he says.

In the control room, glass shattered in several gauges, and the quarter-inch bolts sheared off an overhead light fixture, which crashed to the deck. Earl Watkins thought the depth charges sounded "like hitting a sledge hammer on the steel deck right over the top of your head." Watkins considered himself fairly innocent, never having been on patrol before, "but when I looked over at guys who I thought were pretty salty, and saw them scared, I knew things were not too good."

Up above, the explosions bent the periscope shears, knocking them out of alignment and damaging the packing glands. In the conning tower, Van Atta stood clutching another quartermaster, reluctantly preparing to meet his maker. Suddenly he realized that the sequence of crashing explosions had ended. He relaxed his grip. Summers estimated that the charges were close on the starboard side, with two straddles.

The patrol report records at 1406: "We can definitely hear two escorts now pinging on us." In the forward torpedo room, George Ingram stepped through the watertight door from the forward battery room and secured it behind him. He approached Weaver.

"Boy we sure are giving 'em hell up there today," he said.

Woody explained to him that "we" were not giving anybody hell—those were depth charges exploding—they're trying to kill us. "Ingram's eyes got big," said Woody, "and he hurried back to the forward battery and stayed there."

For the next two hours *Pampanito* continued evasive maneuvers at nearly 450 feet, attempting to point her bow away from the echo-ranging escorts, keeping as narrow a profile as possible. Summers searched for a temperature gradient but was still unable to find a layer of cold water. Now they waited—the hardest part. The *Chidoris* came in and out intermittently but seemed to have lost their enthusiasm. Had they been simply holding down the submarine long enough for the convoy to escape, or had they run out of depth charges? Pappas wrote, "He must have thought he got us or else he didn't have time to fool around."

In any case, the crew was grateful. At 1600, sound reported high-speed screws moving out. Summers had McClaskey slowly bring *Pampanito* up to periscope depth. The boat felt very heavy and sluggish, but they thought it unwise to use the trim pump at that time. Forty minutes later, the boat's periscope broke the surface. All clear.

Summers swept his poorly responding scope around the horizon. There were no gray *Chidori* bows to be seen. At 1700, *Pampanito* finally broke the surface and put her engines on line, full speed. The convoy had a forty-mile head start. It would be impossible to catch it before sunset, at 1842. Summers set the course to 240 degrees, the last estimated base course of the convoy. He guessed it would head on a straight route between Guam and Yap, and he hoped to beat it there.

By 0200 on 8 April, *Pampanito* had been pounding the waves south-westerly toward Yap for nine hours with nothing in sight. Had the convoy followed that course at twelve knots, it would have been about 108 miles beyond the initial contact point, perhaps less if zigzagging. At flank speed of about twenty knots, *Pampanito* should have been abreast of it after five to six hours. Certainly nine hours would have brought a sighting—unless the convoy had changed course. If it had broken south for Woleai right after *Pampanito* was driven down, it might be 160 miles southeast of the submarine. Reluctantly, Summers brought the chase to a halt. He decided to head north, back to the Saipan-Palau shipping route. At 0300 he radioed a contact report to Pearl Harbor, a report that was fourteen hours too late. By that time he had no idea where the convoy had gone, and it would have been almost impossible to vector any other submarines in for possible interception.

Those awake on mid watch (0000 to 0400) speculated about their close call. McGuire wondered how that escort could have gotten so close to drop his "cans" virtually without warning. He figured the Japanese must have gotten Y guns, which projected depth charges out in front of the attacking ship. Summers also considered that possibility. He didn't believe he had held up his scope long enough to be seen.[28]

When Summers closed his eyes, he could still see the bow wave of that damn *Chidori* bearing down on him, a ship that he called "one of the most famous escorts the Japs had." Many skippers came to fear the little torpedo boat as one of Japan's best ASW warships, likening it to the American destroyer escort, "designed solely to sink submarines." Usually one experience with a *Chidori* and a skipper would maintain proper respect from that time on.[29]

When Summers awoke from a fitful sleep at 0600, he dove *Pampanito* for the day. The torpedoes were due for routine maintenance. Upon pulling those in the forward torpedo room, the torpedomen found that the fish in number two tube had its exploder flooded, while those in tubes five and six had flooded afterbodies. Summers couldn't account for the flooding besides speculating that the shock from the depth charging may have broken the exhaust valve seals. He did not believe the pressure in the tubes exceeded 20 to 25 pounds per square inch (psi). Yet no torpedoes in the after room had flooded out. Since only the forward torpedo tube outer doors were opened before the abortive attack, they had probably remained open for the two hours *Pampanito* had gone deep. If so, the torpedoes were subjected not to 25 psi but to 225 psi. One of the Mark 18 electric torpedoes in the after room did have cracks in its battery cells, most likely because of the jarring of the depth charges. Yet the damage to the torpedoes in the forward room most likely came from inadvertently leaving the outer doors open. Summers stayed submerged during the daylight hours of 8 and 9 April while the grumbling torpedomen cleaned, oiled, and baked the gyros and engines on their flooded fish.

Finally, the repair job done, they surfaced and headed for the southeast edge of the patrol area, about two hundred miles south of Guam. Before midnight the men began changing shifts, and Paul Pappas gladly left the duty to Electrician's Mate Second Class Bartlett N. Davenport as he sleepily headed for his bunk. As the clock hands passed the top of the dial,

Pappas thought of the folks at home. He hoped they would all be in church, because back in the States this day would be Easter Sunday.

At 0325 the SJ radar picked up a surface contact at twenty-four thousand yards, bearing 192 degrees. There would be no more sleep this morning. The radar tracking party made a first stop at the ever-present coffee pot to get ready for another long day. As *Pampanito* closed, the screen refined the contact into several ships, two large ones and four escorts, one ahead, two on the flanks, and one astern. Four escorts for two ships? This must be something important. The two large ships were in column, zigzagging on a base course of about 195 degrees at a speed of nine knots.

Summers hauled the boat around in an arc to place it in front of the convoy's estimated course. The maneuver was called an end-around run, which derived from football terminology and was a standard submarine approach tactic. After calculating base course and speed of the convoy, the sub would remain at the limits of visibility, using her lower profile and superior surface speed to run parallel with the convoy. If the base course was predicted reasonably well, the sub would eventually pull ahead, then angle in to place itself directly ahead of, or slightly off the bow of the approaching target, where it could leisurely wait while calculating firing angles. Simple in theory, it was not so cut-and-dried in practice.

George Moffett knew it was a difficult and time-consuming task. If the convoy was moving fast, the difference in relative speeds between it and the sub could make for an end-around of several hours. The difficulty increased if the convoy was close in to shore or if it had air cover or escorts or made radical course changes. The weather was also a factor, for rainstorms or squalls reduced visibility and could diminish the effectiveness of the radar. Rough seas reduced visual accuracy and made torpedo settings less reliable. On paper it looked simple, Moffett explained, "and this is the way Hollywood and TV tend to depict it." But finding, tracking, and successfully attacking a ship were a fortuitous combination of chance and skill.

During this end-around, *Pampanito* was aided by heavy smoke trailing from the target's stacks, slightly darker than the background skies. Although the sub had been trying to head off the convoy for over an hour, when dawn broke at 0503, the better light and an updated calculation showed the convoy bearing 275, range about 16,500 yards—much too far off. *Pampanito* had chased the ships from astern, closing until she was broad off the starboard beam, but morning light revealed that she would have to open out again for another, wider end-around—and a daylight submerged attack. She secured from battle stations, put all four engines on line, and tracked the targets on radar out as far as 34,000 yards. There the sub could buck through the seas, raising all the white water she wanted, and still not be seen by the convoy's lookouts.

At top speed it took four more hours gradually to pull ahead to a position where they could dive directly in front and wait for the proper setup. At 0912, with the convoy bearing directly at them at thirty-five thousand yards' range, Summers took the boat down to look for a temperature gradient.

As the convoy closed, *Pampanito* dipped down to four hundred feet, while McClaskey watched the BT needle. It was a wonderful little instrument, but the ocean was deep, and the sun had not heated the upper layers. The track showed a straight isotherm down to four hundred feet. There was no gradient. At 0925 he brought the boat back up to fifty feet. Once again they would have to make a daylight submerged attack with no protective thermocline in which to evade.

At 1020, sound picked up echo-ranging, bearing 340, and ten minutes later, smoke was sighted. By a check in the ONI manual, the targets appeared to be two seven-thousand-ton freighters similar to the *Tokiwa Maru* and *Toyama Maru*. They were using short, simultaneous zigzags and were protected by a roving destroyer screen on the flanks, a single destroyer using constant helm about fifteen hundred yards ahead of the target group, and a single subchaser astern. All the destroyers appeared to be of the *Fubuki* class. Pappas listened to the description piped to the crew and jotted in his diary: "Looks as if we're in for a little trouble, as convoy has three destroyers and one subchaser for escorts."[30]

In fact, the destroyers were not *Fubukis*, but of the slightly older *Mutsuki* class, and there were two of them, not three. Regardless, the escort commander, commander of Destroyer Division 30, was assuredly not in a good mood, and his charges were extra alert. The convoy, which had originally consisted of *Matsue Maru*, *Aratama Maru*, and *Kizugawa Maru*, escorted by destroyers *Minazuki* and *Yuzuki*; *Takunan Maru No. 2*, formerly a 343-ton steam whaler now serving as a subchaser; and *Subchaser No. 30*, had left Saipan on 7 April with army reinforcements, base personnel, and supplies for Woleai. Early in the morning of April 8 they were jumped by USS *Seahorse* (SS 304). *Aratama Maru* was heavily damaged and drifted ashore at Guam, a total loss. *Kizugawa Maru* was hit and went dead in the water. *Minazuki* and *Subchaser No.30* went off in pursuit of *Seahorse*, while *Yuzuki* escorted *Matsue Maru* to Guam. After a futile chase, *Minazuki* towed the damaged *Kizugawa Maru* to Guam, where she would be sunk in June by U.S. aircraft.

At dawn on 9 April the convoy reassembled to try again. *Sanyo Maru*, which was at Saipan the day before and heading for the same destination, may have joined them at Guam. Whatever items could be salvaged from *Kizugawa Maru* and *Aratama Maru* were hastily loaded on *Matsue Maru*. The 7,061-ton army-controlled cargo ship was packed with supplies as well as three thousand garrison troops. The escort was smarting from its treatment by *Seahorse* and determined not to let another American sub slip past its screen.[31]

At 1128 the target group was dead ahead, with zero angle on the bow and *Minazuki* at five thousand yards and closing. Did Summers entertain the thought of a bow-to-bow, down-the-throat torpedo shot? As far as he knew, it had never been done, and he wouldn't try it now. Down went *Pampanito* to one hundred feet. Summers would attempt to pass under the screen. If he could get under the lead destroyer, he could swing right to 90 degrees and open up a stern shot at the first freighter. As they maneuvered, sound picked up the lead destroyer dropping back to the port bow of the freighter. Now both destroyers were blocking that side. Had *Pampanito* been detected, or was this just a lucky shift for the escorts? Within a few minutes both destroyers were moving back and forth, ahead and astern of the sub. Summers decided to make a U-turn, trying to pass behind the port flank escort and go for a bow shot at the second freighter in the column.

When the periscope next poked the surface it was ten minutes to noon and twenty minutes too late. The convoy had zigged away to the west, presenting Summers with a 150-degree angle on the bow and a range of over six thousand yards. *Pampanito* was out in right field, and she sat for another one and a half hours while the convoy steamed away. Pappas thought the move under the destroyer was rather foolish. "Lucky their

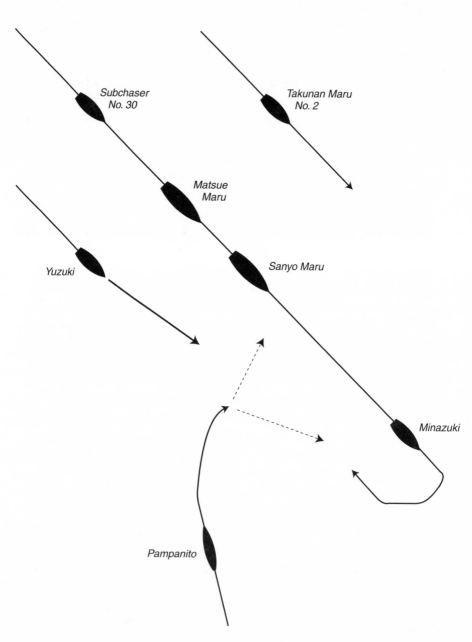

Subchaser
No. 30

Takunan Maru
No. 2

Matsue
Maru

Yuzuki

Sanyo Maru

Minazuki

Pampanito

Convoy attack, 10 April 1944

sound man didn't pick us up," he wrote, "or we'd more than likely be taking charges from now till next Easter."[32] Others were not in the same frame of mind. It was getting downright dispiriting to spend another ten hours tracking a convoy only to blow the attack in twenty minutes of close-in maneuvering.

For another six hours *Pampanito* pounded through the waves, again trying to attain an attack position ahead. At 1936 radar picked up a contact at 22,700 yards, bearing 028, and a sigh of relief went through the conning tower. They had found it. After a few minutes, however, they discovered that the convoy had changed its base course. It was heading southeast, course 125, with the same ship disposition as before. With the moon rising in the east, Summers decided to approach from the west side to keep the targets silhouetted against its tropical brightness. He ran on the surface for another hour to work the sub to the proper quarter. Pappas's wish for the folks back home to be in church should soon be fulfilled, for off of Guam about eight o'clock Monday evening, 10 April 1944, was ten o'clock Easter Sunday morning, 9 April, back in the eastern United States, ten time zones and one International Date Line away.

At 2058, Summers conned *Pampanito* on a course to approach the convoy from its starboard bow, away from the moon, and dove. The full moon could be a friend and an enemy. Summers could not chance remaining on the surface and being spotted in its bright glow, yet it should have provided enough light to allow use of the periscope during a submerged attack. He liked his position. He came in for a 70-degree track on the first freighter and all the while kept his bow pointing at the leading destroyer. "Set up looks pretty good," he logged.

Nearly an hour later, at 2154, all six bow tubes were ready. The leading freighter was about twenty-five hundred yards away with an 80-degree starboard track. Through the scope Summers watched the van destroyer cross in front of the target. The merged ships were black against the moonlit eastern horizon, while the wavelets rippled in silver. The destroyer pulled ahead, and one silhouette became two. The target was left wide open. The trailing freighter bore about 300 degrees relative to *Pampanito*. The starboard destroyer was bearing about 270 degrees relative to the sub, and its range was close, about a thousand yards. The ships gave no indication that they were aware of a submarine in their midst.

The after torpedo room crew prepared tubes seven through ten. Two torpedoes, which were meant for the freighter, were set for twelve feet, and two were set for eight feet—gifts for the destroyer. The torpedomen speculated whether they would be able to fire this time before getting ash cans dropped on them.

"If the folks back home could see us now, they wouldn't believe it," Pappas heard one of them say. "Hell," says another, "I'd much rather be getting ready to take my girl out to the big dance than routining a damn torpedo." Pappas also thought of home and that he, too, would much rather be with his family.

Angle and range readings were transmitted to the after torpedo room. They were ready to fire, and they wondered which room would get the first call. The escorts were close. Pappas wrote, "They are pinging away with their sound gear, but haven't picked us up yet."

At 2155 a final check showed an 81-degree starboard track to the leading freighter, with a torpedo run of 2,450 yards. Summers fired a four-torpedo salvo from the forward room. He spread them so that the four fish were designed to get two sure hits. The quick loss of six tons forward lightened the boat's bow, but trim was quickly adjusted, and it never broke the surface. Four steam torpedoes streaked toward the target at 46 knots. Their bubbling wakes should not be seen until it was too late.

Traveling about twenty-five yards per second, the fish would cover the 2,450 yards to the target in about a hundred seconds. Quartermaster First Class John B. Schilling and Al Van Atta were in the conning tower. Van Atta handled the stopwatch. Jeff Davis was in the control room, while Lieutenant Francis M. Fives, a graduate of the Carnegie Institute of Technology with a degree in mechanical engineering, worked the TDC. Summers swung the scope right to get a look at *Minazuki* in the van, and the words of his old captain, Bud Moore, flashed through his mind: "Don't try to sink a destroyer." But no, no more hiding. Pete got a quick setup on the destroyer, and Fives worked the course and speed into the TDC, which automatically fed the information to the remaining two forward torpedoes. The new track for a shot at the destroyer was 102 degrees starboard, with a torpedo run of 2,400 yards. The gyro angle was 17 degrees right. Fives fired torpedoes five and six.

In the forward torpedo room, the successive firings called for fast work. A torpedo was ejected from the flooded tube by compressed air. The air blast moved it forward about six inches, tripping the engine starting mechanism, and the torpedo continued out of the tube on its own power. The air used to give the initial push was vented inboard to prevent a bubble from rising to the surface and revealing the sub's location. A poppet valve automatically vented the air into the bilges as the torpedo was on its way out. The poppet valve, in turn, had to be closed to prevent inrushing water from flooding the bilges. The poppet was closed by hand operation of a lever vent valve on the blow and vent manifold positioned above and aft of the tubes.

The blow and vent manifold was the domain of the torpedoman in charge, Torpedoman's Mate First Class Howard E. George. As the torpedoes were fired, he listened for the splash of water coming through the poppet valve and into the bilges. It took but two or three seconds. He then grabbed the lever and closed the poppet valve. The days of training and practice should have rendered this procedure automatic. Yet for some reason George was distracted. The torpedoes were off, but several seconds elapsed before the noise of seawater splashing heavily in the bilges prodded George into snapping closed the poppets. Too much water had been taken aboard. Still, the excess water should have been of no consequence—at that time.

A minute after firing the first torpedoes, Summers swung the scope around, determined not to let another escort sneak up. To his left the convoy's starboard flank destroyer, *Yuzuki,* no longer steamed along unconcernedly. She was coming in fast on *Pampanito*'s port beam, "too close for comfort," Summers recorded. She couldn't have seen the torpedoes. Did she see the sub's periscope or detect her with her sound gear? *Yuzuki* signaled *Minazuki,* which *Pampanito* had just fired at, and *Minazuki* got the word, for immediately she sliced her bow to the right. Would she be quick enough to evade the two fish streaking toward her? The angle on the bow was 20 degrees, then 10, then zero—another angry destroyer with a bone in her teeth. "Take her down, emergency. Rig for depth charge," the order went out.

Van Atta was counting the seconds of the torpedo run—99, 100, 101. He glanced up at Schilling. Had they missed? His thought was answered by a piercing explosion that rang through the hull. Sound travels through water about four times faster than through the air, about fifteen hundred yards per second, so the hit on the freighter was announced within two seconds of impact. The timing was almost perfect.

Within seconds a violent concussion rocked the sub, not yet a hundred feet below the surface. In the after engine room Kaup let out with a "Whooeee!" He slapped hands with Michno as the pressure wave physically tilted the boat and made both of them grab hold of "Miss Molly" and "Miss Jean" to keep their feet. "We must've hit an ammo ship," Michno said, and Grady and Kaup concurred.

In the after torpedo room the concussion from the exploding ship jolted the crew. Pappas watched a little bit of cork and paint shake from the bulkheads, almost as if a depth charge had gone off nearby. In the conning tower, Summers believed the target was carrying high-test aviation gasoline in its tanks.

Wham! The second blast followed eighteen seconds after the first. All smiled, for they were certain the attack was a success.

At 2157 sound reported that the target screws had stopped. The freighter or transport, or whatever it was, was dead in the water. Certainly it would go down, if the tremendous explosion was any indication of the damage it had sustained. Now the men listened for the second set of explosions that would announce the destroyer's destruction. But there was no sound except that of destroyer screws coming on fast from the port beam.

Two minutes later, one distant depth charge went off. Perhaps it was an announcement from a flanking destroyer, letting them know she was on the way. A minute after that, a cacophony of noise emanated from the direction of the stricken maru. An escort's high-speed screws mingled with underwater rumblings and noises of breaking up. Nearby, a closer set of screws was heard charging overhead. *Pampanito* passed 300 feet, and Summers told Lieutenant McClaskey: "Take her to 350 feet."

Recently McClaskey has read the latest ONI bulletin that said the Japanese were now setting their charges deeper, down to 350 feet. He told Summers.

"Okay," Pete said, "Then take her to 450."

No sooner had Summers ordered deeper submergence than Whoomp!—Whoomp!—Whoomp! a pattern of three depth charges rocked them, all close. Hubert Brown was in the control room, his battle station on the master gyro plot. He heard the explosions of the torpedoes and imagined what was occurring above. The three depth-charge blasts caught him unexpectedly. He stood underneath a drip pan used to catch water and oil from the piping and machinery above the plotting table. The first explosion jarred the drip pan from its moorings, and it came crashing down on his head. Knocked dizzy for a few seconds, Brown thought, "My God, the hull is caving in!" The sub swayed, but he regained his senses and was relieved to find it was only the drip pan.

At 2202, at 350 feet, *Pampanito* had not evaded the angry destroyers. Whoomp!—Whoomp!—Whoomp! three more ash cans walked across her trajectory, even closer than the last batch. In the heat of the after engine room, Mike Carmody, stripped to his skivvies, heard a horrible bump and grating noise. He wondered if a depth charge was rolling across the deck. The explosion rocked him. It looked like the hull had bent in over number four engine, driving the inboard exhaust valve wheel into the top of "Miss Jean" and putting it out of commission. The main induction flapper valves to the engine rooms buckled. Water dripped to the deck. Carmody quickly glanced up and down the length of the room, then ran over to the section of buckled hull. It was holding. "God bless the builders at Portsmouth Naval Shipyard," he said.

A commotion aft made Carmody rush to the maneuvering room, where he helped the men control a small electrical fire. Beneath them the jolt of the charges damaged some teeth on the port reduction gear. In the after torpedo room, gaskets blew on the outer doors of number nine tube, and the sea rushed in, subjecting the Mark 18 in it to heavy pressure.

In the conning tower the permanent magnet broke loose from the bridge speaker, and part of the wave guide and the lobe-switching motor in the SJ radar were flooded out. In the forward torpedo room the number one sanitary tank was leaking. Down in the pump room, one of the air compressors was out of commission.

In the forward engine room the freshwater evaporator was out. Little John E. Wilson, a motor machinist's mate third class, watched aghast as another engineman let out with a scream. They were all frightened, but the man's loss of control threatened everyone. The wailing went on for only a few seconds when a third engineman laid the man out cold with a wrench. Wilson didn't know which action surprised him most, but he shut up about it.

After another minute, another depth charge crashed above. *Pampanito* was diving beneath it, but the downward concussion, combined with her own steep dive angle on the bow planes, forced her deeper than intended.

*Pampanito* had gone down 300 feet in five minutes. There were no port-holes, and the men could not see the engulfing blackness that surrounded them. At 400 feet she reached test depth, but the downward plunge was not controlled. Pete's order to go to 450 feet was soon exceeded. Suddenly, from somewhere within the miles of tubing, piping, and ductwork, came a low wailing sound. Quiet at first, it increased in intensity and took on a higher pitch. The sub descended. The vibrating wail grew louder, and Hubie Brown likened it to a siren. What the hell was it? One man closed his hands over his ears. Electrician's Mate Third Class Otto P. Aimone, Jr., couldn't stand it. It was not deafening, but its eerie banshee wail evoked visions too frightening for him to continue to function competently. He retreated into a shell and could not move. Bennett thought the compressed air flasks were ruptured.

The culprit was in the induction. Somewhere above the engine rooms there was a rupture in the neoprene gaskets and seals in the joints of the main induction. The piping ran along under the deck but outside the pressure hull from the main induction valve located in the bridge super-structure. It was sealed at the hull upon diving, and hence was dry and at atmospheric pressure. Water pressure increases about one-half pound per square inch for every foot of depth. As *Pampanito* sank below four hundred feet, the atmospheric pressure of about fifteen pounds per square inch inside the induction was being pressed by the water outside at two hundred pounds per square inch. A gasket failed. Water started spurting through the rupture, and the induction began to fill. The water Carmody saw dripping through the induction drains was the first indication of trouble. The wail continued until the entire induction was filled.

Summers was naturally concerned about the inability to bring the dive under control. "Had to close the hull induction drains in Engine Rooms and Maneuvering Room, as water is coming in too fast," he recorded. "The boat is getting very heavy." Typically, he sought a scapegoat: "Our diving officer took her down, but froze at the controls," he said. It was a stale excuse. "I sensed something wrong," Summers explained, "and ran in and saw the depth needle hit 630 feet—400 was max by the rules. Another 20 feet and we'd have been crushed."

At 2207, eleven minutes after the dive was begun, Chief Smith was in the control room. He looked at the depth gauge, calibrated in pounds per square inch, and calculated that they were down near six hundred feet. He tapped the gauge, but it failed to move. All the depth needles were hard against the right edges of their dials. They were below six hundred feet, but no one knew how far below. During the last four minutes of their descent, about twenty-five more charges had exploded above them. The boat's great depth kept the crew safe from the detonations above but presented additional problems. Men heard creaks and groans from the pressure hull.

To regain neutral buoyancy, ballast was blown from the negative tank. The tank held about seven and one-half tons of water and was kept flooded while the submarine was surfaced to give negative buoyancy upon diving. However, for the water to be expelled at deep submergence, the tank had to be blown noisily with high-pressure air. *Pampanito* pulled out of her dive and gained an even keel for a moment, but the stern began to sink because of the water in the induction. Blowing negative was not enough. Summers crept the sub ahead at ninety to one hundred shaft turns per minute—about one-third speed—too loud to evade in a "silent running" mode. He looked at the BT card; there was still no gradient.

The boat's nose lifted while the stern dropped. Steward's Mate George Ingram peered through the glass on the bulkhead door to the forward torpedo room. Water was spilling out of the bilges; they were having trouble in there. He ran back to report.

In a minute, Lieutenant Junior Grade Edward J. Hannon, Jr., the torpedo and gunnery officer, made his way to the forward room. When he entered he saw water in the bilges nearly up to the deck plates. With the up angle, the bilge water flowed back to the sound head controls and grounded out both motors. Hannon asked what had happened. Howard George, who had neglected to close the poppets when the torpedoes were fired, came up with a story. The valves stuck, he said; he had tried to close them right away, but they wouldn't work. Standing nearby, Woody Weaver frowned. Hannon bought the story, and Weaver saw no point in revealing the truth. The damage was done, and it would serve no purpose to get George in trouble over a brief mental lapse. But now the boat had no supersonic detection capability.

The next two hours were pure hell. Down at six hundred feet or more, with water pressure at twenty tons per square foot, the wailing in the induction drove some men to the verge of madness. Lieutenant Bill Bruckart went aft to check the main induction drains. They were shut but still spewing water. The noise was intolerable. "It is the most alarming sound of a low frequency vibration one ever heard," he stated. "And under these circumstances, I became scared more than I can describe." Bruckart headed for the captain's stateroom, stepped inside, and pulled the curtain. Athletic and strong at six feet and 190 pounds, he was able to take a lot of physical punishment, but this was another matter. He took a deep breath and offered up a prayer.

Hubie Brown continued to stand by the gyro plot. He was stripped down to his sandals and skivvies and was terribly hot. The deck was wet with moisture and very slippery. He couldn't breathe. He heard a frightening noise. It was his heart—he could feel his heart pounding right in his temples. His head hurt something awful.

Frank Michno in the after engine room was dripping with sweat. The temperature was surely over 120 degrees. He hadn't bargained on this when he had tried so hard to get off those sweatbox S-boats. Coming from a Polish Catholic family, he thought about how his mother would be returning from church that morning and bringing home the eggs and kielbasa for their meal. He said his own prayer.

Nine thousand miles away, in the same church where he got married, Frank's wife Marian was attending High Mass. She repeated the Latin phrases that she had memorized since she was a little girl, then she added an extra Lord's Prayer for her husband and his shipmates on *Pampanito,* wherever they might be.

In the after torpedo room, Pappas broke out his Bible and began to read. He got no more than a passage into it when Ralph Attaway exploded at him. "Shut up, damn it," he yelled, "Shut up!" Pappas closed the book, not wishing to provoke Attaway. What was comfort to one only served to frighten another. Now all he could do was sit and listen to the screws, still audible far above. He heard a string of about twelve charges explode in a line, but way off the mark. Later, seven more went off, but scattered. He estimated that anywhere between thirty and fifty depth charges had been dropped on them. He thought they were deep enough to evade the destroyers if it weren't for the whistling in the induction.

Rather than sit and let his mind dwell on their predicament, Torpedoman's Mate First Class Lenny Baron stripped down to his shorts and worked on repairing the leaky gaskets in number nine torpedo tube. The rest of the torpedomen stripped down, and Pappas followed suit, which was out of character for him, for he always wore a skivvy shirt and a long-sleeved blue denim outer shirt buttoned up to the neck. This time, Pappas removed his shirt and took turns with the other electricians, going in shifts into the maneuvering room to mind the controllers. It was so hot they could stay only a few minutes. When the hatch was opened, the "cool" air from the after torpedo room rolled in to create a fog. The electricians relished the comfort of the after torpedo room, where it was only about 100 degrees.

Bill McCollum realized the boat was below six hundred feet. He knew it was supposedly good for that depth, but some Navy Yard people had told him that three hundred would be more realistic, and he was quite upset. "I thought this was the end," he said. He had been through several depth charge attacks before, but he concluded, "I was never as scared as I was then. The boat leaked like a sieve."

Off battle stations and with the sound gear shorted out, Roger Walters sat in his bunk and broke open his diary. Born in February 1923 in Clear Lake, Iowa, he had worked several small jobs after high school. However, within six months he was itching to have a little adventure. He enlisted in December 1941 and served for a time on *S-16* out of Coco Solo, Panama. Now, he wondered why he had ever wanted to get into submarine service. In his diary he tallied one hundred depth charges.

Charles McGuire could not sit still. He headed aft to the source of the wailing, bracing himself at every step, for it seemed like the boat sloped at 25 degrees. Suddenly, with a last high squeal, the noise abruptly ceased. In the strange silence he straddled the bulkhead into the forward engine room. There he saw chief motor mac Dinty Moore examining the main induction vent.

"What's the matter?" McGuire asked.

"Come here." Moore waved him over. "Put your hand up here."

McGuire placed his hand on the induction vent. "It's moving—it's shaking!" he exclaimed.

"Right," said Moore. "The damn thing is chock full of water." He looked McGuire in the eye and said, "If that thing breaks loose, there's no way we'll be saved."

Moore was an old salt, about thirty-five years old, and if Moore was frightened, McGuire was frightened. McGuire looked at the vent and backed out of the room. He went to the crew's mess, sat on a bench, and waited—which was all he could do.

Fright is contagious. It spreads like a prairie fire. "Others would catch it," McGuire says, "and they'd do something stupid, and it would lessen everyone's chances. It was terrible." He thought about the job he had in the Caribbean, being a courier and wearing that natty Panama hat. He thought he was out of his mind getting on a submarine. Why did he do it? Because he was young and stupid? No, he thought, the only real reason I'm here getting my butt whomped is because I wanted a few extra bucks for hazardous duty pay. Well, he concluded, "I got it."

Now that the induction was completely filled with about sixteen tons of seawater and the squealing had stopped, the men were better able to hear the escorts crossing above, which gave them more to worry about. Suffering through the ordeal was a unique experience. Unlike a traditional battle with its attendant noise, chaos, and violence, submerged evasion is quite the opposite. There is nothing to pump adrenaline into the system. The handful of men who were active did their jobs in dead silence. Shoes were removed and motors and equipment stilled, and every sound seemed magnified a hundred times. External noises were clearly heard, and every time a propeller passed overhead, it "put a knot in the gizzard." The only thing active was the imagination, and few could escape their own thoughts and fears.

Someone dropped a tin cup to the floor. The stares that greeted this dastardly deed could have killed the man twice. The tension was unbearable. Just then, George Ingram walked into the crew's mess. He was a good sailor and quite a character. McGuire used to race against him in track back in high school in Philadelphia. In the Navy in the 1940s it was nearly

In the After Engine Room, the outlet to the Main Induction at the top.
(Photo by author.)

impossible for a black man to attain a rating other than that of steward. But Good Kid Ingram took his job seriously and performed it with enthusiasm and panache. While the men hunkered down wondering if they were about to meet their maker, Ingram strolled in. He looked down at the sailors, then rolled his head back and stretched out his arms as if imploring the destroyers above. He said: "I don't understand. I have no complaint against you Japanese. How come you're trying to kill me just because I'm with these white guys? You're mad at them, not me!"

It was wonderful, McGuire says. He got them laughing, and the guys really got a kick out of it. "He was worth his weight in gold." Ingram broke the ice. Maybe the men would start concentrating on getting out of this alive, instead of resigning themselves to death.[33]

The six-hour convoy chase that *Pampanito* made before the attack placed her about two hundred miles southwest of Guam. Purely by chance, she was hovering over the Challenger Deep in the Marianas Trench, trying to maintain neutral buoyancy, poised over the absolutely deepest part of any ocean on the planet. Six hundred feet above was the surface, and over thirty-five thousand feet below was the stygian black abyss. Had she gone down here, she would without a doubt have sunk deeper than any other ship in history. Ten cubic feet of seawater weighs about the same as one cubic foot of lead. Had the men dwelt on the possibility of a seven-mile plunge, squeezed by pressures of nine tons per square inch that would crush them to atoms, it would surely have pushed some of them over the edge of sanity.[34]

The revolving props and the up angle on the bow planes kept the boat from sinking any deeper. Whenever Summers attempted to blow more air into the safety tank, it brought on the destroyers. Even after Ingram injected some life into the crew, they could not erase morose thoughts and sullen countenances. The worst feeling for McGuire was being helpless. "There is nothing you can do," he says. "You know the guy above you is trying to blast you, punch a hole in you, kill you. And you can't come up, because he'll shoot you out of the water before you can even man your gun. It's terrifying."

*Pampanito* struggled to hold her ground, stuck between Scylla and Charybdis, between a fiery death on the surface or the icy black maw beneath her. The crew could only hope the tenacious destroyers would tire of the game and, like good shepherd dogs, return to guard their flock. The time passed ever so slowly. Was it only twenty-four hours ago that Pappas noted the coming of Easter with a smile and a thought of home? The clock again ticked past midnight. Easter was over. And truly, joy of joys, the ship's log read: "0015. Destroyer screws going away."

As the Japanese destroyers faded away, it was with difficulty that the men stifled their cheers. Now the number one priority was to get the submarine to the surface. Were the destroyers really gone, though? Had they run out of depth charges or headed back to the convoy? Had they just pulled off a few miles and shut down to listen on their own hydrophones? The men could not hear their screws, but the more acute ears of the sound equipment that might have picked up faint propellers were shorted out and useless.

The bow and stern planes were set at maximum rise angles, and a few more revolutions were given to the props. *Pampanito* sped up another knot. It was no good. The depth gauge still rested hard against the right edge. The great pressure at that depth compressed the hull and decreased the boat's buoyant volume.

Most of the crew understood that they might be far below the bottom line on the gauges. During the course of a dive, air pressure built up inside the boat from a number of sources: air swallowed from the poppets, leaks from the air banks or other pneumatic sources such as the torpedoes, venting of the negative tank, and even the rise in temperature. The depth gauges, which measure the difference between water pressure outside and air pressure inside, will show a progressively shallower depth as the inside pressure increases. Gordon Hopper and others in the forward torpedo room believed their stern was probably close to seven hundred feet.[35]

They would have to blow the ballast tanks if they wanted to surface. Negative tank had been blown first, which had slowed the initial downward plunge to gain temporary neutral buoyancy. Unfortunately, even after negative was blown the submarine hadn't risen. Seven and one-half tons ejected had not compensated for the sixteen tons in the main induction.[36]

Normally, water was blown out of the tanks through the flood ports by compressed air stored in steel flasks located in the ballast tanks. Air under pressures up to three thousand pounds per square inch was fed through a distributing manifold to various tanks, where reducing valves lowered the working pressures. Six hundred pounds of pressure was used for the main ballast tank system and would enable the crew to blow the tanks while submerged at six hundred feet.

Unless a compartment was flooding, blowing mains with high-pressure air at deep submergence was avoided. The use of air would be excessive, and it would take a long time to recharge the air flasks. The crew hoped the sub could be maneuvered to periscope depth before they had to blow the main ballast. Then, the low-pressure, "turbo-blow" system, at ten pounds per square inch, would take over and complete the task, conserving the high-pressure air.[37]

*Pampanito*'s solution should have been to blow the safety tank, a special ballast tank located amidships below the magazine and built with the strength of the pressure hull.

"Permission to blow safety?" McClaskey asked Summers.

"Granted," the captain answered.

Walters heard the bleeding of air into the tank. After an uncomfortable wait, they all could feel the boat come to life. "She's going up!" someone called out.

*Pampanito* broke loose from the ocean's grip. The depth needles began to move counterclockwise, slowly at first, then faster. As high-pressure air expelled enough water to attain positive buoyancy, the submarine rose. But as always, physical laws had the last word. As the submarine rose, lower water pressure allowed the air in the tanks to expand. As the tanks emptied of water, the boat rose faster. The faster it rose, the less the water pressure, which accelerated the process. It was a chain reaction that was hard to stall once started.

Instead of trying to slow the dive, they now needed to slow the ascent. Hubie Brown was relieved when blowing safety made them start to rise. "We got buoyancy all right," he said, "but now there ain't no stopping it."

"We came up," McClaskey said, "faster and faster." He realized that venting would probably not work fast enough, but he thought to try it.

"Permission to vent tanks?" McClaskey asked Summers.

"Like Hell!" Pete answered.

Had anyone looked at the manometer in the control room to see what the inboard air pressure was? Normally, at the end of a long submergence, air compressors were run to charge up the air banks and draw down some of the pressure in the boat, about a half-hour procedure, but it was impossible while heading up as if in an express elevator. Who would pop open the conning tower hatch? The sudden pressure release could blow a man right through. When time was not an issue, the hatch could be cracked open while still dogged down, and the pressure could be slowly equalized, though it might sound like a whistling foghorn. They had to get out quickly to man the guns in case a destroyer was waiting for them.

Summers called for volunteer bridge lookouts—and peered right at Hubie Brown. Hubie knew it was going to be impossible to avoid it, so he grabbed the binoculars, went up to the conning tower, and stood next to Bennett, who would rush to man the 20-mm gun.

The depth needle was cruising, 150 . . . 100 . . . 50 . . . whoosh! *Pampanito* broke the surface. If it was not an uncontrolled broaching, it was about as close as they could get. They cracked the hatch, and the force of the air rushing out was tremendous. "Out, out, out!" urged an officer. Brown undogged the hatch. Below him, someone held his legs, but the force nearly shot him through like a cork out of a bottle. The splashes of water against his bare skin stung like needles. Later, he noticed scores of little red welts on his arms and torso.

Bennett was on the ladder. When the hatch popped open, an officer directly below him almost shoved his head up "Smilin' Bob's" rear end. Bennett flew to the deck and was doused with cold water splashing down his neck. Clambering to the 20-mm gun, he thought, "Boy, someone's going to machine-gun me as soon as I stick my head up."

But it was still dark. The moon had moved halfway across the sky. No orange gun flashes and explosions announced that the Japanese had caught them in a trap. Brown swept the binoculars across the dark horizon and the darker ocean. Nothing. It was 0043, and the Japanese were gone.

"God, or luck, or both, were on our side," said motor mac Ed Stockslader, "for the enemy had left the area. They probably left thinking no one could survive the pounding they gave us. We became veterans in a hurry."

As quickly and as quietly as possible, one of the engines was brought on line. It coughed and sputtered and sent a small puff of smoke out of the exhaust. Because they were unable to use the induction for an air supply, men were stationed at the compartment hatches to see that they did not swing closed. The air was drawn all the way to the oxygen-hungry engines from the open conning tower hatch. The sub slowly pulled away from the last known position of the destroyers. The great majority of the crew were young and resilient. They bounced back from this episode. Yet for some, the trauma left an indelible impression, and they bore mental scars from the experience for years to come.

In an introspective mood after the ordeal, Summers announced to the men in the control room: "Fellows, I never took a shellacking like this in my life. I don't intend to take another one like it." Then, perhaps thinking of the implication, he added, "But if you don't think I won't sacrifice this crew and boat if the prize is worth it, just think again—I will." Time would tell how committed Summers was to that avowal.[38]

While a complete damage report was compiled, Summers decided that further pursuit of the convoy would not be wise. His chief concerns were the flooded induction, the inoperable sound heads, and the flooded Mark 18 torpedo in number nine tube. Woody Weaver did not believe that Summers had any choice in the matter. "A submarine with flooded induction lines, and lacking the ability to control its depth, is in no position to attack a convoy," he said. "It was clearly a case of discretion being the greater part of valor." Then he added, "There was much that went on which was not reflected in the official patrol reports."

At 0300, 11 April, *Pampanito* sent a contact report to ComSubPac and *Harder*, which was patrolling near Woleai. Summers hoped *Harder*'s skipper, Sam Dealey, would get the message and could pick up the convoy. He thought he had sunk the ship that had exploded with such a great crash, but he could not confirm it. He hoped Dealey could verify that the ship was missing from the convoy. Meanwhile, *Pampanito* headed north for the Saipan–Palau shipping route.

The men passed stories of their experiences—what they were doing when the depth charges went off. McGuire had been frightened, and he admitted it, but he thought that a lot of them put up a false bravado, saying things like, "Oh, hell, it was a piece of cake." Some talked about the eerie wailing in the induction. Bill Grady dismissed it as a case of beginner's nerves. "If anybody heard any squealing," he said, "it was their own assholes during their first depth charging. After you have experienced a few depth chargings you know that the ones that you hear did not get you—it is the anticipation of the one that you do not hear that kills."

The after engine room gang rigged the chainfall to straighten out the buckled induction flappers and levered the inboard exhaust valve wheel away from the top of "Miss Jean." After surfacing for the night, the induction was drained into the bilges, and they were pumped dry. To find the leak, someone had to get into the main induction while the boat submerged. Since he was in charge of the after engine room and was of slight build, Bill Grady volunteered. As the boat went down, he wriggled through the pipe. About sixteen feet forward of the after engine room induction outlet he found the leaking flanged joint. Water was jetting in heavily, and he banged a wrench to show he had located it. *Pampanito* surfaced, and Grady backed out of the pipe.

He made his report to the exec, Jeff Davis, who thanked him for his efforts and asked, "Who is going to fix it?" They all looked at Grady, but the little motor mac waved them off and pointed at Motor Machinist's Mate First Class William Merryman, who was assigned to the forward engine room.

"I found it," he said. "You can fix it."

Since volunteers were lacking, Summers got them in his own way. He called on Chief Moore to come to his stateroom. Moore also grabbed Ed Stockslader, a third-class motor mac who was in charge of the auxiliary gang. In his stateroom, Summers explained the problem to them. Said Stockslader: "This was my first volunteer job. The Captain wanted to see me, as he had a job for me and 'Dinty' Moore." He wanted them to go topside, under the superstructure. It would be a slow and tedious task, but he wanted the leaks stopped. And, said Summers, if there were any plane contacts that closed within ten miles, he would have to dive the boat. "Of course," said Stockslader, "we had this in the back of our minds as we entered the superstructure, but we had one job, and that was to fix the Main Induction."

Bill Merryman joined them. They crawled between the deck and the pressure hull, fully appreciating Summers's warning. "This was a 24-inch diameter pipe and not fixable in two or three minutes," Stockslader said, and what was worse, "the opening to get out of the superstructure looked miles away." They welded wherever they discovered split seams, tightened up loose bolts on several flanges, and returned none the worse for the wear. Inside, Moffett was able to replace the bridge speaker, the SJ radar wave guide, and the lobe-switching motor.

The torpedo was finally jimmied backwards out of number nine tube. It, said Pappas, "was warped like a roller coaster due to pressure in the tube from going so deep." The warhead casing was dished in, and the battery cells were cracked and flooded. They threw the battery cells overboard but cleaned and salvaged the remaining parts. The armatures and field coils of both sound head training motors had zero grounds and open circuits and remained out of commission.

The next morning McClaskey cautiously took the boat down to 250 feet, but the induction still leaked. They would have to avoid deep submergence or else go in for an attack after a deep submergence trim, with the induction already flooded. Afterwards they would have to surface to drain the water into the bilges and then pump it dry, time after time. McClaskey went to work on solving the compensation problem, and the crew went back to the mundane routine of policing the boat. Pappas recorded: "'Doc' O'Neill took himself off sick list long enough to direct Field Day in the After Battery."

In the meantime, *Pampanito*'s call to *Harder* brought some action. After plucking a downed aviator off the reefs at Woleai on 1 April, *Harder* patrolled eleven days without a contact. Receiving the radio message, Dealey conned his submarine to the area and managed to pick up a convoy on 12 April—very likely the same one that *Pampanito* had attacked. However, he could not get into a favorable attack position against "the heavily protected fox." Early on 13 April, ComSubPac broadcast a directive giving destroyers high target priority, under capital ships but over merchant ships of all types. To keep up the morale of his crew, Dealey thought of a stratagem; he would go "fishing" for a destroyer. He kept the sub loafing around on the surface all day until he was spotted several times by planes. Knowing that the planes would radio for a destroyer to rush in, he planned to sit tight and wait for one to show up. Sure enough, shortly after 1800 an obliging destroyer came along, pinging away with its sonar.

The destroyer was *Ikazuchi,* whose captain, Lieutenant Commander Kunio Ikunaga, was probably in just as foul a mood as the skippers of the destroyers that had pummeled *Pampanito* in almost the same location three days earlier. Late on 9 April, *Ikazuchi* and the minelayer *Sokuten* were chasing *Seahorse* off Saipan. *Ikazuchi* finished that chore and was sent to Guam when on 13 April a Japanese plane located an American sub bearing 190 degrees and 188 miles south of that island. *Ikazuchi* again went on antisubmarine patrol. The contact could have been *Pampanito* or *Harder;* however, by 13 April the sub that *Ikazuchi* actually found was *Harder.*

Dealey waited until the range was down to about nine hundred yards and let go four bow torpedoes. Two tremendous explosions followed, and almost immediately the destroyer's nose dropped underwater while its stern popped into the air. In four minutes it was gone. On the way down, its own depth charges exploded at the preset depths where it had hoped to catch the Yankee submarine. There were no survivors. At least *Harder* had exacted some revenge for *Pampanito*'s ordeal.[39]

While *Harder* "fished" for a destroyer during the daylight hours of 13 April, *Pampanito* remained submerged. George Moffett spent several hours stripping the motor from the boat's lathe and reinstalling it on the JK hydrophone. The substitution worked, and *Pampanito* could hear again—at least in one ear.

Summers was dissatisfied with the lack of targets and moved closer to Guam. However, five days' patrolling in that area proved no more fruitful. The only noteworthy incident was another breakdown—this time the SJ surface radar. Moffett went to work again, but for two days the cantankerous instrument defied repair. Unless *Pampanito* was very close to a target, she would not be likely to spot anything.

By 20 April, Moffett had managed to jury-rig the SJ. The voltage transformer used to generate anode voltage for the PPI had gone out, and there were no spares. Moffett unsuccessfully tried to wind a replacement transformer. Finally, selecting the best of his options, he disconnected the PPI and used the power source to run the SJ with the "A" scope only. Now *Pampanito* had one ear and one eye. And, as if they hadn't had enough problems, about twelve hours later the number three engine, "Miss Molly," developed a freshwater leak in its exhaust nozzle, and at 2300 they radioed Pearl that they were running low on fuel.

Late in the evening of 21 April, ComSubPac sent a welcome message: depart the area and head for Midway. It had been a long, tough patrol. They weren't allowed to run for the barn, however; numerous plane contacts kept *Pampanito* bobbing up and down like a yo-yo—nine times before noon on 22 April. The last dive was followed by three bomb explosions well astern. That was enough. Summers stayed under for an hour, because, he recorded, "it looks like those planes have us pretty well spotted in." Perhaps the water was crystal clear or they were leaking oil or the induction was sending a trail of air bubbles to the surface, for at 1318 another depth bomb exploded off the starboard quarter. *Pampanito* stayed down until nightfall.

Upon surfacing they were more than ready to put all four engines on line and make up for lost time, but no such luck. New orders assigned *Pampanito* to Guam for another lifeguard mission.

Down the next morning at sunrise, Summers patrolled submerged for over thirteen hours. At sunset they had hardly commenced charging batteries when a saltwater leak was discovered in the exhaust of number one main engine, knocking it out of commission. Was there nothing that would go right for them?

Almost as if on cue, the "A" scope picked up two small pips at twelve thousand yards. Closer in, they identified the targets as two patrol craft heading toward Guam at ten knots. For the first time in nearly two weeks, *Pampanito* had made a ship contact—just eight minutes after an engine breakdown. With the tropical night quickly descending, it would soon be too black for a submerged periscope attack. Could *Pampanito* outrun them on the surface with one engine out? There was no use stirring things up, Summers rationalized. He turned away from the targets and recorded: "Avoided due to pending lifeguard operations in this area tomorrow."

The morning of 24 April dawned with high expectations. The disappointment of letting the Japanese patrol boats pass would be assuaged by a successful rescue of a downed pilot. But once again, hopes were dashed when ComSubPac sent another radio message: the Guam strike and lifeguard mission had been postponed. *Pampanito* cooled her heels by floating underwater for almost fourteen more hours.

By now the men's dispositions ranged from subdued to raw. Even McGuire, usually gregarious and effervescent, had shut up since the depth-charging two weeks before. Otto Aimone had snapped out of his semicomatose state but since then had contracted a skin rash that Doc O'Neill could not diagnose. He was isolated rather than being allowed to risk infecting the rest of the crew. But poor Aimone's ordeal was not over. Early one morning during mid watch he had been assigned to blow the sanitary tank, flush it with sea water, and blow it out again. Evidently he forgot to close the sea valves and flappers, for urine and excrement-filled sea water from the tanks backed into the sleeping quarters and mess hall. Aimone went to his bunk unaware of the flood he had started. Fortunately (or unfortunately), one crewman got up to use the head and stepped in it. All hands had to get up to swab the deck with rags and clean it with torpedo alcohol. The sea water was on the deck directly above the after batteries. Had it seeped down into them, it might have generated deadly chlorine gas. What was simply an amusing incident could have turned into ignominious tragedy had men died because of the improper use of a toilet.

More than one sailor felt the repercussions of the depth chargings. Napping in his bunk, Electrician's Mate Third Class Don Ferguson was jolted awake when someone dropped a deck storage plate. The sharp clang made him bolt upright as he threw his arms over his head, certain that the pressure hull was caving in on him. He was breathing heavily and was soaked with perspiration. He couldn't get back to sleep.

New Yorker Renard J. Lombardi, a seaman first class, was one of five brothers who served in the armed forces. Coming from a good Italian Catholic family, Renard found comfort in his religion. He tried to make his surroundings more familiar and relaxing by setting up an altar in the after torpedo room. He draped a towel around his shoulders as if it were a surplice and tried to conduct a mass. This unglued a couple of men who were already on edge. McGuire, in an understatement, said, "It made the guys even more nervous," and they quickly disabused Lombardi of his notion to become a shipboard priest.

George Moffett explained that submarine duty took a toll on the crew in a number of ways. Some could not function as trained during and shortly after a depth-charging. Later, some men became very quiet and associated with no one. There were cases when off-duty men would retreat directly to their bunks and do nothing but sleep until it was time to go back on watch. Some would later become alcoholics. However, the great majority of the men buckled down and persevered.

Finally, on 25 April, *Pampanito* surfaced about ten miles south of Guam to conduct her belated lifeguard mission. In Japan that day, thousands of people made their pilgrimage to Yasukuni Shrine to make offerings to the gallant war dead. As they prayed for the souls of the departed, flights of Liberators swept over *Pampanito,* heading for Guam to take photographs and drop bombs in preparation for the coming invasion of the Marianas. Just after noon, nine Liberators flew close enough for a visual sighting, and the radiomen picked up numerous voice communications among the planes, but no word was received about any planes being downed.

At 1207 the SD radar contacted three planes closing from five miles. The lookouts were unable to see anything, because the boat had just gone under a low-hanging cloud bank. When the planes had closed to three miles, the officer of the deck hit the diving alarm. Two blasts sent those topside tumbling below. Hubie Brown knew the drill well. "It's a wonder I'm not six inches shorter from jumping off those damn periscope shears," he said. Five men converged at the ladder almost simultaneously. "If you used the rungs," Brown said, "you'd have three guys sitting on your neck." He learned to curl his hands and feet around the outside vertical bars and use them almost as if sliding down a pole in a firehouse.

Thirty minutes later, Brown was topside again. Summers had planned to stay up as much as possible in the hope of rescuing at least one downed pilot. At 1307, radar picked up two more planes moving in fast from ten miles. The low clouds precluded visual sighting until suddenly, about three miles out, they broke through an opening. Brown, on port lookout, spotted them. "I've got two Jap planes closing," Brown shouted down to the bridge.

"They're probably ours," the OOD said. "Just keep an eye on them."

The planes dipped lower, and one swung toward the sub. Brown could make out a red meatball on the fuselage. "No, those are Jap planes!" he shouted again. Suddenly, two more planes popped out of the cloud bank—Americans. They peeled off after the Japanese planes, which were coming toward *Pampanito.* Brown watched the closest Japanese plane flying so low he could see water vapor trailing off its wings. Finally the dive alarm sounded, and again they all scrambled down the hatch.

As the boat went beneath the waves, Brown heard bullets hitting the sides of the fairwater around the bridge, possibly ricocheting off the shears where he had been standing just seconds before. The sound was audible below. Seaman Lombardi, no longer in the guise of a priest, said that a

Japanese plane appeared to come out of nowhere, and as they dove, "I heard machine gun bullets rattling off the hull."

Whose plane was it? Don Ferguson said that the sub's plane recognition signals were incorrect, and it was one of our own planes that did the strafing. "The Captain," he said, "finally had enough and took us down."

Summers also thought that an American plane strafed them. "One was not a Zero," he explained. "It was U.S."[40] Brown heard one loud crash astern and thought the Japanese plane had either gone down or dropped a bomb or perhaps had tried to crash dive into the submarine. Summers heard two explosions within a minute after diving, one of them very close.

"The hell with it," he said. He told McClaskey to take her deep. He was done with lifeguarding. This time he'd stay down for the rest of the day. There was no way he'd fight both Japanese and American planes.

Summers headed for his stateroom while Chief Turk Rahner watched him, unable to disguise his contempt. As Summers ducked through the hatch, Rahner turned to the men in the control room and stated: "I hope that SOB goes in his bunk and stays there. He's going to get us all killed."

Summers heard the remark. Stifling his anger, he continued to his cabin and threw back the curtain. Boiling inside, he made a mental note that he would get rid of Rahner at first opportunity.[41]

With the air raid on Guam over, *Pampanito* was officially relieved of lifeguard duty and again turned toward Midway. Finally, Summers ran on the surface as much as possible. The first radar contact on the morning of 26 April sent the sub down. Through the periscope the plane was identified as a "Kate" two-engine bomber.[42]

Twice more that day *Pampanito* was driven down. The last time, as the boat passed seventy-five feet, two bombs exploded to port. Pappas wrote in his diary: "The Nip air force must have our course pretty well plotted, as they are giving us a little trouble. At 1620 they came the closest with two aerial bombs, than any time before." Regardless, an hour later Summers had the boat up and running to Midway at three-engine speed.

On 27 April some excitement was supplied when a lookout spotted what appeared to be a periscope about one thousand yards off the starboard quarter. *Pampanito* made a radical turn to port and dove but could not pick up any screw sounds. Upon surfacing, she rang up full speed and barreled out of the area on a zigzag course.

The high speeds would certainly get the weary crew home faster, but fuel consumption had become a factor. Perhaps the boat had been leaking oil or maybe there was a miscalculation, but on 28 April a serious discrepancy of over six thousand gallons was discovered. Fuel consumption on ships was not spoken of in terms of miles per gallon, but rather in gallons per mile. A submarine at full speed would consume about eighteen gallons per mile. *Pampanito* slowed to one-engine speed. If everything went smoothly, she would just be able to crawl into Midway on fuel-oil fumes.[43]

The monotony of the slow ride was overcome in a number of ways. Paul Pappas, although he considered himself in excellent health, had lost a few pounds and thought he looked "bleached out like a bed sheet." He needed some distraction in which to channel his nervous energy, and he found it when he discovered the enginemen building a still.

The issue of allowing liquor on board ships had gone through several phases from the 1790s, when all American seamen looked forward to their daily allotment of grog, to the prohibition-minded U.S. Navy of World War II.[44] Of course, tell an American he can't have something, and he'll figure out a way to get it. When sailors got their hands on rice and raisins, they didn't think of rice pudding, but rather of a powerful homemade whiskey called "tuba." Some senior officers (such as William Halsey) overlooked minor infractions and even procured extra bottles of hard liquor for "medicinal purposes." Others, such as Lieutenant Commander Thomas M. Dykers of *Jack*, went strictly by the book. When a Filipino steward on board brewed up a pineapple alcohol drink, it was literally sniffed out and thrown overboard.[45]

It did not take long for submariners to discover that the alcohol that fueled their torpedoes was drinkable, at least after it had been distilled. On 2 May, when it looked like *Pampanito* was going to make it safely to Midway after all, Summers broke out two bottles of "medicinal" rum to celebrate the end of the patrol. However, this barely amounted to a shot apiece for those inclined to drink it. They would have to figure out a way to get more.

In the after engine room, Bill Grady, Frank Michno, and Tex Kaup built a still. Bill Grady had made one while on *Plunger*, and he realized that with a still he would have a way to keep his promise that he would get all the boys drunk after his wife gave birth. The three of them procured a Silex hot plate and coffee-maker from the galley. They stopped up the top and spiraled some 3/8-inch copper tubing through a tin can filled with water. The boiling torpedo juice would steam, travel up the tubing, cool, condense, and then drip down the tubing and out. Cool water was kept circulating in the tin can by hooking it to the overflow condensate from the air conditioner. All the motor macs took turns watching it "cook" while on duty.

The torpedomen supplied the torpedo alcohol, called "pink lady" because of the faint hue caused by denaturing agents added for the express purpose of making it undrinkable. As the pink lady condensed, it was collected in bottles, crystal clear and almost 200 proof. The bottles, also from the torpedomen, had once contained vinegar. Woodrow Weaver had discovered that vinegar could clean the galvanized metal borders on the deck plates in the forward torpedo room. He had pestered the cooks for so much vinegar that the men began to call him "Vinegar Weaver." Woody would use the vinegar, then pass the empties along to the motor macs. They would fill the bottles with cooked pink lady, now called "gilly," and store them away. Michno discovered a perfect place to hide the breakable treasure. He tied one end of a cord around the bottle necks and the other around bolts that extended from the inside cover on the freshwater tank. The capped gilly bottles hung suspended, swaying in their watery environment, impervious to depth charges and prying eyes. No one ever brought attention to the strange fact that so much "vinegar" was off-loaded after a patrol.

Crossing the International Date Line, the submariners had a chance to live one day over again and used the opportunity to test the gilly. It was extremely harsh without enough fruit juice to dilute it, but it worked just fine.

In the early afternoon of 2 May, *Pampanito* worked through the reef to Midway. The boat was met at the pier by the base band. "It was a good feeling to have a brass band serenading the crew as they tied up to the dock," said Woody Weaver. Another morale booster was the immediate distribution of mail. All activities stopped while the men caught up on news from home. Fresh fruit, especially oranges and bananas, were delivered to be devoured by the vitamin C–starved submariners. *Pampanito* had more damage than could be repaired by the limited facilities on Midway. After two days' rest, and after thirty thousand gallons of fuel oil were pumped aboard, she was sent to Pearl Harbor for a complete overhaul. Early in the afternoon on 8 May, after an uneventful four-day run, Bob Bennett, once more topside on anchor detail, could appreciate those beautiful green mountains of Oahu even more the second time around.

## CHAPTER FOUR

# *To the Empire*

Rest and recuperation in Honolulu provided the crew with considerably more entertainment possibilities than did the female-deficient, sandy speck of Midway Island. Admiral Lockwood paid his customary visit, discussing the patrol with Summers over a cup of coffee while the men headed for the Royal Hawaiian Hotel. One of the last to leave, Lieutenant Grommet, was finishing his duty in the conning tower. He was thirsty, and he called down to the control room: "Hey Canty, will you please get me a drink of water?"

"Sure, Mr. Grommet," came the reply.

Bill Canty, the man who felt he had been shanghaied back in New London, wasn't going to be anyone's servant. He got one of the "vinegar" bottles and poured a cupful. Canty handed it to Grommet and hurried away. The lieutenant took a couple of big gulps and nearly vomited it back up. Canty hightailed it down the pier and got on the bus leaving for the Royal Hawaiian. Later, Lieutenant Bruckart never could find Canty while making his inspection of the crew's rooms. He thought he had deserted.[1]

As far as the men were concerned, Admiral Nimitz had done them a favor by requisitioning the Royal Hawaiian as a rest camp for submariners and aviators. Officers were assigned suites, some of which posted the tariff on the door: $105 per day. But for the submarine officers, the cost was

$2 a day, food included. For the enlisted men, the charge was only twenty-five cents a week. The crew moved into the "Pink Palace" two, three, or four to a room, taking over an entire wing of the building. It was luxurious to have a "bunk" that didn't roll with the sea and no reveille calls or duty hours. There were some drawbacks; the men had little chance to meet local girls, who were already preempted by the soldiers and sailors stationed on Oahu. Most girls had dates booked a month in advance. Women were not allowed in the rooms but were permitted on the ground floor during happy hours, 1700 to 1900. The military police watched the stairways and elevators to make sure no one misbehaved; females were harder to smuggle upstairs than bottles of gilly.

For those young men in need of sex, it might be found at the infamous New Senator Hotel or in the brothels of Iwilei, which were carefully monitored by the army for the health of the garrisons at Fort Shafter or Schofield Barracks. However, as the war progressed, citizens concerned with immorality lobbied for a crackdown. Because Honolulu served as the fleet naval base, it escaped the "Brothel Blitz" until 1944.

The Oahu brothels were reputed to take in millions of dollars a year, and the fifty thousand prophylactic treatments administered each month indicated the extent of their business. Some of the girls did not wait for the men to come to them but advertised unashamedly. The most notorious, Mamie Stover, often strolled the beaches in a seductive Hawaiian muumuu, successfully enticing the servicemen.

"One, two, three, four/Mamie's what we're fighting for," the GIs and sailors would chant in cadence. Mamie's House, with its specially constructed "Bull Ring" consisting of four adjacent Pullman-sized compartments with red couches, maximized Mamie's profits. Even at an average of three dollars a session, Mamie managed to retire as a half-millionaire.

However, the thousands of Armed Forces personnel swamping the brothels created the embarrassing problem of having men lined up in the streets. The spectacle led the city officials and the military to shut the brothels down. By 1944 the assembly lines were closed, but men could still find the occasional lady working "free-lance" or even a house or two that still remained in business.

Walt Richter enjoyed his time at the Royal Hawaiian. He relished sleeping as long as he wanted and being able to go to the kitchen at any

*Pampanito's* crew on deck, 4 May 1944. Tied up at Midway next to sub tender *Proteus*. Seated, left to right: Frank Lederer, Joseph Austin, Robert Matheny, Roger Bourgeois, Lloyd MacVane, James Behney, Renard Lombardi, Louis Bobb, Hubert Brown, Edmund Stockslader, William McCullom, Frank Michno, Clarence Carmody, Harold Chinn, William Yagemann, Norbert Kaup, Duncan Brown, Otto Aimone, John Wilson, Roger Walters, Irving Costello. Standing, left to right: Bernard Zalusky, Lynn Martin, Edward Tonkin, Walter Cordon, Robert Bennett, Anthony Hauptman, Milton Meyers, Paul Pappas, Theodas King, William Canty, Albert Van Atta, Lawrence Langin, Ralph Attaway, Gordon Hopper, Ralph Herber, Isaac Robinson, Ray Mosey. (Photo courtesy of Gordon Hopper.)

time to order a meal. He claimed to have won four thousand dollars gambling on the first patrol. "So if we wanted to go to the whorehouse," he said, "we'd get up a little early before all the other sailors came in so we didn't have to wait in line." Richter chuckled at his good fortune. "Ha! At that time it was only three dollars for a piece of tail. They had parties for us; hula girls performing and all those good things."

Sailors returning to the Royal Hawaiian had to get back by 2200, for barbed wire encircled the grounds, and wartime Oahu was still blacked out and under a curfew. After the gates were locked, anyone out late was picked up by the police.[2]

On their first postpatrol liberty, Norm Arcement and Ralph Attaway were looking for some action. At an intersection not far from the Royal Hawaiian they were approached by a shady-looking character.

"I got two bottles of whiskey, and I want five bucks apiece for them," he said, and showed them the tops of the bottles from inside his jacket.

"Sounds good," Attaway answered. They each produced a five-dollar bill, but the man said, "No, no. I can't take it here." He said he was being watched. He would put the whiskey down by the lamp post on the corner, walk over to them, take the money, and they could go over and pick up the bottles.

Arcement and Attaway watched the man put the two bottles down. He walked by them, they passed him the cash, and he kept going. When the sailors got to the bottles, they took them to an alley and opened them up. "We got the bottles, all right," said Arcement. "Vinegar!" They had been stung, and they threw down the bottles and sped off after the con man. They saw him running, but he already had a block's head start, and he soon disappeared. "Boy, we chased that sucker," Norm said. "I wish we could have caught him."

As electricians, Attaway and Arcement tended to "run" together on liberties. Such was the case with all the ratings. According to Harold Chinn, most of them stuck together and associated with their own kind. It wasn't a matter of snobbery, just a result of where one worked and with whom one shared one's watches. Chinn said the chiefs ran with the chiefs, first class ran with first class, and second and third class mingled some, but most ran with mates of the same rating. Said Chinn: "Firemen and seamen were at the bottom of the ladder. And that was me."

Electrician Paul Pappas and electrician striker Andy Currier were assigned a room overlooking Waikiki Beach. Quartermaster striker Al Van Atta roomed with Quartermaster Second Class Albert J. Bacskay, one of his best friends, who hailed from Perth-Amboy, New Jersey, and was known to the men as "the Wild Hungarian Eagle." The hotel was terrific, but somehow the beach didn't live up to expectations, being narrower than Van Atta had imagined. The change of pace was welcome, but a healthy young sailor can only take so much sand and sunshine. With women at a premium, many decided to fall back on what might have been the next best attraction: alcohol. Van Atta and the other quartermasters went out to do the town. A popular song at the time was the Andrews Sisters' "Rum and Coca Cola." Al, not much of a drinker, decided he would find out if he and the gang could reduce the rum and Coke supply on Oahu. They didn't. Al remembered nothing more until Schilling helped deposit him in his bed many hours later.

Within twenty-four hours of checking in to the Royal, several makeshift gilly cookers were in operation. Most agreed that George Moffett ran the best still, but the quality of the product was still a matter of taste. Carmody claimed it was good with grapefruit juice mixer. Walters said it was a decent drink with orange or pineapple juice, then added, "Yum!" Hopper, whom the men had nicknamed "Clod," had a different opinion. Gilly was "bad stuff!"

Torpedoman Howard George figured he could cook gilly better in a hotel room than on the boat, and Joe Eichner assisted him. "We had the tureen to put the pink stuff into," Eichner said. "We had the pie plate with an indentation in the middle of the pan, a soup bowl to collect the white stuff that dripped down from the bottom of the pie plate, and the ice cubes to put on top. Oh yes," said Joe, "and we had the stove to cook it on, too." Big George would come around once in awhile to pour the alcohol into a blue agate pitcher and refill the tureen. He had quite a bit collected when Harold Chinn came in looking for a pitcher to mix up a concoction of his own. Chinn, said Eichner, "took the pitcher with the gilly and poured it down the sink. Needless to say, it was a most discouraging evening for Big George."

The crew arrived at the Royal Hawaiian on 9 May. One day later, Pappas succinctly recorded in his diary: "Gilly party going full blast, 60 percent of crew lit up."

The idea of separating the submarine crews in the hotel made sense. There was a natural rivalry among them, but it was generally good-natured, at least until alcohol entered the equation. Sharing the fifth floor with *Pampanito* was the *Thresher* crew. Under Lieutenant Commander Duncan C. MacMillan, *Thresher* had just finished a fifty-one-day patrol off Truk. She, too, had come up empty-handed, but she was a veteran boat with twelve patrols and had sunk a dozen ships.

On Sunday, 14 May, the inevitable happened. Taunts were exchanged in the crowded elevators and hallways. A punch was thrown, and a melee started. Both crews pulled out fire hoses, sending a river coursing down the stairwell. The water ran down to the first floor, ruining carpets and causing thousands of dollars in damage. In addition, said Frank Michno, louver doors had been kicked in, and the men were charged one dollar for each broken slat. The next day, Admiral Lockwood's staff paid them an angry visit. The ass-chewing was concluded by the wish that the submariners would fight the Japanese as much as they fought among themselves. If they did, the war would have been over by now. The men apologized—then went back upstairs to cook more gilly.

That evening, Lieutenant Bruckart, on his first rotation as duty officer, walked the halls to check the men's behavior. In a few of the rooms the men were peacefully playing cards, reading, or sleeping, but in most the partying was still going strong. In one of the rooms men were assembled around a naked crew member, who was lying in the middle of the carpet, intent on finding how much alcohol he could pour down his throat without coming up for air.

"Hi, Mr. Bruckart," one of them said. "This is fun." They invited him in, but he declined. Bruckart went back to his own room, wondering how so many men could find fun in drinking themselves into oblivion. After Bruckart had made his rounds, a fire was started by men playing "Indian" around a campfire—whether on purpose or from an overturned gilly cooker, no one would say.

The *Pampanito* and *Thresher* crews were not the only ones keeping the Royal Hawaiian in an uproar in May 1944, for crews from *Harder, Tang,* and *Seahorse* were also there. In *Tang*'s wing, officers discovered a stolen five-gallon can of machine alcohol. Lieutenant Commander Richard H. O'Kane was concerned, not so much with catching the thief but about passing the word that the stuff was 200 proof and would be dangerous to drink unless cut with a diluting mixer.[3]

However, not all submariners looked upon drinking as a priority. The greatest number used their two-week liberty to go to movies, play sports, or soak up the sun and enjoy the beach and ocean. Paul Pappas popped roll after roll of Kodachrome into his camera, snapping scores of pictures of the men at play. Several of them made unsuccessful attempts at surfing, and Pappas also admitted that he "did not do so good on the surfboard." Most of them just floated around lazily in the water between Waikiki's first and second reefs, enjoying the moment.

Before Paul Summers could relax, he visited Admiral Nimitz, giving the admiral a personal appraisal of his experiences. He regretted missing the first convoy and blamed it on the *Chidori* that got in his way. He was sure, however, that he had sunk a freighter in the second convoy, even though he hadn't been able to watch it go down. When Nimitz asked him what he thought about lifeguarding, Summers replied, "I think it stinks, Admiral."

Other skippers had complained about lifeguarding, including *Tang*'s Dick O'Kane, who believed that operating as an adjunct of the surface fleet was not compatible to a submarine's main purpose, which was to sink enemy ships. Some thought it may have been a strategic error even to send submarines out after capital ships. Arguably, the proper task for a submarine force may have been to wage *guerre de course*, all-out war on the enemy merchant fleet. Subs were diverted to heavily defended base areas, however, or sent on special supply, guerrilla, or lifeguarding missions when they may have been more gainfully employed sinking merchant ships.

In 1944, submarines spent 469 days on lifeguard station, rescuing 117 aviators.[4] Certainly this was a morale booster for the airmen, and the saving of 117 lives was no trivial matter. But if only one additional *maru* heading to the Marianas had been sunk with three thousand soldiers and their accompanying arms and artillery, it might have saved the lives of several hundred American troops during the invasions. Those 469 days spent lifeguarding in 1944 represented 4 percent of the 11,700 submarine days spent on offensive patrol. Submarines sank 2,388,709 tons of Japanese shipping that year. Had the lifeguard days been used in attacking the Japanese merchant marine, possibly another 95,000 tons would have been eliminated—a much more profitable use of the submarine force.

The disturbing increase in shipping losses finally convinced the Japanese to initiate convoys in late 1942 and a Grand Escort Headquarters to protect them in late 1943. By April 1944, Imperial Navy officers were appointed to serve in a rotating pool of convoy commanders, and ships were held in port until larger numbers of *marus* and accompanying escorts could be gathered. Increasing convoy sizes meant decreasing the number of convoys and permitted a higher concentration of escorts. It was a sound idea that worked well, at least in the Allied Atlantic convoys.

In January and February 1944, submarines sank 249,000 tons and 236,000 tons, respectively, of Japanese shipping. The losses in March were cut to 133,000 tons. In April, losses went down to 94,000 tons. There was optimism in Japan that the new techniques were having the desired effect. The real reason, however, was that so many submarines had been pulled for lifeguard missions. When freed of this task in May, Japanese ship losses immediately ballooned back up to 230,000 tons. The brief jubilation of the Grand Escort Command and Imperial Navy staff was over.[5]

With major lifeguarding operations concluded for the time being, where would Lockwood send *Pampanito* for her second patrol? Now that the United States controlled the Gilberts, Marshalls, and Eastern Carolines and had broken through the Bismarcks, and with more submarines coming out each month, it was possible to concentrate on the shipping lanes closer to Japan. Lockwood dropped his earlier method of assigning hot subs to hot areas, and in mid-April he instituted what became known as the Rotating Patrol Plan, informally called the XYZ Plan. Japanese-controlled waters were divided into sectors, and submarines were placed on a shifting patrol, inshore to offshore, north to south, and from active to inactive areas in order to give all the boats an equal share of both the dangers and the opportunities. The areas were given names, such as Convoy College south of Formosa, Maru's Morgue along the Nansei Shoto Islands, Hit Parade off Japan, Dunker's Derby in the Bonin Islands, and the Pentathlon Patrol in the southern Marianas.[6] Summers carried his sealed orders with him.

Before another patrol began, the business of crew transfer had to be completed. This was a submarine command policy that bothered many skippers and execs, but it served several purposes: it supplied trained nucleus crews for new construction, allowed remaining veterans to teach the fresh arrivals, and potentially allowed for the entire crew to be rotated ashore after five patrols. However, a boat might lose 10 percent to 25 percent of its men after each patrol, and going to sea with a full veteran crew was never possible. Jeff Davis took care of most of the picks, but Pete Summers would have his say. The force never tolerated slackers, and one word from a commanding officer that a man was unfit for sub duty would mark him for immediate transfer. The captain's judgment was never questioned.[7]

In fact, after the depth charging *Pampanito* took, it was possible that her entire crew might be redistributed. Such was the experience of USS *Puffer* (SS 268), when, north of Makassar Strait in October 1943, she had been held down for over thirty-one hours by Japanese escorts. She suffered significant damage, but the factor that made her ordeal so extraordinary was the psychological damage to the crew. Many assumed they were going to die and refused to carry out their duties. The skipper lost control of his men.

*Puffer* managed to slip away, but the mental scars remained. After studying the situation, submarine command determined that when a boat had gone through such an experience, its crew should be disbanded and sent to other boats. The sharing of the ordeal welded the men together in a mystic bond, and no newcomer would ever be able to penetrate the circle, for he had not gone through the experience. Another observation was that one should not hastily form an opinion of a man's value before seeing him under stress. The so-called leaders in good times were not necessarily those who would take over in an emergency. Sometimes the more phlegmatic were also the more reliable.[8]

On *Pampanito*, too, men would always remember *the* depth charging, but control was never lost, and the men were judged fit to continue as a crew. Eleven men were routinely transferred. In addition, now that everyone definitely had depth charge experience, Summers felt there was no need to keep any troublemakers aboard. Ed Kubacki was sent to ComSubDiv Relief Crew 202, far away on Midway.

One sailor who wished he could have gotten off was Bill Grady. He never requested a transfer, however, because he figured he would just be placed on another boat. The problem was not with *Pampanito*, but with superstition. Grady couldn't shake the ominous thought that his eighth

Pearl Harbor, May 1944. The Motormacs. Seated, left to right: Earl Watkins, William Merryman, Norbert Kaup, Clarence Carmody. Standing, left to right: William Grady, John Wilson, John Madaras, Frank Michno. (Photo by Paul Pappas.)

patrol would be his last. "I just had the feeling that we were going to buy the farm on the next run," he said. Since he was sure he would not return, Grady borrowed all the money he could get, then spent every cent during a few days of riotous living. Later he was sorry. Said Bill: "We made it back to port and I had to pay back everything that I had earned for two months."

Summers also found an excuse to dump Turk Rahner. On 23 May most of the regulars had returned to the boat. That morning, after a long night on the town, Rahner was having trouble calling the roll. In fact, he was having trouble standing up straight, and the mustered men thought it would be a good time for a few laughs. When Rahner called out the name "Brown" or "Smith," an anonymous voice would answer, "Which one?" They feigned an inability to understand the names as Rahner slurred the pronunciations, and they went into their "Which one?" routine at all the appropriate places. Soon they started on even the most one-of-a-kind names, like "Bourgeois," "Stockslader," "Yagemann," or "Zalusky." Rahner's poor handling of the situation, punctuated by muffled guffaws from the assembly, was witnessed by Summers. It was all the excuse he needed. Rahner was gone.

"The Chief of the Boat was lousy," Summers said. "That's why I got rid of him. I promoted my engineer [Clarence H. Smith] to Chief of the Boat."[9]

The SubDiv 42 relief crew had a tough job repairing *Pampanito*. The outer torpedo tube doors were realigned. All the rubber flange gaskets in the main induction piping under the superstructure were replaced with Consolco gaskets. The engine room received a new water pump.

Improvements were made as well. A small bunk was installed in the conning tower, where the skipper could sack out at the base of the TDC. A dead reckoning indicator (DRI) was installed in the conning tower. A very high frequency (VHF) receiver and transmitter were installed. The CUO, a hand-tuned radar receiver, was replaced by the APR, an enhanced "black box" that was motor driven and had the added attraction of a visual display screen (CRT) to discern the pulse width of enemy radar.

The fuel problem experienced by *Pampanito* on her first patrol was common to many submarines, and a solution was found to extend the cruising radius. The number 4 main ballast tank (MBT) was modified so it could be used either as an MBT or as a fuel ballast tank (FBT). Dual use allowed the addition of twenty-four thousand gallons of fuel oil, which could give the sub an extra two thousand miles of range. When the fuel was consumed, the tank could be converted back to an MBT.[10]

For the next five days *Pampanito* was put through her paces while the crew tested the new equipment, checked the integrity of the repairs, and

Pearl Harbor, May 1944. The Torpedomen. Kneeling, left to right: Robert Bennett, Harold Rahner, Frank Lederer, Edward Tonkin. Standing, left to right: Robert Matheny, Howard George, James Behney, Bernard Zalusky, Woodrow Weaver. (Photo by Paul Pappas.)

broke in one dozen new shipmates. Among the new arrivals was Lieutenant Junior Grade Ted Nier Swain. Born in Helena, Montana, in 1919, Swain attended the U.S. Naval Academy in the first three-year class and was commissioned as an ensign in June 1942. He had served aboard *S-48* for one and one-half years as torpedo and gunnery officer before being assigned to *Pampanito*.

Swain's forte was in the professional handling of the deck gun. When commissioned, *Pampanito* was equipped with a four-inch dry gun located forward of the conning tower. "Dry" meant that the barrel was sealed with a watertight plug (tampion) and the breech by a watertight cover. Both had to be removed before the gun could be fired.

The order "battle surface" called for the gun crew to assemble in the access trunk in the forward part of the control room, ready to rush out on deck. Woody Weaver was gun trainer and first man out. McGuire, as sight setter, was second. He wore a set of headphones to communicate with the conning tower. Next were Torpedoman's Mate Third Class Edward Tonkin as pointer, Jim Behney as shellman, and Tony Hauptman as gun captain. They had practiced the exercise many times, and Swain was pleased with their performance. On the last day of practice, Admiral Lockwood accompanied them, and Summers and Swain wanted to impress him. As the gun crew assembled, Summers called the trainer aside. "Weaver," he said, "when the surfacing alarm sounds, start undogging the gun access door."

Summers bled excess air into the boat to raise the pressure. He hoped the air would help blow the men out the door and keep the water from draining back in, even with the deck awash. At the sound of the surfacing signal, Weaver undogged the hatch. As soon as the boat was shallow enough for the air pressure inside to overcome the sea pressure outside, the door flew open and practically lifted Weaver out onto the deck in a bubble of air. As the pressure quickly equalized and the little pocket collapsed, the water rushed back through the open hatch and caught McGuire full force. Angry as hell, he regained his composure, plugged in his headphones, and started setting the gun sights.

Summers got the results he wanted, for the gun crew got the first round off while the deck was still awash and even before the captain and the admiral could get to the bridge. That was some quick action.

After the exercise, McGuire was still livid. He went up to Weaver, shook his finger in his face, and said, "Weaver, if you ever do that again, I will punch you in the nose!" Woody just laughed. There was no way McGuire would be punching the big torpedoman. As for the gun exercise, they had it down to perfection. Unfortunately, or fortunately, depending on how one looks at it, they were never called upon to use their expertise in combat.

In port, *Pampanito* was surprised by a visit from Captain "Swede" Momsen. She had received three endorsements, including one each by Momsen and Lockwood. The crew was congratulated for excellent damage control and at-sea repair work, for thorough coverage of assigned areas, for lifeguarding, for persistence in the face of tenacious antisubmarine tactics, and for a successful attack resulting in damage to one 7,000-ton *Toyama Maru*–class freighter. While the men were hastily assembled, still informally clad in dungarees and work clothes, Momsen presented all of the pleasantly surprised sailors with submarine combat pins. After Momsen left, Summers passed the word: he had gotten the area he wanted for his next patrol, and although he couldn't reveal where, the men had better prepare themselves, for they could all expect a hot time.

The last night before sailing, the crew managed to squeeze in one more celebration. Roger Walters was sitting on the pier with Tony Hauptman and a few other sailors. They had been drinking, and Tony was feeling melancholy. They spoke of a submariner's chances of surviving the war, when Tony said that some of them may die, but he was indestructible. To prove how tough he was, he went down to the sub and brought back a razor. "He was drunk as a skunk," said Walters, and he sat down on the dock and proceeded to make four or five slashes across his forearm.

"Christ, knock it off, Tony!" Walters ordered. They finally stopped him, but Hauptman sat there unmoved, staring at the blood and indicating that he was made of steel. Nothing hurt him. To prove it again, Tony told them he would climb the underwater escape tower and jump. When he headed for the structure, they had to gang tackle him and haul him back to the sub. He finally passed out in his bunk. Still, many of the crew thought Tony could back up his boasts. "He was the ultimate submariner," said Gordon Hopper. "He could do just about anything."

Joe Eichner was another one of the midnight revelers. "Most likely," Joe said, "I had more than I could handle that evening." The next morning no one could get Joe out of his bunk. He was ordered to the bridge to speak to the captain, and he only climbed the ladders with the assistance of his mates.

Summers was standing with his arms folded. "All right, sailor," he asked, "Where'd you get the booze?"

"What booze?" Eichner pleaded ignorance. Summers grilled him, but Eichner insisted on his innocence. "I couldn't look him in the face," Joe said, "for if I did, my breath would have knocked him over for sure."

Summers said that he would sweat it out of him and sent him down to the pump room to clean the bilges. Joe banged on the machinery for a while, then found a place between the air compressors and fell asleep. He didn't know how long he had been out, when a noise made him open his eyes just in time to see Pete's starched khaki trousers coming down the ladder. Eichner rolled off his fanny to his hands and knees as if he were repairing something down at deck level.

"Okay sailor," Summers said, "you've had enough. Go back up, and let this be a lesson to you." As the boat got underway, Eichner filled a pitcher with ice water, took a seat in the crew's mess, and drank it down. His hangover was finally going away.

On the afternoon of 3 June, *Pampanito* passed Barber's Point, Oahu, and headed west with her escort, *PC-485*. The first test dive flooded the SJ radar mast and proved that the engine saltwater sea valves were still leaking. The depth charging had damaged the periscopes, for they were extremely rough in train, with considerable noise and vibration while slicing through the water at periscope depth (about fifty-four feet). At 2000, *PC-485* headed back to Oahu, and *Pampanito* proceeded independently to Midway.

On the morning of 7 June, Summers conned the boat through the dredged coral reef and tied up at the Sand Island Pier. He was granted a twenty-four-hour delay so the sub tender, USS *Proteus* (AS 19), could work on the periscopes, the SJ radar, and the leaky sea valves. The boat also took on another twenty thousand gallons of fuel oil. That night, many of the crew went aboard *Proteus* to take in a movie: *The Fallen Sparrow*, with John Garfield and Maureen O'Hara.

With the addition of Lieutenant Swain as torpedo and gunnery officer, Lieutenant Hannon's position was superfluous, and Hannon, a Naval

Academy classmate of Swain, was detached from the boat. Also detached was William McClaskey, who had recently been promoted to lieutenant commander. There always appeared to be hard feelings between McClaskey and Summers. Pete accused him of "freezing" on the near-disastrous six-hundred-foot dive and later told the story that it was he, Summers, who blew ballast and saved the boat. Of McClaskey's detachment, Pete said: "He transferred after the patrol. I never put the incident in his record."

McClaskey had a different recollection. He was an experienced submariner, having made as many patrols on *Swordfish* as Pete had on *Stingray*. McClaskey was navigator for most of the patrol, and he knew he was being prepped for command. Plus, there was no need for three lieutenant commanders on one boat. Far from being booted off, McClaskey's orders came through, and he was flown back to Pearl Harbor to take over as exec of USS *Burrfish* (SS 312).

Taking McClaskey's place was Lieutenant McMillan Houston Johnson, a one-time English professor at Florida State Teachers College now in the Naval Reserve. Johnson would not have an easy time of it either, for Summers never looked upon reservists as true officers. As far as Pete was concerned, the Academy men—he, Lieutenant Commander Davis, and Lieutenant Swain—were the three senior men on board. Swain respected Johnson's position, but he couldn't help feel a little resentment, for he had gotten out of the Academy on 19 June 1942, while Johnson, a "Ninety-Day Wonder," had been commissioned on 15 June, giving him four days' seniority. Johnson had the promotion advantage, but not the same submarine experience.[11]

By 8 June the repairs were completed, and *Pampanito* went to sea. Summers opened his orders and called the crew together: *Pampanito* would be heading for the Empire of Japan. As Pappas remembered the captain's words, they would operate near Tokyo and all along the southern coast, the area known as Hit Parade, on a free-patrolling basis. There would be plenty of targets, and *Pampanito* would surely come back with a broom (signifying a clean sweep) affixed to her shears.

As the boat crossed the date line heading west, 9 June was scratched off the calendar. As the crew settled into its daily routine, Gordon Hopper speculated upon a patrol of the empire. He took the news in stride, convinced, as most young men are, of his own invulnerability. He was just happy to have an opportunity to make a killing right in the emperor's own front yard.

Not having such a sanguine outlook was Motor Machinist's Mate Third Class Clyde B. Markham, who had come aboard in Pearl Harbor. The eighteen-year-old from Marianna, Arkansas, was now the second youngest man on board, after Walt Cordon. He was feeling good about himself and his future. The tall, slim, blond-haired Markham was perched topside as lookout. His shoes were shined, and his trousers were creased. He gave a quick adjustment to his green ball cap. He looked sharp. Markham's reverie about being the Errol Flynn of the sub service was brought to a halt, however, by two blasts of the diving alarm. As he snapped back to reality, he realized he was the only one left topside while the decks were going awash. He went quickly for the open hatch, but ducking down, caught the brim of his cap on the railing. It sailed back and landed on the far edge of the cigarette deck. He ran back to get it. There was no way he'd lose his sharp green cap. He finally scrambled down the hatch, nearly into the arms of Captain Summers, who proceeded to chew him out. Young Clyde Boyd Markham received an epithet-punctuated lecture about intelligence, responsibility, safety, and discipline. Suddenly his future on board did not appear so rosy.

The cooks were also having a rough time. Ship's Cook First Class Bonham D. Large, Ship's Cook Second Class William F. Morrow, Jr., and newly rated Ship's Cook Third Class Joe Eichner were at their wit's end trying to satisfy their hungry shipmates. Storeroom and refrigerator space was at a premium, and once stowed, supplies could not be shuffled about easily. Even the showers were packed full of food. Unless supplies were carefully stored, the crew could find itself eating through a wall of carrots, tomato soup, or Spam until some other variety of food could be unearthed.

Lieutenant Bruckart thought the cooks did an admirable job. Jack Large was a baker, he said, "and good—he was kind to me."

"Mr. Bruckart," Large once asked him, "do you like Jell-O?"

"You bet," the lieutenant answered. The next morning when Bruckart came off watch, he found "a wash pan full of red Jell-O on the wardroom table for me."

It has been said that submarine food was the best in the navy. The cooks took great pride in their reputation and tried hard to cater to the whims of sometimes finicky shipmates. On the first patrol the food storage was done well, so the men had an ample variety. On the first night out, however, someone mixed up a batch of tuna fish and mayonnaise. It looked good and tasted better. Thereafter, the galley was raided by men wanting tuna sandwiches, and within a few weeks all the canned tuna was gone. The cooks had to put up with griping men for another month. On the second patrol, the cooks got smart and loaded tuna and mayo in every nook and cranny. The sailors wouldn't touch it. This time, chocolate mixed with canned condensed milk caught everyone's fancy. Very soon they ran out of condensed milk, which was a true disaster, for almost everyone used it in his coffee. The sailors griped, and the cooks were in hot water again.

Joe Eichner had second thoughts about rating up to cook. He and Morrow had cooked a great batch of chicken and french fries, and although the crew helped with peeling the spuds, Eichner sliced every potato himself. "It took an awful lot of fries to feed about eighty men," he said. He proudly served six heaping bowls of hot, golden-brown potatoes. Before he could turn around, all six platters had been emptied and shoved back through the window into the galley, with twenty-four men clamoring for more. Disgusted, Eichner threw the bowls back at them and told them they could cook the next batch themselves. The ruckus they caused made Joe wish he had remained a seaman.[12]

On 14 June, *Pampanito* was running west along the thirtieth parallel about three hundred miles north of Marcus Island. Lookouts spotted several large glass balls floating nearby, and Summers headed in. They were floats for a Japanese fishing seine, perhaps broken free as the result of a storm. The skipper decided he wanted to get a souvenir, and several of the crew had to manhandle one of the balls to the forward hatch, where part of the ladder had to be removed so it could be lowered into the forward torpedo room. The episode took place in broad daylight, said Lieutenant Bruckart, who was on the bridge unhappily watching the affair. "I thought we were sitting ducks," he said.

The next day began with solid gray overcast skies. Those versed in old mariners' wisdom might have recalled the saying, "Evening red and morning gray, help the sailor on his way." A gray morning sky indicated a blanket of fog, which presaged a clear day—at least according to nautical lore. However, by forenoon, the sky was still gray, with a light haze around the horizon, and seas were moderate but making up.

By the time lunch was over, a fresh breeze of Force 5 had sprung up. The waves had increased to about six feet, with long, rolling whitecaps and spray. When Steward's Mate Ingram was finished with his duties, Summers had him go into the forward torpedo room. He wanted his souvenir glass ball cleaned and polished. Although Ingram was not pleased with the job, he got some rags and alcohol and went to work. Summers could be condescending and outright rude to him, but Ingram tried to shrug it off. While he polished the globe, a heavy sea caught the boat. The ball slipped from his hands, rolled, and banged against a torpedo skid, where it crashed and broke into a hundred pieces. Summers, who seldom went beyond officer's country, happened to be making one of his rare excursions forward. He entered just in time to see Ingram sweeping up the broken pieces.

"Why, you dumb son-of-a-bitch," Summers called out to him, complaining that Ingram couldn't even complete a simple task without screwing it up. McGuire was nearby and heard Pete cursing at Ingram. Good Kid had his head lowered, and McGuire could tell that the dressing down had hurt him. Summers stomped off, and from that time on, the steward's dislike for the captain began to change into hatred.

By that afternoon, everyone had more pressing matters to think about, for the wind was building up in intensity and the seas were becoming mountainous. The barometer dropped rapidly. It looked as if they were about to sail into a full-fledged typhoon, and *Pampanito* sent out a weather report to ComSubPac.

The storm was running north, toward Japan, which meant the sub would cross its path perpendicularly. If she could run on the surface, it would not take long to break free from its grip. By suppertime, however, Summers took the boat below so they could eat without the nauseating rolling. Afterwards, the pots and pans were battened down, and *Pampanito* broke the surface to pound through the seas. The last hundred miles to the Nampo Shoto, the chain of islands running 750 miles south from Tokyo Bay, was like being on a never-ending roller coaster ride. Pappas recorded: "There's one hell of a storm going on. Can't stand up without almost breaking a leg. The waves are coming way over our periscope shears." Since the tops of the shears were about forty feet high, then they were truly riding out a full typhoon, with attendant Force 12 winds of over seventy-five miles per hour.

No one had to tell Walt Richter that they were in a typhoon. After supper he was on lookout, hanging on for dear life. He became nauseated. The rolling waves got worse, and his churning stomach followed suit. In no time he was horribly seasick. As dizzy as he was, he could only hold on and hope for the best. If he were to vomit, he would have to do it standing in place. Sure enough, the next moment Richter felt like he had expelled everything inside of him onto the deck. Lieutenant Grommet, seeing Richter's distress, sidled down the rail and came to him. Instead of assisting, Grommet chewed him out, yelling over the intensity of the howling wind: "Sailor! The next time you have to throw up, ask for permission and go over the side!" His order was almost immediately followed by a huge wave which crashed over the bridge, washing away the vomit and almost everyone else. Richter was finally allowed to go below. Later, he thought about the ludicrousness of the situation, rhetorically asking, "Can you imagine anybody being that stupid and saying something like that?"

By 2028, *Pampanito*'s SJ radar picked up an island of the Nampo Shoto: Tori Shima. The wind and seas moderated after they passed to the west side of the island chain, but the typhoon lashed out with a final gasp, sending one last wave splashing down the main induction and the open conning tower hatch. The bilges and pumps handled it, and there was no damage.[13]

For the next four days *Pampanito* headed due west toward the southern main Japanese island of Kyushu. The seas moderated each day, but on 16 June it was still too overcast to take navigational readings. The fuel in number 4 FBT had been consumed, and it was converted back to an MBT. Several flushings cleared the remaining oil out of the tank so that it would not leave tell-tale traces for the enemy to follow.

Concern grew over the incessant rain squalls with no celestial sightings. Finally, on 19 June they spotted the mountainous Tanega Shima, a forty-mile-long island separated from the southern tip of Kyushu by the twenty-mile-wide Osumi (Van Diemen) Strait. That evening, *Pampanito* surfaced and headed north up the coast to Toi Misaki. There she spent two grueling days, submerged for up to sixteen hours at a time, struggling with heavy overcast, frequent rain squalls, and heavy seas, straddling the one-hundred-fathom curve. It would exemplify her monthly routine.

On 21 June they sighted a fifteen-hundred-ton interisland steamer. This was a target worthy of at least one torpedo. It was running close to the beach, north around a small island named O Shima, but the range was about nine thousand yards. Summers was unable to close because running interference between them was a small motor torpedo boat, patrolling seaward of the steamer. They avoided it.

During the evening, the APR picked up Japanese radar emanations, which caused Summers to limit the use of his own radar to foil enemy detection efforts. Yet there was little chance of locating Japanese shipping at night without it, and Pampanito continued to send out periodic radar sweeps.

Late on the night of 21 June the SJ screen lit up, bringing everyone in the conning tower to attention. There was a large but hazy pip—too large for a ship, and not distinct. Was it simply a rain squall? If it moved slowly, and in the direction of the wind, it probably was a squall. They moved closer and discovered it to be a light squall with a heavy cloud bank in the distance. Squalls could also hide lurking ASW vessels. These radar "gremlins" were distracting as well as eerie, and they were to be experienced almost nightly.

Radar operation was still a relatively new science, and not all boats made full use of it. George Moffett did not believe Captain Summers trusted it during the first few patrols, for it did have its idiosyncrasies. Wise use of radar would definitely give American submarines an advantage. As radar improved, and as skippers became more comfortable with it, there was a dramatic shift from day to night attacks. Because Japanese surface radar was ineffective, U.S. submarines could operate freely on the surface at night, even in the face of escorts. In 1942, when few subs had SJ, only 30 percent of the attacks were at night, but by 1944 the figure rose to 57 percent.[14]

Although the Americans had radar, it was an advantage only when its foibles were understood. Moffett was becoming an expert with it, and on this patrol he had the help of Radio Technician Second Class Spencer H. Stimler, who had come aboard at Midway. Stimler, born in Foley, Minnesota, in 1923, the second of nine children, joined the navy in November

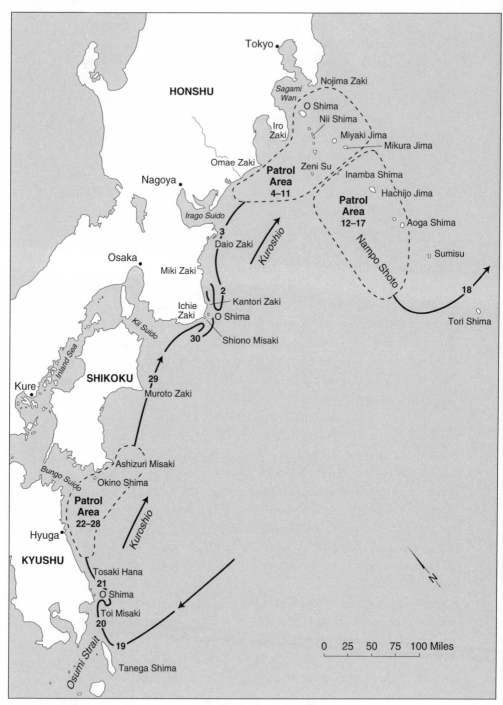

Detail of second patrol, 19 June–18 July 1944

1942. He went to electrical, radio, and radar school and finished his training in New London on submarine sound equipment. He had no previous sea experience, but Moffett checked him out and found he understood the systems enough to stand regular watches. Stimler discovered that if one cranked up the gain on the radar, it could pick up almost everything, including waves. One night, with the power turned up, Stimler discovered a good-sized pip, called out "Radar contact," and gave the bearing and range.

The OOD informed the captain, and the tracking party was called in. Moffett came up and took over the radar, while Stimler, now assistant, showed him his find. The "contact" was tracked another few minutes until it broke up and disappeared. They had been chasing a large wave. Stimler did this a couple of times until he became seasoned. Those in charge consoled him that it was better to be safe than sorry. "However," said Stimler, "to my fellow crewmates, it was a source of constant needling. They never let me forget it."

While playing hide-and-seek with radar gremlins, Pampanito moved up the east coast of Kyushu to the Bungo Suido. The properly tuned SJ picked up the mountainous little Okino Shima, thirty-six miles away at the far eastern end of the strait. At dawn of 22 June, *Pampanito* submerged east of Miyazaki, Kyushu, to patrol the southern approaches to Bungo Suido.

Bungo Suido, Area Seven in the patrol sector known as Hit Parade, was a busy channel between the islands of Kyushu and Shikoku and a very important focal point for Japanese shipping, comparable to the Virginia Capes–Chesapeake Bay region of the United States. Even the name brought a tingle to the spine of submariners, for it was there that our boats had received some of their worst drubbings. It was a most dangerous place to be. The waters were shallow and treacherous north of the one-hundred-fathom curve, the currents were swift and contradictory, patrol traffic was heavy, numerous air bases and radar installations were nearby, and there was the likelihood of encountering "Bungo Pete." The stories of Bungo Pete were legion in the submarine service. Supposedly, Pete was a crafty Japanese destroyer captain who plied the waters, working in conjunction with a Japanese submarine, using one or the other to lure an unsuspecting American submarine into an attack, whereupon either the destroyer or the submarine would close in for the kill.

Although Bungo Pete was apocryphal, there were many shipbuilding facilities and submarine bases surrounding the Inland Sea, including navy yards at Kure and Sasebo, and the Mitsubishi and Kawasaki company yards were at Kobe. The Japanese were very sensitive about this wide open entrance to their private sea, and they did have destroyer and submarine patrols there to defend it. As early as December 1941, false sightings convinced some Japanese navy men that American submarines had sneaked into the Inland Sea via the Bungo Suido, and they resolved to strengthen the channel defenses. Vice Admiral Matome Ugaki believed that if only they could perfect their submarine detection devices, the Imperial Japanese Navy would be invincible. The Bungo Suido was a source of apprehension for both sides.[15]

At the western edge of the channel, *Pampanito* sighted a small, nondescript patrol boat of the kind the American sailors called a spit kit moving parallel to the coast at a range of three thousand yards. It had some type of sweep device outboard that made a whirring sound whenever it got underway and was easily detected by the sound gear. The heavy weather of the past week was finally gone, and the seas were glassy calm under a hot, windless sky. Periscope exposures would have to be kept to a minimum. Summers avoided the little vessel.

Three hours later they sighted another spit kit, a small, open motor sampan, about four thousand yards away and trailing a sweep similar to that of the previous one. Summers got a good look at it. He could see a dozen or more men lined up along the gunwales, evidently doing nothing but watching for submarines. Again, he avoided it. At 1037 the men heard a distant explosion, but a periscope observation disclosed nothing. At 1512 a "Betty," a two-engined Japanese navy bomber, was seen heading north about four miles away. They watched it disappear, but it was five more hours before *Pampanito* surfaced, slowly heading east across the mouth of the channel. To the northwest, one hour before midnight, the lighthouse at Shiminoura twinkled in the darkness.

At two o'clock in the morning on 23 June, the SJ picked up numerous pips at various ranges and bearings. One of the pips looked solid, and since the sea was a mirror of glass and there were very few clouds, *Pampanito* closed to investigate several miles south of Okino Shima. Like a desert mirage, though, the pip became hazy and faded out when approached. The officers figured these gremlins were caused by ionized conditions of the atmosphere.

In the quiet night the APR picked up enemy radar that seemed to settle in on the sub. Since the APR was nondirectional, they assumed the transmissions were either emanating from Okino Shima or from just beyond at Ashizuri Misaki, a peninsula of land on the southwest coast of Shikoku. In either case, it was fairly certain that *Pampanito* had been spotted.

Lieutenant Bruckart was in the conning tower watching the screen. "It was showing signs that we were under surveillance," he said. He discussed the situation with Jeff Davis and Lieutenant Fives, and they wondered if the source might be from an American submarine, because the signal was on the approximate frequency of their own system. They tried to zero in, "but no source could be found when we searched in that direction." Still, Bruckart concluded, "There obviously was someone out there."

Hubert Brown was topside port lookout, and he was getting tired of straining his eyes for targets of which he could see neither hide nor hair. In fact, it was 0350, and his mid watch relief ought to have been up by now. Actually, Brown didn't mind the watch this morning, when the sea was putting on such a dazzling show for his viewing pleasure. It was rather mysterious, but fascinating. The surface, he said, was "black as the ace of spades." But he had never seen such a show of phosphorescence, as the propellers stirred up millions of phytoplankton. The submarine's wake, Brown said, "looked like a low voltage neon sign. Even the flying fish made sparks in the sea as they took off and landed." It was beautiful.

It was also very deadly. Behind Brown, Tony Hauptman swept his binoculars across the horizon astern. *Pampanito* had just turned on the latest leg of its routine zigzag course when Hauptman spotted two faint, luminous silver arrows.

"Torpedoes!" he shouted.

Brown looked aft to see one phosphorescent track rapidly closing, parallel with their own wake. Everyone topside was yelling. The OOD, Jeff Davis, stuck his head down the hatch and called to Summers, who was asleep in his newly installed bunk in the conning tower.

"Captain! Captain! Torpedoes! Right full rudder!" Summers bolted upright, but there was not much he could do; Davis had the conn, and it was his call. They would all quickly find out if the maneuver had been correct. Summers caustically observed: "Davis watched the wakes with his binoculars. He went right between them and almost pissed in his pants."

Almost everyone reported the incident differently. The patrol report officially recorded: "OOD, Navigator and one lookout sighted a torpedo wake crossing our bow. Changed course to left with full rudder at flank speed, paralleling this track only to find another wake proceeding up our starboard side." Paul Pappas wrote in his diary: "Jap sub fired two torpedoes at us. One went past our bow. We swung right at flank speed and the other one went right down our side." Lieutenant Bruckart thought that one torpedo went by to port. They turned to parallel its track, sped up, and another torpedo passed by to starboard.

Hubert Brown saw it all and insisted that the boat never changed course at all. "We did not maneuver," he said. "We might have just zigged, but not after the wakes were seen. It is real clear in my mind." One torpedo sped along, paralleling them to port. It was close, but as long as the sub stayed on course, it would not hit. The second torpedo paralleled them to starboard. They only turned after they dove. Had they radically altered course on the surface, they might have run into one of the torpedoes. The patrol report did not match Brown's observations. Perhaps in this case it simply looked better on paper to show that a quick human decision had saved the boat, rather than blind luck.

At 0402, *Pampanito* submerged and unsuccessfully tried to locate the enemy submarine. George Moffet and Tony Hauptman could not pick up screw noises on sonar. The silence was eerie. Word of the encounter quickly spread through the boat. Frank Michno was coming off duty in the after engine room and got the word. He went into the mess, where he found his buddy Jacques Bouchard. Frenchie, just waking up to go on duty, was pouring himself a hot cup of coffee.

"I was going on watch when Frank came in the mess hall and told me," he said. "It shook me up so much, my cup of java spilled and ran through my fingers." Bob Bennett didn't like hanging around the Inland Sea either. "Looking for Japanese subs at night is spooky duty," he said. "It's like two guys in a pitch black coal mine. The first one that sees the other is the winner."

Yeoman McGuire had just crawled into his bunk when the commotion began. He couldn't sleep a wink. He lay there, tense as a wound-up spring, waiting for the big boom. Every time someone made a noise, he was sure it was a torpedo striking home. The patrol was nerve-wracking. "The Inland Sea was too shallow," he said. "You scrape bottom. You never know if you're following a ship into a trap. You seldom have an escape route. You live in fear all the time." It was strange, he thought. "Everyone is afraid of submarines, but we're just as afraid to be on them too."

*Pampanito* listened on sonar for an hour before resuming a slow patrol between Okino Shima and Ashizuri Misaki. After 0700, they avoided a small motor sampan that chugged by about three thousand yards away. An enemy plane was hovering over the Shikoku coast around noon. Since it may have been scouting the area in front of a convoy, *Pampanito* hung around the area for two hours. Sure enough, at 1440 they sighted the masts of a ship over the horizon. As they closed, they discovered the masts belonged to a destroyer escort, which was barreling along the coast. As Summers recorded in the log, the ship was "evidently running the measured mile off Okino Shima, because at 1515 he had disappeared to the northward . . . and I was never able to pick him up again." He conned the sub north around Okino Shima, hoping to find shipping well inside the hundred-fathom curve. They came close enough to shore to see Okino Shima's camouflaged lighthouse and see Japanese homes with laundry drying on outside lines, but the sea remained deserted. *Pampanito* surfaced south of the island. Two steady white lights beamed from Ashizuri Misaki to the east. Also, the pesky radar from that same peninsula periodically swept over them, making everyone uneasy. Summers may have thought about changing sectors, but at 2300 the radio crackled with a message from ComSubPac, telling him to remain in Area Seven until the night of 27 June. Apparently a crippled enemy task force was heading their way.[16]

Unknown to the men aboard *Pampanito,* a decisive battle had been fought between Japanese and American forces in the Philippine Sea on 19–20 June. It was a major loss for the Japanese fleet under Vice Admiral Jisaburo Ozawa, who entered battle with a force only half the size of that of the Americans. The slight chance of Japanese victory was lessened on the morning of 19 June, when USS *Albacore* (SS 218) torpedoed the heavy carrier *Taiho. Taiho* probably could have been saved, but fuel oil fumes were sent by the ventilation system throughout the ship. Six hours later, a spark set off a tremendous explosion, which doomed her and 1,650 of her crew.

At noon of the same day, USS *Cavalla* (SS 244) put four torpedoes into the heavy carrier *Shokaku*, and she, too, blew up and sank. After the battle, in which the Japanese also lost the light carrier *Hiyo*, Ozawa retreated northwest to Okinawa. It was the first time any nation's submarines had participated effectively in a combined fleet action.

Fleeing north, Ozawa eluded USS *Finback* (SS 230) and the wolf pack "Blair's Blasters," at this date consisting of *Pilotfish* (SS 386), *Pintado* (SS 387), and *Tunny* (SS 282). Even though they failed to connect, Lockwood still had four more boats patrolling the southern entrances to the Inland Sea: *Grouper* (SS 214), *Batfish* (SS 310), *Whale* (SS 239), and *Pampanito*.[17]

At 1300 on 22 June, while *Pampanito* was dodging sampans off Kyushu, the Japanese Mobile Fleet, amidst rain, high waves, and strong winds, anchored at Okinawa. The next day, its attack force and main force were ordered to the Inland Sea for repairs. The same morning that they headed north, *Pampanito* had nearly been sunk by a submarine. Very likely the Japanese boat sent a contact report, because at 1900, while south of Kyushu, Vice Admiral Ugaki, in command of Battleship Division 1 (*Yamato* and *Musashi*), received "advice from Sasebo Naval Base" to change course to 040 degrees. It would be safer for the ships to navigate fifty to sixty miles off the coast. There, escort planes and antisubmarine efforts would be concentrated. The fleet headed for the eastern shore of the Bungo Suido, directly toward *Pampanito*.[18]

Radio intelligence is a double-edged sword, for while *Pampanito* was directed to remain in the area for the approach of a crippled Japanese fleet, the same "crippled" fleet was pounding the waves home, aware of the presence of American submarines and quite prepared to take ASW or evasive action. Summers had been ordered to keep his boat in Area Seven, but the sector stretched from Ashizuri Misaki in the east to the southeastern coast of Kyushu in the west. Forsaking the chance of another encounter with a submarine off Okino Shima, Summers headed west, across the mouth of Bungo Suido. Perhaps the Japanese ships would be just as likely to enter the west side of the forty-mile-wide strait as the east side.

Near sunup on 24 June, *Pampanito* dove on the hundred-fathom curve about ten miles off Kyushu. The entire morning she played tag with numerous sampans and planes. One "Rufe" (the floatplane modification of the Zero fighter) drove her down, and about 1000, a "Betty" was seen east of them and heading south, possibly on her way to cover the approaching Japanese fleet. Had Summers been a little farther off the coast, or had he been surfaced with a high-periscope watch, he may have spotted them barreling in. Better yet, had there been no near miss by Japanese torpedoes the previous day, he might still have been near Okino Shima, probably watching wide-eyed as a submariner's jackpot moved straight toward his torpedo tubes.

Leading the van was Destroyer Squadron 2, with Rear Admiral Mikio Hayakawa in light cruiser *Noshiro*. It consisted of Destroyer Division 31, with *Asashio*, *Okinami*, and *Kishinami*, and Destroyer Division 32, with *Tamanami*, *Fujinami*, *Shimikaze*, and *Hamakaze*. Next came Vice Admiral Shintaro Hashimoto's Cruiser Division 5, with heavy cruisers *Myoko* and *Haguro*. Following was Battleship Division 3, under Vice Admiral Yoshio Suzuki, with *Kongo* and *Haruna*, and Ugaki's Battleship Division 1, with *Yamato* and *Musashi*. Slightly behind, because of time spent refueling, was Vice Admiral Kurita's Cruiser Division 4, consisting of *Atago*, *Maya*, *Takao*, and *Chokai*, and Cruiser Division 7 under Vice Admiral Kazutaka Shiraishi, with *Kumano*, *Suzuya*, *Tone*, and *Chikuma*. It was an awe-inspiring array of warships, and the experienced navy captains commanding the fleet destroyers would have made it rough for any attacking submarine.

At 1140, Ugaki sighted the island of Okino Shima off the port bow. At 1220, the men on *Pampanito* heard several distant explosions, but periscope observations disclosed nothing. The explosions were warning depth charges dropped by the van destroyers, letting any lurking submarines know that they had better stand clear, for the Imperial Japanese Navy was coming through. At 1230 the entire northbound force began passing the eastern shore of Okino Shima. Here was the main Japanese door to the Inland Sea: the eight-mile-wide, mine-swept channel between Okino Shima and the mainland of Shikoku. *Pampanito* had unknowingly left the gate open.

The rest of the afternoon, periscope watch disclosed continued plane and sampan contacts. Summers complained in the log: "This has been a hectic day—and we still haven't seen any traffic moving up and down the coast." Finally, at 0207 on 25 June, Summers surfaced under a bright moon and began heading back east across Bungo Suido's mouth, "hoping," he recorded, "to intercept [the] crippled enemy task force." That task force had already tied up in the Inland Sea's Hashira Jima anchorage six hours earlier.[19]

*Pampanito* continued to ply the waters south of Bungo Suido, but her luck did not improve. While hunting for that elusive task force, the lobing motor in the SJ gave up the ghost, making accurate bearing data very unlikely. The Japanese radar, however, did not appear to have any problems, for it was trained on them intermittently for a full hour before they dove at 0412, only two hours after surfacing. Haze and overcast skies made periscope visibility poor, and while Summers complained about the difficult currents, the crew was concerned about the bad air.

A submarine is a difficult boat to ventilate while submerged, with heat, humidity, and slow evaporation. The amount of carbon dioxide a man can breathe in safety varies with the person and the conditions. Commander Beach (*Trigger* and *Piper*) believed that 4 percent $CO_2$ could kill. Vice Admiral Lockwood said that life would cease at 7 percent. Captain Ruhe (*Seadragon* and *Crevalle*) said that it was easy to make foolish mistakes when breathing air with a low percentage of oxygen, and the ill effects on thinking processes could be disastrous.

The usual rate of breathing is sixteen to eighteen times per minute, but physical activity affects that rate, and a working man will consume thirty to fifty times more oxygen. A concentration of 7 percent $CO_2$ in the air will cause a man to breathe 200 percent more per minute. Carbon dioxide was not poisonous in itself, but it stimulated breathing, which in turn used up the oxygen faster, eventually causing asphyxia.[20]

It was another sixteen hours before *Pampanito* surfaced. The long summer days and short nights with the resultant heat, waiting, boredom, and bad air took their toll. Roger Walters said that by the end of the day it was not even possible to light a cigarette. You could strike a match and watch the sulfur be consumed on the head, but no flame would burst forth. Frank Michno dreaded those long submerged days, because he always got terrible headaches. "It seemed like it took an hour to walk from one end of the engine room to the other," he said. Every step made his head throb, and he trod as softly as possible. "It felt like I had on a steel clamp for a headband, and with every step, someone would tighten it another notch." According to Spence Stimler:

Sometimes between the foul air due to lack of oxygen and the odorous sanitary tanks, you almost wanted to transfer to surface craft where you could at least smell clean air once in awhile. The air would become very foul and they would spread a carbon-dioxide eater around the boat. This chemical had a very pungent odor and affected breathing and the eyes. They would turn the smoking light out. Can you imagine smoking in a submerged submarine? I was one of the culprits. The first thing we did coming off watch was to head for the crew's mess for coffee and a smoke.

The odor produced aboard a submarine is unique, to say the least. Diesel fumes permeated the clothing, and the "Three Fs," feet, fart and fanny, particularly assaulted the sensitive nose. Some thought that USS *Tang* was named after its smell. The odor of the sanitary tanks affected Walt Richter. He believed the waste had frozen inside the tanks while *Pampanito* was on her icy shakedown cruises in the Atlantic and that it took six months to thaw out. "What a smell!" he said. "You could hardly stand it when you went by the heads, and I slept in the after torpedo room right next to the head." Submarine odor was always with them, and little could be done about it.

One plus was the addition of the Kleinschmidt stills. The batteries needed most of the fresh water, but the submariners got a bonus in being able to use the excess for food, drink, and a rare shower. The stills, both about the size of a two-hundred-gallon drum, were located with the forward engines. They were electric, heating salt water with enormous coils shaped like inverted peach baskets one above the other. The chamber was kept under a partial vacuum, and the salt water was boiled at a low temperature. The vapor was pumped out and condensed to fresh water.[21] Clyde Markham liked working on the engines, but as a low rate, he was always nursemaid to the Kleinschmidts. "I didn't like monkeying around with the fresh water evaporators," he said. "It seemed like they always broke down when I was on duty."

Bob Bennett said they never had enough fresh water, but even when it was available, all they got was a "GI shower," in which they would wet down, turn off the water and soap up, then turn it on again to rinse. Bennett tried to wash in the air conditioning condensate—once. The diving alarm sounded. "I busted my head and burned myself," he said, "running naked out of those cramped spaces below decks."

Most of the time, said Lieutenant Bruckart, all the men on the sub could do was to swab down their crotch in a procedure he termed "an alcohol douche."

Surfacing for the evening was enjoyed by all. Some skippers preferred drawing a suction through the conning tower hatch. On *Pampanito* air was drawn through the forward torpedo room hatch. The tremendous amount of air needed by the engines created a small gale that sucked the stale air from every compartment. Papers, blankets, and anything not tied down usually ended up in the engine rooms.

The outside air, according to Spence Stimler, had a very sweet smell. He might go to the engine room to see his brother-in-law, Motor Machinist's Mate Second Class Roger Bourgeois. "We would stand in the airway and suck in the fresh air like a drunk with a new bottle of wine," he said. "At its time, it even rivaled sex for extreme gratification."

George Moffett, however, did not think that sea air was so invigorating and clean. Granted, it was a cool blast to the nostrils, but it was rank with the odor of salt and fish, much like the experience of walking at night along a seashore marina. The air plainly stank to Moffett, but it was welcome, nevertheless.

Woody Weaver enjoyed poking his head through the open forward hatch with the fresh air flowing by, looking out at the beach. In the darkness, Weaver could sometimes see the breakers making white lines of foam as they rolled ashore. It seemed bizarre to him that he was so close to the Japanese mainland, watching the lights twinkling from homes not yet blacked out because of the war.

At sunup on 26 June, *Pampanito* submerged off the hundred-fathom curve and attempted to close Okino Shima again, but the current pushed her west toward Kyushu. The waters flowing along the southern and eastern coasts of Japan are analogous to those along the eastern seaboard of the United States. As the warm Gulf Stream flows north along the U.S. coast in the Atlantic, the warm Kuroshio (the Black Current) follows a similar path on Japan's east coast in the Pacific. And as the cold Labrador Current flows south along the Canadian coast to meet the Gulf Stream, so the Oyashio (the Cold Current) flows south along the Kurile Islands to meet the Kuroshio. The system spins in a giant clockwise circle around the Pacific Rim in the Northern Hemisphere.[22]

The Kuroshio's speed and direction vary, influenced by the shape of the shoreline. Off the mouth of Bungo Suido, it runs northeasterly. However, as one approaches land, a counter-current sweeps in the opposite direction. This eddy flows west past Okino Shima and across the mouth of Bungo Suido to Shiminoura Point on Kyushu, where it is deflected south. This stubborn little counterclockwise eddy, noted *Pampanito*'s log, was not affected by the tides. Every time Summers tried to close Okino Shima, he would be carried back across to Kyushu.

As if there wasn't enough to keep the crew in a foul mood, they discovered the water from the air conditioner had backed up and flooded out four bunks in the after battery room. As Pappas recorded: "Boy, what a mess! And what a howl was made. Someone had the vents plugged up."

During the early morning hours of 27 June, the Japanese radar from Ashizuri Misaki swept over them once more. It was at this location and time four nights earlier that torpedoes had nearly struck them, and it was with some relief that they safely dove at 0412. This time Summers bucked the current and held the boat southeast of Okino Shima. He was plumb in the middle of the swept channel that the Imperial Japanese Navy used for entrance and egress from the Inland Sea. The visibility for the day, however, was limited by overcast skies and intermittent rain squalls.

The men were as depressed as the low barometer. Moffett, thinking back on the near miss by the torpedoes, commented: "It is episodes such as this that can be interpreted as luck, fate, or the will of God. These factors seem to affect the outcome of many things in all our lives. We continued the patrol, but it always seemed that things did not work favorably for us as we encountered patrol aircraft and unfavorable seas."

Woody Weaver pondered the fact that the patrol area had proven to be productive hunting grounds for other submarines. "Things seemed to have quieted down about the time of our arrival," he said. "Enemy shipping was almost non-existent and it turned out to be a disappointing patrol." Men wondered why the sector had been thought of as such a shooting gallery.

At 2002, *Pampanito* surfaced. Summers had kept the boat in the area looking for a crippled Japanese task force just as he had been ordered. He had seen nothing, and now he would head east into Area Six.[23]

The entire day of 29 June was spent submerged, dodging sampans off what was thought to be Ashizuri Misaki. However, upon surfacing for the night, they found that the Kuroshio had set them about forty miles to the northeast. The sampans they had seen that morning were actually off Muroto Zaki. By 2000 they were swept past Shikoku and across the mouth of Kii Suido, the eastern entrance to the Inland Sea. As they patrolled across the mouth of Kii Suido, the APR detected another Japanese radar sweeping toward them, probably from Shiono Misaki, a small peninsula on the Honshu coast.

At 2217 the SJ radar picked up a small pip at twelve thousand yards, and the boat came to life. The target was on course 290, making about eight knots. Again, the sea was glassy calm, and Summers realized he would be between the target and the bright moon. When the range closed to eight thousand yards, he was able to identify the target through binoculars as either a small trawler or a submarine. Uncomfortable with his relative position in the moonlight, Summers decided to try an end-around. Suddenly the target changed course to the north, into Kii Suido, and disappeared from the radar screen. *Pampanito* followed directly behind. However, about five thousand yards from the point where the contact had vanished, Summers got the notion that perhaps it was an enemy submarine that had purposely dived and was now waiting patiently for a shot at him. He did not relish another hide-and-seek game with a Japanese sub. It was only the third solid ship contact they had made in three weeks of patrolling, but they pulled away.

On the morning of 30 June, a "Rufe" floatplane was sighted, and shortly after, swinging around the peninsula at Shiono Misaki, came a *Fubuki*-type destroyer. At sixteen thousand yards, however, and heading away from *Pampanito* toward Kii Suido, it was almost impossible to overtake. Only a radical course change by the destroyer, or a high-speed surface chase by the submarine, would have closed the range, and neither skipper chose those options.

The destroyer disappeared. Thirty minutes later a medium-sized, mast-funnel-mast freighter was coming along the hundred-fathom curve on a course opposite the destroyer's, about twelve thousand yards away. A "Rufe" appeared overhead, and a *Chidori* steamed seaward of the freighter. *Pampanito* came right on a normal approach course, but the freighter swung around Shiono Misaki and hugged the shoreline toward Kantori Zaki, another point about ten miles up the coast. Again, Summers was frustrated. He kept trying to close the point of land at Shiono Misaki, where traffic would have to pass while heading up or down the coast, but the four-knot current would not let him approach. The little convoy disappeared beyond O Shima, a small island east of Shiono Misaki.[24]

Thwarted again, Summers jockeyed the boat about six miles south of O Shima, where he sighted another small convoy of two freighters, one *Chidori*, and three trawlers, with two "Rufes" overhead. They were just east of O Shima and heading west at twelve thousand yards. Summers had closed the range to ten thousand yards when three more trawlers, which had appeared to be fishing off Shiono Misaki, joined the convoy. All the escorts patrolled to seaward of the freighters, nicely blocking *Pampanito*. Summers gave it a shot, however, and managed to close to seventy-five hundred yards. Yet the westward-traveling convoy and the four-knot easterly current would not allow him to attain a favorable position. The high speed necessary to get ahead would have exhausted the batteries with twelve hours of daylight remaining.

Paul Pappas complained that they never could seem to get in a good firing position. "In fact," he said, "every time we tried to raise the periscope we'd about put it through the bottom of some small craft running around." Summers recorded: "Very thoroughly disgusted at this point with the whole set-up; decided to proceed up to the northeast of O Shima between there and Kantori Saki and patrol where the current isn't nearly so bad." The maelstrom of currents contributed to extreme variations of water temperature. On the first patrol off Guam, Summers had hoped for a gradient where none was to be found. Now, with no ships to attack, the BT drew patterns showing a fourteen-degree change in temperature within one hundred feet of the surface.[25]

That night, two more problems awaited them. As soon as the SJ was powered up, the PPI fizzled out. The transformer had burned out again, and there were no spares. The batteries, too, were dangerously low. Had a ship or plane contact forced them down, the time spent below could only have been counted in minutes.

If the World War II submarine had a weak link, it was the necessity to come up every day to recharge batteries. The diesel engines could drive it on the surface as long as the fuel oil lasted, but the batteries might only drive the boat underwater from twenty-four to thirty hours at two to three knots. At ten knots the batteries would be exhausted in thirty minutes. The problem of getting clear of the enemy to surface and recharge batteries was one of the most important faced by a submarine commander.

A submarine battery was not much different in makeup from an ordinary car battery, but each one was about five feet high and weighed sixteen hundred pounds—and there were 252 of them on board. While charging or discharging, hydrogen and hydrogen sulfide gas were produced. Hydrogen burns at a 4 percent to 7 percent concentration in the air, but at 7 percent it is as unstable as nitroglycerin and can be easily set off by a spark. Hydrogen gas is colorless, odorless, and tasteless. However, the distinctive smell of rotten eggs when hydrogen sulfide was present was a good indication that the batteries needed ventilation.

The electric current passing through the batteries heated them, and the water rapidly evaporated from each cell. In warm weather, distilled water had to be added to each cell every two or three days. Loss of distilled water meant that the patrol would have to be terminated—another reason to make sure the Kleinschmidt stills were running properly. As mentioned, salt water that made its way into the batteries could produce poisonous chlorine gas. It was so deadly that submariners were not allowed to use chlorine bleach on their clothes, for fear that its odor might disguise the telltale smell of chlorine gas.[26]

As *Pampanito* bobbed on the surface early in the morning of 1 July, it took almost seven hours to bring her nearly dead batteries back to life. She drifted along the coast to Kantori Zaki, where a tall stack belching white smoke was a good landmark. Since the Kuroshio pushed them in that direction, Summers patrolled between there and Kuki Zaki, another point of land about thirty miles beyond.

The change of scenery produced nothing dramatically new. More sampans were avoided. At 1018, a *Mutsuki*-class destroyer was sighted, bearing 260 degrees, range nine thousand yards. Summers brought the boat right in case the destroyer should open out from the coast, but it hugged the beach, following the coastline northeast. Summers could only close to seventy-five hundred yards. "Will be unable to get in a position for attack," he wrote. By 1120 the destroyer disappeared to the north.

The remainder of the day, *Pampanito* was plagued by numerous spit kits and trawlers. The log read: "We were driven down once in the afternoon by these pests when they evidently thought they had seen our periscope but weren't sure. So they came over and milled around for an hour or so forcing us to use evasion tactics."

Summers pulled the boat to the open sea south of Shiono Misaki for the night. There were a number of things to accomplish before sunrise. The first task was to fix the radar. The lobing motor was repairable, but the burned out transformer for the PPI was a lost cause. Spence Stimler figured there was no way to fix it, "but the Captain," he said, "didn't see it that way."

"Since humans made it, humans ought to be able to fix it," Summers argued. Moffett and Stimler were joined by Warrant Officer Percy Pike and radar officer Lieutenant Bruckart. After an hour of crawling around on their hands and knees with parts spread all over the conning tower and control room decks, they were making progress. The transformer was a goner, but they did have a spare lobing motor. However, to fix it meant opening the antenna mast at the reflector while perched atop the shears. The sea was reasonably calm, and Lieutenant Bruckart climbed atop the housed periscope, working in the darkness. He became lulled by the quiet, beautiful scene. The gentle swells rocked him, and he moved his head in rhythm with the motion, looking alternately to port and starboard, watching the eerie neon lights from the plankton. The stars were brilliant, and the Milky Way was dappled across the sky like a silver ribbon from horizon to horizon. On the beach, several miles away, Bruckart could see the bright lights from what appeared to be a race track in full operation. Again, the Japanese did not seem to be overly concerned about the dangers of silhouetting their shipping for the prowling American submarines. Somehow, Bruckart accomplished his objective, which also included binding up the vibrating number one periscope, while Moffett and Stimler jury-rigged and reassembled the SJ.

While this operation was proceeding, another party was out on deck trying to fix rattles in the superstructure and locate a peculiar buzzing noise that seemed to emanate from the propellers. Having some training in diving, Charlie McGuire reluctantly prepared himself to go over the side to investigate. He was relieved when Summers called Hauptman for the job. The two propellers were about seven feet in diameter, each with four very sharp blades. McGuire cautioned Hauptman. Tony was the ship's barber and charged everyone one dollar for a haircut, but he always cut McGuire's hair for free. Now McGuire told Tony to stay away from those blades. He didn't trust Summers and didn't want Tony to get an unwanted "haircut."

"You know if we spot a plane, the skipper's going to start up the props and dive. Be careful," McGuire warned him. "Stay out of the way." Hauptman swam around the stern, feeling for any imperfections that might be causing the noise. On one of the blades he found a large knot, perhaps a marine growth, that he was able to chip off. Although he feigned indifference, Tony was relieved when he safely climbed back aboard. Later, McGuire asked Summers why he had chosen Hauptman for the job.

"I don't trust you," the captain answered bluntly. McGuire was startled but realized that the feeling was mutual. If he had gone below, he would never have played with the screws with Summers at the helm. He would have lied and told him he couldn't find anything wrong. Both men understood each other.

With the latest round of repairs completed, *Pampanito* headed toward the mouth of the Irago Suido, which led to the city of Nagoya. On 3 July they dove about ten miles southeast of the Miki Zaki lighthouse. The sea remained smooth, and fishing craft were in sight almost continuously. That night, the ever-present radar swept over them, and they figured it was emanating from the peninsula at Daio Zaki. As they closed within ten miles of the Daio Zaki light, the radar settled in on them. It was like playing a game of hide-and-seek, and the person who was "it" never closed his eyes when you were trying to find a hiding place.

In the wee hours of America's Independence Day, Summers pushed *Pampanito* about forty miles east to clear the area. At daybreak he dove west of Omae Zaki, a peninsula on the west side of Suruga Wan, where previous patrolling submarines had found ships. Of course the only "ship" spotted by *Pampanito* was a small trawler. Summers, his patience stretched thin because of the lack of opportunities to fire a torpedo, itched to send a fish at the Japanese ship. But he decided against it, "because there is the possibility that something bigger might be coming through."

No ships appeared. Perhaps in frustration, Summers allowed no celebration on the Fourth of July. Instead, he ordered a field day, and the entire crew had to clean and polish the boat from bow to stern. Among the milder comments this elicited was that from radioman Bill McCollum. *Pampanito*, he said, was noted for its many field days, "and we didn't like it." He added, "The Captain was a bit of a martinet."

The constant cleaning prompted Gordon Hopper to compose a poem entitled "Field Day"—one out of many written by the sensitive but loquacious man:

> We are the crew of the *Pampanito*,
> Trying to whip Hitler and Hirohito.
> We haven't done much, but from what they say,
> We'll sure give 'em hell if we keep
> Holding Field Day.
>
> She leaks just a little, and the screws may be
> Shot.
> Yet she rides like a dream,
> And is never too hot.
> The crew is first-class and the chow is O.K.
> But the bunks are just excess,
> We keep holding Field Day.
>
> We're getting a bit tired,
> But we never complain.
> We'll ride her thru depth charges,
> Snowstorms and rain.
> But we can't get much shipping
> If the officers all say;
> Keep dogging the watch,
> And start holding Field Day.

In the waning hours of the Fourth of July, his cleaning done for the day, Bill McCollum was on the radio when a Fox schedule message came in. These messages, reserved for submarines, would contain a variety of intelligence information regarding enemy targets, friendly forces, assignment changes, ASW tactics, and even personal information for crew members if time permitted. The Fox "skeds" came at fixed hours from more than one station and at various frequencies to circumvent enemy jamming attempts and weather vagaries. The copying submarines maintained radio silence, acknowledging a message only if directed to do so. Depending on conditions, reception of very low frequency (VLF) signals, which were not attenuated as easily as VHF transmissions, could be made with the antenna fifteen to twenty feet below the surface and at a range of up to three thousand miles.[27]

Normally the radiomen copied Morse code encoded into groups of five letters, which had to be decoded by the communications officer. He used an electric coding machine (ECM) that resembled an oversized typewriter with slots in the top to hold about ten wheels. The officer would place the correct wheel in the top slot and type out what the radioman had copied in code. The machine would spit out a paper tape, and the officer would then glue it to a message blank and take it to the captain.

If the submarine was scheduled to patrol in shallow waters that could be reached by salvagers, the ECM would be removed and a strip cipher would be substituted. The removal and switch were done surreptitiously, but word always got around, and the crew would know they were in for a rough patrol when the ECM was off-loaded. Sometimes a sub would carry both systems, and if patrolling in shallow waters, the communications officer would simply throw the ECM overboard and burn the code books.

The strip cipher consisted of twenty numbered strips, each with full alphabets but with the letters in different scrambled orders. The order in which a strip was placed into grooves on the board was stipulated in a booklet, with a different order for each day of the year. Changing the strip cipher was not an easy task.

"Oh, how we hated that," said Lieutenant Bruckart, "which we were obligated to do after getting off watch." The letters from the message's five-letter group were set against a vertical tape by sliding the strips to the proper position. On the right, the plain language decoded message would appear in a vertical column. For the patrol in Hit Parade, *Pampanito*'s ECM was replaced by the strip cipher.

This evening McCollum helped copy the latest Fox schedule message. A large Japanese convoy, including twelve cargo ships with escorts, was traveling north along the Nampo Shoto heading toward Tokyo. The convoy would pass about seventy miles east of them, but Summers decided to try to reach it. "This will be a long run with slim chance of intercepting," he wrote, "and yet I think it worthwhile to try, as 12 AKs aren't easy to find these days."

Putting all four engines on line, they plowed through the sea, and within five hours they slipped through the channel between Nii Shima and Kozu Shima in the Izu Shoto, a chain of small islands stringing south from Tokyo Bay. By morning on 5 July, Summers dove, eagerly awaiting the convoy of cargo ships supposedly heading his way. But, typical of the string of misfortunes that had plagued them, both periscopes developed leaks and began fogging up.

The Kollmorgen-built Type 2 attack scope, with adjustable elevation and a 32-degree field of vision in low power, could cover the entire sky from horizon to zenith. In good visibility, exposing about two feet of scope would allow one to see the top of a *maru*'s mast at three or four miles. This meant that the diameter of observation was six to eight miles—not a large viewing circle. With rain or fog or scopes that were clouding up with condensate, the visibility was cut significantly. In fact, sonar would probably pick up enemy screws before a sighting could be made. The best chance *Pampanito* had was to look for smoke, which could be seen at a much greater distance than a ship itself. Summers rued his luck: "Pressure in number one periscope is less than two lbs. and we have no nitrogen aboard to dry it out. Range of visibility . . . is greatly hampered by this condition." They could not find one ship or one puff of smoke.

At 1941, *Pampanito* broke the surface, and this time Moffett and Stimler went scurrying up the shears to make repairs. Stimler thought the view was magnificent. The moon was bright, and he could actually see the dark profile of the volcano Fujiyama on the horizon far to the north. Their fluorescent wake sparkled behind them, but although it was stunning, it was also a guide for any aircraft snooping in the darkness; so thin was the line separating beauty and danger. Up on the shears, Stimler and Moffett were too far away to get down in time if a plane was contacted. "The Captain," Stimler said, "admonished us that we would probably be left if we had to dive." Understandably, they climbed back down, unable to effect any repairs.

With uncharacteristic wild abandon, Summers drove the boat back west through the eight-mile-wide passage between Nii Shima and Kozu Shima, oblivious to the possibility of being spotted from the nearby islands in the bright moonlight.[28]

*Pampanito* returned to Omae Zaki. This was almost dead center in Area Five in the fabled Hit Parade, which stretched from Shiono Misaki in the west to Iro Zaki in the east.[29] About six in the morning, 6 July, she sighted a trawler at seven thousand yards but avoided it. An hour and a half later, a "Betty" bomber flew by, and one or two more trawlers came out to comb the area. Perhaps something was in the offing. *Pampanito* got a fix on a large white tower on the beach about twenty-one miles west of Omae Zaki and slowly headed west.

At 1255 periscope observation disclosed a three-ship convoy ten thousand yards away. *Pampanito* was on a reciprocal course, heading west, about twenty-five miles west of Omae Zaki, not far from the mouth of the Tenryu River. For the first time in what seemed like ages, general quarters, a somewhat melodious series of notes that has been called the "Bells of St. Mary's," rang over the 1MC, the submarine's announcing system. Signalman Bill Canty and yeoman Charlie McGuire were in the control room. Both were surprised by the alarm but had different reactions. McGuire was itching to sink a Japanese ship and was elated. Not Canty.

"Oh shit!" he exclaimed. "I hope they get away."

McGuire couldn't believe it. After suffering from heat, boredom, bad air, danger, and frustration for a month, he wanted to take it out on someone. "What do you mean, you hope they get away?" McGuire shot back. "Are you crazy or something?"

Canty, who McGuire called "a little guy," never answered him. Instead, he turned around and punched Charlie a glancing blow to the side of his head. More surprised than hurt, McGuire thought about going after Canty, but just then Summers came out of officers' country, heading for the conning tower. He glanced over at the two men, and Canty and McGuire quickly resumed their stations. They'd be in serious trouble for fighting at general quarters, so they'd have to settle up later. McGuire steamed in silence, his face turning as red as his hair.

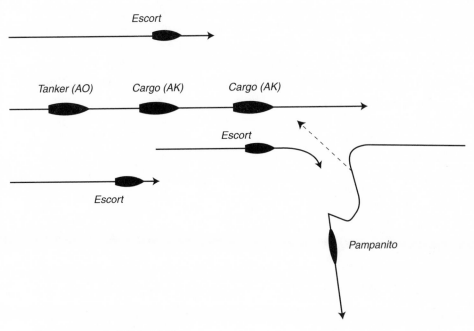

Convoy attack, 6 July 1944

Checking the ONI manual led the crew to believe they had found *Toyokawa Maru*–class (fifty-one hundred tons) and *Kenyo Maru*–class (sixty-one hundred tons) cargo (AK) ships. The third ship, which they were unable to identify clearly, looked like a four-thousand-ton tanker (AO) with engines aft. The escorts appeared to be one destroyer, using radical constant-helm zigs starboard of the formation, and one gunboat and one trawler trailing on either quarter. Three "Rufes" flew lazily over the convoy at different altitudes, one as low as one hundred feet.

The convoy passed the city of Hamamatsu heading east. Summers moved closer, again hampered by the glassy sea and aircraft, which limited periscope observation. The convoy's base course was 90, and *Pampanito* remained ahead and slightly to seaward of its track.

Summers planned to attack the leading escort with three bow tubes, fire the other three bow tubes at the second ship in the convoy, then swing left to bring the after tubes to bear on the trailing tanker. Torpedo depths were set at six, eight, and ten feet.

The covering aircraft kept the sub down too long, and their converging courses brought them too close too soon. The next check showed that the leading escort was dead ahead with zero angle on the bow and only 1,200 yards away. There would be no time to get firing solutions for shots at three ships. Summers swung the boat left and opened the range for a stern salvo. At 1325, getting final bearings before firing, they noticed that their destroyer was not a destroyer at all, but an *Otori* torpedo boat.[30] Although the torpedo boat might draw three feet less water than a destroyer, the setup was changing too fast to correct the depth settings. Tubes seven, eight, and nine were fired, sending off three Mark 18 electric fish. Gyro angles were 20 degrees left, with a 60-degree starboard track and a 2-degree divergent spread. The range was 1,250 yards.

*Pampanito* came right for a bow shot. A periscope check at 1327 showed the last ship in the convoy with a 90-degree starboard angle on the bow. Perhaps they could get off another salvo. Just then, Summers's vision was blotted out as the scope dipped beneath the sea. They had lost depth control. The Kuroshio, mixing with the lighter fresh water from the mouth of the Tenryu River, played havoc with their trim. A sharp temperature gradient at sixty-five feet was giving Lieutenant Johnson fits. Too much ballast had been pumped aft, and the stern dropped down. Minutes passed as they tried to gain an even keel and swing right to present the bow tubes toward the second and third ships in the convoy. Sound tracked the torpedoes beyond the *Otori*—if they were on target, they had gone under the shallow-draught vessel—and toward the cargo ship's screws until they began to fade out. Finally, at 1332 there was one loud distant torpedo explosion, and one set of heavy target screws stopped. In spite of the poor setup and rushed shot, it sounded like they had connected.

Summers desperately wanted to get to the surface for a look. The minutes dragged—1333 . . . 1334 . . . 1335—but Johnson could not get control to bring the boat above seventy feet. They hung there, tantalizingly close to the surface, waiting, for what Summers said "seemed to be ages." High-speed screws approaching from two different bearings dictated their next action. Slamming his fist against the periscope shaft, Summers ordered them to come left and head for deeper water. Disgusted, he wrote: "Since I could not get a look, [I] had to order deep submergence."

*Pampanito* headed south for five minutes before the first depth charges began falling. Pappas wrote in his diary that another plan had gone haywire. We were going to pick off the escort with three electric fish, he said. "But as usual, we slipped up a little by setting our fish for destroyers when the escort was a *Chidori,* so our fish passed under it." Pappas had timed seven minutes between firing and the hit. A Mark 18 traveled about 15.5 yards per second. In seven minutes it would have traveled over sixty-three hundred yards. However, the Mark 18's range was only about four thousand yards. The figures did not add up, yet there was no denying that they had hit something. Pappas said that "our soundmen could hear the freighter's screws stop and could hear the ship cracking up and going down."

While they listened to the results of their torpedo work, *Pampanito* shook free from the pesky surface gradients and went near the bottom at 250 feet, where an ASW vessel would have a tougher time detecting them. A shallow, sandy bottom would make echo-ranging and listening possible at long ranges. A rocky or muddy bottom, while it did not provide the sub a safe place to rest, did confound enemy sonar. Mud provided little bottom reflection, while rocks made for strong reverberations, reduced reliable echo ranges, and played havoc with passive listening gear. Bottom conditions, plus the thermoclines above, made it nearly impossible for the escorts to home in on *Pampanito*. Plus, Summers believed, because he had used electric torpedoes, "the enemy had no idea where we were."[31]

Still, the angry escorts would not give up. Depth charges began exploding above them at one-minute intervals. They all sounded like the newer, heavier charges, but they were set far too shallow, and none were very close. Pappas made ten check marks in his diary, one for each explosion, and he, Jack Wilkerson, Larry Langin, Andy Currier, and Ralph Attaway signed it as witnesses and dated it Thursday, 1330–1400, 6 July 1944. Summers recorded that "it was the most half-hearted depth-charging I have ever witnessed."

McMillan Johnson brought the boat up cautiously, mindful of the tricky surface currents. Finally, at 1442 the periscope broke the surface and they were able to see one gunboat four thousand yards astern on the true bearing of the explosion. A "Rufe" was circling overhead at five hundred feet, while the gunboat appeared to be picking up survivors. Summers believed he had hit the leading ship, the *Toyokawa Maru* type, with either the second or third torpedoes, which evidently had gone under the gunboat. With the smooth sea and presence of the plane, Summers took the boat back down and cleared the area.

That evening, *Pampanito* ran east under a bright moon in the usual mirror-smooth ocean. Very unusual however, was a plane contact at 2015, which prompted Summers to write: "Evidently the Nips are mad about today's attack and are out looking for us."

The plane bore in. Walt Richter was on lookout with Red McGuire. Richter saw the plane approaching and called out a warning. The usual scramble down the hatch ensued, but this time there was a glitch. "I got kicked off the ladder on the dive and fell on top of the Yeoman," Richter said. Caroming off McGuire, he was thrown back-first to the floor. "I was hurt quite badly," he said. "I developed muscle spasms so bad that I could hardly walk." Richter told Jeff Davis that he didn't think he could climb the shears anymore. The exec removed him from duty.

Other crewmen were a bit more cynical about Richter's accidental fall. In fact, they were sick of his constant winning at cards and dice, and more than one man believed there was some cheating going on. When they mentioned the possibility to an officer, the remark was made: "You mean he hasn't fallen down a ladder yet?" Wally Cordon, for one, firmly believed that Richter was "helped" down the ladder during that dive.

That surprising nighttime plane contact also caused further trouble for Clyde Markham. He had just come in from second dog watch (1800 to 2000) and had rotated down to the helm. Markham was smoking. When the dive order came, he paused to pass the cigarette from his hand to his mouth, then grabbed the wheel. It couldn't have taken more than three seconds, yet it was not missed by the eagle-eyed skipper. Once again, as when he had almost lost his ball cap, Markham got chewed out with a lecture on responsibility. Worse yet, Summers ordered that the crew would no longer be allowed to smoke on duty while operating equipment. Summers stormed away, and Markham stood there, red-faced. Now everyone would be angry with him.

*Pampanito* surfaced only fifteen minutes after the plane had driven them down. Five minutes later a lookout spotted what appeared to be a periscope about fifteen hundred yards to port. The lookout was positive he had it in sight for over a minute, but no one else on the bridge could confirm it. Everyone was jumpy, and the sub turned away at flank speed, just in case. Ten minutes later another plane appeared, and Summers pulled the plug again. They must have stirred something up, for they had never seen this much nighttime activity. Summers headed east to clear the area.

On a new day and in a new sector, *Pampanito* dove thirteen miles north of Inamba Shima. Restricted by the many islands running perpendicular to the current, the Kuroshio seemed to pick up speed as it channeled between them. The five-knot set carried them through the day of 7 July on course 065, so by evening they had been pushed well east of Mikura Jima.

Hoping things had cooled off, Summers decided to circle back to Omae Zaki. Heading northwest, they picked up a strong land-based radar apparently coming from Miyaki Jima. Turning west to avoid it, they stumbled across what appeared to be a convoy. At midnight the tracking party snapped to attention, and the boat began maneuvering to intercept. There appeared to be about five slow-moving ships. The setup and attack would be a breeze. Finally, the lookouts could make out the targets, but they didn't look like ships. They immediately realized that they had been tracking the five little islands of Zeni Su and abruptly changed course before they grounded on the shoals. The dead reckoning indicator (DRI) showed that there should have been no islands near their position.

While circling around the rocks at Zeni Su, *Pampanito* was found by a small motor sampan burning a bright light. Apparently it had radar and a good engine, for it stayed a few miles back in the sub's wake throughout the night, even though Summers was making four-engine speed. Unable to shake the persistent little craft, Summers gave up his plan to patrol at Omae Zaki, because he would not be able to get there before dawn, and that damn little sampan knew right where he was. It dogged them for the rest of the day. Finally, *Pampanito* surfaced at 1931 to find it had shaken off its shadow.

On 9 July, finding a quiet place about fifteen miles southwest of Iro Zaki, Summers submerged for another daylight periscope patrol. They saw nothing but fishing vessels, motor sampans, and a one-hundred-ton schooner that appeared to be patrolling up and back across the mouth of Suruga Wan. That same morning, back in Bungo Suido, battleships *Yamato, Musashi, Kongo,* and *Nagato,* and attendant cruisers and destroyers, swung out of the channel east of Okino Shima, heading for Singapore. Again, no U.S. submarines were there to slow them down.[32]

*Pampanito* hung off Iro Zaki, where she sighted smoke and then a mast with a very prominent crow's nest. They went to battle stations only to find that it was simply another small trawler. Surfacing, they picked up SJ radar interference bearing 261. Since it was within the wave band of an American submarine and was coming from Area Five, they decided it was probably from USS *Gabilan* (SS 252), which was patrolling in that sector.

Heading southeast about two hours later, they sighted another small motor sampan burning a bright light—perhaps the same one that had dogged them the day before. In any case, it was time to work off a little frustration. With a rising moon, and the pesky sampan in sight, the gun crews manned the 20-mm cannons and the .30-caliber machine guns, and the chase began. The run started about ten miles north of Zeni Su, and the sampan coughed smoke, put on a burst of speed, and headed straight south. There may have been only a one-knot difference in their speeds, so ever so slowly, after a nineteen-minute pursuit, *Pampanito* was catching up. Looming ahead, however were the rocks of Zeni Su, the tallest being only forty-two feet above sea level. The sampan cut between the shoals. Six thousand yards away, *Pampanito* would not be suckered into following. She swung away and headed back toward the Honshu coast. While leaving, they picked up a weak signal at 500 kilocycles, certainly a contact report of an American sub hovering around Zeni Su. Sure enough, within the hour the SJ detected one patrol trawler, then a second motor sampan, converging on the spot. They apparently knew *Pampanito*'s planned route, so Summers swung southeast to clear the area.

They put fifty miles behind them before diving on the morning of 10 July, east of Mikura Jima, an island eight miles in diameter with a volcanic cone rising three thousand feet above the sea. Then they ran north during the day, following the east side of the Izu Shoto, where they could cover the shipping lanes from Tokyo Bay. Supposedly this was the prime spot to find swarms of Japanese ships, but the only thing *Pampanito* picked up were enemy radar sweeps and airplanes. Two days in the area convinced Summers that his boat had been spotted and traffic had been routed around him. He headed south. At least the waves had become moderate to heavy, breaking up the mirrorlike face they had presented for almost three weeks.

Back in the vicinity of Mikura Jima the SJ showed a pip at thirty-eight hundred yards. In the clear dark night before moonrise, they closed to twenty-eight hundred yards but saw nothing. Thinking they might be tiptoeing with another submarine, they pulled out. For the next two days, *Pampanito* patrolled west of Hachijo Jima. More SJ interference suggested the possibility that there was another submarine out there; whether it was friendly or enemy was unknown. By dusk of 15 July, *Pampanito* was working her way northwest toward Zeni Su. The SJ was picking up more disturbing interference all evening, and they lowered the sound heads to listen for propeller noise. The interference continued through the wee hours of the next morning.

Occasionally, *Pampanito* would chase these elusive gremlins at full speed only to have the target definition become weaker. Summers was convinced they were chasing their own reciprocal radar pulses—or else there was something out there, baiting them and always pulling just out of reach when they got close. It was a nerve-wracking night. They backed off on a retiring search curve. Perhaps dawn might allow them to see what they had been playing tag with.

It was just 0340 on this early Sunday morning, but a gibbous moon in a brightening eastern sky boosted the spirits of those topside. Hubie Brown was at his customary spot on the port periscope shears. The sea was a little rougher eighty miles off the coast, with small rollers that broke in curls, often looking like torpedo wakes. Watching those rollers had become tedious, and Brown waited anxiously for his relief. Several times he thought he had seen splashing waves that resembled torpedo wakes but did not sound a warning. He swept his binoculars along the horizon in his quarter, from 270 to 360 degrees relative. Just then he caught a glimpse of a peculiarly splashing curl.

"You don't wait to thoroughly identify what you see," Brown explained. "You just report it." He called down to the bridge: "I've got what looks like a torpedo wake about 30 degrees off the port bow."

The OOD this morning, Lieutenant Ted Swain, had heard the warning before. "Just keep your eye on it," he answered, which was the standard response. Brown furrowed his brow and peered through the glasses.

"It's definitely a torpedo wake," he called down again.

"Keep your eye on it," the OOD repeated.

Al Van Atta was on the bridge with Swain and heard Brown's warning. They looked to port but could see nothing.

Brown was getting agitated. There was certainly a streak in the water, straighter and longer than any breaking roller, and it was heading right at them. He knew he could see it better than any damn OOD on the bridge. Several more seconds passed, which seemed to Brown like an eternity, and still nothing was done. He put his glasses down, plainly viewing the track coming right at him. He called down a third time, but by now it would be too late to take any evasive action. The torpedo wake and the submarine's bow were about to meet. Brown grabbed the shears and waited for the blast. "Which way am I gonna fly?" he wondered, looking down at the wake that was now almost directly beneath the bridge.

Nothing happened. When he started to breathe again he realized that a torpedo traveling at forty-five to fifty knots is a good distance ahead of the wake of bubbles rising behind it. The torpedo was either set too deep or it had already crossed in front of the boat's bow when the bubble trail rose and the sub sliced through it. Besides the animated conversation, Brown averred, "No one on the bridge made a move. Finally, Pete heard the commotion and came blasting up to the bridge, but by that time it was all over."

Van Atta did not see the torpedo track running almost perpendicular to their own course until they had crossed over it. Only then did Swain call for a hard turn and flank speed.[33]

Belatedly, *Pampanito* swung in the direction of the track. They had been zigzagging at the time, and Summers was convinced that it had saved them from a certain torpedo hit. They made another quick visual sweep, but Summers decided that the light was not good enough to spot a periscope at any distance, and within two minutes he dove. Sound could not pick up submarine screws. When the sun rose high enough to allow the lookouts better vision topside, *Pampanito* uncharacteristically surfaced and charged south at full speed for six hours, hoping to leave her adversary far behind.

Just how readily could those "Japanese" torpedoes have been spotted in the dark early mornings of 23 June and 16 July? The typical Japanese submarine torpedo was a Type 95, twenty-one inches in diameter, with a forty-nine-knot speed and with a range of over nine thousand yards. It ran on liquid hydrogen peroxide and was almost wakeless. The other models were either battery-powered or ran on kerosene fuel with a compressed air drive. None of them produced the telltale bubble trail of the U.S. Mark 14 steam torpedo. If they were Japanese torpedoes, they may have been spotted only because of the phosphorescent plankton they disturbed.[34]

There was no respite. Shortly after sunset they again picked up radar interference. Summers closed to investigate, but the numerous, confusing contacts that had plagued them the past month left Summers in a quandary. Neither he nor his officers could determine if the contact was friend or foe. Not fully trusting his radar, Summers decided to shut down the SJ transmitter. He believed that the Japanese had tracked his radar emanations almost every night, and he hoped that sending out only an occasional pulse would prevent him from being located. He was convinced they knew where he was, had rerouted their ships around him, and had sent out planes, patrol boats, and submarines to sink him.[35]

Even after ceasing constant operation, the next intermittent sweep at 2037 showed a small pip at twelve thousand yards. Reluctantly, Summers closed, but at seven thousand yards the lookouts could not see a thing. Summers had had enough. He put his stern to the contact and moved out. As a last resort, he tried sending out a short signal on the SJ to establish if it was a friendly submarine. There was no response from the mysterious stranger.

"This is either a submarine or a very small escort as he gives a very small pip at relatively close range," Summers wrote. "He has radar and knows we are definitely in the vicinity." *Pampanito* closed once more, but the pip moved away. It was maddening, and the officers and men in the tracking party were nervous and irritable. Summers imagined his adversary was trying to lure him into a trap or maybe was trying to lure him away from bigger game. The indecisiveness on board was troubling. The men had just about reached their limit, and *Pampanito* had ceased to be an offensive weapon. She needed to go home.

On the evening of 18 July, Summers set course for Midway, with Tori Shima to starboard, twenty-two miles away. They had last passed the island running out of a typhoon, over one month before, in high hopes of sending a slew of the emperor's ships to the bottom of the sea. Nothing had worked out as planned.

On 20 July the SJ showed radar interference, and as they were supposed to be passing a friendly sub in the area, they made only a cursory investigation. Closing to eighteen thousand yards, they made out a gray-colored superstructure, assumed it was American, and continued on their way.

Many of the men felt as if it had been their worst patrol. Gordon Hopper thought it was the least productive, mainly because all the targets they encountered were "closer to the beach than Captain Summers dared to go." They had been attacked more than attacking and had nothing to show for all those weeks in Japanese home waters. Woody Weaver thought the patrol was the most physically demanding. "Those long hours of submerged operations with the resultant bad air conditions are forever etched in my memory," he said. "It was one time we really earned our hazardous duty pay." Earl Watkins said he never smoked or drank. However, going through such an ordeal, he could understand why many men did. Watkins did not go topside or see daylight for six and a half weeks. Paul Summers had one major complaint about the patrol area: the current. There were plenty of ship contacts, but the current was so bad "that I'd make an approach and end up going backwards." They were all thankful to be heading for Midway.[36]

As the submarine headed east for the next four days, the crew had time to wind down and reflect on their performance. The patrol had nearly exhausted George Moffett. Even with Stimler there to help, it seemed like every spare minute of his "off" hours was spent repairing the radar, sonar, fathometer, radios, transmitters, and ship's communication systems. Charlie McGuire saw Moffett many nights, sometimes until after midnight, working on broken-down equipment with parts spread all over the deck. McGuire would have some wisecrack for him, and Molly Moffett would snap out a rejoinder. This usually prompted Red to threaten: "You give me any crap and I'll get Stimler to replace you," which would get Moffett even madder. The radiomen and radar technicians were usually given names that suited what the electricians or motor macs thought about their jobs; hence, Molly Moffett or Sally Stimler.

McGuire didn't think a yeoman's job was a piece of cake, either. He claimed Summers had him up night and day typing and retyping the patrol reports. Pharmacist's Mate O'Neill was detailed to help him out, but somehow, whenever it came time for reports to be written, Doc would put himself on sick call. McGuire would finish the report and be ready to sack out when Summers would find him and say: "McGuire, this is good, but I want you to make a few changes here and there." Then, McGuire said, "I'd get stuck re-typing about 40 pages. Pete was not considerate," he added.[37]

Summers had his own trials and tribulations, and much of his time was spent mulling over them in his cabin. According to Lieutenant Bruckart, the officers all got along well, and the wardroom was an informal meeting place where all could relax with a game of cribbage or acey-deucey— except when Pete was present. Summers developed no rapport with his subordinates. There were few times, however, when all of them had the opportunity to get together, because the watch schedule was grueling and sack time was more important. Bruckart, for one, tended to avoid Summers. Yet he could not help feeling a tinge of pity for the captain after hearing a conversation held shortly before arriving at Midway.

It was after noon, and Summers had gone to his bunk for a rest. The daily noontime routine called for the navigator to advise the commanding officer that the chronometers had been wound and compared. Bruckart was lying in his bunk across from Summers's stateroom. A seaman messenger knocked on the bulkhead, and Summers answered in his customary, drawled, "Yeesss?"

The seaman answered: "Captain, the navigator reports twelve o'clock. All chronometers are round and repaired."

There were several seconds of silence, then Bruckart heard Pete's constrained reply: "Seaman, go back and get your report straight."

"Aye, aye, sir," the sailor answered. Bruckart heard his steps recede down the passage and couldn't help but chuckle.

On 22 July, which was to be a double day because of crossing the date line, Summers called for another field day. Naturally, the men grumbled. Why in hell clean the boat when in two days the relief crew would tear it apart? Gordon Hopper felt down in the dumps. He picked up his pencil and jotted down his thoughts in an ironic verse he titled, "My Diary", which surely echoed the frustrations of almost everyone on board:

> A hundred fathoms from the bottom
> And two hundred to the top
> We're a lot more scared of pressure

Than the ash cans that they drop.
(All our nice clean cork might crack)

The lousy battery's gassing
The sound gear's on the blink
The fresh water line's discharging
Fuel oil into the sink.
· (Couldn't fix it, Field Day)

The cook is busy making stew
The only meal he knows.
And someone has the wash bowl
Jammed with dirty clothes.
(Never mind your face; clean the boat)

We've tried to rise a little
For a looksee and a shot,
But the god-damned boat won't surface
And the torpedoes won't run hot.
(Well it's clean, so there!)

We've never even seen a Jap
But all hands on board will swear
We'll exterminate all nasty dirt,
Fight a cockroach fair and square.
We're the joy of all the ladies,
With this clean and spotless ship.
But give your heart and soul to God,
Because your ass goes to the Nip.

Hubert Brown, who had complained so much about the unbearable cold in the Atlantic, now had another problem as his feet broke out in sores and fungus. Roger Walters also contracted an unidentified, severe tropical fungus on one foot. It was so bad that he would have to be hospitalized.

To pick up their spirits and get ready for liberty on Midway, the gilly cookers went to work. Electrician Don Ferguson of Philadelphia, who had made runs on USS *Drum* (SS 228) and USS *Haddo* (SS 255), rationalized that since only the officers were allowed to buy hard liquor at the rest camps, "we poor 'white hats' had to make do for ourselves." Because they knew that the torpedo fuel and much of the food would be tossed out when they reached base, they made use of as much as they could, confiscating the alcohol and dumping jars of vinegar, ketchup, and mayonnaise to refill with gilly. Grady, Kaup, and Michno set up another still and allowed other drinkers to stand two-hour watches over the cooker. "This practice, I am certain," said Ferguson, "insured we kept our sanity for the next patrol."

Unlike many crew members, who played cards for recreation, Bill McCollum, a nineteen-year-old from Saint Paul, Minnesota, was an avid reader. He spent the days heading back to Midway catching up on his studies. "When we would come into Pearl for R&R," he said, "I would hit the book stores and buy a sea bag full of books and stash them away in the radio shack." He finished high school on patrol by getting his lessons at the Armed Forces Institute at the University of Hawaii, studying them on patrol, and taking his exams when he came back to port. While some of the fellows took GED tests, McCollum was the only one to get his diploma by completing regular classwork, homework, and tests.

McCollum did not consider himself an intellectual, but rather "just a curious lad, intrigued by books." He supposed he could get as rowdy as the rest, but that was typical behavior, for they all knew the dangers they faced. He heard that the average survival time was five patrols; after that, "you began to wonder when you were going to be killed. I lost a lot of friends." When off duty and not reading, McCollum sometimes volunteered to stand lookout. He had exceptional eyesight and enjoyed going topside for fresh air. Although still below the horizon, Midway announced its presence by reflecting a patch of aquamarine sky above. McCollum, caught up in the romance of the moment, composed some verses of poetry and reflected on the new friends he had discovered tucked away within the pages of his books.

As the island came in sight on the afternoon of 23 July, McCollum went below to gather his belongings. Even though it had been a nonproductive, rough patrol, he felt proud of his personal achievements. He had finished his course work, he had read several novels, he had just finished *A Tree*

*Grows in Brooklyn,* and he knew that he would be forever in debt to quartermaster John Schilling, who introduced him to the works of Thomas Wolfe. He took time to think of the men he had known in his albeit short life—those who had already become like the lost, wind-grieved ghosts haunting the pages of a novel. Amidst the cursing, the gambling, the diesel fumes, and the submarine smells, the incongruous, sweet, lilting prose of the Carolina pines lifted the thoughts of at least a few wayward angels homeward.

## CHAPTER FIVE

# First Course in Convoy College

Midway Island could not compare to Oahu in many respects, but for the returning sailors landfall was very sweet indeed. First, however, they had to conn the boat through Midway's coral reef, a task that not every skipper had found to his liking. Midway is a small atoll, less than six miles in diameter. It consists of only two islands large enough to be of any use: Sand Island to the west, less than two miles long, and Eastern Island, even smaller. Midway housed a cable station and was a stopover point for Pan American Airlines' trans-Pacific clippers. When the navy realized the atoll was a strategic spot, it built seaplane ramps, hotels, barracks, hangars, fuel tanks, water towers, and an artificial harbor. A fifty-three-hundred-foot runway was added on Eastern Island, and Sand Island became a small town shared by hundreds of workers and sub-marine and aviation personnel. Where the vegetation once was little else but the scaevola bush, now imported soils grew ironwood trees, eucalyptus, shrubs, and lawns.

Just a few feet beyond the coral reef, the bottom drops off quickly. There are no hidden shoals or other perils if one uses a sharp seaman's eye. Yet many a boat had found trouble there, including *Trigger* (SS 237), *Flier* (SS 250), and *Scorpion* (SS 278), resulting in punctured ballast tanks, broken sound heads, damaged reputations, and loss of command. As *Pampanito* approached the reefs on 23 July, the seas were running high, crashing over the coral to port and starboard. Yet, for all her previous troubles, *Pampanito* shot through the opening as smooth as silk and within minutes was pulling into the fuel pier on Sand Island to the accompaniment of a spirited brass band.[1]

The officers headed for the old Pan American Clipper Hotel, which had been taken over by the navy and nicknamed the Gooneyville Lodge. It was of tropical construction, with screens for windows, twin beds, and a shower stall between each pair of rooms—hardly the luxury of the Royal Hawaiian. The recreation room had a refrigerator, three or four card tables, and piles of old, dog-eared magazines. There were beer, liquor, and soft drinks, self-served on an honor system. Free booze was great, but it was an off brand of bourbon the officers called "Schenley's Black Death," and there was no mix, no ice, and only brackish water. Good liquor went on the black market for fifty dollars a bottle.

The enlisted men were quartered in barracks, row upon row of tenementlike structures set on blocks above the sand. The beds were double-deck bunks. There was also a standard navy mess hall. The food was decent but predictable, with eggs, bacon, and ham for breakfast except on Wednesdays and Saturdays, when beans were served. The men were issued beer chits, good for two beers a day, but they could save them up or trade for more. The beer was usually Primo brand, brewed in Honolulu, or Stateside brands like Fort Pitt and Iron City. The men claimed that Midway served the worst beer in any theater of the war and likened the beverage to embalming fluid.

One of the favorite pastimes on Midway was bird-watching. The island, which had been featured in *National Geographic*, was famous as a bird sanctuary. Snow white terns fluttered through the air, and white boatswain birds with two long red tail feathers were abundant, though unpopular because of their nasty tempers. The frigate birds looked like distant airplanes as they hung almost motionless on the air currents.

The most popular however, was the albatross, Midway's famous "gooney bird." The Laysan albatross looked magnificent sailing in the air currents. On land, however, it became the gooney bird. A bevy of goonies could be seen jogging down the sand like a flight of overloaded bombers, kicking up dust all the way. Some would stumble and bump into one another, and all would crash-land in a heap of fuss and feathers. One had to check

Enlisted barracks on Midway, May 1944. The crew listens to a tale by Ed Kubacki. (Photo by Paul Pappas.)

between his sheets at night, for more than one sailor was greeted with a baby gooney, and the attendant mess, tucked underneath his pillow.²

One noteworthy occurrence on Midway in late July was the appearance of trumpeter Ray Anthony and his jazz band. The men used up their beer chits and danced in the sand with each other to some good old jazz and swing music. The next day a team from *Pampanito* won a high-stakes volleyball match against the team from the *Sealion II* (SS 315). They used the five hundred dollars in winnings to buy beer, burgers, and hot dogs for an outdoor picnic under the ironwood trees.

Celebrating his promotion to chief radioman was Mervin Hill, who received his back pay, spruced up in his new uniform, and had a bit too much to drink. Hill staggered back aboard the boat, where he was grabbed and tossed into the lagoon. On deck, Lieutenant Bruckart looked down and saw nothing except Hill's new chief's cap floating on the waves. He began to get worried before Hill finally bobbed to the surface. Hill was having such a rough time staying afloat that he stripped off his new duds. Chief's uniform and almost three hundred dollars in pay went to the bottom. Divers went overboard but could not find his money. Frenchie Bouchard also helped throw his buddy Frank Michno into the drink to "celebrate" his having made motor mac first class, and another wallet was consigned to Midway's lagoon.

Occasionally the men amused themselves with boxing matches. At one of the picnic beer busts, Mike Carmody and Ed Tonkin, two well-muscled men, were put up to a match. They got the gloves on and squared off. Everyone was expecting a real donnybrook from these highly conditioned competitors, but neither man wanted to hurt the other. "It turned out," Roger Walters said, "to be the powderpuff championship of the week." Yet all was well, he added, for they became very good friends afterwards.

Another boxing match occurred in the barracks. Late one night a group of chiefs returned to find most of the men sacked out. Feeling devilish, they broke out a fire hose and decided to spray the sleeping men. Many of the men high-tailed it out the back door, but some fought to defend their turf. In the ruckus, Chief Motor Mac Smith got knocked down the wet stoop in a slippery crash. Carmody swung a roundhouse right at the nearest man with a hose and broke Chief Electrician Attaway's jaw. The situation was brought under control, and Carmody dismissed it as an unfortunate, but minor, incident. "Some men came into the barracks feeling too good and started washing us out of our bunks," he said. "A fight ensued, and that was about it."

That wasn't quite it, because now Summers had to replace his chief electrician. He searched for a way to court-martial Carmody but couldn't figure out how to explain why the chiefs were all drunk and spraying a fire hose into the barracks.

Fifteen men transferred off to the ComSubDiv 202 relief crew. Electrician Walt Cordon was detached but came back aboard when Attaway was scratched. Roger Walters went to sick bay on *Proteus* for treatment for his persistent foot fungus.

Before *Pampanito* pulled out, Walters was visited by Mervin Hill. "He came to say good-bye," said Roger, "but he was worried sick that something was going to happen." It was the first time that his old radio gang would not be together, and Hill couldn't help but feel that his number was up. Roger tried his best to allay his fears. "Merv, old buddy, cheer up," he said. "I got a message from the Man upstairs. He says everything's going to be all right. You're in good hands." Hill left, seemingly in brighter spirits, and Roger hoped his little pep talk had helped.

One transfer that might not have been routine was that of Walt Richter. He was sent to the relief crew, but first stop was at *Proteus* to have his injured back examined. Scuttlebutt was that his constant gambling and winning would no longer be tolerated, and Richter might have left the sub for his own safety. However, it did not curtail his gambling. He did more business while operating aboard *Proteus*. "Midway was a gambling paradise," Richter said, and before the gambling "dried up," he claimed to have mailed three thousand dollars home to his sister.

Transferring aboard to replace Pharmacist's Mate O'Neill was Pharmacist's Mate First Class Maurice L. Demers. Demers had already packed many war experiences into his twenty-six years. He was raised in New Hampshire, but jobs were few during the Depression, and he found employment on a British cruise ship. He was laid off when the war began, and he joined the navy. Demers was a hospital corpsman at Brooklyn Navy Yard before being assigned to the store ship USS *Yukon* (AF 9). In the North Atlantic he helped haul torpedoed sailors from the icy waters and assisted in the removal of frozen limbs. He saw a U-boat surface in the middle of his convoy and said to himself, "Now that is the place for me. Those sailors are safe and sound underwater."

Demers served in Iceland for one year, all the while thinking of submarine service and wishing he was in the warm Pacific. He finally got into sub school, where he was thoroughly trained for every emergency he might encounter, from gas poisoning to appendicitis. Orders were not to operate on possible appendicitis cases. Pharmacist's mates had performed the procedure previously, aboard *Seadragon*, *Grayback* (SS 208) and *Silversides* (SS 236). A very angry navy surgeon general, Rear Admiral Ross McIntire, in a 1943 directive demanded that all appendectomies cease.

In January 1944, Demers went to Midway and served on *Proteus* until August, when he was sent to see Lieutenant Commander Summers. Demers first thought that Summers wanted him aboard because of his qualifications, but soon learned that "the CO was mad at the old Pharmacist's Mate and kicked him off." Still, Demers thought Summers was "a nice guy, intelligent, but not a friendly man. He was pretty shaky after seven or eight patrols. He was edgy and stern. He could drink and fool around, but business was business—no fooling around. He was the strictest skipper I ever had."[3]

Other personnel changes included Ensign Pike, who was detached from the boat because of illness. Most surprised at his own transfer was Bill Bruckart. He had no idea Summers designed to get him off the ship. He had been examined by Summers and by a board that included Captain Frank Fenno. Summers gave Bruckart a very good fitness report and a good recommendation. He was also designated as "qualified in submarines" (as were Lieutenants John H. Red, Jr., and Francis Fives). Yet Summers apparently made some unfavorable comments, for Mike Fenno later mentioned to Bruckart that he "should not tell the CO how to run his ship." Bruckart never realized he might have been guilty of that indiscretion. "Pete had no sense of humor, and he developed a barrier between him and the officers," said Bruckart. "He was very touchy when no one else would give a second thought to chance remarks."

In place of Pike and Bruckart came Ensign Charles K. Bartholomew, USN, and Ensign Richard J. Sherlock, USNR. Bartholomew had worked his way through Rice Institute as a civil engineer before joining the navy. Dick Sherlock was born in Youngstown, Ohio, in 1920, and was a 1942 graduate of Case School of Applied Science (now Case Western Reserve University) in Cleveland. He enlisted in March 1943, went to electronics schools at Princeton and MIT, then to sub school in New London. The first time he had ever been in the Pacific was in July 1944, and within weeks he had been assigned to *Pampanito* for his first war patrol.

Sherlock and Bartholomew felt an immediate bond. "Since all the other officers were at least Lt. (jg)s and had two patrols under their belts," said Sherlock, "we lowly ensigns had to band together for mutual protection." Sherlock enjoyed "Black Bart" and his wry sense of humor that helped keep the wardroom loose. "Needless to say," he added, "Bart and I became great friends."

Maurice Demers, too, found his first submarine assignment satisfying and challenging. They had been training off Midway for only a few days when he got an opportunity to make his first major diagnosis. Chief Smith, a big man with an expansive girth, went to Doc with a pain in his abdomen that he thought might be appendicitis. Demers told him it was only a stomach ache; he only needed a good bowel movement.

A few days later the pain had increased, and when Demers had Smith lift his leg, it hurt even more, a possible sign of appendix trouble. Demers wondered if he had incorrectly diagnosed his first case. Smith was sent aboard *Proteus*. The doctors said it was his appendix and scheduled an operation that very day. Demers was embarrassed that he had misdiagnosed the condition, and he was anxious for Smith's safety. Then, surprisingly, an hour later Smith came strolling down the gangplank to the sub. He only needed some exercise, had a healthy movement, and was fine. Demers felt vindicated, and his career as the "doc" was off to a good start. Yet there was not much glory in diagnosing constipation. In fact, Demers believed constipation was the worst thing men had to worry about when starting out on patrol. After shore leave it took a week before everybody got regular again. Also, all headaches, coughs, and colds seemed to disappear after about two weeks when all the men got used to each other's "diseases." Demers wondered if he would ever get the opportunity to show his mettle.[4]

No one would see any action until the relief crew finished with the boat. The major work included replacing damaged gaskets in the conning tower hatch, in the main induction hull valve, and on flood valves in No.

4A FBT. All main-motor brushes were replaced, and the remainder of the Mark 18 torpedo-charging equipment was installed in the forward torpedo room. The SJ was equipped with a new transformer, and a radio key was installed in the radar circuit for communications. The S-band tunable cavity made focusing the SJ easier and made it more sensitive. The radio key permitted boat-to-boat communications in Morse code at S-band frequency. Dots and dashes were slower, but the SJ had greater range than the VHF radio.

Loading for the next patrol began 14 August, and the men gathered back at the boat to square away their gear. Pappas set up his record player in the crew's mess. One record he brought along to play during their next attack—if they ever had a next attack—was the "William Tell Overture," better known to the crew as the theme from the radio show *The Lone Ranger.* He figured it should get them in the spirit.

Those not disposed to listen to Pappas's records could switch on the radio, where Pacific atmospheric conditions were usually good enough to allow almost world-wide reception. They listened to San Francisco's KGEI for war news and entertainment; programs such as *Command Performance, Musicale Americana,* or *Your News from Home.* When they tired of American "propaganda," they could tune in to the other side, Radio Tokyo's "Rose" being a favorite.

Submariners remembered Tokyo Rose almost from the first day of the war, and almost everyone remembered her differently. She had a sweet voice, a sexy voice, a husky voice, or a squeaky voice. She spoke impeccable English. She spoke poorly and mispronounced words. She was on all day or only at certain times. She was enjoyed for her clumsy propaganda and her popular music. She played too many unpopular English recordings. She was an evil temptress, reviled for spreading lies and sowing dissension in the Allied ranks. She was corny and harmless, and there was no objection to her music or her chitchat. No two men had the same recollections.

In fact, in spite of all of the men's memories, there was no Tokyo Rose. The name was a GI invention, much as Kilroy was, or calling an Englishman "Limey," or a German "Jerry," or an American Southerner a "Johnny Reb." There were twenty-seven female disc jockeys who worked for Japanese radio stations during the war. The one who was finally singled out and labeled the infamous Rose was Iva Toguri, a Los Angeles–born graduate of UCLA who was stuck in Japan when the war began and, to make a living, ended up on NHK Radio Tokyo broadcasting as "Orphan Annie." Her boss and script writer actually thought she had a metallic voice that sounded like Gracie Allen's.

Her slot was called *Zero Hour,* and it began 1 March 1943. It was a weekday, early evening, fifteen-minute program that eventually expanded to an hour. Pappas and his shipmates listened to Rose the evening of 14 August: "Hello you fighting orphans of the Pacific. How's tricks? This is the after-the-weekend Annie back on the air, strictly on the *Zero Hour.* Reception okay? Well, it had better be because this is an all-request night and I've got a pretty nice program for all my little family—the wandering bone-heads of the Pacific Islands. The first request is made by none other than the boss. . . . He wants Bonnie Baker . . . 'My Resistance is Low.'" If that was sly propaganda, the submariners couldn't care less. It would get them away from Pappas's 78s and help them pass away another night of watching gooney birds crash land on the beach.[5]

While the new crew members were becoming familiarized with submarine protocol, Paul Summers had some anxious days awaiting his fate. He had commanded a boat for two patrols. Policy was to give every commander a chance to prove his worth; if he failed to perform after two patrols, he was relieved. Summers was credited with damaging only one freighter on the first patrol. The kindest endorsement for Patrol Two came from Mike Fenno, who conceded good area coverage despite heavy enemy air and surface patrols. Fenno thought the hit claim for the Mark 18 that ran over six minutes was stretching credibility. Admiral Lockwood was concerned that only one attack was made out of seven worthy chances, but he believed that enemy submarine activity off Japan was heavy, and he made it mandatory that henceforth all U.S. submarines operating in Hit Parade would zigzag while on surface patrol. He granted damage to one freighter but did not believe the patrol worthy of a combat insignia.

With two patrols and only two damaged freighters to his credit, was Summers on his way out? Author Clay Blair, Jr., contended that "the boat was known throughout the fleet as 'The Peaceful *Pamp.*'" However, many a submarine had gone through two or more patrols without a confirmed sinking, and no such appellation had been placed on them.[6] At this early stage of her career, *Pampanito* was comparatively unknown. Moffett had only heard the term "Peaceful *Pamp*" used by a couple of disgruntled shipmates. Even so, he felt it was unwarranted. George had been in the conning tower during every approach, and he personally knew how much time, effort, and sweat went into every attack. To him, *Pampanito*'s lack of success was the result of bad luck. Regardless, two patrols without any confirmed sinkings would place any captain on tenuous ground.

Lockwood was unhappy with recent empire patrols. The next sub scheduled there was *Tang*. She left Midway on the last day of July, when her commander, Dick O'Kane, opened up a penned note from Lockwood. The admiral explained why he was sending *Tang* to the empire: "We have had two poor, and now a dry patrol in these areas, the boats reporting a dearth of shipping," Lockwood wrote. He said that intelligence sources knew there was shipping in the area, and he wanted *Tang* to find it. O'Kane knew it was a rough area from the reports of other skippers who had patrolled there, but he would do his best. *Tang* returned from the patrol with contacts on twenty marus, thirty-one escorts, and twenty-two separate patrol craft. She sank four *marus*.[7]

Although Lockwood had misgivings, he let Summers take *Pampanito* out for her third patrol. Pete must have realized he was walking on thin ice. He needed to score big this time.

*Pampanito* was already two days behind schedule, because on the last trial run, one of the main motors failed. Pappas succinctly commented: "Number four main motor shorted out while we were going full speed and we got a big explosion." A section of the compensating winding shorted across the series field winding, burning both insulation and brushes. Smoke filled the maneuvering room, and carbon dust coated the motors. No one could determine the cause of the short.

While a repair crew frantically worked, members of the sub crew couldn't resist some last-minute mischief. The story may be apocryphal, for it is remembered in various versions. It seems that there were some unattended jeeps, and even a motorcycle, parked on the island. Wouldn't it be great if the men could have their own transportation on other islands they might visit? Someone subsequently stole a jeep or a motorcycle and drove it back to the sub, where a number of motor macs began to disassemble it and haul the parts down the hatches. The scheme was halted, however, when the Marines noticed a vehicle was missing and traced it to the submarine dock. The dolphin-wearers were caught again, but no one would admit who stole the vehicle, and before they could pursue the matter, it was time to sail. An alternate ending had the thief either driving the stolen jeep off the dock to dispose of the evidence or else crashing the cycle into a tree right in front of headquarters. In any case, the scheme failed, the motor was repaired, and *Pampanito* was finally able to pull away for her third patrol.

This run would offer a new twist, for Summers and crew would be part of a wolf pack. On 17 August, *Pampanito* was finally underway in the company of *Growler* (SS 215) and *Sealion II*. They would be heading for Convoy College, an area where Japanese shipping bottlenecked as it passed between southern Formosa and northern Luzon.

Commanding *Sealion II* was Eli T. Reich. Reich had served with Summers for three patrols on *Stingray* in early 1942 and was later exec of USS *Lapon* (SS 260) and was instrumental in testing the new Mark 18 torpedoes. Summers described Reich as, "a philosopher. He read on *Stingray* all the time." Eli took pleasure in his books and was somewhat low-key and soft-spoken, but underneath the veneer was an aggressive commander. On Reich's first patrol in the East China Sea he sank four ships, and he was out to add to that score on this, his second patrol.

Commanding *Growler* and in charge of the wolf pack, was Thomas Benjamin Oakley, Jr., who had formerly served on *Cachalot* (SS 170) and *Tinosa* (SS 283) and had commanded *Tarpon* (SS 175) for one patrol. This was his second patrol on *Growler*, and although he had sunk only one ship on his first patrol, Summers had misgivings about him, thinking he was too flamboyant and aggressive, perhaps even careless. Oakley, as the senior skipper, named the wolf pack "Ben's Busters." All three boats carried electric fish.

They were a week behind another pack, heading to the same area, consisting of Eugene Fluckey's *Barb;* the new boat *Queenfish* (SS 393), commanded by Charles E. Loughlin, who had spent time in Panama on the old *S-14;* and *Tunny,* under George Pierce. In command of the pack and riding on *Barb* was Lockwood's flag secretary, Edwin R. Swinburne, who had never made a war patrol. Swinburne had named his group "Ed's Eradicators." In a typical bit of submariner humor, two of the boats in the pack were also known as the "Boob" and the "Queerfish."

The "Busters" headed west at two-engine speed. On the first day, *Pampanito* discovered that wolf pack communications with the VHF voice communications system were not satisfactory, and again Moffett had to tinker with the equipment. Although *Pampanito* could hear *Growler's* communications, the reverse was not true when the range exceeded eight thousand yards. Both *Sealion II* and *Growler* had navy-type VHF's, while *Pampanito* had an army unit. The poor performance of the army radio would spell trouble later.

Next, they discovered a full-voltage ground in the number two main motor. Summers wrote: "Can't seem to dodge this bugaboo in spite of all the work done during refit and past repair periods." It took two days to repair. On 24 August, *Pampanito* passed close aboard and exchanged signals with USS *Rasher* (SS 269), homeward bound on an opposite course after a stellar patrol in which she sank five ships, including the twenty-thousand-ton escort carrier *Taiyo*.[8]

The next day, SD radar picked up an "Emily" at six miles. It was a surprise, being so far from a Japanese air base, but the plane's thirty-eight-hundred-mile range meant that the big craft could patrol almost every corner of the Pacific. A quartermaster was up on the shears, greasing the scope. The OOD, Lieutenant Swain, who had been a football blocking back at the Academy, had once injured his knee in a game. It had bothered him from time to time throughout the entire war, and it was throbbing today. The plane contact was announced, and Swain sounded the diving alarm. The lookouts scrambled below, but the quartermaster kicked over the grease bucket onto the bridge deck. As Swain headed for the hatch, he slipped in the grease, twisted his knee, and jammed a finger. Doc Demers checked Swain. His sprained knee wasn't too bad, but his finger was broken. Demers gave him a shot of morphine, put a splint on his hand, and sent him to his bunk. Later, Swain got up to go to the head, became dizzy, and collapsed in the passageway. The men helped him back to bed. He would be off duty for the next two weeks.

On the way out, Maurice Demers had the 1200 to 0400 radar watch. He learned that by clicking on the SJ key, he could send out a radar impulse that would make the "grass" jump on the screen. Demers had a plan. On board *Growler* was his sub school classmate, a man named Thompson, who also had the 1200 to 0400 radar watch. Since they couldn't talk to each other whenever they were surfaced, they conspired to send out "clicks" once an hour on the high-frequency SJ. That way, Demers and Thompson figured they would know that the other one was alive and well. Demers's clandestine signaling would have bought him a severe reprimand if discovered. As it was, the radiomen had their hands full guarding the Fox schedules.

On 29 August, *Pampanito* entered the patrol area between Formosa and Luzon, and the next morning she dived for a submerged patrol in Bashi Channel about forty miles north of Batan Island. Apparently radio conditions were not good, or *Pampanito* was too deep to pick up a message that came in about noon. A convoy was departing Takao, Formosa, and heading for Manila. *Barb* received the message and passed the word to the other "Eradicator" pack members. The "Busters" also got the message, and for the first time in the war, two wolf packs were converging on one convoy—that is, two packs minus one boat. Somehow, *Pampanito* failed to receive the word. Only after surfacing about 1930, twenty-two miles from Itbayat Island, did she get notice. The other five subs had seven hours' head start.

Loughlin in *Queenfish*, which had never before fired a torpedo in anger, got in the first attack at 0223 on 31 August, sinking the forty-seven-hundred-ton *Chiyoda Maru* on his first try. Within the next few hours *Sealion II* and *Growler* both put torpedoes into the nine-thousand-ton oiler *Rikko Maru*. *Barb* then sank the fifty-six-hundred-ton cargo ship *Taikoku Maru*, *Growler* attacked a destroyer, and *Sealion II* sank the thirteen-hundred-ton frigate *Shirataka*. The convoy, designated MI-15, scattered, with the remaining ships heading individually back to Takao. Later in the day, *Barb* hung on to sink *Hinode Maru No. 20*, a converted minesweeper, which was heading out to help the convoy. Only *Tunny* failed to attack a ship, and only because she was lining up *Taikoku Maru* for a shot when *Barb*'s torpedoes connected first.[9]

Where was *Pampanito*? At 2100 on 30 August she was still heading north under a clear sky and bright moon, dodging plane contacts. *Growler* had changed course to the west. Oakley, using the agreed-upon 2,000-kilocycle band, had been trying to raise Summers all evening. He sent a blind message spelling out the positions of his patrol line, hoping it would be received.

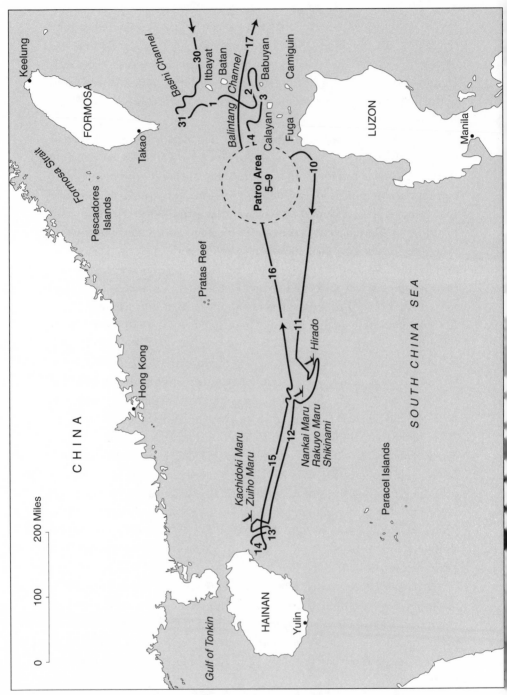

Detail of third patrol, 30 August–17 September 1944

The next day, Oakley recorded in his log: "The daily patrol stations of *Sealion* and *Pampanito* are in good position. They should both make contact before we get there." But *Pampanito* did not get the word. By 0200 she had already moved far to the north and east of the spot where the other five boats were about to jump the convoy. She picked up SJ interference bearing 250 and turned west to investigate. By 0330 the men on the bridge could see fires and smoke on the horizon. As they closed, Summers recorded: "Moon was down, and the sight was something for those seeing their first torpedoed ship." Less concerned with the aesthetics were several of the officers who would rather have done the shooting than passively watch the results.

Lieutenant Ted Swain was agitated. It seemed to him that they were constantly going in the wrong direction. "We had a skipper that didn't listen to us," he complained. "We'd have a big conference in the wardroom. We'd tell him which way we thought he ought to go, and he'd go the other way—literally."

Summers pulled back and decided to patrol on an east-west axis to the south of the burning ship. Meanwhile, the convoy was fleeing north, with five subs in pursuit. Swain's temper was nearly as hot as the flaming *maru*. Summers, noting Swain's discontent, tried to change the subject by asking about his broken finger. Did Swain realize that the injury during a war patrol could make him eligible for a Purple Heart? Barely hiding his contempt, Swain retreated to his bunk.

While on the new course, *Pampanito*'s SJ picked up another contact. Closing, she identified *Growler*, which had just finished making her attack. Summers made no attempt to establish communications. Instead, he hung around in the same vicinity, noting bright flashes from "quite a gun battle" taking place off his starboard bow. Hopper was on lookout and could see haphazard Japanese tracers arcing to all compass points. Like orange streamers, they appeared to float lazily into the ocean— except for the close ones that seemed to pick up speed and noisily whiz over the sub. Planes appeared at dawn, and while the other submarines were chasing the convoy remnants toward Formosa, Summers dove on course 140. It was an incomprehensible decision considering the SJ contacts to the north. "Decided to proceed southeast to clear immediate area," he wrote. "Believe convoy must have headed eastward although we have been unable to make contact nor have we received any contact report."

Paul Pappas had finally gone to bed after the excitement of the evening. His sleep was disturbed by distant depth charges, approximately forty-six of them, which went off between 0730 and 0930. When he awoke, the boat had been rigged for silent running, and the temperature was up to 114 degrees. He surmised that *Growler* and *Sealion II* had hit something and were getting worked over for their efforts. Unfortunately, *Pampanito* also had to suffer for it.

While at deep submergence, sound reported a loud air noise forward, but a search failed to find the cause. Then Lieutenant Johnson discovered that the forward trim tank was about two thousand pounds heavy. They suspected a small water leak had been spraying against metal, causing the noise and slowly filling the tank. The noise would impact on any future evasion attempts, and all hands in the forward torpedo room searched for the leak.

Before noon they secured from depth charge and made a periscope observation. All was clear until 1227, when a mast was sighted at ten thousand yards. Summers hoped he finally had found the elusive convoy, but it proved to be a small trawler. Nothing else appeared, so they surfaced early, skirted Itbayat Island, and headed south, guessing that the fleeing convoy might have gone in that direction.

Just after midnight on 1 September the APR picked up another sub's radar, and a minute later *Pampanito* exchanged recognition signals with *Queenfish*. Summers had found another submarine—but it was from the wrong wolf pack. Several times he tried to contact *Growler*, which hadn't been heard from for six days. He did raise *Sealion II* and learned that Reich had expended almost all of his torpedoes and was proceeding to Saipan for more. This was another blow. One of their pack mates was going for a reload while they hadn't fired one damned torpedo. Was Summers getting paranoid, or were Oakley and Reich purposely cutting him out of the action? There seemed to be no reason for the lack of communication.

On *Growler*, however, Oakley was as concerned as Summers. Had *Pampanito* been sunk? Several times on 1 September he had sent blind messages to her with no response.

On 2 September, *Pampanito* played tag with planes in Balintang Channel while *Growler* spent the day unsuccessfully calling her. Finally, after surfacing about eleven miles northeast of Babuyan Island, *Pampanito* made contact. *Growler* said they would change patrol stations during *Sealion*'s absence. With the assurance that he had not been abandoned, Summers patrolled Balintang Channel, ending up fifteen miles from Calayan Island at dusk on 3 September.[10]

The next day did not augur well for Pete Summers's thirty-first birthday. The leak in the forward trim tank was worse, and the source could not be pinpointed. Flooding the tank as much as possible did not seem to slow the leak or stop the noise. The only way to plug it was to find it, and that meant someone would have to go into the trim tank while the boat submerged. It was dangerous, but two men volunteered: Lieutenant Howard Fulton and Motor Machinist Mate Second Class Ed Stockslader.

Fulton had come aboard before the second patrol. Born in Los Angeles, he had received an A.B. degree at Fresno State College, had attended midshipman school at Northwestern University, and had been commissioned as an ensign in June 1941. He had attended Naval Mine Warfare School and had served for a time as a naval observer at the American embassy in London. Fulton made his indoctrination patrols on USS *Mackerel* (SS 204), and was currently *Pampanito*'s assistant gunnery and engineering officer.

Stockslader had little concern about his second "volunteer" job since mending the main induction on the first patrol. "I had no thoughts, no qualms; a job had to be done and so I did it." Then he added: "I volunteered like I usually did. The Captain would say, 'See me in my stateroom, I have a job for you.' I ask you, is this volunteering or not?"

The first job for the twenty-six-year-old Fulton and the twenty-two-year-old Stockslader was to make sure the manhole cover on the top of the trim tank wasn't leaking. Finding that the cover's gaskets and bolts were secure, and knowing that pressurized air could be blown into the tank, they made preparations.

After surfacing at 1945, a work party went topside and under the superstructure to unbolt the cover. Extra lookouts went up to search for planes. As usual, the men knew that they might be left behind in an emergency dive. Down inside the trim tank, Fulton and Stockslader switched on their flashlights while the cover was sealed above them. The final tightening of the bolt and a rap on the hull for good luck echoed with the cold finality of being sealed alive in a tomb. Inside the forward torpedo room, another cover that connected with the after end of the forward trim tank was removed, opening a tenuous channel for voice communications. When they gave the okay, Lieutenant Johnson slowly took the boat down.

A little more pressure was built up in the forward torpedo room and trim tank. No water came in, and Johnson took her down to sixty feet. Men called to Fulton and Stockslader through the open connection, but there was no answer. After a few tense minutes they called back; all was okay, they were still searching. The pressure at sixty feet evidently wasn't enough to reveal the leak. Johnson took her down to two hundred feet. The minutes passed slowly. After nearly an hour, word came through; they had found the leak. It was in a packing gland surrounding a rod that operated the outer door of number five torpedo tube and that extended through the bulkhead of the forward trim tank. Said Stockslader: "We found the leak at a depth of 200 feet, but to add a little spice I had them go down to 400 feet on the pretense that I wanted to make sure." At 2115, *Pampanito* surfaced, and Fulton and Stockslader happily emerged from the tank. Now they knew what the problem was, but somehow they had to fix it.

The daylight hours of 5 September were spent submerged on station while blueprints of the tank and torpedo tubes were studied. That evening Gunner Hauptman again donned his diving gear and went under the superstructure into the void on the starboard side of the chain locker. A line secured around his waist led up the ladder and onto the deck, where Hubie Brown grasped the other end. Brown tried to keep it at just the right tautness, giving Tony his leeway but not leaving too much slack in which to get tangled. While Hauptman worked underwater, tightening the bolts around the packing gland, the tropical night closed in. Another officer came out for moral support, but Brown couldn't even identify him in the darkness. Brown payed out and pulled back on the lifeline, all the while thinking Tony was a little crazy, wishing he would hurry up, and swearing that no one would ever get him down in there in that predicament. Suddenly the line went slack. A lump rose in Brown's throat, but shortly after, Hauptman appeared at the ladder. Everyone hurried below.

At the cost of a few barnacle scratches, Hauptman had tightened all the bolts except one.

One final evening was needed to complete the repair. A specially designed wrench was rigged up to allow ratcheting the bolt at a sharp angle. Hauptman went down one more time and by 2000 had completed tightening the final bolt. Fulton's, Stockslader's and Hauptman's services would earn each of them a letter of commendation.[11]

From 5 to 9 September, "Ben's Busters" patrolled in a 120-mile-diameter circle off the northwest coast of Luzon. This quadrant of Convoy College had traditionally been an area of numerous ship contacts, but the sorry luck that seemed to follow *Pampanito* continued unabated. In the early morning of 7 September she saw a flashing light on the ocean, but when she chased, the light disappeared. During the day, *Pampanito* came upon a lone, abandoned lifeboat. It was painted gray and had a weathered number 4 or an *A* on its side. She could find a half-sunken lifeboat, but no ships.

On the evening of 9 September, sound detected distant explosions. Nothing was sighted when they surfaced, but subsequent SJ radar interference was eventually identified as *Queenfish*. Although communications were garbled, *Pampanito* determined that the "Eradicators" had picked up a Japanese convoy near Luzon. In fact, *Queenfish* was having quite a first patrol, having sunk two more ships in the vicinity of Calayan Island. *Pampanito* was having an easier time contacting "Eradicator" boats than those in her own pack. That same evening, Oakley had unsuccessfully tried to raise *Pampanito* for two hours. He had received an important message from ComSubPac regarding interception of a convoy, but it would require shifting the wolf pack three hundred miles to the west.

Hoping to sink any stragglers that the "Eradicators" might have left behind, *Pampanito* headed in the opposite direction, toward Cape Bojeador on Luzon's northwest coast. Oakley gave up trying to contact Summers. He sent a request to ComSubPac asking if it could get through to *Pampanito* regarding the ULTRA and the pending rendezvous of the "Busters." Meanwhile, skulking along the Luzon beaches throughout the day of 10 September, *Pampanito* saw nothing but aircraft patrolling the coast. Distant intermittent depth charges were heard during the morning, constantly reminding the men that other boats seemed to have no problem finding enemy ships. A patrolling "Rufe" forced *Pampanito* down. At 0938, when rising to periscope depth, the sub was rocked by an aerial bomb that exploded nearby and caught everyone off guard. They rigged for depth charge and went deep for another hour and a half.

It was 1907 before *Pampanito* popped to the surface, and very unexpectedly, radio messages began coming in fast and furious. She exchanged signals with *Barb*, picked up a message from ComSubPac, and received a similar note from *Growler*. There was a message about a big convoy heading north through the South China Sea. A quick plot of the rendezvous point showed *Pampanito* would have about twenty-six hours to make a 350-mile run. They were finding no ships while marking time off a Luzon beach, so Summers called for four-engine speed, and they were off to the races.[12]

"Ben's Busters" headed for a point in the South China Sea about two hundred miles south of Hong Kong and two hundred miles east of Hainan Island. *Growler* was closest to the spot and only needed moderate speed. *Sealion II* was farthest, returning with a batch of Mark 14 torpedoes from Saipan. She had six hundred miles to travel, but because Reich had stayed on the surface and picked up the message on 10 September, he had an extra day to pound the waves west at seventeen knots. Although the situation called for alacrity, Summers still spent nine hours submerged during the daylight hours of 11 September.

Surfacing at 1800, *Pampanito* sighted another surfaced submarine about ten miles away. Summers promptly dove, then assumed it was either *Growler* or *Sealion II* and resurfaced, continuing on to the rendezvous. The mystery submarine was *Sealion II*, which had already made up the two-hundred-mile deficit and had passed *Pampanito* on her race to the meeting.

At 2131, *Pampanito* pulled up to *Growler*, over one and one-half hours after *Sealion II*. The "Busters" were finally together. Maneuvering within one hundred yards of *Growler*, *Pampanito* received her instructions by megaphone: "Use 2006 Kcs until zero hours Zebra 14th. If jammed, shift to 2880 Kcs. Use channel 144 for contact reports. Course 213 (T), speed 13 knots until 0200; then reverse. *Sealion* open out 8 miles to the west, *Pampanito* 8 miles to the east of *Growler*. Spend the 12th as follows: *Growler*-George 23, *Sealion*-How 23, *Pampanito*-Fox 23. Rendezvous 1400 Zebra 13th at 20-30 N, 117-40 W. Whoever makes contact send contact report and attack! Good luck."

The scouting formation was a line abreast eight miles between subs, heading southwest at 13 knots on a course reciprocal of that of the expected convoy. With radar on, they would cover a thirty-two-mile front. If nothing was sighted by 0200 of 13 September, they would reverse course and head northeast toward Pratas Reef. Behind them about seventy miles to the northeast were "Ed's Eradicators," minus *Tunny*, which had been sent home after taking bomb damage. The first "Buster" to make contact would break radio silence and announce the contact for both wolf packs. The night was dark, with half the sky covered with rain clouds. The quarter-moon would not rise until about 0230, and the sea was a relatively calm Force 3. It was shaping up to be a fine night for a submarine attack.[13]

The "Busters" moved southwest for over two hours, crossing the boundary from SubPac to SubSoWesPac territory. That was normally a prohibited action, but there were no Seventh Fleet submarines in the area, and they were in "hot pursuit." Shortly after 0100, 12 September, *Growler* picked up a radar contact dead ahead at almost fifteen miles. At 0130, *Pampanito*, eight miles to the east, made her own contact at over fifteen miles, bearing 250, to the west-southwest. She headed northwest to get ahead of it.

The message over the Fox schedules that had brought them to this point was an ULTRA, a top secret communication with information derived from a decoded Japanese radio transmission. Quartermaster Al Van Atta marveled at the accuracy of the ULTRA. These special messages, decoded by the communications officer, and for the captain's eyes only, were always a source of scuttlebutt for the crew. Van Atta thought there was some courageous American spy working at the Japanese headquarters and living in great danger, passing out this information through secret radio transmissions. The precision could be uncanny: convoy departure time, course, speed, numbers of ships, and so on. Not until after the war did Van Atta learn that the source was from intercepted and decoded Japanese radio transmissions. The people at Pearl Harbor, Van Atta said, "probably knew as much about enemy shipping as the Japanese did themselves."

As assistant communications officer, Dick Sherlock was privy to much of the ULTRA information. He was amazed that Pearl could tell them the daily noontime positions of the convoy for every day it approached the interception point. And there it was, right on schedule.

*Pampanito* heard a contact report from *Growler,* but it was garbled, and Communications Officer Red could not decode it. Yet the gist of it was surely understood; convoy found, commence attack. Following Oakley's instructions, *Pampanito* immediately sent out a contact report. Unfortunately, "Ed's Eradicators" heard neither of the reports. *Sealion II* assumed sending out a third report on the same convoy would be redundant and kept silent.

*Growler* made the first attack. Oakley was lining up a tanker in the center column when an escort on the starboard beam of the convoy saw him and headed in. Oakley quickly shifted targets and worked a set-up for a down-the-throat shot at the rapidly oncoming frigate. The tactic had been used before; Mush Morton's *Wahoo* had done a down-the-throat with a Japanese destroyer off New Guinea, William S. Post's *Gudgeon* (SS 211) had attempted it twice in one day against destroyers south of Tokyo, and Sam Dealey's *Harder* had done the same to a destroyer off Tawi Tawi. No one had ever done it bow-to-bow and on the surface, however. Oakley fired three torpedoes from only 1,150 yards and hoped for the best—if he missed, the two ships would probably collide. Forty-nine seconds later the first torpedo struck with a brilliant explosion and flash. The frigate heeled over and started going down immediately. *Growler* passed by as close as 200 yards, near enough for the men on the bridge to feel the intense heat. It was the end of *Hirado,* the current flagship of the Number Six Escort Convoy commander.[14]

At 0155, *Pampanito* was north of the convoy and almost in position to fire her own torpedoes when the night was lit up by a blinding flash, followed by several explosions. Wild gunfire erupted from several ships. Summers thought he was in a good attack position, but the exploding frigate sent the convoy off in a panic. He was angry. He did not believe anyone had given him an adequate report before starting the attack, and *Growler* spoiled it for everyone by charging in and scattering the quail. On the bridge, they could see Oakley's boat quite plainly, illuminated by the glow of the burning patrol frigate and apparently only yards away from it. Pete turned to Jeff Davis and said of Oakley, "That guy's a damned fool!"

Summers had to make a quick decision. The escorts were fanning out, and the convoy was dispersing rapidly. He logged: "Since both the *Growler* and *Sealion* had been to the west of us, I assumed the attack had been made from that side, and that the convoy would probably head east away from the direction of the attack. As a result I headed east at full speed to get in position ahead of convoy if and when they headed in that direction."

It was the wrong decision. The convoy turned northwest, not east, and once again *Pampanito* was cutting the waves in the wrong direction. The officers recommended that Summers head west, but Pete would not listen. Was he pondering other phantoms? Was he being purposely cut out by two New Yorkers, a robust athlete and a soft-spoken intellectual, who both looked down their sophisticated East Coast noses at a Southern country boy? Pete couldn't, and wouldn't, emulate them. To be effective, one has to be cool-headed, Summers insisted. He likened Ben Oakley to Sam Dealey, whom he sarcastically labeled a "so-called destroyer-killer."

"I never tried a down-the-throat," he said. "I used a small angle sometimes, but never direct." He lumped Oakley in with others he thought too hot-headed. "I never did anything so drastic as 'Mush' Morton or Dick O'Kane. I never had to get a ship or else." Then he added, "My crew was too important to me."

Thinking he was being given a raw deal by his fellow skippers, being questioned by his officers only made Summers more adamant. No one was going to tell him which way to go or how to run his boat. If some men thought him cautious, it was too bad. Yet, he admitted, "I may have been a little conservative, based on the fact of my experiences on seven other patrols. It calmed me down. If I hadn't been hit by so many depth charges on *Stingray*, I might have been different too."

Ted Swain would have smiled at that assessment, but he would have agreed. "We always knew that with Pete Summers we'd get home, because we'd never get close enough to find anything," he averred.

Doc Demers finished up his sonar watch and left the conning tower amid much "bitching and bellyaching" among the officers concerning which was the proper course of action. Summers rejected their advice to turn west, did an about-face, and retreated to his stateroom. *Pampanito* headed east for an hour, away from the action. Several officers, including Swain, Sherlock, Bartholomew, and Davis, quietly called a meeting. Ted Swain was the most vocal and became the leader.

"The man did not do the right thing at the right time," he argued. They, the junior officers, figured they should make a report to the division commander. "How can you give him a fitness report?" Swain asked rhetorically. "How do you know what he is like?" The incipient mutineers believed that they knew. "We thought he had a problem. We thought he was incompetent."

As *Pampanito* drew further away from the enemy, Sherlock thought about the Navy Articles. One of them required the commanding officer "to do his utmost to overtake and capture or destroy any vessel which it is his duty to encounter." Certainly they had Summers on that one. But there was another one that threatened court martial for persons found guilty of disobedience and mutiny.

Even so, the thought was on everyone's mind, and it was finally spoken: they ought to remove Summers from command and take over. "We thought a couple of times about putting him in the tank," Swain said. "We'd let 'Jeff' take over the boat. That's how bad we felt about it." Fortunately, they mulled over their proposed action. "Cooler heads prevailed," Swain concluded. "'Jeff' and I decided it was the wrong thing to do."

There would be no outright mutiny, but the episode was not over. Dick Sherlock said they elected Ted Swain as their spokesman, and they all marched to Pete's stateroom. With grim determination, they stated their case: "We told the Captain we felt we should reverse course. We indicated that if he persisted on the present heading and failed to make contact we would request an official review upon our return to port." Having made their announcement, they walked back to their stations to await his response. Sherlock thought about it later. "In retrospect," he said, "I think we were on very thin ice."[15]

Was Summers's obduracy a lesson to his officers to prove they could not dictate to him? Maybe he had already figured that reversing course was the proper action, or possibly the officers' ultimatum had its desired effect. In any event, at 0340, Summers ordered a course change. The report gave no hint of the little drama that had preceded it: "By tracking, found the convoy was proceeding on base course 325 T. This put us back on their starboard quarter with the moon well up in the east. Commenced making end around to south and west of convoy to get on dark side away from the moon. One escort pulled out toward us and closed to about eight thousand yards before rejoining convoy. No evidence of enemy radar."

With that crisis over, *Pampanito* was back in the chase. However, heading east for one hour and forty minutes meant that she had to make a two-hour full-speed run in the other direction just to pull abreast again—and by then it would be dawn.

By 0527 they had closed sufficiently to begin another attack approach. The brightening eastern horizon caused Summers to opt for a submerged radar attack. They were ready. The OOD had his hand on the diving alarm when another explosion rent the early morning quiet. Within the minute successive detonations lit up a second ship. This time it was *Sealion II* that had hit the convoy just minutes before *Pampanito* could fire. She had put two torpedoes out of five into the eighty-four-hundred-ton naval transport *Nankai Maru*, and two out of three into the ninety-four-hundred-ton passenger-cargo ship *Rakuyo Maru*.

Again the convoy altered course, this time from northwest to west. Summers fumed. Another setup was ruined. The crew echoed Summers's discontent. Said Bill Yagemann: "We'd sit as a flanker while the two glory-happy boys were knocking off the ducks." They had suffered as much indignation as they were going to take. "We were all ticked-off about this."

In the maneuvering room the feeling was mutual. Pappas was anticipating the attack when he heard distant torpedo hits and depth charges. Immediately he thought that *Sealion II* and *Growler* had "cut us out again." The crew, he said, "is plenty mad," first because the other subs did not give them the word that they had picked up the convoy, and second, because "them two ——— pulled this trick on us before."

In addition to feeling that they were being short-changed by their packmates, the men were becoming frustrated with their skipper's lack of aggressiveness. Said Gordon Hopper: "For some time the crew had believed that Captain Pete Summers was too conservative and this experience confirmed our doubts."

Summers watched the escorts dashing about in the glow of the fires. One of them switched on a red light and charged across the sea. Guns were fired and depth charges dropped haphazardly, for the escorts did not yet know where the attack had originated. For fifteen minutes Summers explored his options; he could still charge into the melee while it was relatively dark and maybe get some hits amid the confusion.

No. Instead, he decided to pull to the north and try another end-around. The decision meant that they would be attacking submerged in the daylight or they could track and pursue for fifteen hours until night-fall. Neither course was appealing. The officers were ready to pull their hair out in dismay.

Everyone was tired after a night of pursuit, battle stations, argument, near mutiny, and disappointment. Summers crawled into his bunk in the conning tower for a little shut-eye, and at 0545, *Pampanito* was off again in pursuit.[16]

As the sun rose, the submarine paralleled the westward-moving convoy toward Hainan. They could count at least four ships and several escorts. Daylight forced them down, and by periscope they tracked the convoy's smoke. Slowly the ships drew out of range, and when *Pampanito* popped up at 1122, they had disappeared. There would be hell to pay if they lost the convoy again. They raced west until high noon, when smoke was seen once more. The tracking party breathed a sigh of relief. Now they could travel on the surface, hull down over the horizon, and work ahead into position for an evening attack. For three hours they slowly pulled ahead, always keeping the high smoke in sight.

After *Growler* sank *Hirado,* she was chased by the angry escorts and headed east into the darkness at nineteen knots. By the time Oakley circled back for a second attack, the convoy had fled northwest, and he was lucky to find its position by seeing the glow from the burning *marus* that *Sealion II* had hit. It was almost seven in the morning when he worked close enough to see two escorts standing by the stricken ships. One of them he identified as a seventeen-hundred-ton *Fubuki*-class destroyer. Oakley had already sunk a frigate in this fight, and he felt pretty confident about getting another one. Then *Growler* could be known as a bona fide destroyer buster. He closed in, fired six electric fish for two hits, and sank the destroyer *Shikinami.* As the ship went down, five of its own depth charges exploded within a few seconds, helping it on its way. With only one torpedo left, Oakley pulled clear. Late on 13 September, ComSubPac turned over command of the pack to Eli Reich and, to the joy of *Growler*'s crew, allowed Oakley to head to Australia for liberty.

*Sealion II,* in the meantime, after hitting the two *marus,* was chased off by the escorts and kept down for four hours. When Reich surfaced, he spotted a small corvette about seven miles away and heading northeast. Erroneously assuming it was part of the convoy he had been attacking, he surfaced and began the chase. About noon, *Sealion II* picked up a contact report sent by *Pampanito*. It was puzzling, because if it was correct, then Summers was tracking the convoy about sixty miles due west of Reich's position. Eli decided the report was inaccurate or obsolete and continued heading northeast, thus taking himself out of the picture for the next twelve hours. In the afternoon, *Barb* and *Queenfish* saw *Sealion II* heading north in their vicinity and assumed she was patrolling independently along the convoy's projected track. Neither "Eradicator" contacted *Sealion* for confirmation. The next day when no ships materialized, Ed Swinburn gave his pack orders to head back to the Bashi Channel. *Barb*'s skipper, Gene Fluckey, was quite critical. He thought they had wasted three days and four hundred miles, all because the "Busters" had not radioed a contact report to them.[17]

*Pampanito* continued tracking the convoy when at 1508 it made a radical zig to the north. Summers thought it was changing base course to head for Hong Kong, and the change would put the submarine on and slightly ahead of its new track. He dove for a daylight attack. However, another half hour disclosed that the convoy had zigged back to its original course, about 280 degrees. Perhaps they were still heading for Hainan. Back on the surface, the lookouts could clearly distinguish one large transport, two medium cargo ships, and one small cargo ship.

*Pampanito* continued west for three more hours, staying just ahead of the convoy. Another hour would bring twilight and an ideal setup for the attack. However, now they were in range of land-based air from Hainan, and sure enough, at 1839 a plane bore in on them and forced them down. They surfaced after half an hour, but another plane was sighted from the bridge, the twentieth plane contact of the patrol. Down they went again. At 1955, Summers brought the boat up—this time, they hoped, for the remainder of the evening.

The convoy was gone.

They couldn't believe it. The two planes had kept them bobbing up and down for only about an hour and a quarter, but the convoy had disappeared from their field of vision. In an understatement, the log simply read: "Felt very discouraged over possibility of losing convoy after long chase." What happened? Had the planes seen *Pampanito* and radioed a warning? Had the convoy made a routine course change at twilight to throw off pursuers, as was the wont of many Japanese commanders? Did it change destinations from Hainan to Hong Kong? Because it had been unmolested for over twelve hours, was it returning to its original northeast course, bound for Japan? What was *Pampanito*'s proper course of action?

A serious mistake in any military operation is to base your tactics on an enemy's intentions instead of his capabilities—that is, unless you possess the ability to correct a wrong guess. *Pampanito*'s trump card was her speed. Theoretically, if she poured on the coal at twenty knots and headed directly for the last known position of the convoy moving at eleven knots, she could get there before the convoy could get out of radar range. It was the safest play, but it would take longer to reacquire another attack position ahead of the convoy, for essentially the submarine would be following two sides of a triangle. A correct guess based on intentions would allow the sub to cut along the hypotenuse of that triangle. She would get there sooner and be better able to approach from ahead. A wrong guess, however, would cause the sub to miss the convoy by twice its radar range without any hope of reacquiring it. After a twenty-hour chase, and given the mental and physical state of the officers and crew, a cautious, safe choice based on capabilities may have looked like cowardice.

So what was the best guess of intentions? *Pampanito* had been ahead of a westerly traveling convoy at 1839. Two plane contacts kept her underwater for a total of forty-nine minutes. Had the convoy stayed on the same course at eleven knots, it would have moved 8.9 nautical miles and would have been even closer, perhaps almost right on top of the sub. The fact that it had disappeared means it had to have made a radical departure almost at the moment of the first plane contact. Would it have reversed course? That would have taken it farther away from land and closer to the scene of the earlier attacks. Would it have headed south? That would have been taking it back in the direction of Singapore. It obviously was not going west anymore. Summers and the tracking party finally concurred: "Took a chance that convoy had changed course at dark to head for Hong Kong and put submarine on a northeasterly course." Swain, however, was still not convinced. He thought heading north was a desperation move.[18]

Although they had made the most logical choice, the mood of the officers was growing as dark as the descending tropical night. How many times had they made mistakes, blown attacks, or gone the wrong way? The tension was heavy in the quiet conning tower. Thirty minutes passed, then sixty, then seventy. Finally, one hour and eleven minutes after losing the convoy, George Moffett announced he had a blip on the "A" scope. There it was, almost thirty thousand yards away, over seventeen statute miles, and still dead north at 000 degrees. The convoy had made a radical course deviation, and if *Pampanito* had gone east towards its last known position, she would most likely have lost it for good. Even Lieutenant Swain conceded, "A guy can't have bad luck all the time."[19]

Spirits soared again, and congratulations were in order, especially for the radar work. Radar Officer Dick Sherlock, himself fresh out of electronics school, came to rely on Moffett's expertise. Once, when the radar was malfunctioning, Sherlock suggested a solution, but Moffett indicated that he did not appreciate the lieutenant's interference. Sherlock said he would stay away—but only if Moffett and Stimler could make repairs in twenty-five minutes or less. Sherlock called Moffett the "maverick of the crew" and its "unofficial spokesman." He believed Moffett was just testing him, "trying him on for size." When they both understood each other, however, Sherlock knew he had a man of extraordinary ability to rely on. Quartermaster Third Class John H. Greene praised Moffett: "He could pick up a bird with our radar, it was that sensitive and finely tuned."[20]

Congratulations may have been in order, but there was no cause for celebration yet. They had been in this position before. *Pampanito* closed in. At 2152 one escort fired off a green rocket. Not knowing its purpose, Summers angled off northwest for a short time to see whether he had been discovered. The flare may have signaled a course change to the west, for *Pampanito* was able to bear in quickly from the south, approaching the convoy on its port bow.

After having tracked this convoy for twenty-one hours, they finally went to battle stations. It was 2225 and another fine night for an attack, with the sea light and a cloudy, dark, moonless sky. On the bridge, Summers operated the Target Bearing Transmitter (TBT), which was a set of binoculars mounted over a gyro compass. When the captain lined up a target, he pressed a button that sent the bearing information to the conning tower, where it was input into the TDC.

The TDC, looking rather like a vertical pinball machine tucked against the bulkhead on the port side of the conning tower, absorbed data such as course, speed, range, bearing, and angle; displayed it visually; and generated a firing solution. It was operated by two men, usually Lieutenants Francis Fives and Ted Swain but occasionally in conjunction with Fire Controlman Bill Yagemann. Lieutenant Sherlock was plotting officer, and Davis was assistant approach officer or would work on the plot or the TDC. The TDC continuously computed gyro angles for the torpedoes and electrically sent the solutions to the gyro angle setters in the respective torpedo rooms.

On the horizon there appeared to be four ships with four escorts. Summers, in a school-boat maneuver, planned to approach the targets, fire all six bow tubes at the near ships in the near port column, then swing right and unload the remaining four stern tubes at the two ships in the starboard column. At 2235 they were getting ready to fire, when, for the umpteenth time, another potential catastrophe struck.

In the forward torpedo room they received the order to "make ready the forward tubes." Howard George was now chief torpedoman, and Woody Weaver had become torpedoman first class, taking over the forward room. Weaver was positioned at the blow and vent manifold. Bob Bennett manned the flood valves for tubes one, three, and five (starboard), and Ike Robinson was on the flood valves for tubes two, four, and six (port). Jim Behney was between the tubes operating the interlocks, which had to be aligned to open the outer doors, and Joe Austin was at the gyro setter. They had a full load of electric fish, which Summers preferred because they left no telltale wake.

Upon orders to "make ready," they began flooding the tubes, but the water pouring into tube number four caused the torpedo to slide forward past the stop bolt. This tripped the starting lever, and the torpedo began a "hot run." The outer door was still closed, so the torpedo had nowhere to go.

Immediately Weaver called the bridge, and Summers coolly ordered, "Secure tube four." Lieutenant Swain heard the exchange from the telephone talker in the conning tower. When he saw that the TDC gyro indicator did not show a match in tube four, he assumed it was jammed.

He had Bill Yagemann step over to the TDC, and he headed for the forward torpedo room.

Up front, the whine of the running fish had unnerved the torpedo reload crew. Weaver looked back to see them disappearing through the hatch. The "hot" fish, however, was more of a nuisance than a danger. Weaver explained that the torpedo carried about one thousand pounds of torpex, enough explosive to disintegrate half of the submarine, but it required an initiating explosion—a fulminate of mercury detonator and a booster charge—to set it off. The detonator and booster were set into a cavity in the warhead, but several inches away from the torpex. The warhead could only be armed by an impeller, which was rather like a miniature waterwheel. As water streamed by the impeller, it would screw the detonator down until fully mated with the booster. Not until then was the warhead fully armed, and not until it had traveled through the water for about four hundred yards could it arm. The torpedo propeller could spin, but as long as the outer door was closed, there was no water flowing by to turn the impeller.

The reload crew, mainly seamen and stewards, heard the sound of a wild torpedo and naturally began to vacate the compartment. As they headed for the exit, Little Joe Austin, sitting on a wooden stool in front the gyro setters, caught the contagion and tried to follow them out. Before Little Joe could get off his stool, the old alligator wrestler, Jim Behney, lifted his foot onto Joe's chest and said, "You little son-of-a-bitch, sit down there and match pointers."

Within a minute or two, Austin had calmed down and had finished matching the gyros by hand. The entire sequence took only four minutes, and at 2239 the log read: "Gyros matched forward." The unmatched gyro that Swain could see on the TDC was simply the result of the hot run and the delay in setting the gyro by hand. The other five tubes were not affected. The reload crew came back when it realized the bow was not going to be blown off. The small crisis was over before Ted Swain could get involved. Behney and Weaver repaired the tube the next day by installing a new gyro setting spindle.[21]

It may have been well that Howard George was not in charge of the forward room. There had been a few occasions when his lack of concentration had caused them trouble, such as his tardiness in closing the poppet valve on the first run. He knew his business, or else he would not have been chief torpedoman. Yet George had a way of pushing his weight around and making himself disliked. Pappas said that George would often enter the crew's mess, sit down on a table in his sweaty skivvies, pass gas, then walk away roaring in laughter. He had been Hubert Brown's boss for the first two patrols, and Brown thought George was just "a big, obnoxious guy" who would go out of his way to be aggravating.

The hot run, however, cut George down a peg. The uninitiated seamen had swarmed out of the forward torpedo room when the electric motor started to whine. However, the chief, who should have known better, ran just as fast. He found Doc Demers in the after battery. "Portugee," as Demers called George, was so upset he couldn't say a word, but just "sat there shaking." Demers finally realized that the big guy "was afraid of the hot run." The crew had seen him and realized his bluster was just a facade, and they began to ostracize him.[22]

*Pampanito* bore in from the southwest side of the convoy. Lieutenant Red, the communications officer, reminded Summers that orders called for them to radio a contact report before attacking. Summers declined. He wouldn't cooperate after the way he felt Oakley and Reich had cut him out. It was the competitive way, he said. "It's the way they did it to me."

From the bridge at 2240, Summers gave the go-ahead to fire. Swain, Sherlock, and Fives were surprised, for they thought they were still too far away—thirty-eight hundred yards was the extreme limit of the Mark 18s. Swain was about to protest, but Jeff Davis, the ever-present buffer, cautioned him, and Swain punched the figures into the TDC. "I'll never forget it," Swain said, "because I matched the numbers." Lieutenant Sherlock, also in the conning tower, thought the range was even farther, more like an astonishing five thousand yards.

Swain hit the firing buttons. The forward salvo was reduced by one because of the disabled number four tube, but five torpedoes were off; three for the big transport and two for the large freighter in the port column. Immediately they swung hard right rudder and brought the stern tubes to bear. Two torpedoes shot out for each of the medium freighters in the starboard column. The quartermaster looked at his stopwatch. At twenty-nine knots the torpedoes would take about four minutes to connect—if they would ever connect at this range.

Surprisingly, at 2244 the first of the fish began to hit. Three grand explosions walked down the length of the big transport, the 10,500-ton *Kachidoki Maru*. Shortly after, it appeared that two torpedoes struck a trailing freighter. Within a minute another torpedo appeared to strike the trailing ship in the starboard column, and then, still another seemed to hit the lead ship of the far column. The last explosion was timed to coincide with the last torpedo, although they couldn't see it strike because that ship was obscured by the brilliantly exploding *Kachidoki Maru* in front of it. Seven out of nine torpedoes had hit. Sherlock was amazed: "When they struck the targets we all felt that Pete was the luckiest man alive." Even Lieutenant Swain had to smile at the irony of the situation.

Up on the bridge, Summers was soaking in the awesome beauty of exploding and burning ships on a black ocean. Within ten minutes he saw the large transport and the closest freighter go down. Another great detonation sent the after deckhouse of the trailing freighter high into the sky. Summers said that it "went up light as day." The fourth cargo ship leading the far column could still not be seen clearly even after the *Kachidoki Maru* had gone down because of the remaining smoke, flame, and debris. Finally the escorts began dropping depth charges at random, and Summers logged, "but for once we didn't mind."

One of those topside was not so infatuated with the situation. Signalman Third Class Herman J. Bixler was a twenty-one-year-old from Geneva, Indiana. He had recently left the University of Illinois and had only joined the boat at Midway before the third run. It was his first war patrol and, as bridge watch this evening, he admitted being "scared to death."

On the controllers, Electrician's Mate First Class Jack Wilkerson and Paul Pappas slapped hands in jubilation. They heard seven beautiful hits and heard the battle description over the intercom: one ten-thousand-ton transport going down in a few minutes, one seventy-five-hundred-ton freighter going down by the stern, and two hits on what was possibly a tanker. Studying the radar screen, however, Moffett could not confirm Summers's assessment. "I saw two target blips on radar disappear and felt that represented the sinking of two ships." Up on top as a lookout, Tony Hauptman was also taking in the scene, which impressed him enough that he would later make several drawings of the attack. "He was a good artist,"

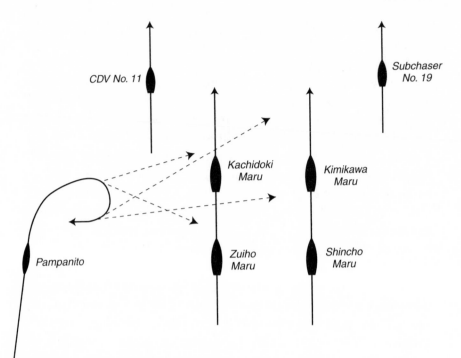

Attack on Convoy HI 72, 12 September 1944

Pete contended, and he encouraged Hauptman to make the drawings to verify what they had seen.

Summers desperately wanted credit for these ship sinkings—and the awards that would follow. One ship sinking would win a Secretary of the Navy's Letter of Commendation. Two ships would get a Silver Star, and three ships or more, a Navy Cross. The Navy Cross would also permit secondary medals: two Silver Stars and two Bronze Stars, to be given out with the captain's recommendation. Ted Swain thought Summers was overly concerned with verification when he had other business to take care of, such as sinking more of the convoy. "All he wanted," Swain said of Summers, "was to be a Commander and get a Navy Cross." This evening, it finally looked like he might have both.[23]

At 2253, while the topside watch was basking in the fiery glow, the submarine was rocked by an explosion that seemed to come out of nowhere. They thought it must have been a thrown depth charge, but they were nearly two miles from the nearest escort. Most likely, amid the smoke and confusion, they had been surprised by a night-bomber from Hainan. Lookouts and radar watch had probably been preoccupied with the burning convoy in front of them. Had the bombardier been a little more accurate, *Pampanito* might have ended her career right then. Incredibly, the possibility of a plane had not crossed their minds. Summers remained on the surface, picking up two escorts on the SJ at forty-six hundred yards. At 2300 he decided to pull clear to the southwest to get rid of the "hot" torpedo and to reload the tubes.

As they headed into the darkness, billowing flames, smoke, and occasional gunfire punctuated the scene. Hubert Brown watched the Japanese fire Very pistols, and it looked like they were shooting into their own ships. The gun flashes and tracers streaming across the sky looked like a Fourth of July celebration. Moffett kept the radar zeroed in on one large and one small intermittent pip out to nineteen thousand yards. To Summers, it meant that one more of the damaged ships had sunk, and the last, accompanied by a destroyer, was steaming away on a westerly course. Finally, he ordered a radio report sent out on the wolf pack frequency.

Down in the torpedo rooms, the mood was much more buoyant than it had been an hour ago. The forward torpedo room crew managed to extract the gyro spindle, open the outer door of tube four, and fire the torpedo out with a shot of compressed air. The reload crews happily jockeyed ten more torpedoes into place. Hubie Brown entered the forward room to find the steward, George Ingram, clad only in skivvies and down on his hands and knees, lending his muscles to the chore.

"Iggy," he asked, "What the hell are you doing here?"

"You don't think," the steward answered, "that I'm going to tell my kids that my battle station was the coffee pot, do you?" Brown joined Good Kid, as they worked the fish into their tubes.

Reloading ten torpedoes is labor-intensive and time-consuming. *Pampanito* had been heading steadily away from the convoy for half an hour before she lost radar contact with the last ship at twenty-eight thousand yards. Finally, at twenty minutes to midnight the loading was completed, and the sub headed back to the attack site.

At 0010, 13 September, radar again picked up two small pips at 053, range fourteen thousand yards. Summers thought they were escorts. As they tracked the pips and closed in, one stopped, leading him to believe it was picking up survivors. The other pip appeared to be maneuvering around in a small circle but was still about five miles away. They approached the stopped ship and identified it through the binoculars as a destroyer escort.[24]

Ever since his bad experience with a torpedo boat on *Pampanito*'s first patrol, Summers was reluctant to engage small, hard-to-hit craft. He observed for twenty minutes while slowly working his way in for a good setup. At half past midnight the escorts began radio chatter and commenced moving away at six knots. The chance to fire at a stationary target was gone. Now Summers logged: "Decided to attack as soon as possible and get clear." Even so, it was twenty more minutes before he fired three bow torpedoes, at the excessive range of thirty-five hundred yards. He had gotten away with it before, so perhaps he thought he could do it again. The first time, however, he fired nine torpedoes at four large, overlapping targets, with the *Kachidoki Maru* over 500 feet in length. Now, three torpedoes were streaking toward what might have been a subchaser about 167 feet long. Pete's flirtation with Lady Luck during this patrol was over. All the torpedoes missed.

So be it. He had done enough for one night. He assumed the two remaining contacts were small escorts and would not be worth a torpedo. But wait. Again, the officers had other thoughts. How did they know for sure they were small escorts? And if one was worth three torpedoes already, why not try again? There were eight ships in the convoy when they first struck. Even if three or four had been sunk, there were still four or five out there. They simply needed to move toward the last known bearing and find out. Six torpedoes were ready to fire, and five more waited to be loaded. The officers wanted to head in for an aggressive follow-up attack.

Fire Controlman Bill Yagemann was angry. He believed Summers was too conservative. "He was a goddamned good technician when it came to making an attack," he said, but he wouldn't push it to the limit. Later, when Yagemann thought about the distance from which they fired in the initial attack, he said, "We were lucky to sink the *Kachidoki Maru*."

The repeated vacillations of the skipper had even gotten to Frank Fives. The twenty-six-year-old lieutenant, born in Dunmore, Pennsylvania on Christmas Day, 1917, was an unassuming, soft-spoken man. He was so unobtrusive, Charlie McGuire could rarely get a rise out of him, describing him as "almost a non-entity. He never said more than five words to anyone." Dick Sherlock, who came to know the reclusive lieutenant better than most, noted how silent and morose Fives could become, especially after receiving ULTRA messages. Fives, said Sherlock, "was a brilliant engineer. He was a no-nonsense, reserved, solid performer. He was greatly admired by the crew and his fellow officers." It was not until after the war that Sherlock learned the reason behind his reticence. Fives was a strict Quaker and a pacifist. He had hated almost every minute of the war and wanted no reminders of it. Fives was saddened because impending battles meant that he might have to play a part in killing other human beings. An antiwar Quaker on a submarine was incongruous to say the least, but this time Summers had finally angered him.

"Everybody felt we should have done more than we did," said Fives. "We should not have broken off. Everybody was upset. Davis, spoke right up, saying, 'Let's go.' But by that time, Pete had had it. Everybody felt we should have done more."

The long chase, the lack of sleep, complaining officers, and battle stress had again taken their toll. Summers ordered them to pull clear to the southeast to join up with the rest of the pack the following night, and he wearily retreated to his cabin. Unaware of the little drama being played out among the officers, the majority of the crew were happy with the battle results. "It was celebration time," said Gordon Hopper. "Brandied eggnog was prepared in the galley and poured for all hands."[25]

As *Pampanito* cleared the battle area, those not on duty caught up on some long overdue sack time. Still within aircraft range of Hainan at sunup, they submerged for another routine periscope patrol. First order of the day was to log in the battle action of the last twenty-four hours. The reports were serious business. According to Vice Admiral James F. Calvert (*Jack* and *Haddo*), the task of writing was never delegated but almost always done personally by the skipper. Although they were not always literary masterpieces, the reports were detailed descriptions and analyses of every action, submarine and enemy tactics, and difficulties experienced. An accurate and thorough record was essential, for every patrol report was copied, duplicated, and sent to the sub school and to the skippers to teach and learn from. Calvert acknowledged their significance: "I read each one so many times that I almost memorized them."[26]

Besides being a learning tool, the report would obviously reflect the skipper's performance. Summers delegated the typing to Yeoman McGuire, but only after he had assured it was written up "by the book."

"He looked for perfect shots," McGuire said, "but you don't get perfect shots." The result was a continuous altering of the numbers until everything harmonized, and to McGuire, it was all a farce. He explained: "It was like Pete saying, 'You want a medal? You'll get it if we acted aggressively, and not otherwise.'"

Lieutenant Swain was pleasantly surprised when Summers dogged the convoy for twenty-four hours, and although the attack turned out satisfactorily, he was not happy with the firing ranges, and he detested fudging the reports to make the skipper look more aggressive. Said Lieutenant Sherlock: "We'd shoot at 5,000 yards, and by the time the reports were rewritten, the shooting would be at 1,500 yards. It took a hell of a lot of retracing on the plot and TDC to rewrite the facts and figures to jibe." As usual, Swain seemed the most affected. "It drove Ted wild," said Sherlock. "He thought it would come out and reflect on his record. Swain was furious over the patrol reports." When Sherlock reconsidered, however, he laughed and said, "We probably had better luck at 5,000 yards."[27]

The entire day of 13 September, *Pampanito* patrolled submerged, heading away from the attack site. The steel shark had finally bared her teeth and become a killer, but for many men it was not enough. Because of their animosity toward Summers, it seemed impossible for the men to give their best. Dick Sherlock felt that it was senseless to continuously go in harm's way and return home with nothing to show for it. He wished his captain was more aggressive. Ted Swain believed the officers were good people, but "it was not a happy wardroom" because of the captain. "I didn't have any confidence in him," he said.

There were those who defended Summers, stating that they would rather come home safe and sound than be a dead hero—certainly an understandable sentiment. When all was said and done, Sherlock said that

Summers just wanted to be able to someday know his grandchildren, and, he concluded, "I can't hate him for that."

One of the most telling idiosyncrasies that showed the inseparable gulf between the captain and his crew was Summers's habit of putting on a pair of gloves whenever he ventured beyond the control room. Some officers traditionally wore white gloves during compartment inspections, but Summers seemed to go to the extreme. "The crew," said Sherlock, "claimed that he was afraid of catching a disease from them."[28]

In fact, the real reason for the gloves was discovered months later. Chief Smith had been instructing Motor Machinist's Mate Third Class Walter R. Madison, a twenty-two-year-old from North Platte, Nebraska. Madison had made runs on *Trigger* and *Snook* as a fireman, but Smitty took him under his wing to show him his duties as a new motor mac. Touring the compartments, they had discovered Summers applying a topical cream to his hands and carefully covering them with his gloves. The captain confided to them that he had a persistent fungus, the "jungle rot" so often spoken of by men who served in the South Pacific.[29] Far from trying to avoid a disease, Summers had been protecting his men. It was a side of their reticent, yet considerate, captain that few men came to know.

After *Pampanito* surfaced for the evening, she picked up a message from *Sealion II*. Reich informed Summers that *Growler* was heading for Australia, that he, Reich, was now pack commander, and that he would patrol off Hainan. Suddenly the coastal waters did not seem so inhospitable, and Summers put the boat into a 180-degree turn. He was returning as much to protect his "territory" as to make a rendezvous with Reich.

Summers had mixed feelings about the wolf pack concept. In his later years he thought that it was a good idea and that sinkings ought to have been maximized under a proper coordinator. He thought it best to have the senior skipper command the pack from his own boat, as Oakley did from *Growler*. He did not want a supernumerary wolf pack commander on his boat—as pack leader Ed Swinburne was on *Barb*. Perhaps Summers finally realized just how uneasy Charlie Jackson must have felt knowing another officer was breathing down his neck.

However, on 14 September 1944, in the South China Sea, Pete Summers was anything but happy with the wolf pack concept. He was angry with his packmates, he was glad that Oakley had pulled out, and he wanted to get back to the site of his own attacks should Reich be snooping around for any crippled ships still afloat.

Near Hainan at sunup, *Pampanito* sighted a heavy black column of smoke issuing from "huge flames bubbling up from the surface of the water." Summers reckoned that this must have been the remains of one of the ships he had hit. He made a note to ask Reich if he had made an attack anywhere in the vicinity.

At 1540 lookouts sighted two small "smokes" over the horizon in the direction of Hainan. Since the burning ship was a total loss, *Pampanito* headed after them. After they had run west-southwest for an hour, the lookouts suddenly sighted several lifeboats and rafts about eight thousand yards to the north. All but one appeared to be empty. The choice was to investigate the lifeboats or head for the smoking ships. Since Summers assumed the boats were probably filled with Japanese survivors from the torpedoed ships, he saw no real need to run in for a closer look, and he kept the bow pointed west.

Through the high periscope at 1700 they sighted the masts of two ships underneath heavy, high columns of smoke. They pounded the waves to try and head them off before they reached Hainan. At 1915 *Pampanito* dove about thirty miles from the coast, ahead of the ships' track. After sunset, two small pips appeared at fifteen thousand yards. As they closed, however, Summers recorded: "Looked as though we had been fooled." His ships proved to be nothing but trawlers with high masts and smokestacks apparently burning poor, unrefined fuel oil. They were too small for torpedoes. Summers wrote: "It was too dark to attempt a gun battle, so reversed course and opened the coast. Very disheartening." Apparently *Pampanito* was up to her old tricks.

At 0530, 15 September, *Pampanito* received orders from *Sealion II* for a rendezvous, and one hour later the two boats pulled into hailing distance. The burning ship Summers had seen the day before was, incredibly, still smoldering nearby. Reich said he had seen the ship as early as 13 September, and from its persistent flames and thick black smoke he had assumed it was carrying a cargo of raw rubber. Summers agreed it was a cargo ship of about four thousand tons, because he had seen it fairly close up. Reich, perhaps testing Summers's resolve, exclaimed, "Well, there's another ship I should have claimed sinking."

This raised Pete's hackles. "Eli," he called back. "Don't you go claiming sinking that ship, because you weren't anywhere in the area at all." He had Davis check the navigational charts. "Hell," Pete called again to Eli, "this wreck is within two or three miles of my attack." Later, when asked if anyone credited Reich for the sinking, Summers remarked, "Well, I hope they didn't."

After these "pleasantries," Reich laid out the day's patrol plan. The subs would stay on the surface four hundred miles east to Bashi Channel. They cruised at twelve knots, *Pampanito* about twenty miles south of *Sealion,* searching for cripples or possibly a new convoy.[30]

The bridge watch on *Pampanito* was tense. It was crystal clear, with a calm sea, and certainly the Japanese knew that submarines were in the area. Naturally, patrol planes caused them trouble, and twice the APR indicated radar sweeps. *Pampanito* secured its air search radar. If they would sight anything it would have to be through the sharp eyes of the lookouts.

About one hour after the SD was shut down, the first dog watch (1600 to 1800) was settling in for a two-hour shift. After being broken in during the night torpedo attack three days earlier, Herman Bixler knew his watch duties well. He conscientiously searched his sector of horizon, and within a few minutes of coming topside he spotted something floating in the water. He looked again and determined that the object was a lifeboat. Bixler told the OOD, McMillan Johnson, who notified Summers and began to close the lifeboat. They were about thirty miles northwest of the spot where *Sealion* had torpedoed her ships on the morning of 12 September and assumed the lifeboat might contain some survivors of those sinkings. Cruising past the small boat, however, they found it was abandoned and swung back to resume their course.

Only a few minutes later, quartermaster Johnny Greene, another newcomer who had first transferred aboard from the relief crew on Midway, made a second discovery. "Two rafts with men on them!" he called out. Those topside swung their binoculars and found a group of men frantically waving at them.

Men on rafts. It was a situation to be approached cautiously, for American sailors had heard stories about treacherous Japanese who often used lifeboats as lures to bring a submarine in close where a waiting

Japanese submarine could torpedo it. No one ever had proof of this, but all floating rafts and boats had to be approached with skepticism, especially those with people aboard. Summers wrote: "It was naturally believed that these would be Japanese, so small arms were broken out and preparations made for taking prisoners."

Officially, Summers was out to take prisoners, and a party of men was armed for its own safety. There was no set policy for this situation. If a skipper could capture useful equipment from a ship, or gain information from a prisoner, all the better. If he saw fit to destroy the ship along with the survivors, it was up to him. It was not ostensibly condoned or disapproved.

Submarine skippers had always acted inconsistently in this situation. In the Atlantic and Mediterranean, British submarines and German U-boats had gunned down floating survivors, but only on rare occasions. The Japanese were not so cognizant of or caring about the tenets of the Geneva Convention. Off the coast of India in December 1943, Lieutenant Kazuro Ebato machine-gunned and rammed his submarine *RO-110* into the lifeboats of the survivors of the British cargo ship *Daisy Moller*. In 1944 in the Indian Ocean, Captain Tatsunosuke Ariizumi, commander of the *I-8*, had massacred ninety-eight survivors of the Dutch merchantman *Tjisalak* and had also tortured and killed survivors from the American freighter *Jean Nicolet*. There were more than one dozen similar incidents as Japanese submarines ran wild in the Indian Ocean.[31]

After an attack by USS *Sculpin* (SS 191), Lieutenant Corwin G. Mendenhall stopped the crew from taking pot shots at Japanese in the water. Lieutenant William Ruhe on *Crevalle* once saw his captain shove aside a crewman's gun when the man aimed it at floating survivors. Ruhe was thankful, for he believed "there was no place for that in submarine warfare." On the other hand, Lieutenant Commander Morton on *Wahoo* figured that every enemy who gained shore from a sunken ship was one more enemy who must be killed by the ground forces. He figured that by not shooting survivors, he was aiding and abetting the enemy. In January 1943, Morton had his crew fire the four-inch gun, a 20-mm cannon, and two Browning automatic rifles at about twenty lifeboats of Japanese troops who managed to escape from a ship *Wahoo* had just sunk. Ostensibly, they were only trying to smash up the boats to prevent the troops from reaching land; incredibly, the exec, Dick O'Kane, claimed that "no individual was deliberately shot in the boats or in the sea."[32]

On *Pampanito,* word of the discovery of men on rafts flashed through the boat. If Summers officially was looking to pick up prisoners, unofficially he may have had other thoughts in mind. Lieutenant Sherlock heard Pete order them to break open the gun locker. "Anyone who wants to shoot Japs, get yourself a Tommy gun and come out on deck," Summers called out. Shortly after, said Sherlock, "A whole bunch of guys came out from the Gun Access hatch under the Conning Tower with Tommy guns, all set to have a ball."

Lieutenant Swain was below, finishing up his decoding watch when he got the word. In fact, he had just completed his first regular duty shift since getting the splint off his broken finger. It was tender and sore, but he massaged it to loosen it up and convinced Summers that he could climb the ladder and operate all the necessary equipment. When Swain thought he heard the call, "Prepare to repel boarders," he quickly went to the gun locker. His fingers were quite limber enough to handle a .45.

Reserve officer Lieutenant John Red, Jr., who Dick Sherlock described as "fresh out of Yale," said that they all thought the men on the rafts were Japanese. He heard Summers pass the word to break out the small arms and say, "We'll have some target practice."

Bill Yagemann was on the bridge, tinkering with the malfunctioning TBT. While he worked, the starboard lookout called out that he saw wreckage in the water. At first Yagemann could see only debris floating amidst a mile-wide spread of brown crude oil. Gunner's Mate Tony Hauptman went past him and climbed down to the deck carrying a twelve-gauge, double-barreled shotgun. Hauptman was followed by Torpedoman Jim Behney with a Thompson submachine gun. Mike Carmody and a half-dozen others followed suit. "We were not going to pick them up," said Hauptman. "The captain told me to do away with them. I was going to shoot them." Tony walked forward to the bullnose and stood there waiting, shotgun leveled at the approaching life rafts.

One man not particularly thrilled about the situation was Gordon Hopper. It was his job to man the 20-mm gun, and the order he heard given to all the topside gunners was that "we would sweep past the rafts and shoot the survivors upon the captain's command." As Hopper loaded and adjusted the gun, many thoughts raced through his mind. He never considered himself overly religious. Although his father was a minister, he never seemed to have the calling himself. Yet a man did not have to be a preacher or a pacifist to have an aversion to killing. Were there Japanese on life rafts out there? They were still human beings, and they represented no potential threat to Hopper. He couldn't kill them. He was "appalled at the prospect of shooting helpless men on rafts in the middle of the South China Sea." But this was war, another voice told him. He had to obey orders. "Waiting for the captain's word," Hopper explained, "I was debating what to do, knowing that if I refused to fire or fired wildly I could be court-martialed or even shot on the spot for disobeying an order during combat."

The sub moved closer to the waving men. Hopper could almost make out their individual faces. He lined up the gunsight on the nearest one. A burst from a 20-mm could cut the man in half. My God, what would he do? Hopper set the sights on the man's chest and waited for the word from Summers that he hoped would never come. His temples throbbed and he tried swallowing, but his throat was too dry. Hopper's finger tightened on the trigger. The man on the raft began to speak.[33]

CHAPTER SIX

# POWs, Convoy HI 72,
# and ULTRA

The mysterious beings floating on life rafts in the middle of the South China Sea had gone down a hellish road to end up in this predicament. They were not Japanese, but British and Australian. Their ordeal began in February 1942 with the fall of Singapore, an event that Prime Minister Winston Churchill called "the greatest disaster and capitulation in British history." Conversely, it was the greatest land victory in Japanese history. In one swoop, 130,000 men surrendered to the Japanese.

In 1929, ideas about the humane treatment of prisoners of war had been advanced by the Red Cross at Geneva, Switzerland. Japan, along with forty other nations, signed the accords, but its home government never ratified the convention's stance on POWs. In 1941, General and Prime Minister Hideki Tojo sent strict orders to the heads of the prison camps: they must not succumb to mistaken ideas of humanitarianism. Treatment of the captives was at the discretion of the local army commanders, much as the disposition of prisoners was left to the discretion of the U.S. Navy submarine commanders. The Japanese, faced with a labor shortage for the growing needs of the Greater East Asia Co-Prosperity Sphere, quickly found a use for their prisoners. Once the Imperial Army swept across Thailand and into Burma, additional supply lines were needed. What better way to save twelve hundred miles of sailing around the Malay Peninsula than to have those prisoners of war build a railroad?[1]

The track, which was to connect Bangkok to Rangoon, was begun in October 1942 by three thousand Australian prisoners working east from Burma and a similar number of British working west from Siam. The job brought misery and death, for the line traversed some of the most hostile terrain imaginable, including mountains, malaria-ridden swamps, ravines, and rivers. It was the worst jungle in the world apart from the Amazon Basin. And the POWs had little choice. "No work, no food," declared Prime Minister Tojo.

At construction's peak, perhaps sixty thousand prisoners and two hundred thousand *romusha*—Malay, Chinese, Burmese, and Javanese laborers—worked on the "Death Railway." Hundreds of thousands of tons of earth were moved, carried a basket at a time, to build railroad embankments over the swamps. Thousands of logs were felled, hewn, and measured to build innumerable bridges over chasms and rivers. About thirteen thousand prisoners and perhaps ninety thousand natives died because of brutal taskmasters, sadistic guards, inadequate food, and diseases.

In November 1943 the railway was opened. Over 150 million cubic feet of earth had been moved and nine miles of bridges built. The most famous span, immortalized in a book by Pierre Boulle, from which was made the movie *The Bridge on the River Kwai*, was actually built across the Mae Klong near the POW camp at Tamarkan, Thailand. In reality it was a minor operation that took about two months in the spring of 1943. In April 1945 the Allies bombed the bridge to pieces. It was said that the railway cost one life for every sleeper (railroad tie) laid down. After the war, the British sold the railroad to the Thais for six million dollars. Most of the track in the border area was torn up, and the sleepers were used for firewood or housing. Today, the line runs about sixty miles into the jungle and stops—the apotheosis of "utter futility," according to one former POW. In the end, the railroad, the suffering, and the death were all pointless.

After the railway was completed, ten thousand of the most "fit" remaining POWs were selected to be shipped to Japan. The Britons who had done a major share of the building of the famous bridge left their camp as defiantly as they had arrived. After much bowing and official ceremony, they marched off, singing the insultingly obscene words of "Colonel Bogey's March" to the uncomprehending Japanese.[2]

While awaiting transportation to Japan, old railway plagues returned in the forms of beriberi, pellagra, cholera, dengue and blackwater fevers, malaria, and tropical ulcers. C. "Andy" Anderson, Lance Corporal in the Fifth Bedfordshire and Hertfordshire Regiment of the British Army, worked on the Singapore docks for four months before shipping was available. Harry Jones, a twenty-eight-year-old sergeant in the Royal Signal Corps, was eager to go. He believed that somewhere, even at sea, he would be able to make his escape.

To supplement their meager rations, many POWs who worked on the docks became adept at robbery. Thomas Smith, a twenty-three-year-old former haberdasher, and now a private in the 125th Anti-tank Regiment of the Royal Artillery, participated in a cigarette heist. He and his mates smashed open some crates and stashed their clothes full of the valuable smokes. The guards discovered them. Smith got away, but several were caught and severely beaten and had their rations cut for punishment.[3]

K. C. Renton, a private in the 2/2 Pioneer Battalion, Australian Imperial Force (AIF), was taken prisoner on Java. A high point of his captivity was the Christmas dinner served after completing the railway—rice and radishes—which elicited the comment, "Oh boy, what a feed!" Selected as one of the "fit" men to go to Japan, Renton was first taken to Saigon, where he spent three more months working on the wharves before being sent back to Singapore.[4]

Ken Williams was already thirty-six years old and had a wife and two children when he joined the AIF in 1940. Captured in the massive surrender of Singapore, Williams and hundreds of his mates were packed aboard the *Celebes Maru* and shipped to Mergui, Burma. It was his first experience on a Japanese "hell ship."

Williams called working on the railway sixteen months of "one of the grimmest tragedies man could witness." They ate rice and more rice, some limed to keep out weevils; when boiled, it tasted like glue. "In Australia, you would not have fed it to the pigs," he said.

After the railway was finished, Williams was given clean clothes and forced to sing for what he called "a propaganda farce." The Japanese filmed them whistling while they worked. But as the cameras rolled, the defiant Aussies sang out in what Williams called, "an unprintable parody of 'Bless 'em All.'" When the Japanese learned what was being sung, they gave the men more bashings and forced them to sing a more recognizable version of "Tipperary."[5]

Cliff L. Farlow, corporal in the 2/19 Battalion, AIF, was born in Sydney in April 1922. Cliff left high school at age fourteen to milk cows and work on his father's farm. When he turned eighteen, he joined the army. "In those days you joined up because you had a cause and believed in your history," he said, "and I still do."

Like Williams, Farlow worked the railway with three thousand other Australians in "A Force." After the task was complete, he was allowed to bathe in the Kwai Noi, not far from the bridge later to become famous. He then went by rail to Bangkok and by river to Saigon, where he worked on the wharves.

Harold D. "Curly" Martin, of the 2/10 Field Ordinance, AIF, sarcastically said that he was lucky to go directly to Burma after being captured, so he never had the chance to "get soft" in the Changi, Singapore, prison camp. The thing he remembered most was how the prisoners tried to trick the guards—for example, by shortening the rows of pegs the Japanese had staked out to show how much dirt the men had to dig in one day.

Tricks were fine, but there was no escaping the sickness brought on by overwork, lack of medicine, and poor food. Said Martin: "Each worker would take with him in the morning, cooked rice molded into a lump about the size of a tennis ball." However, he added, if natives were working nearby, "we would usually be surrounded at lunch time by starving kids and would end up giving the rice balls to them. What else could we do?"[6]

The time the Australians spent in Saigon was one of the few "bright" spots of their captivity. The POWs made contact with some natives and were able to obtain a few bottles of rice wine. Thirty-year-old Alfred D. Winter, a private in the 2/4 Battalion, AIF, said that everybody had "a whale of a time singing and dancing." In their malnourished, weakened condition, the wine hit them like a pile driver. When the guards inquired what the problem was, Winter replied, "Malaria."

Roydon C. Cornford, from New South Wales, Australia, was a private in the 2/19 Battalion, AIF. Cornford had been chosen to go to Japan, and he was issued his first clothing in two years; a Dutch army shirt, shorts, Japanese T-shirt, and split-toed rubber sandals. In April 1944, Cornford's group went to the Mekong River to a large, new-looking freighter. However, the captain decided he would not be responsible for the lives of so many men if his ship was torpedoed, and he refused to sail. The next morning they were all herded back to Saigon, where the opportunities for thieving were limitless. Roy celebrated his twenty-second birthday on 24 May, when his mate swiped a can of condensed milk from under the nose of a Japanese guard who was in the middle of a lecture about why the Australians should stop their stealing.

M. Robert "Bob" Farrands, a former auto mechanic and now a corporal in the 2/19 Battalion, AIF, had spent his twenty-first birthday working on the railroad at 105 Kilo Camp. In Saigon one year later, Farrands thought they would all be shipped to Japan, but a friendly guard told him that their column was too large, and "too many ships were being sunk as they left Saigon." Instead, they would all have to be sent by rail back to Singapore.

Reginald J. Harris and Ronald C. Miscamble, both twenty-seven-year-old gunners in the 2/10 Field Regiment, Royal Australian Artillery (RAA), were assigned to a Saigon airfield. While they thought about sabotaging planes, they actually found the Japanese airmen quite sympathetic to their plight. They felt sorry for them because they were so thin, said Harris. "They gave us food and cigarettes."

William H. "Mac" McKittrick was born in England and was a merchant seamen before emigrating to New South Wales, Australia. Now a twenty-seven-year-old private in the 2/12 Field Company, Royal Australian Engineers (RAE), Mac got the relatively easy assignment of painting a Japanese colonel's house. Every morning a Free Frenchman would drive by on his bicycle and slip McKittrick a package with cigarettes, money, or war news. Once he took McKittrick's canteen and returned it brimming with red wine. The POWs took their food and drink from whatever source was handy.[7]

In June 1944 the "good life" in Saigon was over, and the prisoners were hauled back to Singapore. While backtracking to Phnom Penh, Sergeant William D. Cuneen, Thirteenth Battalion, 4 Anti-tank Regiment, AIF, made a tense contact with an Allied agent. The twenty-eight-year-old former farmer, now camp cook, was approached by the man right under the watchful eyes of the Japanese guards. The agent passed him medicine and war news: Normandy and Saipan had been invaded. The agent wanted to know who was in the POW party and where they were headed. Brigadier General Arthur L. Varley, with Cuneen, passed the man a list of the POWs written on a roll of toilet paper. The agent moved away, and the train continued on its journey.

As they passed through Bangkok and turned south down the Malay peninsula, the POWs learned that the country had been devastated economically, and the natives were nearly as destitute as the POWs. Roy Cornford said that Bangkok had been badly damaged by Allied air raids, and the coolies threw stones at them, blaming them for the extra work they had to do to repair the railroad. In Kuala Lumpur, POWs gave the natives rice in exchange for fruit. On 4 July 1944, America's Independence Day, the train finally reached Singapore.

Singapore was a poor place compared to Saigon, and the Australians joining the British already there only exacerbated a bad situation. There was not enough food, and those who had regained their strength began to fall ill again. Most of the POWs were assigned to work on the docks, where they learned from the Chinese and Malay coolies that few ships were available because the "Americana boom-boom" destroyed them at sea.

Finally, on 4 September the men were herded to the docks. Roy Cornford saw thousands of Red Cross parcels, and the Japanese distributed a portion of them. They got their first mail in years, and Cornford was thrilled to get five letters. They were to embark on some of the same ships they had been loading with tin, rubber, copra, and scrap iron during the past few days. Said Ken Williams, "Many Japs told us we would finish up as 'fish *makan* [food],' which was quite a nice send off."

It was grim humor, but true. American submarines had already taken such a toll of the Japanese merchant marine that it was said a person could walk on periscopes from Singapore to Japan without getting his feet wet. As the POWs boarded, many were relieved of their last few possessions. While most were destitute, some still managed to hide away the fruits of their labors. Harry Pickett, a twenty-eight-year-old former musician, now a signalman in the 2/4 Battalion, AIF, had saved several hundred piasters. He and his mates had found a way to cut up mosquito netting and make it into ersatz shorts to sell to the natives.

Britisher Charles A. Perry, a former cabinetmaker thirty-one years of age, now in the 125th Anti-tank Regiment of the Royal Artillery, had been assigned to a work party that was burning huge piles of Malayan paper money. Perry hid a stack, which he had heretofore considered as "play" money. Upon reaching Singapore, he discovered that his fifteen thousand dollars in Malayan currency, which he had tucked away in his haversack, was still good.

Another former cabinetmaker and now infantry private in the AIF, twenty-three-year-old Frank J. Coombes, had a small but valuable stash; diamond earrings and bracelets that he had "liberated" from a store in Singapore during the last days of chaos before the surrender. He kept his treasure hidden inside a money belt.

As they boarded the ships, the coolies cautioned them. Sergeant Harry Jones was told that he should live for today, for tomorrow he would be dead. Strangely enough, Jones was encouraged by all the talk of doom, for he believed it implied the Allies had intelligence on the convoy, that they would try to destroy it, and that it would open a way for him to escape. Britisher Tommy Smith, after his successful cigarette robbery, decided to take the advice of the doomsayers. "We had a glorious time smoking up everything we had," he said. Unfortunately, during the ensuing trip they had to scrounge cigarettes from the Australians.

One of the last things each POW was required to do was to haul aboard a thirty-pound block of rubber with a handle attached. These, they were told, were "life preservers." Charles Perry didn't believe it; it was just a clever way to carry more raw materials to Japan. Bob Farrands never trusted the Japanese or the rubber. He said, "I was lucky enough to find a life jacket that I wore all the time."[8]

The convoy, as K. C. Renton remembered it, consisted of eleven ships. According to Roy Cornford, there were ten: two transports, two cargo ships, two oil tankers, and four escorts. Their estimates were very close, for intercepted Japanese messages indicate that at least that number of ships had assembled in Singapore for the long run north through the China Seas. The convoy was designated as HI 72. Some of those same intercepted messages revealed the names of the ships, the destinations, the cargoes, and the estimated daily noontime positions to the interested American eavesdroppers. *Asaka Maru* was a 7,400-ton armed merchant cruiser that carried a cargo of bauxite and 593 passengers; its destination was Moji in the empire. *Shincho Maru,* which carried 573 passengers and a load of fuel oil, was also bound for Moji.[9] *Nankai Maru* was an 8,416-ton transport loaded with bauxite and aviation gas and headed for Miike.

*Zuiho Maru* was a civilian-owned tanker of 5,135 tons loaded with aviation gas and oil and bound for Takao, Formosa. *Kimikawa Maru* was a 6,863-ton seaplane tender that was carrying bauxite, aviation gas, and 273 passengers for Osaka.

Two of the ships at the quay were large passenger-cargo vessels. *Rakuyo Maru* was built by the Mitsubishi Shipbuilding Company in Nagasaki and launched in 1921. She was 477 feet long, displaced 9,418 tons, and was loaded with bauxite and with 601 British, 716 Australians, and one American, Colonel Harry R. Melton, Jr., of the U.S. Army Air Forces. Its destination was Yokohama. Cliff Farlow called it "a dirty, disgraceful looking ship."[10]

Next to *Rakuyo Maru* was the 10,509-ton *Kachidoki Maru*, a ship with a more storied past. She was also built in 1921, but at the Camden, New Jersey, yard of the New York Shipbuilding Company. Originally named *Wolverine State*, she had made only a few trips for the Pacific Mail Steamship Company when she was sold in 1923 to the Dollar Lines for around-the-world service and was renamed *President Harrison*. In 1930 she was reconfigured to her present design, a 524-foot-long ship with well decks, masts, and cranes fore and aft and a central passenger area with a single stack. In 1938 the American President Line bought out the Dollar Line.

As the Pacific war progressed, four of the "presidents" were converted to hospital ships, and two others were lost to groundings. *President Harrison* was on a mission to Chinwangtao, China, to evacuate about two hundred embassy and legation guards from Peking and Tientsin. On 8 December 1941 she was located by Japanese planes and ships. Rather than surrender, the ship's master tried to run her aground on a small island off the coast from Shanghai. Racing at her top speed of fourteen knots, the ship tore a ninety-foot gash in her bottom, but she did not sink. She was patched and towed to Shanghai. Two months later *President Harrison* became *Kakko Maru*, and she was later renamed *Kachidoki Maru*, flying the red and white ensign of the Japanese merchant fleet. Over the next two years she served the Japanese well as the largest American ship ever to fall into enemy hands.[11]

Providing escort for these valuable ships and cargoes were the destroyer *Shikinami;* the frigate *Hirado*, flagship of the commander of Escort Number Six, Rear Admiral Sadamichi Kajioka; the frigates *Mikura* and *Kurahashi, Coast Defense Vessel No. 11,* and *Subchaser No. 19.*[12]

On 4 September, *Kachidoki Maru* was the flagship of the No. 16 Maritime Transportation Command. It was also packed with 900 British prisoners, making a total of 2,218 POWs aboard *Kachidoki Maru* and *Rakuyo Maru*. The prisoners suffered another thirty-six hours down in the dark, hot bowels of the ships before finally getting underway. The Australians would not stand for the cramped quarters. As Bob Farrands went down the stairs, he read an English sign that said the space was designed for 180 third-class passengers, and, said Bob, "they wanted to put 1,315 of us in the hold." Men broke into open revolt and forced their way topside. In order to prevent a possibly deadly confrontation, the Japanese captain agreed to allow, in Farrand's estimation, "about 200 men on deck, which soon tripled." The captain addressed them in English. As long as they behaved, they would be treated well. Farrands remembered his words: "All prisoners not doing what they were told will from now on not be treated as guests of the Japanese people." The POWs thought that was pretty funny. The captain told them there was nothing to worry about, for he had already made eighteen successful trips from Singapore to Japan. At that point, Farrands said, "some wag amongst us yelled out that Ajax, a successful Sydney racehorse, won eighteen straight, and went down on the nineteenth." The men on deck roared in laughter, but the captain was not amused. On 6 September the convoy moved slowly out of the roadstead and headed north into the South China Sea.

Although some men were allowed topside, most were forced deep into the cargo holds. It was then that the Japanese prisoner transports truly earned their appellations as "hell ships." The men became hungry and thirsty as they sweltered in the outside sun or baked below the steel decks. Those with sleeping accommodations were stacked in layers three feet above one another. Many had to sit cross-legged for the duration of the voyage. Toilet facilities were ludicrous. On *Rakuyo Maru* there were six small wooden platforms, called benjos, lashed outboard off the edge of the deck. The exposed seats with difficult access and constant lines made it excruciating for the many men with dysentery.

On the first day of travel, Convoy HI 72 headed due north along the Malayan coast, averaging eleven to twelve knots and covering about 280 miles. By noon of 7 September it was about 150 miles east of Kota Bharu on the Malay Peninsula. On the *Rakuyo Maru*, Bill Cuneen was selected as a cook. He worked in a shack built on the stern and had only two pots. It was nearly impossible for him to make even a cupful of rice for each of the 1,318 prisoners. Billeted aft, near Cuneen, was a covey of Japanese prostitutes called "jig-a-jig" girls. Cuneen kept his distance but could authoritatively tell the men that the girls "wore no underpants."

In the middle of the mouth of the Gulf of Siam, HI 72 altered course to the northeast so that by noon on 8 September it was off the southern tip of French Indochina (Vietnam) and just west of the Poulo Condore Islands (Con Son Islands). By the next day, conforming to the bulge of the Indochina coast, the convoy was closing Cam Ranh Bay. After several days at sea, the men became so gamy they could barely stand their own stench. They pleaded to be allowed to wash, and permission was granted for them to hose down with the topside saltwater pumps. As hundreds of them washed naked on the open deck, the jig-a-jig girls watched, giggled, and teased. Roy Cornford, trying to scrub away his grime, noticed some of the girls laughing, "with some holding their hands apart to show what size they saw." To the men, deprived of so many "necessities" for the past years, the teasing women were another torture.

On 10 September, one problem was temporarily alleviated as an afternoon thunderstorm dumped rain on the convoy, now two hundred miles from shore and angling northeast into the vastness of the South China Sea. The men on decks danced for joy, holding their mouths and canteens wide open, enjoying the largesse from heaven. But even this was short-lived. After dark the rain turned to a cold drizzle, and those topside shivered in a chilled, wet misery.[13]

On 11 September, about one hundred miles northeast of the Paracel Islands, they were joined by three ships from Manila, from a convoy designated MAMO 03. This convoy had left Manila on 10 September under the escort of *Coast Defense Vessels No. 10* and *No. 20* and *Minesweeper No. 21*. As the convoys met, the three escorts turned back to Manila. One of the three ships joining HI 72 was *Kagu Maru,* a 6,800-ton seaplane tender and sister ship of *Kimikawa Maru.* The second ship was the 9,574-ton army landing ship *Kibitsu Maru,* and the third was *Gokoku Maru,* a 10,038-ton armed merchant cruiser.[14] The convoy reconfigured, with the tankers moving to the center of three columns. *Rakuyo Maru* shifted to the rear of the starboard column, the destroyer *Shikinami* was in the van, and the frigates and patrol boats took position on the flanks. Harold Martin thought there were fifteen ships in three columns of five. One Japanese speaking in fair English told him that there would be nothing to worry about, because they were in a fast convoy, and American submarines could not keep up with them. Others were not so sanguine. On *Kachidoki Maru*, men heard one Japanese joke, "This is the day we sink."

During the night of 11 September, many of the POWs were up and restless. Roused out of a sound sleep, Bill Cuneen was told by the guards that someone had stolen some sugar. He had to remain awake to watch the sugar bags. The culprits were Alf Winter and his mate, Walter V. Winter (no kin), also a private in the 2/4 Machine Gun Battalion, AIF. They broke into storage, took a forty-pound bag of sugar, distributed some, and gulped the rest down raw. On another foray, Reg Harris and Ron Miscamble went to the cook shack to see what they could steal, but they ran into the aroused Japanese guards. Miscamble broke free and hid, but Harris was too slow and got smashed by a rifle for his troubles.

By midnight the POWs on *Rakuyo Maru* calmed down and fell into a fitful sleep. However, about 0200, 12 September, their sleep was shattered by a flash and an explosion. Bill Cuneen was startled by an escort ship, which went charging by with its lights blinking. Suddenly it exploded and disappeared. Hilton G. "Harry" Weigand, a thirty-five-year-old sapper in the 2/12 Field Company, RAE, was sleeping on deck by the No. 3 Hold when a terrific explosion on the starboard side woke him with a jolt. By the time he got to the railing, he saw the mainmast of the escort, which was "burning like the devil and sinking fast." The guards and the crew panicked. The ship's forward gun fired a flare that landed on the far side of the escort, but no one could see any submarine. Britisher George K. "Dagger" Ward, a private in Fifth Battalion, Sherwood Foresters, was a coal miner who had been evacuated from the beaches at Dunkirk in 1940. Ward thought the torpedoed victim was a large warship: "The first thing we saw was a Jap cruiser hit amidships by a torpedo. What a lovely sight. It simply snapped in two then sank." The burning escort was the frigate *Hirado*, torpedoed by *Growler.*

Harry Pickett was dozing under a pile of bags near *Rakuyo Maru*'s bow. His mate kicked him awake when he heard the explosion. They went to the rail to see what looked like a destroyer on fire. Suddenly Pickett was grabbed by a Japanese guard. He thought the man might lose his head and throw him over the side, yet strangely enough, the guard just tightened Pickett's life jacket and walked away. Harry Jones was with another group of men standing at the railing, cheering the sinking as if they were at a football game. Stuck down in the hold, English gunner Douglas A. Cresswell of the 148th Field Regiment, Royal Artillery, thought it was wonderful knowing the Allies were out there, yet he hoped another torpedo wouldn't kill them all like rats trapped inside the ship. Finally the crew and guards came to their senses and tried to drive the rest of the topside prisoners down into the holds.

On *Kachidoki Maru,* most of the men were sealed below decks and could not see the sinking. Yet they knew something was happening, for their ship made a radical course change, running from imagined torpedo wakes. Zigzagging wildly in the darkness, *Kachidoki Maru* struck another fleeing ship almost bow to bow. They scraped and rumbled along their full lengths before separating. The men in the hold felt like they had heeled over forty-five degrees before righting. They never knew exactly what had happened, and it was another hour before they calmed down enough to fall back to sleep.[15]

The sun was just rising, and the POWs assumed they had made it safely through the night when *Sealion*'s torpedoes struck *Nankai Maru* and *Rakuyo Maru.* Those who had been cheering when *Hirado* blew up quickly changed their tune. *Nankai Maru* was first. Torpedoes slammed into the No. 3 and No. 6 Holds, the latter of which carried a full load of drummed aviation gas. Fires spread, but the ship stayed up for three hours before sinking with 199 men. Also lost were sixty-five hundred tons of bauxite, four thousand drums of gasoline, 170 tons of oil, and seventy-seven packages of mail.

The first torpedo to hit *Rakuyo Maru* penetrated the No. 1 Hold, which was filled with rubber, and the second one smashed directly into the engine room. The bow hit bent the plates so severely that the front end dug into the sea like a snow plow, cascading water across the decks and into the forward hatches. There was instant hysteria. The POWs tore at each other to be the first up the ladders.

Harry Weigand was sleeping by the hatch to No. 3 Hold when the impact of the explosions threw him up against a winch, gashing open his leg. A great wave of water came up over the forecastle, and Weigand had to hang on for dear life to keep himself from being washed overboard. Bob Farrands found himself riding a tidal wave and getting flattened against the steel deck. He grabbed a winch as the water rushed by, then ran to the hold to help evacuate those below.

Harry Pickett saw a Japanese gun crew get blown over the side, then fought against the water that came up as deep as his chest. Bill Cuneen didn't know if he was still on board or had been washed to sea. John R. Hocking, a corporal in the 2/2 Pioneers, said that down in the hold the torpedoes "sounded like steam trains coming out of a tunnel." One hit amidships, and one forward. Had the forward torpedo hit about thirty feet farther aft, it would have entered No. 2 Hold and killed hundreds of POWs. Harry Smethurst, twenty-three-year-old private in the Royal Army Ordnance Corps, instantly knew what had happened. "Everybody was shouting, 'Let me get out,'" he said, as they all ran for the ladder.[16]

There was chaos aboard the ship. Immediately the Japanese took to the lifeboats, kicking out any prisoners who attempted to join them. Some of the POWs used the opportunity to take out two and one-half years of captivity on their guards. Harry Smethurst said that "one big bloke picked up a sword and chopped up about six Japs. He just went berserk." Harry Jones saw a dozen POWs attack and kill the bow deck gun crew. Bill Cuneen saw another man bashing some Japanese with a two-by-four piece of timber. He applauded as a few other mates tossed the semiconscious Japanese over the side. Reginald S. Stewart, twenty-one-year-old gunner in the 4 Anti-tank Regiment, was looking for a life jacket when he saw three Japanese soldiers steal the life jackets from a like number of prostitutes. Stewart and other prisoners quickly found some metal angle irons, beat the soldiers, and relieved them of the jackets. Cliff Farlow remembered a man named McGregor who was about to go over the side but decided that he would go back and kill some Japanese first. He picked up an iron bar and headed toward the bridge. Farlow never saw him again.

Many of the first men overboard had jumped without any flotation devices. Denny Smith, a twenty-four-year-old in the Royal Northumberland Fusileers, realized that the ship was not going down immediately. He stayed on board for a while to prepare himself, and as he helped other men toss debris over the side that might help them stay afloat, he saw a number of objects hit and kill men who were still bobbing close by the side of the ship. Harry Jones didn't jump recklessly, either. He made his way to the radio shack to see if he could get a message out, but the radio had been smashed. In the captain's cabin, Jones found several other POWs calmly sitting down and helping themselves to the captain's food and cigarettes.

Charles Perry managed to push his way onto one of the first rafts he found. Suddenly he remembered about his fifteen thousand dollars in Malayan currency. He thought someone might steal it, so he had given it to a Lieutenant Keyes to hold for him, but the lieutenant was gone. Another man who jumped early, Alf Winter, nearly broke his neck when his kapok life jacket slammed against his chin when he hit the water. Since the ship didn't go down immediately, Winter decided to return to look for some drinking water. He found six canteens and was able to bring them back to his raft.

Bob Farrands found a wooden "raft" about six feet square and eight inches thick with rope hooks around the circumference. He threw it overboard and jumped behind it. "Down I went," he said. "I thought I would never come up." And the worst part was, "I lost my hat." Frank Coombes found a hatch cover to climb on, which he paddled about "like a surfboard." He felt for his money belt and found that it was still safely buckled around his waist. A Japanese officer tried to climb aboard a nearby raft. "One of the blokes," said Coombes, "called him over and pushed him under and held him down." Britishers Tommy Smith; Thomas Taylor, a private in the Eighteenth Reconnaissance Corps; and Jesse Harrison, a private in the First Battalion, Leicestershire Regiment, all thought it was too dark to rush into the sea. They found a raft on the sun deck, collected some canteens and life jackets, found a half of a coconut, and calmly launched the raft. Denny Smith managed to team up with a few mates, one of them being F. E. "Curly" Wiles, a former prizefighter from London and now a private in the Fifth Battalion, Bedfordshire and Hertfordshire Regiment. They found one of the portable benjos floating by and climbed aboard, sailing the China Sea on an outhouse.[17]

More than one thousand men may have abandoned ship by the time *Growler*'s torpedoes struck *Shikinami* just before 0700. Those fortunate to have been in lifeboats or on rafts gave a hearty three cheers when the destroyer exploded. Those in the water were not so lucky. *Shikinami*'s tremendous disintegration, quickly followed by its depth charges going off, caused brutal shock waves through the sea. "It was like someone kicking you in the stomach," said Reg Harris. Others described it like an electric shock down the spine or like a mule kick. The results ranged from internal injuries to death. Blood vessels burst, and bowels emptied. Frank Coombes said, "I saw many men vomiting blood." Donald F. McArdle, who had been a trainer of racing greyhounds, was now a corporal in the 2/29 Battalion, AIF. McArdle and Ron Miscamble were both severely injured by the blast. McArdle felt a whack in his guts and then a strange trickling inside as blood vessels burst in his stomach. Miscamble came up vomiting and bleeding from the ears. He believed he would have drowned if Reg Harris hadn't held him up for an hour. Roy Cornford, who had drunk as much water as he could before going overboard, now lost it all when the concussion squeezed it all back out of his stomach. It was quite an opening act for the coming ordeal.[18]

Although a good number of people had jumped overboard, many realized *Rakuyo Maru* was not going down immediately. The ship righted itself. There was no fire, and no further explosions, and the men commenced a more orderly evacuation. Some of them returned to try to salvage items that would increase their chances of survival: canteens of water, food, life jackets, bamboo, deck chairs, anything that might float. They quickly found out that when the rubber "life preservers" hit the water, they sank like a stone.

The Japanese were too busy saving themselves to be concerned about the prisoners, although there were cases of murder on each side. In the water, some POWs were allowed into the boats with the Japanese but were forced to row. Other boats refused to allow any POWs on board. Since the Japanese had abandoned the ship first, the remaining men on board saw no reason to rush to judgment. About 1820, thirteen hours after she was torpedoed, *Rakuyo Maru* finally slid to the bottom more than one mile below. Only nine of her crewmen were lost. There were about twelve hundred British and Australians in the water.

The frigate *Kurahashi* had been busy picking up survivors of *Hirado* since early in the morning. While so engaged, HI 72 sped off to the northwest, only to be hit by *Sealion II* and *Growler* once again. This time *Mikura* tried to hold down the submarines while the convoy altered course to the west. At 0920, after realizing two ships had gone down and a third was likely to follow, *Mikura* radioed to the commander of No. 16 Maritime Transport Command on *Kachidoki Maru* that she needed help. *Kurahashi* was told to hurry its rescue of the *Hirado* survivors and head to the next disaster scene. *Kagu Maru* was also detached to assist the two frigates.

*Mikura* hove to, picking up her countrymen. Later, *Kagu Maru* arrived, and finally, about 1600, *Kurahashi* came on the scene. The POWs who tried to climb aboard were kicked or clubbed back into the water. A Japanese officer on *Mikura* called in English to the POWs that they must not come near the ship or they would be shot. Andy Anderson explained: "We took to the rafts and hoped to be picked up by our friends, the dirty yellow devils, but no hope. They were only concerned about their own race of animals." The Japanese, said Ken Williams, "had the cheek to wave as they left us behind." On one raft, when the men realized the escorts were not rescuing any prisoners, they sat on a lone Japanese and held his mouth shut. When the frigates left, the POWs beat their captive to death. A Britisher commented, "Some of the men were already dying of thirst. They drank his blood. It was horrible."

At 1900 *Mikura* radioed to *Kachidoki Maru* that it had rescued everyone it could: eight officers and 120 men from *Shikinami;* 360 men plus the captain off *Nankai Maru;* and 230 men, including the ship's master, from *Rakuyo Maru*. In addition, 90 men from *Hirado* were rescued by *Kurahashi*. Concluding the operation, the Japanese carried out one last act of vitriolic meanness; the frigates tore back through the center of the floating survivors, chopping up some in their propellers and drowning others. Dagger Ward thought they were a bunch of rotten bastards. It was a last straw for many men. "A lot of the boys," said Harry Weigand, "died about an hour after the ships left us." It was as if they had lost the will to live. Some succumbed to their injuries, but others just gave up hope and slid off their rafts and disappeared. Yet when darkness fell that first night, there were still a number of men with spirit enough to sing out in a throaty chorus of, "Rule Britannia."[19]

On the night of 12 September 1944, the remnants of HI 72 must have thought they had escaped the submarines that had attacked them earlier in the day. In the confusion of *Sealion*'s and *Growler*'s attacks, *Asaka Maru,*

*Kibitsu Maru,* and *Gokoku Maru* headed off on a different tangent, first making for Takao, then changing course for Hainan. The main body of HI 72 now consisted of *Kachidoki Maru, Zuiho Maru, Shincho Maru, Kimikawa Maru, Coast Defense Vessel No. 11,* and *Subchaser No. 19.* The convoy reached its rendezvous point at 19 degrees north, 112 degrees east and made a turn to the north to confuse any stalking submarines. It was about to turn toward Yulin on the south coast of Hainan when more ships began exploding left and right, this time victims of *Pampanito.*

*Zuiho Maru* was able to send off a message: "Submarine certain. Torpedo attack, damage at 2250, 12th, in position 19-23 North, 111-50 East." *Zuiho Maru* suffered no casualties, but eight thousand tons of oil would be lost with her.

On *Kachidoki Maru,* things happened fast. On the bridge, three torpedo tracks were seen coming from the port side. A hard turn avoided all but one torpedo, which struck the No. 7 Hold. Split seams along the waterline quickly filled holds six, seven and eight, and by 2310 the engines had flooded and stopped. Most of the nine hundred British POWs were in No. 2 Hold. The Japanese were on deck launching lifeboats and letting the POWs fend for themselves. The captain ordered abandon ship at 2315 and in twenty more minutes she was three-fourths underwater with a forty-degree list. At 2337, *Kachidoki Maru* heeled over to eighty degrees and slid beneath the waves. Six thousand tons of bauxite and the ashes of 582 Japanese war dead went to the bottom. Only twelve crewmen were lost, but 476 POWs and other passengers died.[20]

For the POWs who had made it off *Kachidoki Maru* and *Rakuyo Maru,* it was time to face a new enemy: the sea. The following days were a kaleidoscope of horror. The few lifeboats the POWs managed to secure were dangerously overcrowded. One boat of perhaps thirty to thirty-five men sailed away from the crowd, heading east toward the Philippines. They were never seen again.

Curly Martin found a section of a hatch cover fifteen feet long, one foot wide, and about three inches thick. Others found similar pieces, and they tied them together in a triangle with fasteners and strings from their kapok life jackets. They sat on the edges with their feet to the inside. As they found more planks and timbers, they made a floor and even constructed a makeshift mast with pieces of linen for a sail.

Ken Williams had waited on *Rakuyo Maru* until the last minute. When the starboard deck was going awash, he took some planking and dropped into the water. "Off I went on my four-day sail," he said. He teamed up Martin; Francis E. Farmer, a private in the 2/10 Battalion, AIF; and several others.

As the sun grew hotter, the suffering increased. Heads and faces were burned. Lips cracked and swelled. Those with canteens found that seawater had leaked into them. They became thirsty, ravenous, and exhausted from hanging on to their pitiful bits of flotsam. Roy Cornford considered himself lucky to have a hat and a Japanese T-shirt, and only his arms were badly burned. He saw a dead Japanese floating by with a canteen bobbing around his neck. His mates, Claude Longley and Darcy F. Lynch, warned him not to leave the raft, but Roy went after it. He got the canteen, but the cork was gone, and it was full of seawater. Then he realized he was too weak to swim back to the raft and almost drowned.

At dawn on 13 September the survivors tried to even the odds against them. They tied boats and rafts together when possible, distributed water and food, made token sails, patched oars together, and stretched out canvas in the hopes of catching a few drops of rain. The daily rations for one group measured one billiard-ball-sized lump of rice and two cigarette tins of water. James H. Lansdowne and Strachan M. White, privates in the 2/26 and 2/29 Battalions, AIF, respectively, noticed that a school of fish had collected beneath their raft. They tilted the raft into the water and used their toes as bait, wriggling them until several fish swam over the half-submerged raft. When they quickly tipped the raft up, two fish were caught high and dry. The men hungrily devoured them, but discovered they were so salty they only made them thirstier. Others gulped down seawater and began to go crazy, killing themselves or having to be killed by their comrades to prevent them from harming others.

It was dreadful to hear men talking to nonexistent parents, wives, and children, then "walk" off to pay them a visit and disappear under the waves. But at least there were no sharks. For some strange reason, perhaps because of the jellylike oil that covered the men and the ocean, the sharks stayed away.

By the third and fourth day in the water the survivors began to die by the hundreds, with thirst and despair being the main killers. Those still clinging to life were terribly burned and blinded by sun and oil; tongues and lips were swollen grotesquely. Grasping at any hope of relief, some tried drinking their own urine; it only seemed to make them go insane. Harry Pickett tried it and said, "it was horrible." Don McArdle and Reg Stewart tried to poke holes in dead men's necks to get some blood, but nothing came out. Two other men used penknives to cut into their own veins for blood and died for their efforts. Cannibalism was mentioned but never confirmed. There were perhaps three hundred still alive.[21]

While this was occurring, the three escorts that were detached from Convoy MAMO 03 and returning to Manila were notified of the disaster. *Coast Defense Vessel No. 10, Coast Defense Vessel No. 20,* and *Minesweeper No. 21* retraced their wakes and sped back to the point where HI 72 was first attacked. They arrived in the vicinity of the sinking of the *Rakuyo Maru* about 1045 on 14 September and, to the surprise of the desperate survivors, began to pick them up. *Coast Defense Vessel No. 10,* with a humane, English-speaking captain, hauled 157 men aboard. Some were clubbed by Japanese sailors, but they were fed hot biscuits soaked in a sweet, brandy-flavored liquid and generally treated kindly. It was the last group of POWs picked up by the Japanese. Another group of survivor boats nearby, containing the Australian Brigadier Varley and the American Colonel Melton, were never seen or heard from again. The captains of the *Coast Defense Vessel No. 20* and *Minesweeper No. 21* were apparently not so kind-hearted.[22]

What amount of luck and what amount of deliberate planning had brought about the Convoy HI 72 disaster? Unknown to the Japanese, their American adversaries were well aware of the convoy. Since before the Pearl Harbor attack, intelligence units had broken several Japanese codes. Two and one-half years later, there were few communications sent that were not being decoded.

Cracking Japanese codes had paved the way to a decisive American victory at the Battle of Midway in June 1942. In April 1943, intercepted messages revealed the flight plan of Admiral Isoroku Yamamoto, and P-38s were sent to shoot him down. Code breaking was used in small-scale tactics, as when the New Zealand corvettes *Kiwi* and *Moa* were sent to intercept the Japanese submarine *I-1* off Guadalcanal in the hope of capturing even more code books the *I-1* was known to be carrying.[23]

Radio intelligence involved intercepting radio messages, analyzing traffic, direction finding, translating intercepted signals, collating, and evaluating the material. The intelligence gained from the process was known simply as ULTRA or MAGIC, respectively from the British designation of it as "ultrasecret" and the Americans' reference to the codebreakers as "magicians." By whatever name, radio intelligence was a boon to the Allied war effort; General Douglas MacArthur believed it saved thousands of lives and shortened the war by two years.

The Japanese never remedied fundamental flaws in their communications security, perhaps under the impression that their codes were too complex and numerous to be broken. Major codes included JN 14, a four-digit naval code that revealed both small-scale and major fleet movements; JN 23, a five-digit code devoted to construction and launching of new warships; JN 25, the major five-digit fleet code, from which Yamamoto's flight plan was discerned; JN 36 and JN 37, Japanese meteorological ciphers; JMA, the military attaché code; KA KA KA, the Japanese army field code; CORAL, the naval attaché machine cipher; and PURPLE, the machine cipher of diplomatic traffic broken well before Pearl Harbor. The Imperial Navy might use up to twenty-four codes at one time, while the Japanese army used another thirty or more. Luckily for the Allies however, the maxim appears true which states that human ingenuity cannot concoct a code that it cannot also resolve.[24]

Perhaps most significant for the U.S. submarine effort was the cracking of the Japanese Water Transport Code and JN 40, a merchant shipping code of four-syllable kana groups. The former gave detailed information about Japanese army shipping, while the latter, also called the "*Maru*" code, was the prime source of information for the merchant marine convoys.

Breaking JN 40 allowed the Allies to plot Japanese convoy routes from their positions, which the merchant skippers would obligingly transmit at 0800 and 2000 every day. Before that time, broken naval codes allowed the occasional routing of submarines against major warships, with unsatisfactory results. Cracking the "*Maru*" code enabled submarines to be sent against slower, poorly escorted convoys and thus hiked the sinking tonnage in 1944 up to a quarter of a million tons per month. It was impossible for the Japanese shipbuilding industry to overcome this attrition rate.

Surprisingly, the "*Maru*" code even helped the U.S. Navy to solve its own torpedo problems. Even before the submarine skippers turned in their patrol reports complaining of defective torpedoes, the radio eavesdroppers learned of failed attacks by listening to the Japanese telling of American torpedoes that bounced harmlessly off the sides of their ships. The Bureau of Ordnance, at first blaming reported torpedo failures on the inadequacies of the submarine crews, could not fail to heed this firsthand evidence.[25]

By the summer of 1943 the Joint Intelligence Center, Pacific Ocean Areas (JICPOA) was established to collect worldwide intelligence source materials. Radio traffic was compiled daily, and summaries were made nightly. By the summer of 1944 the operation was a functioning, well-oiled machine, run like a large newspaper. It was said that death was the only excuse for not getting out a daily intelligence product.[26]

Seldom could Japanese ships sail without intelligence knowing about it. Convoy HI 72 was no exception. The first characteristic that would single it out for closer attention was its size. Even early in the war, with all their merchant shipping intact, the Japanese never assembled convoys in the numbers that the Allies would routinely gather. The 1941 invasion of the Philippines at Lingayen Gulf consisted of eighty-four ships—what one seaman considered to have been the largest convoy of the war. In contrast, the 1944 American landing on Saipan, Operation Forager, used 535 ships, and in 1945, Operation Iceberg, the invasion of Okinawa, saw the assembly of 1,200 ships.[27] The Japanese were never again able to muster the amount of shipping that they used in the first six months of the war.

One of the reasons Japan had convoy problems was that it never had enough escorts to protect them. Early in the war, many merchant ships sailed alone and unescorted. The small number of American submarines and the poor performance of their torpedoes may have given the Japanese a false sense of security. In April 1942 the first Maritime Protection Units were created. The First Escort Unit had ten old destroyers, two torpedo boats, and five converted gunboats to protect shipping that stretched from Japan to Singapore. The Second Escort Unit protected the lanes from Tokyo to Truk, over two thousand miles, with four old destroyers, one torpedo boat, and two converted gunboats.

Allied planners calculated escort-to-ship ratios by using the formula $X = M/10 + 3$, where $X$ equals the number of escorts needed and $M$ the number of merchantmen in a convoy. Without air cover, twice the number of escorts was required. The Allies had once assembled a convoy of 164 ships, but 100 ships was an average. For a 100-ship convoy, the formula indicated that 13 escorts should provide adequate protection with air cover and 26 without air cover. Therefore, the number of escorts in an average Allied convoy would outnumber the total number of ships in most Japanese convoys. It took more escorts to protect a large number of small convoys than it did to protect a small number of large convoys, but apparently the Japanese were never able to understand the economies of size.[28]

The important *Take* Convoy No. 1 carrying the Imperial Army's Thirty-second and Thirty-fifth Infantry Divisions to New Guinea in April–May 1944 left Shanghai with nine transports and six escorts. It lost one ship on the way to Manila, but there it picked up another escort. Even so, the eight ships and seven escorts were attacked again, and three more ships were lost. The Japanese had the right idea—the number of escorts provided should have been sufficient—but they were still frustrated by having no unified escort tactics; by poor, old, slow escorts; and by radio communications that were open to the American codebreakers. Increasing the number of escorts could not overcome these shortcomings.[29]

The list of ULTRA-directed sinkings is large. In 1943 in the waters off New Guinea, General George C. Kenney's Fifth Air Force bombers teamed up with the submarines USS *Argonaut* (SS 166) and USS *Grampus* (SS 207) to sink four ships. USS *Triton* (SS 201) sank one army troop transport and damaged another. In March 1943, Kenney's bombers obliterated the sixteen-ship Convoy No. 81 in what was called the Battle of the Bismarck Sea. It was a powerful example of radio intelligence's influence on the course of the war. The strategic initiative in New Guinea passed forever from the hands of the Japanese to the Allies.[30]

In January 1944 almost three thousand Japanese troops were crammed aboard *Denmark Maru*. *Whale* was sent to intercept, and the ship went down with the loss of over a thousand troops. In February and March 1944, ULTRA discoveries from the broken army water transport codes led to the destruction of five convoys heading to New Guinea. Wewak Convoy

No. 20 was caught by *Gato,* and *Daigen Maru* went down, drowning four hundred soldiers. The Hollandia Convoy No. 6 was hit by USS *Peto* (SS 265), with the loss of the troop-laden *Kayo Maru.*

In July 1944, ULTRA information led the wolf pack "Park's Pirates" across the path of Convoy MI 11 off Luzon. Two of the boats, *Parche* and *Steelhead* (SS 280), subtracted five ships and a good portion of five thousand men of the Imperial Army's Twenty-sixth Division out of the emperor's war plans.

Another coup for ULTRA was the discovery of the transfer of the Imperial Army's Twenty-third Division from Manchuria to the Philippines. Two wolf packs were waiting in the East China Sea when HI 81 left Pusan, Korea, in November 1944. *Queenfish* sank *Akitsu Maru, Picuda* got *Mayasan Maru,* and *Spadefish* (SS 411) sank the twenty-one-thousand-ton escort carrier *Jinyo.* Over fourteen hundred soldiers drowned.

The ships did not have to be carrying soldiers to be singled out as targets. Perhaps more important was the economic attrition begun when intelligence discovered that the Japanese were becoming desperately short of oil. In early 1944 tankers were moved to top priority on the submarine hit list. On one occasion, ULTRA directed *Jack* to intercept a convoy in the South China Sea, and *Jack* subtracted four tankers from the dwindling Japanese fleet.

ULTRA targeted single ships as well as large convoys. The Japanese submarine *I-29* was tracked from the empire to Germany and almost all the way back home. Its ports of call, cargo, equipment, and even the people on board were known. It had taken a dozen scientists and engineers to Germany and was returning with blueprints for secret weapons. One passenger, Technical Commander Iwaya, carried plans for the rocket-powered Messerschmitt Me. 163 Komet. Another, Captain Matsui, carried plans for turbosuperchargers and rocket launching accelerators. In Singapore, the men disembarked and were flown to Japan. ULTRA knew. Even so, the bulk of the German scientific cargo remained aboard *I-29:* radar apparatus, Enigma coding machines, rocket launching equipment, and bombsight plans. This time ULTRA disclosed the specific items to the submarine commanders to impress upon them the importance of stopping *I-29.* Three submarines set up an ambush, but it was *Sawfish* that fired first, blowing apart *I-29* with three torpedoes.

By mid-1944 intelligence gathering operations were so successful that the stations were becoming swamped with information, with detail enough to know the very rations eaten by various Japanese garrisons.[31]

The fact that HI 72 consisted of a dozen ships made it noteworthy for the Allied eavesdroppers. Learning of its cargo would also have perked up their ears: thousands of tons of oil, aviation gasoline, and bauxite, with the last perhaps the most important commodity at this stage of the war. Aircraft production required tons of aluminum, economically extracted only from bauxite ore. In 1943, decrypts of the Japanese economic situation revealed a bauxite shortage. Allied war planners realized that cutting imports would cause havoc with plane production. The fact that bauxite was being carried on *Asaka Maru, Nankai Maru, Kimikawa Maru,* and *Rakuyo Maru* was known at least as early as 5 September. Although the ships would have been targeted even if they had been sailing empty, certainly the bauxite made it more imperative that the convoy be stopped. Five days later, "Ben's Busters" were ordered to intercept.

Intelligence knew that the same convoy was also carrying over 2,200 prisoners of war—at least after the sinkings. The interception of a 22 September Japanese water transport communication leaves no doubt. It documented 1,317 prisoners on board *Rakuyo Maru,* with 1,051 missing at sea, along with 750 tons of bauxite. *Kachidoki Maru* was listed as having 950 prisoners, with 431 missing in addition to the loss of 97 cases of carbide, 600 tons of bauxite, and 137 cases of mercury. The intercept also indicated that *Rakuyo Maru, Zuiho Maru,* and *Kachidoki Maru* were equipped with cloth emergency bags and weights for the disposal of secret documents. The message ended with the rather cryptic statement: "Until the common opinion that they were rescued by enemy submarines has been broadcast, it will clearly be necessary to suspend half of the retaliatory measures against encounters of this type."[32]

On 22 September the codebreakers were privy to the fact that HI 72 carried POWs. They knew the bauxite was aboard on 5 September. Would the messages have mentioned all of the cargo except the prisoners? If so, the Japanese would have been breaking their own edicts. Japanese Army Instruction No. 22, regulations for handling POWs, contained over two dozen articles. Articles 15, 16, and 17 specifically ordered that prisoners of war being sent to the rear had to be reported to General Headquarters.

The number of prisoners, the points of embarkation and debarkation, the dates of arrival, and the methods of communication and transportation had to be promptly passed from the sender to the receiver.

Don Wall, author and former Australian POW who worked on the Burma-Thailand Railway, studied the subject for many years. He stated that in addition to the radio intercepts, the news of POWs being loaded on the convoy was reported to the Allies by the Chinese in Singapore. Admiral Lockwood said the same; spies in Singapore often reported the exact cargoes that were loaded and unloaded.[33]

The daily intelligence summary of 12 September even indicated that the commander of Number 16 Maritime Command, under his "secret" code name KO KE A MI, was sailing on *Kachidoki Maru,* and that *Kachidoki Maru* was in fact the "Ex Pres. Harrison." Later, Commander Summers believed that he was the first to discover that one of the ships he sank was originally an American vessel. Those at Pearl Harbor knew it long before he did.

How soon did the codebreakers know about the passengers of HI 72? Did this knowledge come before the fatal ULTRA interception message was transmitted to the "Busters" on 10 September? References to the POWs decrease as one works backwards from 22 September, with no mention at all of HI 72 between the dates of 6 and 10 September. Were there no messages, or are records still being held back for security reasons?

ULTRA itself remained a secret until 1974, but finally, between the years of 1978 and 1988, the National Security Agency released over half a million decrypted Japanese signals. A wartime codebreaker himself, Alan Stripp understood the process but could not fathom the reason for the continued withholding of records. Stripp reasoned that "the Japanese knew their contents because they sent and received them, and we knew because we broke and read them. Who was there left to hide them from, and why?"[34]

Did American submarines sink Japanese ships while following the orders of those who knew that there were British and Australians aboard? The ULTRA information sent to the "Busters" did not disclose specific cargo information, for the submarine commanders did not need to be told of the human freight. Perhaps living in the post-Watergate era obliges one to be overly suspect of clandestine operations, but it does appear likely that those back at Pearl Harbor were well aware of HI 72's passengers.

The destruction of Japanese ships ferrying POWs was not unique to HI 72. Early in the war the Japanese took a rather cavalier attitude about transporting POWs by sea, often routing lone ships across waters that American submarines had not yet made especially dangerous. During the course of the war, 120,000 POWs were moved by sea—at the appalling shipboard space of less than one square yard per man. Eventually, American submarines began hitting them. The first deaths in great quantity came in July 1942, when the 7,266-ton *Montevideo Maru* out of Rabaul was sunk off Luzon by USS *Sturgeon* (SS 187). It was carrying 160 civilians and 1,053 Australian soldiers, the majority from the 2/22 Battalion. They all died. Off Shanghai on 1 October, the 7,053-ton transport *Lisbon Maru* was torpedoed by *Grouper.* About 850 out of 1,800 British POWs were killed. The rescue ships used the swimming prisoners for target practice.

The worst year for a POW to be at sea was 1944. On 24 June, the 6,780-ton freighter *Tamahoko Maru* almost made it to Nagasaki when it was jumped by the ULTRA-directed *Tang. Tamahoko Maru* went down with a loss of 560 out of 772 POWs, including 15 Americans.[35]

The worst month to be a POW at sea was in September 1944. On 7 September the 2,634-ton *Shinyo Maru* was taking 675 American prisoners from Mindanao to Luzon. Two torpedoes from USS *Paddle* (SS 263) sent it to the bottom. Only 85 Americans made it to shore. On 18 September the British submarine HMS *Tradewind* sank the 5,065-ton cargo ship *Junyo Maru* off Sumatra. Over 5,000 men died, including over 1,400 Dutch, British, and Australians and a handful of Americans. On 21 September, *Hofuku Maru,* en route from Manila to Japan, was found by American carrier torpedo planes. They sank it within three minutes, and over 1,000 British and Dutch POWs were lost. The destruction of HI 72 killed another 1,500.

On 24 October 1944, *Arisan Maru* sailed from Manila. About 225 miles from Hong Kong, the 6,886-ton cargo ship was torpedoed by USS *Shark II* (SS 314). The Japanese shut the hatches and abandoned ship. Of the 1,802 prisoners aboard, only eight survived. The last POW convoy out of Manila left on 13 December. The 7,000-ton *Oryoko Maru* carried 1,619 prisoners. American carrier planes damaged it near Subic Bay, Luzon. *Oryoko Maru* pulled into the bay, but the planes returned the next day and finished it off. About 1,350 of the prisoners made shore. Within two weeks they were split up and loaded on *Brazil Maru* and *Enoura Maru*. In January 1945, at Takao, Formosa, *Enoura Maru* was bombed and another 270 were killed and 250 wounded. The survivors were moved to *Brazil Maru*. During the remainder of the two-week voyage, another half of them died in the holds. Only about 400 made it to Moji alive.[36]

In a March 1945 memorandum, Captain Harry L. Pence listed fourteen Japanese ships sunk by Allied forces while carrying POWs. Japanese records indicated that about twenty-five ships carrying POWs were bombed or torpedoed during the war. Admiral Lockwood said, "The sinkings of Japanese merchant ships resulting from Communication Intelligence ran into hundreds of ships and probably amounted to fifty percent of the total of all merchantmen sunk by submarines." If anyone could give an accurate assessment of ULTRA's success, it was Charles Lockwood.[37]

Should one be surprised that so many POWs went to their doom on HI 72? Probably not. We are not here to debate the morality of war. If HI 72 had been left unmolested, the ships, personnel, and cargo that would have reached Japan would have had the potential to do more harm in the future. America and Japan were in a bloody death-struggle, and any means taken to gain victory were justifiable at the time. Both sides had been dehumanized. The psychological distancing that facilitates killing was in evidence not only on the battlefields but also in the plans of the strategists and tacticians. The Pacific war was a Manichaean struggle between completely incompatible antagonists. It was a war without mercy.[38] If any innocent parties got in the way, they would have to suffer. It is harsh, and indubitably heartless, especially when looked at through a fifty-year cushion of time. But such is war. In the grand scheme of things, ships carrying tons of gasoline, oil, and bauxite had to be destroyed, regardless of the possibility that Allied lives would be lost in the process. The fatal ULTRA was sent.

These events were unknown to the POWs. If they realized anything at all, it might have been the ironic fact that they had become free men—but at what price? They were free to drown in the middle of the South China Sea. Some had resigned themselves to their fate and faced the end stoically, but most, K. C. Renton said, "began to go a bit dippy." Two men in his party had just drunk seawater and had thrown themselves off the rafts in despair only a few hours earlier.

On one raft, former schoolteacher Frank Farmer and Curly Martin had been discussing their likely fate. They were interrupted by a raftmate who had been delirious and kept claiming that he saw masts on the horizon. They ignored him. Finally his persistent interruptions caused them to strain their oil-blinded eyes. Martin heard the sound of engines. A ship was coming, and it appeared to be a submarine. At first it went by, and Martin thought it was a U-boat. Farmer stood up and waved his hat, and the submarine closed in. It swept past again, and Farmer could see armed men on the deck. Finally they turned back. Martin waved, too. "I, fortunately," said Martin, "had a lot of fair, curly hair at the time, and they knew I wasn't Japanese and they came back to have another look."

Ken Williams had the same explanation. "One of our men, Curly Martin, had a hat, and when he waved it they could see fair hair, so they reckoned he couldn't be a Nip." K. C. Renton was about to give up when, about five in the afternoon, "a marvelous and wonderful thing happened; a submarine was making straight for us. We did not know whose it was. My eyes were in pain from the oil and I could not see clearly, but when it was right opposite us, I saw a couple of men with machine guns pointing them at us. I did not care because it would have been a quicker way out—and believe me, they looked tough."

Another man on the raft noticed the guns that were trained on them. Not as ready to meet his maker, he called out to the submarine in defiance.[39]

## CHAPTER SEVEN

# *Rescue*

Gordon Hopper was still grasping the trigger of the 20-mm gun, waiting, not knowing what to do if the order came to fire. *Pampanito* had approached the first group of men on a makeshift collection of hatch covers and timbers. There were about fifteen of them, scantily clad and covered in crude oil. Some had Australian "Digger" hats, and a few wore Japanese-style caps. They were waving frantically and shouting all at once so that no words could be distinguished. Most of the crew on deck were startled when they heard an obviously English voice angrily call out: "First you bloody Yanks sink us. Now you're bloody well going to shoot us." Bob Bennett remembered the exchange as: "You sink us, then you save us, you bloody Yanks." On the bullnose, Tony Hauptman lowered his shotgun and called back: "Who are you?"

"Prisoners of war," one yelled. "Australians. British. Prisoners of war. Pick us up, please."

Several men moved to assist them, but Summers was not yet sure. Just one, he cautioned, then yelled out, "Get the one that speaks English."

"You dumb bastards," came the defiant reply, "We all speak English."

Hauptman put down his shotgun, held up one finger, and said, "One man. One man only." A rope was thrown across, and several men broke for it or jumped into the water and began swimming for the submarine.

Hauptman shouted for them to stay put, while Jim Behney raised his machine gun.

Frank Farmer was the first to reach out. "I grasped the rope," he said, "and was hauled across the intervening water to the sub's side, up which I was assisted by two crewmen. When I thanked them in English, they were incredulous." He was escorted to the conning tower, where he met Lieutenant Commander Davis. Farmer's brief story about the POWs' being on the convoy greatly distressed the exec, but the officers were finally convinced that they were not Japanese.

"Take them aboard!" Summers ordered, and Frank Farmer became the first survivor of the "Railway of Death" to return to Allied control. Harold Martin and Ken Williams followed close behind. "They threw us a line," said Williams, "and the three of us were soon on board. After hearing our story, they immediately started searching for more."

Word passed through *Pampanito* like a flash, and almost everyone not on duty tried to come up to help. Fireman Andy Currier was one of the first in the water to help pull the rafts closer to the sub, followed by Bennett, Hauptman, and Behney. Yagemann stopped repairing the TBT and climbed down on the side of the hull. He saw that the men were so weak they couldn't even grab the lines; they'd reach out and fall off the rafts. They were almost impossible to haul up. "It was like trying to capture a greased pig," Yagemann said. Crouched on the side tanks, he cut his knees on barnacles and had his back wrenched by someone using his leg as a ladder. Hopper breathed a great sigh of relief, slid down from the 20-mm gun, and jumped into the water. On deck and along the tanks they were assisted by Mike Carmody, Ed Stockslader, Don Ferguson, John Madaras, Seaman First Class Jack J. Evans, and Motor Machinist's Mate Third Class Richard E. Elliott.

Jeff Davis climbed down and tried to get in the water to help a survivor on board. "I had to call him back to the bridge," Summers said. There was some decorum to be maintained. Besides, if a plane appeared, he might have to leave some of his own crew behind.

More men came topside and helped strip the remnants of clothing off the survivors, while others took rags to swab off the oil and lower them inside. In the forward torpedo room, Clyde Markham had some rags soaked in "pink lady." He was trying to be helpful, but "one POW screamed

The rescue of the POWs begins, 15 September 1944. (Photo U.S. Navy, Paul Pappas.)

when it got into his open sores," Markham said. "After that we used soap and water."

Red McGuire was below when he heard the order, "Stand by to pick up prisoners." One survivor climbed down the ladder under his own power. McGuire saw a short, oil-covered man who barely came up to his chin and thought he was Japanese. Coming from behind, McGuire grabbed him in a headlock and banged his head into the ladder.

"Blimey!" the fellow yelled out. McGuire wiped some oil off his face with a rag and asked, "Who the hell are you?"

"I'm a British prisoner of his Imperial Majesty, the Emperor of Japan," the man smartly answered.

"No you're not," McGuire countered. "Now you're a free man on a United States submarine." The man's eyes lit up, and McGuire, rather embarrassed, said "I'm sorry. Does your head hurt?"

"Oh, no," the man answered. "I'm just fine." And he walked away, McGuire said, "as happy as a lark."

Not everyone could stand seeing the conditions the poor survivors were in. Frank Fives tried to help, but he said, "My stomach couldn't take it. It was terrible." It was the first time he had seen the bloody side of war, and he didn't like it. It was why he had chosen submarines. Fives went back up to the bridge.

*Pampanito* combed her way through more wreckage. The first group of fifteen men was all aboard by 1634. In the patrol report Summers recorded: "A pitiful sight none of us will ever forget."

Heading for a second raft, *Pampanito* broke radio silence and sent out a message to *Sealion II* asking for help. About twenty-eight miles to the northeast, Reich got the word and swung his boat back to the scene at four-engine speed.

Cliff Farlow was having hallucinations from heat and thirst. "I looked out and saw my mother and father milking cows under palm trees in the South China Sea," he said. "Obviously I was getting pretty delirious." One of his mates saw something that looked like a submarine, then they heard the thunder of the engines, but they figured it was "a bloody Jap sub." When it neared, Farlow saw "blokes come out on the deck with machine guns and we thought we were going to be done over." However, one of them called out, "They're Australians!" Two sailors jumped over the side

POW rescue. Pete Summers observes from cigaret deck. (Photo U.S. Navy, Paul Pappas.)

and swam over. As they helped Farlow and his mates aboard, one of them kept saying, "For Chrissake hurry up—we gotta get down!"

About 1720, *Pampanito* had cleared the second raft, and bearings were taken on three others in sight. The second had nine men aboard, and they were less covered in oil, making their boarding a bit easier. While

Oil-covered survivors from the South China Sea. (Photo by Paul Pappas.)

heading for the third raft, the sub passed a small piece of floating debris
that appeared to have a single man aboard. Upon closer inspection the
crew found the occupant to be dead—with part of his head gone.

The raft Bob Farrands was on was thoroughly waterlogged, and he sat
in water up to his chest. He was "thirst crazy," he said. "I would shut my
eyes and see the soda fountain running in a shop back in my home town,

but no one would give me a drink. We always had a water bag on the verandah at my home. Water was running out of it, but still I could not drink." He was going a bit balmy when he heard an engine and saw what appeared to be "a Yank sub."

"A sailor dived in and put a rope around my chest," Bob said. "I was pulled and assisted onto the deck. There I stood stark naked, covered in emulsified oil. A sailor said, 'Are you all right, Aussie?' and I said, 'As good as gold.' Then he let go of me and I fell flat on my face." Farrands was given a water-soaked cloth to suck on and hauled below.

The third and fourth rafts, carrying six men each, were picked up by 1730. Then another small raft was seen with one man lying motionless on his back. A sailor dived in with a line and swam out to him. When he reached him, the survivor sat bolt upright and tried to jump off, perhaps thinking that the Japanese had found him again. He was nearly blind. This was John Campbell, Second Battalion, Gordon Highlanders. He collapsed while being hauled on deck and remained in a semiconscious state.

Roy Cornford saw what appeared to be a small ship in the distance. "It seemed like hours," Roy said, "watching this black looking dot going to the rafts, when we realized it was a submarine." Finally it closed in, and a sailor dived in with a rope and pulled them aboard. "I can remember lifting my hands up, but pleading with the sailors not to grab my arms because they were just blisters and sores." When Cornford got on deck he was surprised he could still walk.

Paul Pappas was topside with his camera and was given the ship's 16-mm movie camera to record the action. He shot all the film and used all three of his own rolls. At 1753 they found another large raft with eleven men. While they were hauling this group aboard, there were about fifty men on deck.

Scanning the horizon were Harry S. Lynch and Clarence Williams, both electrician's mates third class. Williams, who had joined up in Miami, Florida, in March 1943, was a novice at lookout. This was his first patrol on *Pampanito*, and he was diligently searching his sector when suddenly he saw aircraft.

"A flight of low-flying Jap planes!" Williams called out.

Summers shouted to clear the deck. It had happened. The Japanese had found them, and at the most vulnerable time. In moments, crewmen,

Rescue of Aussie POWs. On the ballast tank at left is Bob Bennett. Bill
Yagemann extends his leg. On the raft is Andrew Currier and Gordon
Hopper is at far right. (Photo by Paul Pappas.)

as well as survivors who could hardly walk, somehow came to life and
dashed for the open hatches. Then almost immediately the crisis passed.
Williams shouted: "Never mind. It's a bird!" A flight of frigate birds
hovered almost motionless on the air currents. Williams felt a bit foolish

when he realized his mistake. Summers recorded: "Fortunately one of the planes was seen to flap its wings, proving the formation to be large birds gliding in perfect order."

Chief Clarence Smith strapped on a sidearm when he heard the call about men in the water. But by the time he got ready to go topside, the survivors were coming down. It was hard to carry them, and they couldn't easily be lowered, because they were still too slippery. Smith stood below the after battery hatch and caught the POWs as they were dropped down. Roy Cornford was one of the men given the heave-ho. He had just taken off his clothes to get the oil swabbed off when he heard a shout, "Planes, planes!" A sailor grabbed him, lifted him, and dropped him, Roy said, "down the hatch onto a big plump sailor's stomach." Chief Smith had finally found a use for his belly.

At 1835, *Pampanito* sent a message to ComSubPac notifying them of the situation. Five minutes later, a second minor panic swept topside when a patrol boat was sighted through the high periscope. A closer look showed that the craft appeared to be a submarine, but with a gun aft. *Sealion II* did not have an after four-inch gun, and since it did not answer a challenge, *Pampanito* dove. One of the survivors said that there was a German sub in the area, and Summers tracked the mysterious boat for half an hour. By 1940 they were close enough to see the submarine dead in the water. It was *Sealion*. The "gun" on the after deck was a cluster of rescuers hauling survivors aboard. Summers surfaced, but they had lost valuable rescue time.

In the approaching darkness, they spotted what looked like a man waving a white flag. They moved closer to find the "flag" was really his hand, bleached white from the salt water. He was hauled aboard, and they headed in the direction of where they had seen another raft before they dove. It was 2005 and almost totally dark. Chances were they would never find anyone, but incredibly, looming up out of the black sea was another group of about one dozen men. After taking them aboard, the crew made a cursory head count. They had rescued over seventy men, which almost doubled *Pampanito*'s crew of seventy-nine men and ten officers. Being "cramped for living space," and unable to sight anyone else in the tropical night, Summers broke off the operation.

One of the last men brought aboard was Harry Pickett. He had been on his own for quite a while. "It was darkish," he said. "I could feel the

Bob Bennett at left, cradles John Campbell. (Photo by Paul Pappas.)

regular pulse of a motor through the water. Then I saw a sort of shape."
Pickett heard what he called "a good old American accent" call out to him:
"Can you catch a rope, buddy?" It was the Floridian, Jim Behney. He tossed
Pickett a line and lifted him bodily in his strong but gentle arms. Behney's
name, said Pickett, "I will never forget. He carried me below."

Gordon Hopper didn't return to man the 20-mm gun. "All the rest of
my life," he said, "I have thanked God that I didn't have to make the

decision to fire or not to fire. All the rest of my life I have treasured the memory of helping save lives rather than terminate them."[1]

Three days earlier, *Pampanito* had bared her teeth, sending her first ships to the bottom of the sea and killing hundreds of men. During the past four hours she had plucked seventy-three men from the sea, more than were rescued by any other American submarine during the entire war. A boat of steel with men of flesh and blood can serve two masters. *Pampanito* had become a killer angel.

The wounded, burned, emaciated survivors were carried down the hatches, and Maurice "Doc" Demers got his chance to prove his mettle. Crew members volunteered to be nurses, helping to wash off the oil, administering medicines, feeding, and donating clothing. It was a most moving experience: hardened soldiers and sailors weeping together in sorrow and joy.

The first thing to do was to find a place to put everyone. The crew thought they should quarantine the survivors all aft, but that proved impossible. "There was no way you could fit seventy-three men in the after torpedo room," Hubie Brown said. Many were bunked there, but some went to the crew's quarters and others went to the forward torpedo room. While some of his mates had to give up their bunks, Brown never did, because his was on the top level in the forward torpedo room, and the weakened men couldn't climb up. Some of them were so skinny, however, they could fit two to a bunk.

Torpedoman's Mate Third Class Peder A. Granum was making his first patrol on *Pampanito*. He had been born in Mohall, North Dakota, in 1913. Being thirty-one years old and only five and one-half feet tall, Peder was called "Grandpa" Granum by the crew. He had made one patrol on *Gudgeon* but had broken an ankle while jumping down the hatch. After getting his leg in a cast and going to the States, he was eventually sent back to Midway, where he was assigned to *Pampanito*. Granum was good with electric torpedoes. "The guys thought I was a spy for the Naval Bureau, the way I got quickly added to the boat."

Granum had been in the boat's rubber raft, helping pull in the drifting survivors. He swabbed them off, helped them down the hatch, and heard more than one man thank God for being rescued. Granum used "pink lady" to clean off the oil, carefully avoiding the open tropical ulcers.

Demers broke out the rubbing alcohol to wash down the survivors. The sailors approved; there was no sense in using up good torpedo juice when rubbing alcohol would do the trick.[2]

Summers appointed Lieutenant Swain to oversee placement and care of the survivors. Lieutenant Fulton made a head count. Forty-seven of the men were Australians, and twenty-six were British. Among them were Wally Winter and Alf Winter. Alf thought it was remarkable that two Winters were rescued by a Summers.

Ted Swain had not needed his .45. He had put the weapon away, helped lower men down the hatches, and wished they could have picked up every man on the ocean. When Summers told him, "No more," he felt like disobeying. Swain helped weave rope lines in the torpedo racks to construct makeshift hammocks, then laid blankets on them, and they became fairly decent bunks. The worst cases stayed in the crew's quarters. "They smelled terrible," Swain said.

Still delirious, John Campbell was carried down and placed in Van Atta's bunk, starboard and aft of the galley. Al didn't mind. He also helped clothe Campbell from his own wardrobe.

Demers quickly found himself worked to the limit. He checked his supply locker: atabrine for malaria, aspirin, merthiolate, mineral oil, castor oil, gentian violet, glucose, bismuth, sulfa powder, burn ointment, tincture of benzoate, boric acid, morphine, vitamins, plasma, syringes, gauze, and bandages. Unfortunately, the survivors had numerous maladies that a lone pharmacist's mate was not equipped to deal with.

Most of them were in shock, and they looked like they would pass out or die any minute. He gave fifteen of them morphine shots. Their eyes were gray from vitamin deficiencies. He worked on their eyes, cleaning out the oil and dirt, then moved to the ears, nose, and mouth. Some had globs of oil in their mouths like chaws of tobacco, but they were too weak to even spit them out.

After treating the most obvious physical symptoms, Demers retreated for a few minutes to his medical books, with which he diagnosed a few of the diseases such as beriberi and pellagra. The survivors should have been quarantined, but the crew resigned themselves to the situation and went about their jobs as nurses with a passion. "You didn't have to ask anybody to help," Demers said. "They just did it."

The survivors were first given moist cloths to suck on, then cups of water. Very soon they were asking for something more substantial. Cooks Joe Eichner and Bill Morrow and Ship's Cook Second Class Daniel E. Hayes had their work cut out for them. Dan Hayes in particular, newly arrived on the boat, became a full-time assistant to Demers, serving tea, cocoa, bouillon, and soup. Harry Jones was overcome by the kindness he received. He got a large mug of hot vegetable soup, and even though his lips and tongue were cracked and swollen, he was happy that he could still taste the wonderful brew—"something good and wholesome, the like of which I had not partaken of for the last two and a half years." Jones and some of the more fit ones just sipped their soup in silence, sometimes unable to restrain the tears of joy that came to their eyes.

K. C. Renton thought he was going to be machine-gunned, but "instead of lead," he said, "we got a rope and were taken aboard. Can you imagine the shock? We got water and tomato soup and crackers for our first dinner, something that we never had for two and a half years." He added, "And since then we lived like lords."

Bob Farrands was quartered in the after torpedo room. He perked up rapidly. "The poor bloke that looked after me must have got sick of my voice," he said, "as I never shut up." Farrands was given plenty of hot soup and tea, he said, "but the best meal was a slice of bread and butter; it was beautiful."

Almost everyone but John Campbell responded well. Try as he might, Demers was unable to find a vein substantial enough to give him a glucose injection. It was as if the man didn't have any blood. In one foot there was a hole the size of a silver dollar, going clean through. They speculated that fish had been gnawing on him.

Even so, Campbell became lucid for short intervals. McGuire had the job of going to every man and getting his name, rank, service number, and name of next of kin. When he got to the Scotsman, however, he had a tough time. "I had to ask him his name about twenty times," McGuire said. "He had a burr about a mile long." Finally, McGuire deciphered his name as "Jack" or "Jock," and found out he was with the Gordon High-landers. Attending Campbell was twenty-year-old Seaman First Class George W. Strother. Strother learned that Campbell had been a cook on the Burma Railway. He had a wife and three kids, but he had never seen his youngest child. Strother thought Campbell had a beautiful personality. The man's acceptance of his situation and his thoughts regarding his family made the young seaman think about his own mortality. "I was just a kid then," he said. "I grew up pretty fast."[3]

Back among the rafts, *Sealion II* also had a busy evening 15 September. Reich conned his boat through the waters until 2200. He picked up fifty-four men: twenty-three Australians and thirty-one British. Reich believed no more could be safely taken aboard, and even with others close by and calling for help, he pulled away. "It was heartbreaking to leave so many dying men behind," Reich wrote. Some of his crew who were still on deck in the darkness had recurrent memories of the scene for years afterwards, especially at the plaintive cry of "Over here! Over here!" fading out in the night.

*Sealion* also radioed Pearl, and Lockwood gave both subs permission to head for Saipan, about eighteen hundred miles away. Since Reich reported that many men were still in the water, Admiral Lockwood, at 0300 on 16 September, ordered *Barb* and *Queenfish* to head immediately to the scene of the rescue. On *Barb*, Gene Fluckey, still complaining that the "Busters" had not informed him about the convoy, was irked again because he had to retrace another 450 miles back to the site he had left a couple of days before.

However, about 150 miles from the scene, Fluckey happened across something that would quickly change his disposition: a convoy. *Queenfish* found it first, and *Barb* picked it up minutes later. It was big, and the rescue of any remaining POWs would have to wait.

This convoy, HI 74, had left Singapore on 11 September. It consisted of the *Harima Maru, Omuroyama Maru, Otowayama Maru, Hakko Maru,* and the big tanker *Azusa Maru,* filled with 100,600 barrels of oil. It was escorted by the frigate *Chiburi,* the training cruiser *Kashii,* and *Coast Defense Vessels Nos. 13, 19, 21,* and *27.* Guarding them all was the twenty-thousand-ton escort carrier *Unyo.* On 12 September, while moving north in the wake of HI 72, HI 74 received word of an attack on its sister convoy. The convoy commander, Rear Admiral Yoshitomi Eizo, ordered them to swing about sixty miles to the east to bypass the attack area. They succeeded in avoiding the "Busters," but late on 16 September they ran smack into the "Eradicators."

Swinburne ordered the boats in, and *Barb*'s torpedoes sent down *Azusa Maru* and *Unyo.* When the carrier finally sank about 0700 on 17 September, again the codebreakers knew. Back at Pearl Harbor, Captain Wilfred J.

Holmes, a liaison officer between the Submarine Force and the crypto-graphers, was looking through a batch of the latest Japanese naval messages. He picked up a garbled one about a vice admiral shifting his flag from one ship to another and a second one that commented about the safety of the imperial portrait. Holmes knew that vice admirals rode on carriers, and he knew a carrier had gone down even before the men on the submarine that sank it. *Barb* and *Queenfish*, however, had lost a few more hours in their race to pick up the last survivors.[4]

The POWs had been in the water for five days, and they were in terrible shape. After noon on 17 September, *Barb* and *Queenfish* found them. Now, however, the barometer had dropped and the seas had risen; a typhoon was approaching. Submarines and men were tossed about in the heavy waves. Scenes played on *Pampanito* and *Sealion* were reenacted on *Barb* and *Queenfish* as the dazed, incredulous survivors were hauled below and kindly cared for by men of war suddenly become angels of mercy.

The two subs combed the area. Charles Loughlin picked up eighteen men. Fluckey, having rescued fourteen men, contended that he would have forgone the pleasure of an attack on a Japanese task force to rescue any one of them. "There is little room for sentiment in submarine warfare," he wrote, "but the measure of saving one Allied life against sinking a Japanese ship is one that leaves no question, once experienced." By dawn, with winds the two captains estimated at between sixty and one hundred knots and "skyscraper waves," the rescue was over. All that remained were dead, bloated bodies bobbing grotesquely in the seas. If any man was left alive by that time, Nature would soon eliminate him. *Barb* and *Queenfish* broke off and headed for Saipan.[5]

While Fluckey and Loughlin were attacking HI 74 on the evening of 16 September, Summers was already two hundred miles to the east, approaching Balintang Channel. Most of the men had made remarkable comebacks in the twenty-four hours they had been aboard *Pampanito*. Try as Demers might to ease them back into a regular diet, many of them overdid it. Wally Winters decided he wanted a good old American ham-burger and a Coke, and he sneaked into the galley to look for some. Not seeing the harm in it, Joe Eichner fried him a big burger, complete with onions, relish, and ketchup. Winters wolfed it down and about an hour later was as sick as a dog. Demers could only say, "I told you so."

A similar incident occurred while Hauptman was looking after John Campbell. The Scotsman seemed to take a turn for the worse, and Hauptman called Demers. Demers didn't know what to do but tried again, unsuccessfully, to shoot some glucose into the man. Meanwhile, Tony left and went to see McGuire.

"I think I killed him," a shaken Hauptman confessed. "He looked hungry and I fed him a big piece of bread and butter." Naturally the word got back to Demers, and the order went out: absolutely no one was to feed the survivors without the permission of Doc Demers or Lieutenant Swain.

The unfamiliar food caused havoc with their systems. Within twenty-four hours all of them who did not already have dysentery had diarrhea. Many were berthed in the after torpedo room, and that compartment was serviced by only one head (toilet), which had to be discharged to the sea after each use. Said Ken Williams: "A bit of panic occurred when one of our chaps pushed the button on the toilet when we were submerged—of course we had been told not to."

A sailor was detailed to assist them. Woody Weaver explained: "The poor guys were lining up to use the one head, and we had to have a man on watch to operate the discharge valves for them. The poor sailor on that watch had quite a job. As fast as he took care of one man, there was another ready to sit on the commode."

As daylight waned on 16 September, so did the life signs of John Campbell. He never came out of his latest lapse into unconsciousness, and about 1830 he died, his head supported in George Strother's arms. It was a deeply moving moment, for everyone had tried so hard to save him, and no one had ever died on *Pampanito* before. In the discussion of plans for his burial, a small argument ensued as to how to weigh him down.

"We compromised," said Carmody, "and placed a four-inch shell and a connecting rod with him. We figured 'Jock' deserved the best we could give. We sewed him into a double mattress cover and took him topside." Van Atta knew he would be getting his bunk back when he saw them hauling the bag up the access hatch. "What a way to go," Van Atta thought, "being dumped alone into the South China Sea."

On the after deck a burial ceremony was conducted in the gathering darkness under a beautiful, star-filled sky. The ship was rolling smartly in the swells. A layer of thick, black crude oil remained on the deck, making the footing hazardous. Because the men considered Pappas the cleanest-living crewman, he read a short service by the light of a red flashlight shielded by a sailor's cap. Bill Yagemann remembered that he, Tony Hauptman, Peder Granum, and Lieutenant Swain were in the burial party, but he couldn't see the other faces in the darkness. McGuire watched from above while on lookout. They had draped the bag with an American flag, and they apologized to the British that they had no Union Jack with which to cover him. When the prayers were over, Campbell's body was committed to the deep. But there was one last glitch, for the ship rolled, and the men holding the bag slipped on the oily deck. Campbell's body slid along the ballast tank and hung up on the hull. Carmody observed: "'Jock' didn't want to leave us!" A sailor stretched over the side and kicked the bag free. Campbell's body sank to the depths.

Two days later, one of the men *Queenfish* had rescued and who had been in a coma the entire time finally died. Since they were riding out rough weather, they committed his body to the deep by blowing him out of a torpedo tube.[6]

*Pampanito* cleared Balintang Channel and headed east through the Philippine Sea. The survivors were improving in health by the hour, and many were able to move freely about the boat. Roy Cornford, however, was still bed-ridden. He lay in his bunk for days with nothing to do but listen to the record player. He heard the Al Dexter song, "Pistol Packin' Mama," so many times he memorized it.

Private William Cray was in the Sixteenth Advance Regiment, Royal Artillery. The gunner from Hull, England, took up with Bob Bennett, sharing stories and correspondence. Bennett seemed to have a knack for making friends, for he and Frank Farmer also became close, exchanging letters for another fifty years. Dagger Ward, of Nottingham, England, later wrote a letter to Hubie Brown, closing it with a little verse:

When you're sailing on the deep
And the sun begins to set
When others you are thinking of
Won't you sometimes think of me?

The kindness shown by the submariners needed no repayment. All the survivors had to give was a heartfelt thanks. They were completely destitute, almost to a man. Only Frank Coombes had managed to come through with more than just a few scraps of clothing; he still had his hidden diamonds.

Motor Machinist's Mate First Class Wendell T. Smith, Jr., of Portland, Maine, had served on USS *Jenkins* (DD 447) before coming to *Pampanito*. Smith was on duty in the forward engine room when the survivors came aboard. The first few were so thin and oil-covered, he thought they were Japanese. When he realized they were British and Australian, he selected the next one through as his personal charge and thus became quick friends with Frank Coombes.

As they neared Saipan, Coombes wondered how he could repay Smith's kindness. He reached down for the money belt he still had under his shorts and produced the diamond earrings.

"I have a gift for you," Coombes said to Smith, and he handed him three diamonds that he had extracted from one of the earrings. He told Smith he had "liberated" them from a store in Singapore just before the Japanese had marched in. Coombes also gave some diamonds to two other sailors who had looked after him. After the war, Smith took the diamonds to a jeweler, who pronounced them excellent stones and mounted them in a ring that Smith's wife, Virginia, still wears.

A. John Cocking, a private in the 2/4 Machine Gun Battalion, AIF, was from Perth. He recuperated quickly and got to know several of the crew. Cocking told them that back home he owned some horses for racing and for stud service, and that if they ever got to Australia he'd show them the racing business. He also became friends with Woody Weaver, and the torpedoman gave him a little black book with the crew's names and addresses. Weaver was destined to cross paths with Cocking's son twenty-five years later.[7]

*Pampanito* had been on patrol for a month, and the food was rapidly being consumed. The crew subsisted on sandwiches. The last hot meals, said cook Dan Hayes, were hot dogs and beans, but everyone enjoyed them nevertheless. Ed Stockslader remembered that the pantry was down to mustard and bread.

After noon on 18 September, *Sealion II* caught up with *Pampanito,* and they both made rendezvous with USS *Case* (DD 370). Aboard *Pampanito* came medical officer Lieutenant Commander Paul V. H. Waldo and Chief Pharmacist's Mate Lynn T. Wilcox. Demers had been up for three days; he had lost weight, and his legs had swollen. Summers gave him a shot of brandy and ordered him to go to bed.

They discussed transferring all the POWs to the *Case*, but Reich and Summers decided they had brought them this far, and they might as well take them the rest of the way. The POWs had a say in the matter also. When they were told of a possible transfer to an American destroyer, Curly Martin said they resisted. "We said, 'No way!' The captain picked us up on his sub and we want to stay here. And I believe he [Summers] grew about ten foot at this statement."

The survivors stayed aboard the subs. Unfortunately, the new doctor never examined one man. Ted Swain was tired and not in a diplomatic mood. Lieutenant Commander Waldo asked what he had been feeding the POWs.

"Liquids, soft eggs and toast," Swain answered.

"Why not citrus?" the doctor asked.

"We haven't seen citrus ourselves in thirty days," Swain answered. When Waldo asked for Swain's records, he snapped back, "What records? We've been working, not keeping records!"

Summers directed the doctor and corpsman to remain in the wardroom, then woke Demers. Still groggy, the pharmacist's mate went back to work. Soon he diagnosed another serious problem. Being down in a submarine with air conditioning blowing on them, the survivors had begun to develop coughs, colds, and pneumonia.

Hospital records later indicated that the survivors were an average of sixteen pounds underweight; 95 percent had malaria, 67 percent had dysentery, and 61 percent had tropical ulcers. All had vitamin deficiencies and malnutrition. All had skin lesions, five had scarred corneas from the oil, 20 percent had acute bronchitis, nine had pneumonia, and one had tuberculosis.

The after torpedo room began to smell so bad that Lieutenant Swain called for a field day to clean it. The sailors and the most fit of the POWs lent a hand. The British were a "little uppity" at first, said Swain, but they eventually pitched in. Soon enough, the torpedo room was cleaned up and disinfected like a hospital room. At sunup on 20 September, *Pampanito* met

USS *Dunlap,* and the destroyer escorted her the rest of the way. About 0900 a pilot came aboard and guided her through the torpedo nets and into Tanapag Harbor, Saipan, where she moored next to the tender USS *Fulton* (AS 11).

All but the most seriously ill were allowed topside to witness the docking. They stood on the decks, dressed in submariner's clothes, looking almost part of the crew. Six could still not walk, and basket stretchers were used to haul the last of them topside. Demers was proud of his work. He believed most of the former POWs looked better than the majority of the crew. Lighters came alongside to ferry them to shore. While waiting, ice cream and fresh oranges were brought aboard, giving both the crew and the former POWs quite a treat.

As the submarine emptied, Joe Eichner, still in the galley, thought about giving one of the survivors a memento. "I noticed the oblong plate on the hot water heater in the crew's mess next to the sink," he said. "The idea came to me to unscrew the plate, which read, 'USS *Pampanito,* Hot Water Heater, Crew's Mess.'" Joe grabbed one of the exiting Australians and handed him the plate for a keepsake. He never knew whom he had given it to.

Although most of the survivors appeared relatively fit, one sailor who didn't look so well for wear was Dan Hayes. The cook, thin to begin with and now appearing haggard, stumbled along with the POWs as they were loaded onto a small boat. He was grabbed by a Marine and helped aboard.

"Hey, I'm an American!" Hayes protested. The Marine wouldn't listen, especially when prompted by the laughing sailors still on deck. "No he isn't," they yelled down, "Take him ashore." Eventually the former POWs admitted to the joke, and Hayes was released to climb back on board *Pampanito* to the guffaws of his mates. The boats took the survivors ashore. Summers wrote that they "shoved off with cheers, thumbs up, and a mutual feeling of friendliness that will be hard to exceed anywhere."

Of the British POWs on *Kachidoki Maru,* about 520 were eventually rescued by the Japanese and sent on their journey to Japan. About 157 British and Australians from *Rakuyo Maru* were picked up by the Japanese. Submarines rescued 159 men: *Pampanito,* 73 (one died); *Sealion II,* 54 (four died); *Queenfish,* 18 (two died); and *Barb,* 14.

The British survivors sailed to Hawaii on the liberty ship *Cape Douglas.* From there another ship took them to San Francisco, a train carried them to New York, and another vessel took them to England. The Aussies sailed on the liberty ship *Alcoa Polaris* to Guadalcanal, and from there on the minelayer *Monadnock* to Brisbane. Six of them, including Roy Cornford and Reginald H. Hart, were too sick to leave and spent six weeks in "an American tent hospital where we," said Cornford, "were cared for by lots of American doctors and lovely American nurses." Eventually the liberated men spread the word of the atrocities they had experienced while slaving on the Burma Railway and told of their torpedoing and miraculous rescue by the same men who had sunk them.[8]

The transfer ashore of the former POWs was completed by 1100, 20 September. Ten minutes later, *Sealion II* came in, moored outboard of *Pampanito*, and unloaded her POWs. Demers watched them come up the hatches and was startled. The POWs' heads were shaved, perhaps to counter problems with lice. They hardly had any clothing; some simply wore blankets draped around their shoulders. They looked like walking skeletons. Demers thought *Pampanito*'s POWs looked much better.

The rival crews began ribbing each other. Demers thought that Red McGuire was the loudest yeoman in the navy. If that was true, then he believed *Sealion* had the second loudest, a man he remembered by the name of O'Neill. The two verbally sparred across the decks.

"You glory-hunting sons-a-bitches," McGuire began. "You shot your torpedoes all over the damn ocean and just missed us. You jumped in when we were going to fire and took our ships. You hogged the damn convoy for yourselves." O'Neill jabbered right back that it was a dog-eat-dog world, and that if *Pampanito* couldn't keep up with the big boys, it had better stay on shore. Reich and Summers were on their respective bridges and could hear the shouting. The same thoughts were probably on their own minds. Finally, the captain of *Fulton*, towering several decks above both subs, sent down a message for them all to shut up. The incident ended, but there were still hard feelings between the crews.

Demers went to see a doctor on *Fulton* about his own condition. His feet and legs looked like balloons, and the doctor told him to stay off his feet. He took a hot shower, then marched back to the sub. Summers gave him more brandy and ordered him to go to bed. He slept for thirty-six hours.

Saipan had been a major Japanese base in the Marianas Islands. Marines of the Second and Fourth Divisions and soldiers of the Twenty-seventh

At Saipan, 20 September 1944. Maurice "Doc" Demers, on right, assists ex-
POW out of the hatch. (Photo U.S. Navy, Paul Pappas.)

Division suffered over sixteen thousand casualties taking it, but they buried more than twenty-three thousand Japanese and took over fourteen thousand prisoners, mostly Japanese civilians. The island was invaded in June, but many soldiers and civilians retreated into the jungle mountain recesses and held out for months, and even years later. The loss was such a blow to the Japanese that Prime Minister Tojo and his cabinet resigned, and the Japanese people finally began learning the truth about the deteriorating war situation. For the submariners, the capture of Saipan meant that they had a base thirty-seven hundred miles closer to the war zone than Pearl Harbor.

*Fulton* was becoming quite an establishment in Tanapag Harbor. The Japanese called the tenders "America's secret weapon," but *Fulton* got her own special nickname. She had access to plenty of steaks, but no booze, while the nurses at the army hospitals ashore had access to booze but few steaks. Since the officers' club ashore closed at 1900 each evening, booze, steaks, sailors, and nurses could be seen shifting back and forth on a regular nightly basis. *Fulton* became known as the pigboat "Pussy Palace."

However, *Pampanito*'s men had little time to sample the cuisine. A relief crew swarmed on board to fumigate, decontaminate, and clean the boat from stem to stern. Since there was concern about disease, the bedding and blankets were removed and burned, and new sets of dungarees and skivvies were issued. The crew had only four hours of liberty. A few men visited Charan Kanoa, the internment camp for the Japanese civilians, where their lasting impression was of feces, rotting animal carcasses, and large flies.

It has been said that the Japanese fought for their emperor, the British for glory, and the Americans for souvenirs. Al Van Atta went off into the countryside, a dangerous thing to do, since Japanese would occasionally come down out of the hills and make one-man banzai charges at unsuspecting soldiers. Van Atta found a Japanese boot in a ditch, and he thought he'd get it as a keepsake. The Japanese were known to leave booby-trapped items around, waiting for a curious American. This one was not trapped, but when Al picked it up he saw that it still had a man's foot in it. That effectively ended his souvenir hunting. He decided he would simply trade items with the Marines from then on.[9]

By 1600 *Pampanito* had taken on fresh provisions, fuel, and lube oil and made her way out of the harbor, escorted by USS *Cassin* (DD 372). A half-dozen men were still on deck as the sub went out through the torpedo nets. Standing near the stern was Clyde Markham. As the engines kicked over, Markham's lifeline became unbuckled, and he slipped overboard. If he had been daydreaming again, a splash in the cold water certainly woke him up with a jolt. "The first thing I thought of was getting chewed up by the propellers," he said. "So I kicked with all my might off the side of the hull and began to swim away as hard as I could."

Bob Bennett looked aft and saw "someone swimming like hell off the side." They had been swimming near the beach, he said, "but this was crazy. He must have been sitting on the guy wire and fell over backwards." Bennett ran to the bridge to point out the man overboard.

Meanwhile, Markham swam for a buoy marking the channel near the torpedo nets. He figured if he could get there he could cling to it and eventually someone would come back to get him. Markham grabbed the buoy. *Pampanito* looked very tiny, but finally she turned around. He was all smiles as the sub loomed near, but the officers on deck were not so blithe. They were stopped outside the nets like a sitting duck in a spot where Japanese subs were known to operate. On the bridge, Clyde was raked over the coals again, this time by both Davis and Summers. It was the worst ass-chewing he had had to date, and he was really getting to dislike the captain. Some of the crew thought it was kind of funny, however, and they began calling him "the seventy-fourth survivor."

The next seven days were devoid of enemy contact, and *Pampanito* raced for Pearl Harbor. It was a chance for the men to relax and swap stories of the ship sinkings and the rescues. However, not everyone was content. Pete Summers sank his ships, but the stress of running a sub while being constantly second-guessed by his officers had frayed his nerves. He had eaten next to nothing during the past few weeks and survived practically on coffee and cigarettes. His weight had dropped from 165 to 145 pounds, and he growled at the most trivial offenses. He had dressed down Markham and steward Ingram on several occasions.

Lieutenant Sherlock tried to put it in perspective. With few exceptions, he said, no one on board had made more than a few war patrols. "Your life expectancy was slightly over four runs," Sherlock said, "while Pete was twice dead. He was on his tenth patrol in September 1944 and openly admitted that he would never make a thirteenth. We really had a man who was completely 'burned out' but too proud to admit it. Thank God the rest of us didn't have to make ten or more runs. I wonder if any of us could have handled it as well."

The crew could never fully appreciate the pressures Summers was under. An incident that illustrated his sorry state was reminiscent of an episode that author Herman Wouk would later write of in his book *The Caine Mutiny.* While on Saipan, Summers obtained several quarts of fresh strawberries, which he looked forward to dining on. Having an ample supply, Pete decided to share some with the officers. Occasionally the stewards might partake of desserts if there were any leftovers.

After supper, however, not knowing Summers's plans to save the rest for himself, George Ingram and Steward's Mate First Class Robert Byrd ate some of the leftover berries. Ingram, also remembering the bananas that were given to him by the men in the forward torpedo room on the way out from Panama, decided he could now pay back the favor. The remaining quarts were consumed. The next night Summers searched in vain for his dessert. When told it had been eaten, said Lieutenant Sherlock, "he flew into a rage." He immediately held a captain's mast for the two culprit stewards and threatened a court-martial when they returned to Pearl. Once again, Ingram had been embarrassed by Summers, and this time he vowed he would get revenge.

George Moffett thought it was all pretty funny, but he became a little more careful when he saw part of Ingram's vengeance. The stewards would be awakened at all hours of the day or night to bring coffee to Summers or the OOD. Moffett took note when he witnessed Ingram letting go with a big, juicy spit right into Pete's coffee cup before taking it to him. "I guess Summers would not have liked that very much," said Moffett in an understatement, "but he would have been just as upset had he known that the steward used his toothbrush whenever he had the chance." As for himself, Moffett remembered to be careful. "I made it a point to get my own coffee or do without regardless of how long I was on duty."

Thus, the captain and crew were again at loggerheads when *Pampanito* rounded Barber's Point and approached Pearl Harbor for the third time. This would surely be a welcome rest and recuperation.

## CHAPTER EIGHT

# To the South China Sea and Australia

There would be some celebrating. It had been another trying patrol, and the men were tired as usual, but at least this time there was something to boast about. *Pampanito* received an endorsement from Lucius H. Chappell, former skipper of *Sculpin* and now ComSubDiv 281. Chappell doubted that *Pampanito* had been the near victim of a thrown depth charge, for he did not think the Japanese had that capability. He attributed the close explosion during the nighttime convoy attack to aircraft. Chappell also commented that the poor VHF radio performance needed investigation, while other failures of the submarine's equipment seemed to mark that equipment as inferior. Nevertheless, he wrote that *Pampanito* had made a brief but spectacular and effective patrol. He praised the crew for its courage, skill, and devotion and gave special recognition to Pharmacist's Mate Demers.

Squadron commander Charles F. Erck wrote a second endorsement, concurring with Chappell and giving special recognition to Howard Fulton, Ed Stockslader, Tony Hauptman, and Maurice Demers. A third endorsement by E. J. Hynes indicated that *Pampanito* had made a splendid patrol and was credited with three ships sunk and one damaged. He praised the resourceful repairs and the rescues and indicated eligibility for a Combat Insignia Award.

Pete Summers, although physically run down, was elated by the knowledge that he would receive a Navy Cross. In addition, Sherlock and Bartholomew received routine upgrades to lieutenant junior grade and were no longer lowly ensigns. Summers arranged a "wetting down" party to celebrate.

The dinner party would take place at Trader Vic's, followed by a champagne reception at Summers's date's house after dinner. Sherlock looked forward to it—until the day of the party, when Pete presented him, Bart, and John Red with bills for $125 apiece to cover the dinner and the champagne.

Sherlock tried to make the best of it, remaining as cheerful as possible during dinner. Afterwards, when they retired to a beautiful little house in the hills, Sherlock's date developed a terrible headache and went home. Now stag, Sherlock was nominated as the wine steward. He turned morose as he contemplated a night caressing wine bottles while the others laughed and danced with live female companions. Sherlock decided to take his revenge by sampling every bottle. "After spending a month's pay for the Captain's party," he said, "I drank half of each bottle before serving the rest to the guests."

The next afternoon Sherlock found himself in sick bay. He didn't remember what had happened. He was told that on the way back to the base, the jeep they were riding in took a curve on a hillside at high speed. Sherlock was launched into space and bounced along the road a good distance before coming to a halt. "They thought I was dead," he said. "I never felt a thing, but I didn't have much skin on my back."

The men wasted no time heading for the Royal Hawaiian. One evening several men were drinking in the "Pink Palace" when they noticed Lieutenant Commander Davis imbibing alone, and they asked him to join them. Something was bothering Davis, and after a few minutes Doc Demers succeeded in getting his story. His experience as a young lieutenant on *Growler* had been haunting him.

Landon L. Davis, Jr., was born in Bedford, Virginia, on 15 October 1916. He graduated from the Naval Academy, was commissioned an ensign in 1939, and served on USS *Phoenix* (CL 46) for two years. Davis was assigned to *Growler* in March 1942. Unfortunately, on the second patrol in the East China Sea, Davis had a run-in with *Growler*'s skipper, Commander Howard W. Gilmore. One night Gilmore was sleeping in his bunk in the conning tower, and Davis was on the bridge. Twenty-three-year-old fireman Daniel M. Bialko, from Ecorse, Michigan, who would make *Growler*'s first ten patrols, remembered what happened. Lieutenant Davis had been gingerly maneuvering his way through an area of wreckage from sunken ships, seeing no need to announce the minor course changes. However, Gilmore awoke and wondered why Davis never asked about or informed him of his actions. After a few more changes, Gilmore became very angry and stormed up to the bridge, where he confronted Davis and "bitched him out." The crew liked Gilmore, Bialko said, but never knew why he was so hard on Davis on that occasion. From then on Davis could do nothing without Gilmore's jumping on him for the most trivial matters.

On *Growler*'s fourth patrol in February 1943, she was chasing Japanese ships near Rabaul in the western Solomons. Early on the morning of 7 February they spotted a ship about two thousand yards away. Gilmore turned the sub away to ready the tubes, then swung back at seventeen knots to rush in for a shot. As the sub bored in, the nine-hundred-ton provision ship *Hayasaki* had reversed course and was charging toward the sub.

On the bridge were Gilmore, Davis, Ensign William W. Williams, a quartermaster, and three lookouts. Suddenly, before a shooting solution could be determined, the ship was on them and the range was already too short to arm the torpedoes. Gilmore ordered left full rudder, and the collision alarm sounded. In moments, *Growler* rammed the ship's starboard side. In the control room, Bialko was jolted as the sub's nose crumpled and she rolled heavily to port. The exec, Lieutenant Commander Arnold F. Schade, was thrown through the conning tower hatch to the control room deck, where he landed bruised and dazed. There was chaos topside as the Japanese opened up with machine guns. Bullets sprayed the bridge. Ensign Williams was killed immediately while the lookouts scrambled for the hatch. One of them, Fireman Third Class W. F. Kelley, had never been topside before and had just talked the regular lookout into switching places with him. Kelley was hit and remained on the bridge. Two others, who Bialko remembered as Wade and Baxley, were wounded, the former in the arm and the latter with "a big chunk" taken out of his leg.

Lieutenant Davis also got down as the bullets ricocheted above him. At this point, as Davis explained to the submariners at his table in the Royal Hawaiian, the stories begin to diverge. In the standard account, Schade waited at the foot of the ladder as he heard Gilmore order everyone to clear the bridge. He waited for Gilmore, but the commander, apparently badly wounded, could not make it to the hatch. From above they heard Gilmore's last order: "Take her down."

Schade hesitated for a while, unsure whether to save the ship or to go back for the captain. Finally he gave the order to dive, leaving Gilmore, Williams, and Kelley topside. As they dove, Bialko got on the battle phones and called for damage reports. He found that most of the compartments were okay; one small electrical fire was soon under control, and only the conning tower had been punctured by bullets and was leaking water. After a short time, Schade gave the order "battle surface," but the *Hayasaki* had moved away in the darkness and was gone. Gone also were Gilmore and Williams. In a rather grisly discovery however, the crew found Kelley's body wedged in the ladder leading down from the periscope shears. For Gilmore's order sacrificing his life to save the ship, he was posthumously awarded the Medal of Honor.

The submariners were familiar with the story, for word of Gilmore and *Growler* had quickly spread through the service. Unfortunately, said Davis, that was not the way it had happened. Schade was knocked to the control room deck and was out of commission for a time. Davis had managed to get down after the quartermaster and the two wounded lookouts. But, he told Doc Demers, everyone else up there was already dead; the lookout, the assistant OOD, and the captain. "Gilmore never made that famous quote," he said. "He got his head shot off on the bridge." Davis took her down.

The incident had weighed on his mind ever since. Davis gave a nervous laugh. He had received a Silver Star "for gallantry and intrepidity in action" and a Navy and Marine Corps Medal "for extremely heroic and courageous conduct as Officer-of-the-Deck." But instead of medals, Davis said, they should have been court-martialed for getting the boat in that predicament to begin with. It was all a fake, he said. "We made up the story for propaganda purposes."

Demers saw Davis's anger about the incident and the latent problems that had surfaced because of it. Although he did not consider himself able to assess the psychological ramifications of such a trauma, Doc believed the incident contributed to the lieutenant commander's apparent nervousness and occasional sullen moods. Dick Sherlock saw that Davis was obviously plagued by nightmares. Demers never knew which version to believe.[1]

As usual, there were postpatrol transfers; this time seventeen men rotated off the boat. One man who almost got off was George Ingram, but not because of a transfer. McGuire had to pick up the pay records at the base pay office. On the way back, he saw a black man dressed in civilian clothes who looked familiar. He walked closer and saw it was *Pampanito*'s steward.

"What are you doing, Iggy?" McGuire inquired.

"I'm going. I'm jumping ship," Ingram said. "I'm not going back. That man [Summers] is crazy."

McGuire told him to think about it. He'd be a deserter. What was he going to do? How would he get a job? How would he get back to the States? It wasn't worth it, he said. Just mind your own business, stay away from him and you'll be fine, McGuire reasoned. Eventually Ingram saw the wisdom of the advice and agreed. He made his way back to the ship, and no one was ever any wiser.

Before the crew could relax, however, they all had to receive inoculations, because, according to McGuire, they had been in contact with the POWs, "who had all those crazy Asian diseases." McGuire remembered four shots, and they made him sick for one entire day. Hubert Brown thought the yellow fever shot hurt the worst.

Within a few days men were again surreptitiously cooking their gilly. Doc Demers found a party in a second-floor room. A couple of looped sailors were attempting to "tightrope" out on a flagpole that extended horizontally from the window. Electrician Don Ferguson actually managed to wobble out to the end before the pole began to bend, and he could not retreat fast enough to the ledge. Down he went. They rushed to the ground level, hoping Ferguson hadn't seriously hurt himself. Carmody was the first to find him, scratched by the shrubbery and shaken up, but otherwise unhurt.

"Go get 'em, Mike," Ferguson said to Carmody. "They must have hit me."

It was rough on the men who were to be transferred but who had to remain aboard the boat for the first two weeks while former shipmates were partying without them. Howard George was unable to wait. He left the boat and went to the Royal Hawaiian, where he crashed a party and began throwing his weight around. Some of the fellows, never too pleased with George's abrasive manner, indicated he wasn't wanted. George snarled, but seeing he was outnumbered, reluctantly conceded.

"Fine. I'll go," he said. "But first I'm taking this with me." He grabbed a bottle of gin and rushed out of the room. Carmody went after him. The two muscular sailors collided in the hall, crashing off the walls and rolling on the floor. Carmody got in a punch, but George swung the gin bottle and cracked it against Mike's head, knocking him backwards. George got loose, his own hand badly cut from the glass, and crawled forward into the arms of Maurice Demers.

"Help me, 'Doc,'" Howard pleaded.

"I'll help you, all right," Demers answered, and took another punch at George. The blow glanced off George's head, and Demers only succeeded in breaking his own finger.

Hubie Brown came out of the room and helped Carmody to his feet. He had a fine gash in his head, and Brown's stomach turned slightly at the sight. "Every time his pulse pounded," Brown said, "another spurt of blood would shoot all over those nice pink walls."

Woody Weaver and Jim Behney were rooming down the hall. Weaver opened the door, and in ran Howard George. He and Behney managed to get the staggering man calmed down and into the shower, where they cleaned him up, dried him off, and gave him a clean shirt. Later that night they secreted him back to the sub base. In the meantime, Demers patched up Carmody's cut head.

Two days later, Summers got word of the incident. George had been transferred to SubDiv 281 Relief Crew on 1 October. On Friday, 6 October, Summers had George transferred back to *Pampanito,* where the commander held a captain's mast and broke him down from chief. The next day, Summers transferred him back to the relief crew. George's association with *Pampanito* was over, and he never served aboard a submarine again.

Summers verbally blasted the other men involved, but Carmody, once again, dodged a bullet, for George was in the wrong by being away from the sub and at the hotel. Trouble, however, always seemed to find Mike Carmody. He became good friends with Demers, and Doc never knew exactly why. "Somehow we meshed," he said. "We always hung out together on R&R. Mike was my buddy."

A few days later, Doc and his buddy left their room to get a bucket of ice. They filled the container and were heading down the hall when they were confronted by an old chief from *Sealion II*. The chief wasted no time in voicing some obscenities at all *Pampanito* sailors. Demers told Mike to forget about it, but Carmody would not listen. Nobody was going to cuss *Pampanito*'s boys. A few choice phrases passed between them before the old chief knocked the ice bucket out of Mike's hands. In a flash, Carmody, who Demers described as "strong as a bull," had the chief's arm twisted behind his back until Demers heard an ugly snap. Carmody let the man go, and he and Demers hightailed it down the hall and out of sight. From the sound, Demers was sure Mike had broken the chief's arm. This time, however, no one discovered the culprits.[2]

An officer making an unexpected exit from the boat was Clifford Grommet. The relief crew had been working on the boat for a week. Three main engines and the auxiliary engine were overhauled, a Mark 8 TBT was installed, and the SAE 1045 "USN" motor brushes were replaced with the old SAE 1045 brushes. The army VHF communications system was replaced with a navy VHF, and they received new steel rectangle gasket hatches. Engine overhaul and hatch work required access to the sub's interior through the "hard patch," a removable welded section of the pressure hull. When the work was completed, the patch was welded back in place.

Newly promoted Lieutenant Commander Grommet was overseeing the pressure test in the after engine room to see if it was airtight. Liberty time was near, but pressurization and decompression were time-consuming. Moffett explained: "It was an unfortunate fact that Lieutenant Commander Grommet was probably the least liked officer aboard, and the least inclined to take advice from any enlisted personnel." As the time passed, Moffett said, "Grommet became increasingly impatient with the slow process and suggested to one of the motor macs that he open the inboard air induction flapper valve to complete the depressurization." The valve is designed to seat with sea pressure, and releasing the lever lock would be dangerous in a highly pressurized compartment.

"A motor mac informed Grommet that he did not think this would be a good idea—without explaining why." Disinclined to take the advice,

Grommet reached up to the overhead and released the lock on the three-foot levered arm. The compartment pressure forced the suddenly freed flapper valve to snap open, forcing the lever down through its full arc. It caught Grommet full force in his arm and shoulder, badly cutting his biceps and knocking him flat to the deck. He ended up in the naval hospital and was off the boat.

The men increasingly talked of politics during their two weeks of "rest." The elections would be held in less than one month, with President Roosevelt running for an unprecedented fourth term in office against Republican challenger Thomas E. Dewey, the young governor of New York.

Tom Dewey looked for any key that might crack Roosevelt's coalition. Republicans charged that the Roosevelt administration knew of the planned attack against Pearl Harbor and did nothing about it. Dewey believed Roosevelt's knowledge of the episode could lead to his impeachment. This sensitive issue brought the army chief of staff, General George C. Marshall, into the affair. Marshall was afraid that further rhetoric would reveal that the United States had broken the Japanese codes and place the entire radio intelligence operation in jeopardy. Marshall talked to Dewey, explaining the vital importance of keeping the information secret. In a September 1944 letter, "For Mr. Dewey's eyes only," Marshall explained the radio intelligence details. He told Dewey that codebreaking had given America the advantage in the Battle of the Coral Sea and at Midway; that we knew the strengths of Japanese garrisons and the sailing dates and routes of their convoys. The revelations "poleaxed" Dewey, and he agreed to drop the issue for the good of the country. He never made the information public. In taking that course, Dewey probably gave away any chance that he had of winning the election.

Roosevelt had everything going for him in the weeks before the voting. The labor movement, both the AFL and the CIO, was fully committed to the war effort and pledged not to strike for the duration of hostilities. The only organization of any size not to exercise restraint during the war was John L. Lewis's independent miners' union.

Servicemen were not pleased with strikers. They were out fighting for their country while the stay-at-home laborers had access to women and much higher wages. To some, wartime strikes seemed a mixture of blackmail and treason. Commander Galantin, while refitting his sub at the

Bethlehem Steel Company shipyard in San Francisco, wrote that the selfishness and lack of patriotism in some of the unions "is nauseating." The POWs still languishing in Japanese prison camps in the Philippines listened clandestinely on their secret radios, cursed the strikers in Detroit, and ripped apart beetle-browed John L. Lewis and his coal miners. Even Tokyo Rose made mileage out of the coal miners' strike, taunting the sailors, asking if their wives were being faithful while everyone back home was making plenty of money. The bad press about the unions had its effect. According to Red McGuire, the entire *Pampanito* crew thought "all strikers were pricks."[3]

Personnel changes made between patrols were routine but never easy. Old shipmates made their heartfelt goodbyes and good-lucks and moved on. One change that definitely caught the crew by surprise was the replacement of Captain Summers. Skippers left their boats for a number of reasons. Some were removed for a lack of success in sinking enemy shipping. Others, however, were removed because of the stress of the job. Psychiatrists claimed that four patrols in command of a submarine should be the limit. A man, like a steel spring, was only good for so many torsions and tensions without being subject to failure. Will power was like a capital balance that a man expended during a patrol; eventually it would be spent and the man was finished.[4]

After his third patrol in *Pampanito,* and tenth overall, Paul Summers had had enough. Summers said that at his debriefing with Admiral Lockwood and Captain Fenno, "I asked Admiral Lockwood for a leave. I was run down." Thin to begin with, he now looked almost skeletal. There was no problem with his relief. Apparently the decision was made even easier when Fenno thought about it for a minute.

"Hell, I'll take your boat out!" Fenno exclaimed.

Thus, Mike Fenno came to command *Pampanito.*

Frank Wesley Fenno, Jr., was born in Westminster, Massachusetts, 11 September 1902. He went to the University of Maine for two years before attending the Naval Academy. He played baseball for the Academy for three years and was captain of the team in 1925. Fenno served on USS *Utah,* on USS *Florida,* and then on the submarines *S-37* and *S-31.* After a stint as an instructor in electrical engineering at the Naval Academy, he returned to sea duty on *S-12* and *S-45.* In 1940, Fenno assumed command of *Trout.*

In February 1942, Fenno sailed to Corregidor and delivered thirty-five hundred rounds of antiaircraft ammunition to the hard-pressed garrison, along with canned food, grapefruit, and cigarettes. After removal of all the ammo and supplies, *Trout* needed ballast. Before Manila had fallen, the silver and gold was removed from the banks. Perhaps *Trout* could use the bullion as ballast. On the night of 4 February, two tons of gleaming yellow gold bars and eighteen tons of clinking sacks of silver were stowed away in her hold. Heading back to Pearl Harbor, Fenno managed to sink a 200-ton patrol boat and the 2,718-ton *Chuwa Maru*.

For this outstanding patrol Fenno was awarded a Distinguished Service Cross by the army and a Navy Cross by his own service, and every member of the submarine was decorated with the army's Silver Star. For future successes on *Trout*, Fenno received a Gold Star in lieu of a second Navy Cross. He returned to the States in the summer of 1942 to take command of USS *Runner* (SS 275). In two patrols, *Runner* was credited with damaging enough additional Japanese shipping to earn Fenno another Gold Star. Fenno left *Runner* in May 1943, and on the next patrol, under John H. Bourland, the boat was lost with all hands off northeast Honshu after striking a Japanese mine.

Fenno became commander of SubDiv 201 in September 1943, and in May and June of 1944 he commanded the wolf pack "Fenno's Ferrets," consisting of *Picuda, Peto,* and the new boat *Perch II* (SS 313). Operating in Luzon Strait, the "Ferrets" had bad luck. Attack chances were missed, communications were poor, and there was a noticeable lack of aggressiveness among the boats. Only *Picuda* managed to sink the twelve-hundred-ton river gunboat *Hashidate*. In another abortive attack, *Perch II* was badly depth charged and almost lost. After the patrol, the skipper of *Peto*, Paul Van Leunen, was relieved of command, and *Picuda*'s skipper, Albert Raborn, voluntarily stepped down.[5]

Fenno received a Silver Star for his command of the "Ferrets," but it may have been because of that rather dubious award that he jumped at the chance to take out a submarine again. In any event, on 7 October 1944, Captain Fenno took over *Pampanito*. Naturally, the crew was happy. Steward's Mate Ingram was thrilled; maybe he would not have to jump ship. Their new skipper was said to be an enlisted man's friend.

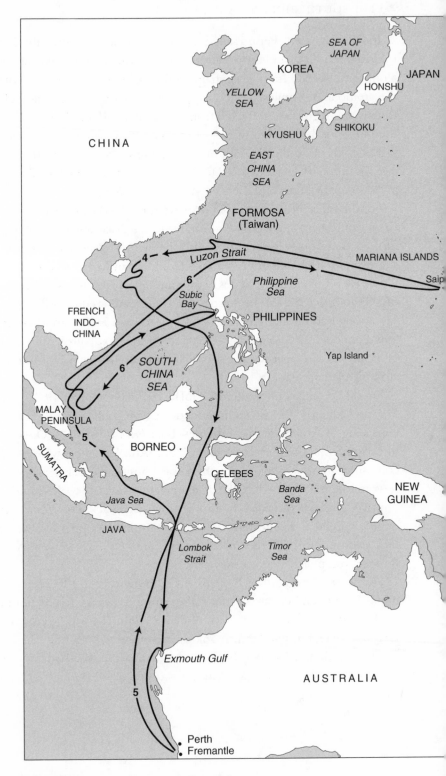

USS *Pampanito* patrol routes 4, 5, and 6

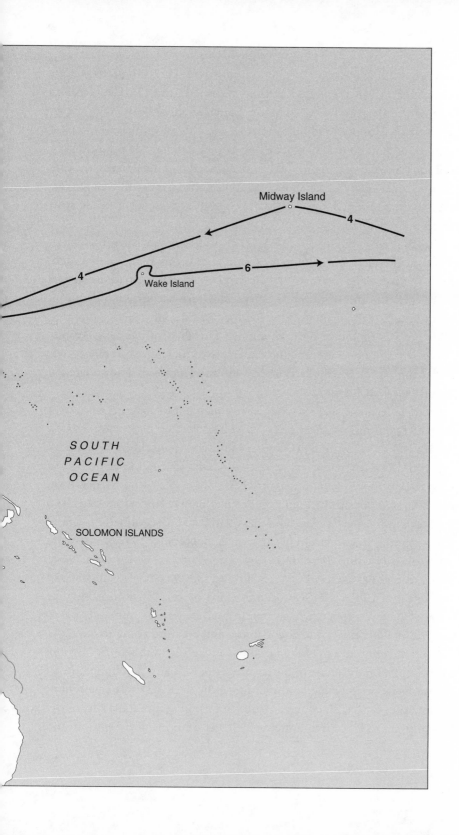

Midway Island

4

4

6

Wake Island

SOUTH
PACIFIC
OCEAN

SOLOMON ISLANDS

When refitting was over, another training period in the endless process of breaking in new men and equipment ensued from 17 to 25 October. Although Fenno may have had better management skills than Summers, said Gordon Hopper, "it didn't mean he took it easy on his crew. To the contrary, he put us through rigorous preparation that made prior training runs look like picnics." They dove and surfaced countless times, seeking to shave off precious seconds in getting to periscope depth. "I still have scars on both shins," Hopper said, "the result of banging into the steel rungs on the ladders."

Shortly before sailing, Red McGuire went to the Navy Exchange wearing a Hawaiian shirt, dungarees, and sandals. Sub Base Security men, whom the crew referred to as "the Gestapo," picked him up for being out of uniform and threw him in the brig. McGuire had no identification. Security had to call the duty officer to verify that McGuire was a submarine sailor on *Pampanito,* as he maintained. The duty officer sent Woody Weaver to the brig to identify the embarrassed McGuire and escort him back to the boat. It was the second time in Pearl Harbor that he had nearly missed *Pampanito*'s sailing.

On the afternoon of 28 October, *Pampanito* got underway for her fourth war patrol, this time leading her own wolf pack. One packmate was USS *Pipefish* (SS 388), on her third patrol and commanded by William N. Deragon. Deragon had served as exec on *Seawolf* for eight patrols before going to Portsmouth to fit out *Pipefish.* USS *Sea Cat* (SS 399) was a new boat, also a Portsmouth product, and on her first patrol. Her skipper was Rob Roy McGregor, from the Academy class of 1929. McGregor had captained *Grouper* for three patrols. On his first, on 21 September 1942, he sank the 4,070-ton cargo ship *Tone Maru.* One week later he sank *Lisbon Maru,* killing about 850 British POWs, a sinking that McGregor said was not directed by ULTRA. His second and third patrols were unproductive because of many torpedo failures, and he was relieved of command, spending staff time in Submarine Squadrons 6 and 8 before going to *Sea Cat.*

Captain Fenno was in charge of the wolf pack he dubbed the "Fenno-mints," a play on the name of the laxative gum Feenamint. Joining him on *Pampanito* as prospective commanding officer (PCO) was Lieutenant Commander Earl T. Hydeman. Hydeman, who had graduated from the Academy in 1932, had spent much of his time in New London and

Washington. It was his first war patrol. Fenno and Hydeman opened their orders and found that their destination would be the South China Sea, near the area of the POW rescue. The submarines headed for Midway.

On 1 November, *Pampanito* reached Sand Island and began topping off her fuel. *Sea Cat* and *Pipefish* soon moored alongside. All ships made minor repairs, while *Sea Cat* needed extra work on her SD radar.

While tied up, *Pampanito* received a visitor. Frank Michno, who had transferred off the boat to the relief crew in July, had come to see his old shipmates. He was tired of Midway and had wondered if his old boat needed another engineman, but there were no vacancies. Frank learned all about the third patrol, the ship sinkings, and the rescue of the POWs.

It figured. He was stranded on a speck of sand in the Pacific while his buddies were out having all the fun. Four days earlier, Michno had hoped to get on *Albacore,* which had stopped for fuel before departing on patrol of the Empire. The boat needed an engineman. They looked for Michno, but he had been playing softball and had fallen asleep at the ball diamond. When he returned to base he learned that *Albacore* had sailed with a motor mac second class. Michno kicked himself in the pants. He had blown another chance to get off Midway—and on a boat that had many past successes, including the sinking of a carrier. It was back to the old routine. "There was nothing to do but save up your beer chits and watch the damn gooney birds," he said.

In truth, Michno's luck wasn't so bad after all. *Albacore,* under Lieutenant Commander Hugh R. Rimmer, was making her eleventh war patrol. On 7 November, off the coast of Honshu near Esan Misaki, a Japanese patrol boat was trailing an American submarine. The submerged boat apparently hit a mine, for there was a large underwater explosion, followed by pools of floating oil and debris bobbing to the surface. *Albacore* was never heard from again.

It was not the first time that fate had smiled on Michno. On the *S-11* he had twice drawn straws with shipmates to see who would go to new construction. One man went to *Scorpion,* and the other went to *Cisco.* Both boats were lost with all hands.

Charlie McGuire, too, had dodged a bullet when he was unable to get on *Golet.* The boat had troubles. McGuire's friend, Lieutenant Commander James S. Clark, was PCO. The first run resulted in no sinkings. Clark met expectations, but Lieutenant Commander Philip H. Ross recommended that several officers and chiefs be removed. Ross left the boat, and Clark became the new skipper, but they kept the men that Ross had found wanting. *Golet* once again went on the "Polar Circuit" off Hokkaido and the Kuriles. An ASW patrol in the area recorded a depth charge attack on 14 June, which produced cork, rafts, oil, and other debris. *Golet* was lost with all hands.[6]

Joining the wolf pack at Midway was the old USS *Searaven* (SS 196), on her thirteenth patrol and commanded by Raymond Berthrong, a 1938 Naval Academy graduate. Three boats headed for Saipan. *Sea Cat* would join them when her radar was repaired. On 5 November, an acute case of appendicitis was reported on board *Pipefish,* and she raced for Saipan at maximum speed. On 7 November, *Archerfish* was sighted, and it joined the group for the remainder of the passage. *Archerfish,* under Commander Joseph F. Enright, was on her fifth war patrol, en route to a spot off Honshu where she would later in the month sink the biggest Japanese ship ever downed by an American submarine, the fifty-nine-thousand-ton aircraft carrier *Shinano.*

On 9 November, *Pampanito* and *Searaven* entered Tanapag Harbor and moored to the tender *Fulton. Pipefish* was already there. She had success-fully delivered her appendicitis patient but had suffered cracked liners on number four engine because of the speedy run. After seeing that the batteries had a fresh supply of water, Pappas and a few mates took a quick tour of the island.

"Everything is all shot up," he wrote. "We inspected Japanese pill boxes along the beach, and also saw a stockyard of Jap airplane engines, search-lights, antitank guns, and five-inch guns that never got unpacked. It is all useless now . . . going to decay for lack of care." Tour over, they returned to the boat.

Construction battalions had been working at full speed on Saipan, trying to build the mile-and-a-half-long runways necessary to accom-modate the B-29s that would be based there for the long-range bombing of Japan. Isolated Japanese soldiers still hiding on the island occasionally tried to disrupt the construction with suicidal attacks. On 2 November, nine twin-engine Japanese bombers flew in at low level to bomb Isley Field. Five days later there were two separate attacks of five planes each. Hubert Brown listened to Tokyo Rose on the night of 9 November. After making some comments about "who was screwing your wife back home," Brown said, Rose commented about the submarines in Tanapag Harbor: "We see all those little guppies tied up alongside the submarine tender in Saipan," she said. "We'll see you tonight, boys." That night everything was blacked out and extra watches were set. The planes did come, said Brown, but they went past the harbor and attacked the airfield.

There is something to be said about the sense of humor of both antagonists. On more than one occasion Rose had apologized for playing the same records over and over again, lamenting that she did not have the most popular songs to entertain her favorite "boneheads of the Pacific." Soon after, on the orders of Lieutenant General Robert Eichelberger, a B-29 was sent over Tokyo with a load of records for her, dropped by parachute. Unfortunately, most of them broke on impact.[7]

On 10 November, *Sea Cat* finally arrived in Tanapag, and by the next day all four boats were ready to go. The submarines headed west, making numerous plane contacts. For a change, *Pampanito*'s SD and IFF were working flawlessly, detecting aircraft at thirty-five miles. Two contacts in the middle of the Philippine Sea did not trigger a friendly response, but Fenno kept *Pampanito* on the surface, heading for Bashi Channel.

The long days fell into a repetitive routine that was, according to George Moffett, very unlike what one usually sees in Hollywood movies. Patrols were tiresome, lengthy, and "not filled with adrenalin-laced approach and attack action." The first few days were taken up with stowing personal gear, training new men, familiarizing the crew with new and modified equipment, and giving qualification instructions. According to Moffett:

Patrol then settled into a monotonous, seemingly endless routine of four hours on duty, eight hours off duty, day and night. Off duty time was spent sleeping, eating, playing cribbage or visiting other departments or crew members. . . . There was a rhythm to a boat on patrol, the sea motion, the sounds of the engines and of the internal equipment such as ventilation blowers, the main motors, and even the periodic slap of the sea against the hull. There was always the ever full coffee urn, the sounds from the crew's radios and the Fox code emanating from the radio shack in the Control Room, along with routine course orders to the helmsman.

Card games were very popular. McGuire considered himself a good pinochle player. He liked three-handed cut-throat, and he figured the only way he could lose was if the other two players ganged up on him. He became so adept at the game that he could find few opponents.

McGuire wanted to learn the finer points of cribbage. His introduction to the game had come during the first patrol at the hands of Walt Richter. In one of their games, Richter came up with a twenty-nine-point hand, the highest possible hand he could be dealt. Odds of its happening were approximately one in a quarter-million. "It cost McGuire quite a penny," Richter said. Needless to say, Charlie shied away from further games with "The Gambler." Now he decided he would learn the game from Woody Weaver, a good and an honest player. McGuire went to the forward torpedo room and made his proposal.

"Sure, I'll teach you," Weaver told him, "but at five cents a hole."

"Come on Woody," McGuire protested, "we're old buddies."

"Correct," Weaver answered, "but if you want to learn, you have to pay for the experience." McGuire reluctantly agreed.

"However, there is still a bit of luck involved in cribbage cards," McGuire chuckled, "and soon enough, Weaver owed me about fifty bucks." Fifty dollars was a lot of money for any enlisted man, and Weaver quit. McGuire got up from the table and laughed. "Gosh!" he exclaimed. "How am I going to ever learn anything from you? You can't play."

Although McGuire was popular with the crew, he was also an agitator. In one of his money-making schemes, Charlie filled his head with trivia from the *World Almanac.* He bet that no one could write down the names of all the states and their capitals within five minutes, then circulated through the boat, taking men for five dollars and ten dollars at a time.

"He started his scam in the crew's mess," Woody Weaver said. "I heard of it via the grapevine, and knew it would not be long before I was challenged. I decided to do a bit of preparation." He looked up the states on his own and wrote down a few capitals he might have trouble with. He had just finished when McGuire burst in with his challenge. Weaver didn't have the time to dispose of his review paper, so he flipped it over. Not wanting to appear too anxious to accept the bet, Weaver demurred for a minute. "Mac wanted to get on with it and asked if I had some paper which could be used. Before I could stop him, he picked up my review paper and turned it over. He had uncovered my trap!"

McGuire's eyes "bugged out," Woody said, "when he realized what he almost walked into. He yelled, 'No bet! No bet!' and charged out of the room. I had a big laugh about that. It was one time I got the best of McGuire." But, Weaver concluded, "It would have been much sweeter if I had managed to take him for five bucks."

Fenno led the wolf pack toward Bashi Channel, and on the morning of 15 November he received an ULTRA about a convoy. He directed the four boats into a scouting line, heading in the direction of the calculated interception point. About 0900 *Pampanito* sighted and exchanged signals with USS *Besugo* (SS 321), out of Pearl Harbor on her second patrol. A half hour later a large Japanese plane came in from dead ahead at low altitude and drove *Pampanito* down for about an hour.

After surfacing, the pack continued on at four-engine speed. At 1250 they sighted and exchanged signals with two more boats, *Pintado* and *Halibut*. The latter, under Commander Pete Galantin, had the day before taken a vicious depth charging from escorts directed by Japanese planes equipped with *jikitanchiki,* a magnetic airborne detection system (MAD). An anomaly in the earth's magnetic field caused by a submarine hull at shallow depths could be detected by planes with MAD equipment. *Halibut* had been found in this manner and nearly destroyed. After shaking her pursuers, *Halibut* was lucky to find *Pintado*, which escorted her to Saipan. She was so badly damaged she would not be worth repairing.

Many subs were in Convoy College, including two additional wolf packs: "Clarey's Crushers," with *Pintado, Jallao* (SS 368) and *Atule* (SS 403), and "Roach's Raiders," with *Haddock* (SS 231), *Halibut,* and *Tuna* (SS 203). The number of submarines was a grim reminder to Japan of the tightening stranglehold that was being placed on its lifelines. During October, American submarines sank over 314,000 tons of Japanese shipping, the highest monthly total of the war. By the end of the year, the Japanese merchant fleet would be down to 2,500,000 tons, only 40 percent of the shipping that had been available in December 1941. It was not just coincidence that caused torpedoman Weaver to announce: "It seemed we sighted a friendly sub every few days."[8]

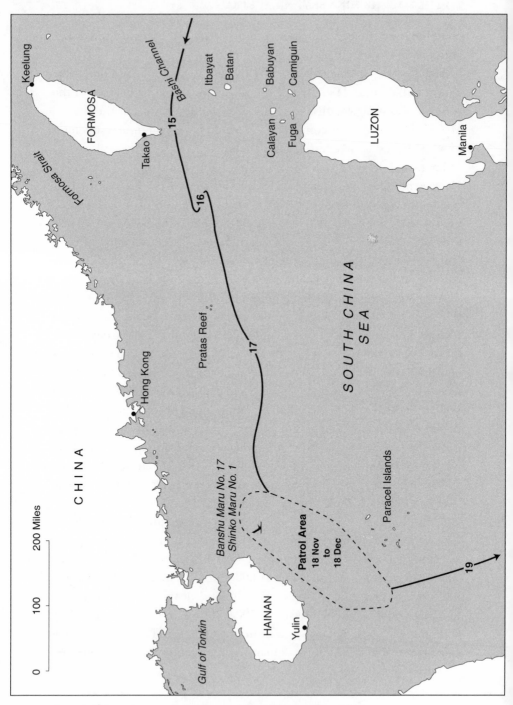

Detail of fourth patrol, 15 November–18 December 1944

The "Fennomints" continued through Bashi Channel, the northern entrance to the South China Sea, completing the transit at midnight. On 16 November they patrolled submerged on their assigned station, hunting for the convoy. Fenno led the pack from a point southwest of Formosa back toward Bashi Channel on course 120, combing perpendicularly across the convoy's projected path. After a day's patrolling, there was not a ship in sight. Even with ULTRA working for them, there was still a bit of luck involved in finding targets on an immense ocean.

Heading for Hainan, *Pampanito* exchanged recognition signals with *Jallao* and *Sailfish*. On 17 November the pack entered its area. Fenno had them conduct surface patrol with SDs manned and using high periscope, roughly paralleling Hainan's east coast. Closest ashore was *Searaven*, then came *Pampanito*, with *Pipefish* and *Sea Cat* eastward.

Unknown to the "Fennomints," major elements of the Japanese fleet were approaching the eastern edge of their patrol area. Having left Brunei, Borneo, on 16 November, the battleships *Kongo*, *Nagato*, and *Yamato*, accompanied by light cruiser *Yahagi* and Destroyer Squadron 2, were heading north for Japan. On 17 November, as Fenno's pack passed south of the Pratas Islands on a southwesterly course, the Japanese battleships were approaching from the south on a northeasterly course. It was in this very area that "Ben's Busters" had sunk four ships two months earlier. Yet at least one officer aboard the *Yamato* did not appear worried. Vice Admiral Ugaki had little fear of submarines, since their force was "well away from the coast of the Philippines." He did not realize that good fortune had allowed him to miss sailing right into a hungry wolf pack of four submarines.[9]

Fenno maintained the formation until 18 November, when *Pampanito* apparently received an ULTRA signal, although it was not mentioned in the log.[10] Fenno abruptly changed course to due west and increased speed to fifteen knots. At 0730 he recorded: "Arrived at position, commenced surface patrol on course 170 T. and 270 T. on half hour legs across the traffic lanes from southern coast of Hainan to Hong Kong." At 0915 a lookout sighted three bombers approaching in formation, and *Pampanito* submerged. Expecting aircraft regularly while operating so close to Hainan and "desiring not to be detected this early in the game," Fenno kept the boat down for the day.

At 1808 Fenno surfaced, and all the subs were ready for action. Apparently his dispositions were sound, for at 1940 *Pipefish* reported a contact at 19 degrees, 32 minutes north, 111 degrees, 50 minutes east. All boats were ordered to intercept and attack. By chance, *Pampanito* was almost on the enemy's track. She changed course to run ahead, then turned to wait. At 2047, Fenno had SJ contact at ten thousand yards. There were three ships, an escort leading a fairly large freighter about one thousand yards astern, and a slightly smaller escort about seven hundred yards off the port quarter of what Fenno called "the big fellow."

*Pampanito*'s maneuverings point to the likelihood that Fenno had been directed by ULTRA. Information gleaned from Japanese radio communications shows that at 1616 on 17 November, a message was sent out from Hong Kong to the Hainan Guard District commander stating that a three-ship convoy, including a special subchaser (name garbled), had departed Hong Kong at 1500 of 17 November to arrive at Yulin at 1600 on 19 November. At Yulin, there was to be a transfer of cargo, and the final destination was to be Saigon. One vessel, the 1,200-ton civilian cargo ship *Shinko Maru No. 1* (garbled as *Sokuko Maru No. 1*) carried 130 tons of miscellaneous freight. The other was the 459-ton depot ship *Banshu Maru No. 17*. Their 18 November noon position was to be 20 degrees, 30 minutes north, 112 degrees, 35 minutes east, and they made a request for patrol arrangements. The message was sent in the familiar JN-40 code, and JICPOA had it translated on 18 November.

The noon position would place the convoy about one hundred miles off the northeast tip of Hainan. The "Fennomints" set up for the evening about fifty miles ahead of that point, directly on the line of the convoy's Hong Kong–Yulin course.

After the first contact, Fenno sat tight, tracking for one and a half hours while waiting for *Pipefish* to attack. No doubt comments were made about the skipper's courtesy in giving the first shot to the boat that made the initial discovery. Meanwhile, the tracking party determined that the Japanese were not zigzagging and were on a course of 220, with a speed of about ten knots.

*Searaven* closed in and took position about three miles off *Pampanito*'s port beam, which boxed in the convoy on three sides. By 2230, the men were getting impatient. Finally the radio crackled with a message from

*Pipefish.* She had picked up persistent interference on her SJ on the same bearing as the target and suspected it might have been a friendly submarine. She broke off contact and made no attack.

Fenno had a different idea. He recorded: "We had a clear picture of the situation and know that any SJ interference in the vicinity of our contacts would have been picked up by this time." There was no more time for courtesy. Two minutes later Fenno sent out a concise, "Am attacking," and headed *Pampanito* in.

The boat was now about ninety-five hundred yards off the track, and Fenno headed west, plunging into the pitch dark night and rough seas at eighteen knots. After a short run, he came to course 010 and bored in from the enemy's port side. His target was the large freighter, now on the port quarter of the escort. At 2323 they were about twenty-seven hundred yards from the target, but the lookouts could not see anything in the blackness. Fenno decided to fire on radar bearings and loosed six bow torpedoes using a one-degree divergent spread, gyro angles at 340 degrees with a 60-degree port track.

While the fish were speeding toward the leading freighter, *Pampanito* came hard right to unmask her stern tubes. The solution for the trailing freighter showed the same range of twenty-seven hundred yards, but with a gyro angle of 205 degrees and a port track of 100 degrees. The torpedoes were set to alternate depths of six and eight feet because of the high seas. At 2325, two more fish were heading to the second target, which was now overlapping the large freighter. The escort was far ahead and out of the way.

Before the last fish were away, the men on the bridge were treated to the sight and sounds of two great explosions. One torpedo had hit slightly abaft the middle of the target, and the other exploded near the stern. A bright orange flash was seen, followed by a huge cloud of smoke that billowed up to about five hundred feet. The ship burned for only two minutes, then disappeared from the radar screen.

One minute later there was another blast. A small flash of flame burst from the second ship. By this time *Pampanito* was about five thousand yards from the targets. However, the illumination from the fires enabled those on the bridge to see the first target go down by the stern. The OOD lost one target from his binoculars at this time, and one blip also disappeared

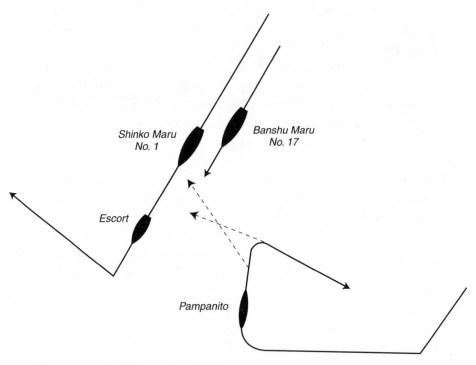

Convoy attack, 18 November 1944

from radar. Paul Pappas heard from the lookouts that they "saw one freighter blow sky high." *Pampanito* withdrew to reload. The bad visibility did not allow Fenno a positive identification, but he thought he had hit a mast-funnel-mast freighter with a block superstructure amidships, weighing about six thousand tons. He guessed the second target was about five thousand tons. The escort and the damaged freighter turned towards Hainan, and Fenno directed Ray Berthrong on *Searaven* to continue the attack. Shortly after midnight, *Banshu Maru No. 17* finally got off an urgent message: "0030, 19th. Torpedo attack with two hits in position 19-00 North, 111-00 East."

*Searaven* chased the fleeing *Banshu Maru No. 17* and the subchaser toward the Hainan coast. At two in the morning, Berthrong reported that he had completed two unsuccessful attacks, and Fenno ordered all boats to return to their previous stations. At 0221, however, Fenno recorded hearing two heavy explosions. No other boat in the pack claimed making an attack. Likely it was the crippled *Banshu Maru No. 17* finally giving up the ghost.[11]

After this quick success, targets almost disappeared during the next eight days. On 23 November, Thanksgiving dinner was interrupted when a lookout spied a raft floating nearby. For the crew who had been involved with the rescue on the previous patrol, the news was provocative; perhaps it was a chance to win more laurels. Unfortunately, the raft was empty. Late that day they got an SJ contact at 11,700 yards, but the ship was moving at high speed, and eventually it pulled away.

On this patrol the crew enjoyed their new captain. Bob Bennett said, "Fenno was not like Summers. He would not wake the stewards up at night to get him food. He'd get his own coffee and sandwiches in the galley." One morning, Gordon Hopper was in the crew's mess when Fenno strolled in and asked the cook for a cup of soup. When he found that none was prepared, he wanted to know what kind of ship it was that didn't have "ten-thirty soup for all hands." And for the rest of the patrol, soup was always ready. Fenno once walked into the crew's mess in his underwear, wondering if the enlisted men's library had anything worth reading. He told them "that he'd read everything in the wardroom and was going to have to read the Bible if he could find nothing else."

Clyde Markham certainly liked Fenno better than Summers, probably because he didn't do anything wrong for Fenno to chew him out about. "He was just a better guy than Pete," Markham said. "He'd mix with the crew. He'd come into the crew's mess in his skivvies, itching and scratching like a sailor, and sit and talk to the men. He was a regular guy."

George Moffett had a reason for liking Fenno: the skipper trusted the radar and Moffett's evaluations. Molly could paint a clear picture of an attack situation for him, as well as locate the other subs from their interference azimuths on the radar. It was one of the reasons that Fenno charged in to attack while *Pipefish* demurred because of an uncertain picture of the tactical layout.

The last few days of November, *Pampanito* patrolled thirty to forty miles from the Hainan coast. On 27 November they sighted four small ships by high periscope at twenty-five thousand yards and moving to the northeast. *Pampanito* and *Searaven* went in pursuit, while *Pipefish* covered the southerly headings, but they lost the ships at dusk and never regained contact. During the past several moonlit nights, the Japanese began sending out patrol planes to harass them. Even so, Fenno used the SD continuously in the daylight and every thirty seconds to one minute during the night.

The morning of 28 November, high periscope again sighted the same four ships that had disappeared the previous night. With better visibility this time, *Pampanito*'s lookouts were able to identify them as small patrol craft. The pack steered clear. However, the next morning they found what Fenno called "our old friends, the patrol vessels of yesterday and the day before, still hanging around the same general area." This time there were six patrol boats, and once more, the pack steered away.

Fenno ran on the surface to increase sighting range. Late on 29 November, *Pampanito* picked up a blip on the SJ at twenty-five thousand yards. The night was crystal clear, with a flat, calm sea and a full moon. The excellent visibility meant that the sub would have to stay beyond twenty thousand yards while making an end-around. They sent out a contact report and commenced the chase.

The convoy was making wild zigzags. Eventually the tracking party determined that the convoy's base course was being altered every hour, its commander apparently cognizant of the difficulty this would cause any trailing submarines. Best estimate of the convoy's course was 220 degrees with a speed of fifteen to sixteen knots.

It was dawn on 30 November before *Pampanito* finally worked her way slightly ahead of the enemy's port bow. The sub was still seven thousand yards off the track, but the brightening eastern sky ruled out a continued surface end-around. The situation, said Fenno, "made it necessary to get things done in a hurry." At 0419 he dove, but the good visibility meant he could not come up to radar depth. He made a periscope approach, but the disparity in speeds only allowed him to close to four thousand yards.

There appeared to be four medium-sized ships in column. The two leaders were tankers, configured with a low stack aft, a low bridge structure well forward of amidships, a cruiser bow, and a low island forward. There were at least three escorts visible: one on the port bow of the formation, one on the port quarter, and one on the starboard bow. They were all actively pinging. The sound operator counted at least five different sonars. The escort commander was apparently serious about protecting his charges.

Fenno got as close as he could and fired the bow tubes. Three fish went off toward the leading ship, and three to the second, using a depth setting of only four feet in the flat seas. The sub swung around to let go the stern fish. Fenno tried for an escort, but it was too far away with a 100-degree angle on the bow, and now he could not get a bearing on the remaining ships.

Five long minutes passed without the sound of a torpedo explosion. Sound was picking up pinging at all compass bearings, yet the escorts seemed to have disappeared from periscope view. Fenno decided to take *Pampanito* deep.

Starting at 0505 and for the next three minutes the men on the submarine heard five torpedo explosions. From the time of the run the quartermaster judged that the first one could have been a hit but that the last four must have been end-of-run explosions. Fenno thought he might have damaged a tanker, but he could not be certain. No depth charges were dropped.

*Pampanito* reloaded and surfaced almost two hours later. The ships were gone, and none of the other boats were able to get into attack position because of the convoy's speed. The chase had taken *Pampanito* out of her area, about 120 miles south of Hainan, and halfway to the Indo-Chinese mainland. They ran north.

During the evening, the radar scope began acting up with "gremlins" the likes of which hadn't been experienced since off the coast of Japan. There were five of them, at ranges of seventeen thousand to sixty-five thousand yards, and Fenno cautiously closed. The weather was calm and clear with bright moonlight, but still nothing was visible, even as close as seven thousand yards to the nearest pip. The "gremlins" faded away. Just before midnight, *Searaven* was sighted at ten thousand yards. All the "Fennomints" were now back in their assigned area.

Perhaps the radar anomalies were a harbinger of changing weather patterns, for as the new month began, the weather began to deteriorate. Some of the old salts said they could feel it in their bones—there definitely was a storm brewing. The skies turned gray on 1 December, but the seas were still strangely calm. Next day the wind picked up out of the north, and the rollers began to grow. Only one plane was seen. At 1243 an empty, unmarked life raft was sighted bobbing in the rising seas about thirty miles south of the position where they had sunk *Kachidoki Maru* two and one-half months before. By the end of the day Fenno recorded: "We were in the throes of a northeast monsoon with high seas and continuous rain."

The monsoon of southern Asia is probably the most impressive weather phenomenon of the tropics. It is not a hurricane, cyclone, or typhoon, which are local names for spiraling, low-pressure tropical disturbances. The monsoon is a seasonal reversal of wind and weather systems caused by temperature contrasts between land and sea areas. In the winter, intense high-pressure areas over the Asian continent blow their heavy cold air south over the warmer seas.

Mid-September to mid-December is a transitional period in the monsoon cycle, with the summer monsoon fading away and unstable weather patterns coming into play. To complicate matters, the "typhoon nursery" in the western Carolines sends an average of twenty-one storms per year across the Philippine Sea, making the Philippine Islands the most tropical storm–battered of any country in the world. Many storms rage across the islands and into the South China Sea, where they can be caught by the northerly monsoon and deflected south. The interminable bad weather experienced by the "Fennomints" over the next two weeks may have been because of these weather patterns. December 1944 was one of the worst months for storms ever experienced by the U.S. Navy during the war in the Pacific.[12]

In the inky darkness early on 3 December, *Searaven* made contact with a convoy, and Fenno ordered all boats to close in and attack. It was quite a ride, for the near gale winds produced rolling waves of fifteen feet. Nevertheless, four bobbing submarines struggled to approach the oncoming convoy of four oilers, one passenger ship, one cargo ship, one more unidentified ship, and four escorts. It was a large group for this stage of the war and, like the convoy of 18 November, it was on a course of 220, apparently heading from Hong Kong to Yulin or points south.

This time *Pampanito* was far from the convoy and remained out of action while the other boats got in their licks. *Searaven* went in first, and at 0410 she reported sinking an 11,600-ton passenger ship during a surface radar attack. Thirty minutes later, *Sea Cat* radioed that she had made her attack, sinking a 10,000-ton oiler. By 0446 *Pipefish* reported she was attacking, and *Searaven* also headed in for her second try. Under a windswept canvas of lead-gray sky, *Pampanito*'s lookouts searched fruitlessly for a sight contact. She had finally attained a position ahead of the targets and slowed down to listen for pinging, but with no results. Slowly she headed northeasterly, up the convoy's estimated track. Two days of monsoon rains had made it impossible to fix an accurate position.

*Pampanito* homed in on SJ interference and at 0506 finally picked up a pip at thirty thousand yards, bearing 076 degrees. One minute later, beyond the horizon, Fenno "heard and saw a beautiful explosion." This time, *Searaven* claimed hitting an oiler of 9,200 tons. Four minutes later, one of *Searaven*'s stern shots hit and damaged another oiler. She reported that three ships and two escorts were heading away from her at thirteen knots. She was remaining behind to finish off the crippled oiler.

At daybreak *Pampanito* could make out five targets on radar, which matched *Searaven*'s report, but the way her packmates were hitting the convoy, there might be nothing left to shoot at. Still bucking the heavy seas, Fenno had the torpedomen set the fish to run at eight feet, hoping they would be deep enough to keep beneath the waves. The order to battle stations rang out. On the scope were three ships and two escorts, holding course 220 at a speed of twelve knots.

At 0544, as they fought the waves to get in position, they heard three more explosions. It was beginning to resemble the third patrol, when all the other subs got in shots while *Pampanito* sat on the sidelines. The latest attack came from *Pipefish*. Deragon believed he had hit a cargo ship, but he actually had sunk the 940-ton *Coast Defense Vessel No. 64*.

Finally, the brightening morning sky forced *Pampanito* to dive for a submerged periscope attack. She had somehow crossed ahead of the convoy's path, and Fenno had to cut back northwest, once more bisecting the track. The enemy, on course 225, crossed the submarine's stern. It was now or never. At 0655 all four of the after tubes were emptied at the first oiler at thirty-two hundred yards. One escort was on the near bow of the oiler and one on the near quarter. The last ship could not be seen because of the high waves, which Fenno estimated at thirty feet. The planesmen and diving officer had all they could do to keep the boat from broaching as it punched through the wave crests.

Before Fenno could come around to fire the remaining four bow torpedoes, one of the escorts peeled off, so he took the boat deep. From

0702 to 0704 the crew heard four torpedo explosions. The first, timed at six minutes, should have been a hit, even though it meant the range was farther than they had estimated. The last three, at eight minutes, were probably more end-of-run detonations. Fenno was disturbed by this. If they were end-of-run explosions, then eight of the last ten torpedoes fired had detonated thus, while none had done so out of the first ten. "How come?" Fenno rhetorically asked.

He had more to think about, however, when at 0720 the first of six depth charges began to go off. In the after torpedo room Pappas recorded that they were "not too close and not too far." Above them, the escorts were having trouble, for they had to keep up sufficient steam in the rough seas to keep from swamping, and thus they could not use their sound gear effectively. *Pampanito* successfully evaded, for at 0755 the last two charges were heard to explode, but at a great distance away. Fenno was despondent over the torpedo misses.[13]

*Pampanito* surfaced at 0903 and began searching to the southwest on the last known convoy heading. Information was broadcast to the pack, and *Pipefish* joined *Pampanito* in a southerly search. Meanwhile, to the north of them, *Sea Cat* was making an end-around on one ship with two escorts moving at twelve knots on course 215. Fenno hoped that this meant his torpedoes had actually sunk the other ships and this was the last of the convoy. *Searaven* actually caught up with the target first, about 2200, but missed with one last torpedo. After midnight on 4 December, the target had slowed to four knots, and *Sea Cat* was finally able to get off four torpedoes. McGregor claimed two hits. Even so, he was not thrilled with Fenno's coordination of the pack. "The one attack that we made," he said, "was on a convoy that we picked up on our radar and attacked singly."

In fact, *Searaven* and *Sea Cat* may have been chasing the same crippled oiler that *Searaven* had hit in her second attack. Thus, Fenno thought, two oilers and one unidentified ship managed to escape. As a group commander, Fenno had not kept tight rein on his boats but had given general orders and let his skippers take the initiative. Out of a seven-ship and four-escort convoy, Fenno thought that *Searaven* had sunk one oiler and one passenger ship and had damaged another oiler; *Sea Cat* had sunk two oilers, including one that *Searaven* had damaged; *Pipefish* had sunk one cargo ship; and *Pampanito* had damaged one oiler. On paper it was quite an accomplishment, but Fenno's rather uncoordinated tactics were not as successful as he thought they would be, at least according to postwar assessments.[14]

As a gray, rainy dawn broke on 4 December, the wolf pack was again southwest of its area, and Fenno directed it to form an east-west scouting line, heading north. The torpedoless *Searaven* was released to head for Midway. The next three days were carbon copies of high northeasterly winds, heavy seas, rain, and poor visibility. The only advantage, said Fenno, was that the Japanese fliers stayed home.

The lookouts dreaded the darkness, high seas, and rain, for all they could do was hang on and hope not to be swept overboard. One night the monsoon seemed to let up, and a new watch went topside without rain gear. An hour later, however, the downpour began again. The lookouts were in misery, with a wind-swept drizzle stinging their faces and drenching their clothes. As OOD, Lieutenant Swain called below for a rain jacket. Later, Captain Fenno visited the bridge and saw the lookouts, who looked much like drowned rats.

"Are you quite comfortable, Ted?" Fenno asked Swain.

"Yes Captain, I'm okay," he replied.

"What about your men?" Fenno continued.

"Well, sir, they're going to be relieved soon," he answered.

"Wrong, Mr. Swain," Fenno said. "They're relieved immediately." Then he chewed the lieutenant out, insisting that he must take care of his men first.

The next night on Swain's watch, the rain began in almost a repeat performance. This time, however, he called for rain gear for everyone. Chief Smith bellowed out Swain's request. "Rain gear for the lookouts," and because of Swain's size, as well as because he was in the captain's "dog house," the chief added: "And one pup tent for Lieutenant Swain!"

The succeeding days blended into painted swirls of gray on a rain-swept canvas. Several times Mike Carmody was drenched by water cascading out of the main induction after particularly high waves crashed over them. The bilges were pumped constantly, little cooking was done, and Carmody ate nothing but cold sandwiches for three days. Many were seasick, and the only way to get a little shut-eye was to strap oneself into the bunk. "In the After Torpedo Room," Carmody said, "you could hear the propellers come out of the water every time we were atop of a wave. What a sound! It was amazing we didn't crack in half."

Sailors were stationed by the conning tower hatch, ready to close it every time the OOD would shout down, "Wave!" As a lookout, Hubie Brown could only hold on and wait until the wave broke over him and subsided. "But at least the water was nice and warm," he conceded.

Moffett spent several doleful days on the radar scope. Regardless of the precautions, waves still broke over the bridge and splashed into the conning tower, making him wet and miserable. Sometimes the inclinometer showed rolls of 30 degrees. In order to eat, they had to place towels on the tables to keep the dishes and utensils from sliding. The boat rolled as much as 10 degrees even two hundred feet underwater.

The elements battered the submarine. Welds were broken on the steel deck, and several plates were lost. On 14 December they noticed that they were leaving an oil slick. Fenno adjusted course and speed to take the waves head-on with as little rolling as possible, while personnel went out on deck to try to diagnose the trouble. Chief Motor Mac Bill Merryman and Carmody, as "oil king," figured that the trouble was in the connections to the No. 4 FBT. Aft of the cigarette deck they removed a section of deck plate to get beneath the superstructure. Before going below, Carmody noted that the waves were about twenty-five feet high. He crawled under the deck and found that the pipeline between an inboard vent and a main vent on the No. 4 FBT had parted. Since the tank was nearly empty, they decided to convert it back to ballast. There were flanges, fuel lines, air lines, and vent valve linkages to hook up, a job that Carmody said would take about an hour to complete. He couldn't work and watch for waves at the same time, so Merryman stood above the opening and handed him tools while listening for warnings from the lookouts.

Carmody was busting his knuckles for a time, trying to remain steady while getting the ride of his life in a caged roller coaster. Suddenly they were both startled to hear the lookouts shouting. Carmody first thought it might be an enemy plane coming in. Merryman stuck his head down and shouted for Mike to get out. As he scrambled for the opening, Carmody looked out a limber hole and saw "a monstrous wave about 40 feet high coming over us." The wall of water crashed down, driving Carmody away from the opening and bouncing him off the forest of structural supports like a pinball. He fought for all he was worth to get back to the deck opening, indicated by a lighter patch of water above him. "It seemed like an eternity that I was underwater," he said. Finally, under the light patch, Carmody kicked for the opening. He shot to the surface about the time the wave receded and ultimately got his head above deck level. He coughed and sputtered, then took a great breath and looked around. "I was shocked to see that the chief was gone!"

Mike scrambled out of the hole. The deck plate and tools had washed away. He grabbed for the tenuous security of the radio antenna line and ran aft to see if he could spot Merryman. "The Captain was screaming at me to get back to the Conning Tower," Mike said, "as he didn't want another man in the water." Carmody ignored him. His mind flashed back to the time he was on *S-17* in the North Atlantic when two lookouts were washed overboard. Carmody was in the rescue party that recovered them, but they had been in the icy water for about twenty minutes, and both of them died of exposure.

Obviously Merryman wouldn't freeze in the tropical sea, but he couldn't last long battling the huge waves. Soon enough his strength would give out. Carmody hung on near the stern and searched. Then he saw Merryman, bobbing briefly on a crest, then down and gone, then up again. Fenno spun the sub around while a rescue party came out on deck. Some expert maneuvering for about twenty minutes got them near enough to throw the chief a line, yet still they couldn't toss it close enough for him to grab. Then, almost providentially, another huge wave lifted him up and nearly placed him right back on the deck. He grabbed a line and was hauled aboard. "By all rights," said Charlie McGuire, "he probably should have died. After that he was living on borrowed time."

Merryman was taken below, and the conversion was completed. Because it was not safe to crawl back in to remove the blanking pads from the vent risers, it was impossible to use the low-pressure blower on this MBT. At 1600 Fenno dove the boat to flush out the last of the oil. Back on the surface an hour later, they picked up a message from Pearl with a contact made by *Bashaw* on a task force about four hundred miles south near Cam Ranh Bay.

The pack moved south to about 17 degrees north latitude and patrolled on an east-west axis between 110 degrees east and 111 degrees east, hoping to cross the path of the northbound task force. It was a long shot that proved fruitless. By 16 December, Fenno decided to reassign the lanes and take them back to Hainan. *Sea Cat* was to patrol the western boundary and *Pipefish* the center, twenty miles to the east, while *Pampanito* moved twenty miles east of *Pipefish*. They swept the Hainan coast that had proved so productive of ship contacts before. This time there was nothing to be seen.

On 17 December the "Fennomints" reversed course. *Pipefish* developed a radar contact on a large freighter making eleven knots along the Hainan coast, but she was not able to attack. *Sea Cat* and *Pampanito* never could get into position, and the chase terminated as the freighter headed into Yulin.

Two days earlier Fenno had requested to remain in the area an extra week because of the poor hunting. Now, dwindling fuel prompted second thoughts. For a fortnight the men had been asking him about the possibility of going to Australia for the next refit. Fenno visited the crew's mess. "Can I sit down, guys?" he asked, then squeezed in and made himself comfortable. He asked what the crew needed.

"We need some damn liberty, Captain! Beg your pardon," Hubert Brown heard a sailor remark.

"Yessir, we'd like to go to Australia," another one exclaimed, while a chorus of other voices chimed in agreement.

"Oh, I don't have that kind of pull, fellas," Fenno said. "I can't get you to Australia." But the crew was insistent. Over the weeks they kept heckling him, and finally their persistence paid off. Fenno's request was granted, but if they finished the week's patrol extension, they would first have to go to Saipan for fuel. To reach Australia with their current fuel they would have to leave immediately.

Spence Stimler thought that Fenno knew all along he would go to Australia and was just stringing the crew along. "Soon thereafter," Stimler said, "we disappeared from radio contact with Pearl, and when we did make contact we had drifted south of our patrol area. Pearl was most gracious in telling Mike to have a good time in Australia. They knew what he was up to and decided to play the game."

Mike Carmody said that Fenno approached him and asked him if they could make it to Australia. After carefully checking, Carmody answered that they could make it to northern Australia, but not to Fremantle. There was a fuel barge at Exmouth Gulf just for such emergencies. Fenno gave the okay, then radioed a request to terminate the patrol. During the morning of 18 December, final permission was granted, and the crew gave a rousing cheer. Fenno turned over command of the pack to Rob Roy McGregor on *Sea Cat* and pointed *Pampanito*'s nose toward the equator.

It would take a week to get to Exmouth Gulf. Targets were scarce; there were no ship or plane contacts for the entire trip, and the men settled into their routines. McGuire was up to his schemes again, studying the almanac and betting the men that they couldn't name the longest rivers, the highest mountains, the fastest trains, and so on. The trouble was, if the bets didn't go McGuire's way, he'd back out of them without paying up. McGuire, the "feather merchant," as Bob Bennett called him, had a tough time waking up for his watches. On one occasion when the sleepy yeoman could not be roused, Bennett and Moffett cranked up the meg-ohmmeter. The device generated four hundred to five hundred volts, but almost no current. Finding a foot protruding above the bunk rail, they hooked one end to the pipe and touched the other end to McGuire's bare toe. McGuire sprang up with a jolt, knocking his skull against the overhead, while Bennett and Moffett beat a hasty retreat into the forward battery.

Moffett also put the "megger" to good use by charging up various capacitors, which he would then scatter on the mess tables. Inevitably a curious sailor would pick one up and, said Moffett, "receive a thrill if he happened to touch both contacts at once."

There were seventeen men making their first patrol on *Pampanito*. Among them was Ona D. Hawkins, born in January 1924 in Boone County, Missouri. In 1943 he joined the navy and went to electrical school in Saint Paul, Minnesota. It was there that Ona met Muriel Mix, his wife to be, who began writing and sending to him the first of a remarkable series of 315 letters. The most exceptional features of the letters, aside from the personal nature of the correspondence between a young couple in love, were the envelopes themselves. Muriel was quite an artist, and she adorned the envelopes with full-color drawings of pretty girls in various attires and poses, each suitable as a pin-up for any lonely sailor.

Ona was assigned to a relief crew in Hunter's Point, California. He scraped and painted subs, stood fire watches, and did one thousand and one other tasks—everything but get into the war. "God, when are we ever going to get on a boat?" Hawkins lamented.

In the late summer of 1944, Hawkins was sent to Pearl Harbor, and finally he was assigned to *Pampanito*. Also coming aboard were three other men who attended electrical school with Hawkins: Patrick H. Bergfeld, John E. Goodson, and Lawrence E. Noker. All four were firemen first class and electrician strikers. As new or unrated men, Hawkins and Bergfeld were assigned to help the mess cooks. Not having learned the fine art of securing food on a rolling submarine, the two men were given a sharp lesson in the South China Sea. They were filling ketchup bottles when a severe roll sent them and the ketchup to the galley deck. The red paste splattered everywhere. "My God," said Hawkins, "It looked like we had a massacre in there."

Hawkins and Larry Noker spent time on lookout. Ona never considered himself a good lookout because he didn't believe he had keen enough eyesight. However, Noker, a twenty-year-old Pennsylvanian, loved it. While Ona avoided going topside, Larry liked to scan the horizon, preferring the fresh air to the diesel fumes and cramped conditions below. Many times his sharp eyes were the first to spot approaching Japanese planes.

Paul Pappas was having a rough patrol. He had a pleasant personality and could get along with almost everyone, including his new shipmates. "I loved the guy," said Ona Hawkins. "He was always good to me." The only problem for the crew was that Pappas never had any money. He drew only a few dollars every payday, then, out of funds, he would start to borrow. However, said Hawkins, "He kept a perfect record to repay everyone. Next pay you'd get back every cent." A saver, a nondrinker, and seemingly without many of the vices common to many sailors, Pappas always had over three thousand dollars on the books.

Pappas's nemesis was Herbert E. Thompson, the new chief electrician's mate (CEM) who had taken the place of Ralph Attaway after Carmody rearranged the latter's jaw. Thompson, who had made runs on *Dolphin* (SS 169), *Whale,* and *Sandlance* (SS 381), was a stocky former prize fighter, and the constant pounding had given him a rough countenance and a rough manner. They called him either "Punchy," or, because he was going bald, "Curly." Walt Madison claimed that Thompson had the most annoying habit of getting in a sailor's face and ramming heads—what Madison called "coco-butts."

Thompson was out to get Pappas. He called him "a damn Greek" and always gave him the worst tasks. The ground meter in the control room was supposed to show no more than fifteen volts, but it always registered high. The officers complained to Thompson that too much current was being drawn. Thompson, who should have known better, would force an electrician to search for the ground. The electrician would explain that ever since the sub had been built, the meter always registered over fifteen volts. Thompson wouldn't listen, and the electrician would have to pretend to make repairs. Pappas was sick of tracking down nonexistent grounds, but it was Wally Cordon who finally took care of the perpetual problem. One day when no one was looking, Cordon went to the ground meter and, with a pair of pliers, twisted the needle so it never showed over fifteen volts again.

When Thompson noticed that the electricians in the maneuvering room never wore their headphones, he complained to Lieutenant Fives. The headsets should always be worn, Thompson said, because if the annunciators, interior communications, and hand phones all went out at the same time, they wouldn't be able to hear the orders. This was the dumbest thing Pappas had ever heard. There was enough redundancy built in to more than cover any failure. And not one of the systems had ever failed. Nevertheless, at Thompson's recommendation Fives ordered the men to don the headphones.

"Okay, Mr. Fives," Pappas said. "We'll wear the headphones. But if you call for flank speed and we trip over these long cords, you just might not get your flank speed." And, Pappas concluded: "That ended the head-phones." Thompson was furious, and he would try to get his revenge.

On 23 December, while heading south through Makassar Strait, *Pampanito* crossed the equator for the first time.[15] The occasion called for more shenanigans as a number of "pollywogs" had to be introduced to the mysteries of the deep. Kentuckian Seaman First Class Ervin O. McGehee was making his first patrol. He received a summons to appear before the Court of Neptunus Rex, Ruler of the Raging Main, charged with "being a non-coffee-making mess cook" and "spreading Pollywog tracks all over the bridge." Ervin dutifully yielded himself to the court.

Ona Hawkins was also summoned. He was given some "foul-tasting liquid, probably Worcestershire sauce and some other junk," which was "hotter than thunder." Hawkins had to crawl down the center passageway on his hands and knees, wearing nothing but his skivvies, as a couple of dozen men took turns paddling his rear end.

Roger Walters, who returned for the fourth patrol after his foot fungus had cleared up, was blindfolded and forced to sit on a "hot seat," which was wired up with a wet towel placed over it. Chief Smith threw a switch that sent a current through the chair. "Boom!" said Walters. "I bounced right onto the deck on my butt and I shook for four hours afterwards."

With the equator-crossing ceremony over, *Pampanito* entered the Java Sea. Those topside were treated to warm weather and beautiful water. Hubie Brown was nervous because there were places so shallow that when they dove, the keel would nearly scrape bottom while the scope was still above water. Al Van Atta seemed more inured to the danger and relished the scene. It was incredible, he said, how green and smooth the sea was, almost like emerald glass. Once they spotted what appeared to be a blimp on the horizon. When they got close enough, they discovered it was only a small, palm-covered island, somehow reflecting its green canopy into the sky.

With shallow water and the upcoming transit of narrow Lombok Strait, Fenno decided to destroy the code machine. They had made use of it for the majority of the patrol, but there was no sense in taking a chance on its possible capture if the submarine happened to run aground. Chief Radioman Mervin Hill broke the machine into pieces and disposed of them over the side. The code books and ciphers were burned. In the after torpedo room Roger Walters found a metal bucket, put the shredded papers in, and set them afire. Lieutenant Red wanted to dump the ashes in the head.

Waste disposal aboard a submarine had always been a concern. Some of the problems were mechanical, but others were a matter of logistics. In July 1941 the captain of the *Skipjack,* James W. Coe, had ordered 150 rolls of toilet paper from the tender USS *Holland* (AS 3). In a typical navy "snafu," the order went unfilled, and it was over ten months later that Coe's requisition came back stamped, "Cancelled—cannot identify." Thereupon Coe wrote up a sarcastic second requisition for some toilet paper, adding that the crew had been forced to implement their own remedy by using most of BuShips' "non-essential paper work" to wipe their rear ends. The story was repeated that forevermore, wherever *Skipjack* pulled in from patrol, she received no fruits, vegetables, or ice cream. Instead, she invariably received mountains of toilet paper.

Yet toilet paper was not a submariner's major concern. The main problem was the operation of the head. No less a skipper than Sam Dealey only half jokingly said that you had to be "a Cal Tech man to know how to operate the head aboard a sub." The German *U-120* actually sank because of a malfunction of her heads while underwater. On *Pampanito,* the officers' head in the forward torpedo room drained into the No. 1 Sanitary Tank, and the crew's head and washroom drained into the No. 2 Sanitary Tank under the after battery. After a long day's collection, the nightly ritual was to blow the tanks' contents out to sea. Through the long tropical days, the tanks had plenty of time to ripen. Care had to be taken to head into the wind when the large No. 2 tank was blown, or the stench could be sucked in through the hull ventilation and piped throughout the boat.

Sometimes "bathroom humor" meant more than just telling off-color jokes. The crew's mess stools were placed side-by-side with a half-wall partition between. To use them, one had to open the sea valves and let water flow into the bowls. To play a trick on the person occupying the next stall, a man dexterous enough could work his hand behind the partition and turn on the other man's valve without his knowledge. Bob Bennett explained: "Soon enough cold salt water would be flowing up the guy's butt and over the bowl."

The after torpedo room head gave everyone the most trouble. It was blown directly to the sea with a number of valve manipulations that needed to be performed in a specific sequence. Incorrect operation caused many a "brownout" to ruin a sailor's evening. McGuire called the after toilet a "blow head" and said it had numbered instructions. "If you were careless you'd get a face full," he said. "It must have happened ten times in a year. It would blow so hard you'd be a week trying to wash it out."[16]

When Walters finished burning the code books, Lieutenant Red took the bucket of ashes to the head. Roger didn't think that Red was familiar with the operation, and he offered to do it for him.

"No Walters," Red said, "I'll take care of that."

Roger watched him open the flapper valve on the toilet and dump in the ashes. He rinsed it down to clear the valve seat and closed the flapper valve. Then Red opened the sea valve and built up the pressure. Walters wasn't sure that Red had completely rinsed the valve seat, because it wasn't fully sealed. He stood back. When the lieutenant, hunched over the head, tripped the blow valve to send the air pressure into the trap, instead of sending the contents out to sea, the flapper blew open. The lieutenant, said Walters, "received a nice shower of ashes and seawater in his face and on his shirt and pants. It was all I could do to keep a straight face." Red "looked like the old-time comic, Edgar Kennedy, in his famous 'slow-burn.'"

"I guess I should have let you do it," Red said, then he turned and hurried forward for a change of clothes.

With the ECM and books destroyed, Fenno could concentrate at getting his boat through the Indonesian island barrier and into the Indian Ocean. There were few practical routes through. Between Sumatra and Java, Sunda Strait was twelve miles wide and seventy miles long, but only 90 feet deep at its shallowest point. Bali Strait between Java and Bali was only two miles wide. Between Bali and Lombok, Lombok Strait was eleven miles wide, twenty-seven miles long, and between 576 feet and 3,800 feet deep. *Pampanito* could head as far east as Timor for a wider channel, but her fuel situation would not allow it.

On a dark Christmas Eve, flooded down to keep a low profile, *Pampanito* dashed through Lombok Strait. If things went well, they could thread their way through on the surface, keeping up a moderate speed and making use of the strong southerly current. In the middle, the channel pinched between Nusa Penida and Point Lombok, and minefields along the shores and gun batteries on Cape Ibus and Cape Abah made it a tight squeeze. Van Atta didn't understand why the Japanese didn't mine across the entire channel, but that was the reason why submarines used the strait so regularly; it was too deep to anchor mines.

Hubert Brown heard scuttlebutt that a sub had recently gone through on a northerly course, radioing: "Be careful. Low flying aircraft and shore batteries. Lousy shots. Merry Christmas." Bob Bennett heard that a sub had gone through before them and had taken a shell for her trouble. Admittedly, scuttlebutt was not always accurate, but in this case Bennett had the story partially correct. USS *Angler* (SS 240), escorting USS *Bergall* (SS 320), had gone through several days earlier. *Bergall* had damaged the

Japanese heavy cruiser *Myoko* in the Gulf of Siam, but an escorting destroyer placed a lucky nine-thousand-yard shot into her forward torpedo room loading hatch, tearing a large hole in the pressure hull. *Bergall* was unable to dive. Orders came to scuttle her, but a skeleton crew was placed aboard. *Angler* came to help, and the boats began a harrowing two-thousand-mile trip to Australia. They slipped through Lombok Strait in the darkness and made Exmouth Gulf on 20 December.

On Christmas Eve, Hubert Brown was at the helm as Fenno took the sub through the strait. Patrol boats skittered around them like water bugs. Fenno stood by Moffett, watching the radar screen and steering around the pips. Brown likened the transit to a pinball game, as the sub banked ten degrees right and ten degrees left, caroming among the contacts. It was a long trip. Before Brown had come down from the shears he had noticed how close the shore appeared and wondered why they had chosen such a tight place to go through. The ten-thousand-foot volcanic mountains on either shore "were so close it looked like you could reach out and touch them." The sea, said Brown, was not too rough, but "there was a hell of a current."

Bob Bennett was jittery at his post on the 40-mm gun. For nourishment as well as to ease his nerves he munched from a can of peanuts, but it seemed that the crunching might be heard all the way to shore. It was pitch dark. Occasional heat lightning flashing over the volcano on Bali illuminated the sky and highlighted the waves like streaks of orange paint on black velvet. Bennett saw many sampans and wondered how they could fail to see the submarine. Signal lights on the shores flashed on and off, twinkling as they passed, appearing to follow them as they headed south. Bennett nervously popped a few more peanuts into his mouth. "It was pretty spooky," he said.[17]

Nevertheless, for all their consternation, *Pampanito* completed the transit undetected. On Christmas Day she was in the Indian Ocean over the twenty-thousand-foot depths of the Java Trench. They had been gone almost two months and had traveled nearly sixteen thousand miles, and supplies were running low. The only thing "fresh" they had to eat was a bushel of potatoes that had been kept in the hatch above the crew's mess. The last potatoes were the highlight of Christmas dinner. By 27 December, with fuel dropping dangerously low, they spotted Northwest Cape, and the sub finally reached the long inlet of Exmouth Gulf. The diesel oil calculations had been cut too closely, and Carmody thought the boat made the last miles to the fuel barge running on her batteries.

Back in 1942 it was thought that Exmouth Gulf could be used as an advance submarine base, similar to Midway Island. Darwin was first choice, but Japanese bombing raids from Timor, only 360 miles away, proved that the city was too exposed. Exmouth was farther from Japanese-controlled bases, but it was desolate and deserted. From September to April it was roughed up by northwest winds that made it difficult for a sub to dock. And most emphatically, submariners did not care to be put in quonset huts in a sea of mud, surrounded by millions of flies, and separated by 750 miles from the girls and pubs of Perth-Fremantle.

However, making Exmouth Gulf an advance base seemed a good idea at the time. The Australian military built landing strips, quarters, anti-aircraft emplacements, an infirmary, a radio shack, a power plant, and water distillers. In May 1943 the tender USS *Pelias* (AS 14) moved up from Fremantle. When the Japanese found out about the operation, they began sending over long-range bombers, which effectively ended Exmouth Gulf's short existence as an advance sub base. The place was abandoned, with a fuel barge and a radio listening station left behind. The fueling operation was manned by convicts of courts-martial or other discipline cases who volunteered for duty instead of going to the stockade.

"My God, what a desolate place," commented Hubie Brown as he came topside. It was the beginning of the Australian summer, and Brown thought he would see some green, but instead he found "just a fuel barge and a desert." Nevertheless, the crew immediately found a diversion; they tossed Charlie McGuire overboard. Apparently Red had been up to his money-making tricks again and reneging on more than a few of his bets. They chased him around the boat, finally cornering him and tying him up in the forward torpedo room. Van Atta compared McGuire to the scarecrow in the Wizard of Oz: tall and lanky, with unkempt red hair and struggling arms and legs awkwardly flailing about.

They hauled him topside. Someone suggested wrapping the rope around his neck, but an officer dissuaded them. They did have to secure a rope around his waist, however, because he couldn't swim. Over the side he went. He wasn't quite keel-hauled, but he was dragged alongside the hull, to the amusement of the men who had lost money to him. McGuire was only hauled back aboard when they figured he had swallowed enough of the Indian Ocean. "He took it pretty well," said Bennett, "and it calmed him down a bit." However, according to Brown, the only mistake they made at Exmouth Gulf "was in hauling McGuire out of the water."

The weather was warm and calm, and that evening a movie was shown on deck. Hubie Brown noticed Lieutenant Swain and some other officers leaving the boat "to go ashore and get drunk." Less than a week after the Australian summer solstice, the hour was quite late before it was dark enough to show the movie. The feature was *Holiday Inn*. It had first come out in the fall of 1942, and it introduced the Irving Berlin song "White Christmas," crooned by Bing Crosby. The tune was quite a hit. Over the next two years the song topped the "Hit Parade" nine times, repeating its dominance during the Christmases of 1943 and again in 1944. The song was appropriate for the wartime mood—sad and yearning—emotions with which homesick soldiers and sailors could identify.

The trouble was that on *Pampanito, Holiday Inn* had been shown about ten times, and while some sailors enjoyed reruns evoking memories of a sentimental white Christmas back home, many were heartily sick of the film. Hubert Brown remembered that they had tried to trade the film to every sub they met up with but had no takers. By the time the movie got rolling, Lieutenant Swain returned to the boat—"bombed," according to Brown. At first he couldn't remember the password, and he wasn't allowed aboard. Eventually Lieutenant Johnson let him up the gangway. When Swain saw the detested movie playing again, he pulled out his .45 and threatened to shoot the projector. While the men on watch tried to calm the lieutenant down, his pith helmet blew into the water. Tony Hauptman got out his own .45 and proceeded to fill the floating cork hat full of holes. This set Swain off complaining about his helmet and "bitching" about the movie again. Finally, Mac Johnson, invoking his authority as officer of the deck, ordered Swain to shut up and go to his cabin. Frank Fenno arrived shortly there-after, and true to his depiction as an enlisted man's captain, hauled aboard a couple of cases of Emu Bitters beer for the crew to enjoy. The men gave a hearty cheer and for the eleventh time settled down to watch *Holiday Inn*.

Early on 28 December, *Pampanito* got underway after receiving suffi-cient fuel to travel the remaining 750 miles to Fremantle. What the men still needed however, was fresh food. On the morning of 30 December, nearing Fremantle, *Pampanito* was met by a small Australian provision ship, no bigger than a cabin cruiser. It sent over just the things the men had been craving. Some crew members cheered the "Aussie beer," and others rushed for the mail, but most relished the fresh fruits and vegetables. Ona Hawkins couldn't remember milk tasting so good. "God, the guys just couldn't get enough milk," he said. "It was great—better than any beer." Soon after the provision ship pulled away, the huge lighthouse on Rottnest Island outside of Fremantle harbor hove into view. It wouldn't be long now. The land down under; food, drink, and women.[18]

## CHAPTER NINE

# To Indo-China and the Philippines

Fremantle, located at the mouth of the Black Swan River, was the seaport of Perth, about ten miles upriver. In 1944, Perth was a bustling city, the center of insurance and merchant banking for the agricultural economy of Western Australia. Fremantle was much smaller, with a frontier-town atmosphere rather strange to the sailors, who likened the homes to what American dwellings looked like in the 1920s. The climate was superb in December; Bennett compared it to June in San Diego, California.

*Pampanito* was welcomed as she pulled in to Fremantle on 30 December. To the crew's surprise, some of the smiling faces on the pier looked familiar. Penetrating the usually strict submarine security rules, a half-dozen of the former POWs who had been rescued three months earlier were dockside. The grinning men, who included Jack Cocking, Harry Pickett, and Wally Winters, dressed in the same dungarees the crew had given them, grabbed the hawsers themselves and tied *Pampanito* securely to the pier.

The sailors had never had such a hospitable welcome. After checking in to their quarters—officers at the Majestic Hotel a few miles outside of Perth and the crew at the Ocean Beach Hotel right on the seashore—they were free to see the sights. What a time they had. The townspeople could not do enough for them. Doc Demers was hugged and kissed by everyone. He went to parties and danced, ate, and drank his fill. "The whole town

was ours," he said. "It was an emotional experience, hard to describe."
Demers shared drinks with Wally Winters, and they laughed about the
time shortly after the rescue when Winters got sick on an American
hamburger. Gordon Hopper rhetorically asked: "Did anybody ever see a
New Year in like we did that one?"[1]

There are many reasons that men fight in wars. However, a case has
been made that in World War II, Americans fought less for abstract
notions of freedom and patriotism than for the emotional values represented by sweethearts, wives, and families. Sexuality played an extensive
role in the war experience. Always in the near background were the pin-
ups of the Hollywood stars, the pictures of the girl back home, Rosie the
Riveter, or the lady at the last port of call. There was something about war
and killing that inflamed the sex drive, and it has been commented upon
by many, including war veterans and authors such as William Manchester
and James Jones. The latter believed that women were always on men's
minds when they were not in combat, and the former knew from personal
experience that even during the thick of a fight, a man could desire a
woman. With the presence of death and extinction just around the corner,
wrote Jones, the comfort of women was of great importance. Combat
opened men's eyes to love as an emotional lifeline of sustenance.

To the soldiers and sailors with a combat-heightened sex drive, Australia
was almost heaven. Many Australians, at least the women whose men were
away fighting, viewed Americans as their saviors. The Australian soldier's
view was not so sanguine. When Australians arrived home after battling
Rommel in the North African desert, all they saw was Americans stealing
their girls. Various "battles" erupted across the country. In the "Battle of
Brisbane," a file of Australian soldiers leaving their country passed by a
company of arriving Americans. The impudent GIs mocked the Diggers,
saying that they would lay every Australian woman they could find. Shots
were fired, and some men were killed, but the incident was hushed up.
Americans won the favors of the Australian girls—and the animosity of
the local male population.[2]

"Talk was," said Charlie McGuire, "that you don't go around with the
Diggers. They'll go out with you, but when they have the chance they'll put
the boot to you and steal your money." He heard that some Americans
had been killed. But such was not the experience of *Pampanito*'s men. "We

could go into the toughest places in Perth," McGuire said, "and if anyone gave us any lip, there'd be three or four Diggers who would jump in with us." McGuire and a few buddies went to town in a taxi. The vehicle, operated from a charcoal boiler towed behind the cab, took them to downtown Perth. As they exited, the driver asked for twenty bob.

Standing nearby, Wally Winters asked, "What did he say?"

"Twenty bob," answered McGuire.

"Give the bloke seven," Winters said, "and I'll give him something else." The cabby got out to argue, and, said McGuire, "Winters beat the hell out him." The driver threatened to call a cop. "Go ahead," said Wally, "I'll wait here while you call him." The driver left, and from then on, the sub-mariners never paid more than seven bob for a ride.[3]

The sailors had free run of Perth, and although women were plentiful, some men did not have the patience for the time-consuming process of finding a date with a "nice girl." They had received their warnings about venereal diseases time and again. Posters, pamphlets, lectures, and films about the dangers of intercourse were ubiquitous. Former boxing champion Gene Tunney, then a navy commander, was appointed by President Roosevelt to develop physical and mental fitness programs for the enlisted men. Tunney admonished the sailors to display moral bravery when confronted by the rouged challenge of "diseased harlots." The men admired Tunney as the heavyweight champion but were merely amused by his antisex campaign.

In the U.S. armed forces, enlisted men were required to submit to the lectures and the ritual of "short-arm" inspection every six months. It didn't help. There were perpetual roadblocks to deter the aims of the moral crusaders, from the condom shortage caused by the Japanese takeover of rubber-producing Malaya in 1942 to the introduction of penicillin on a mass basis in 1944. As the "wonder drug" came into use, the men grew more incautious, figuring the one-shot "magic bullet" of penicillin could cure anything they might catch. Gone were the days when the partial deterrent of long-term, painful injections awaited the man careless enough to contract gonorrhea. When penicillin was made readily available, the venereal disease rate actually increased.

Among those unable to wait for a "nice girl" were Red McGuire and Steward's Mate First Class John Lewis Johnson. Johnson, born in Tennessee, was one of only two black men on *Pampanito*. He and Ingram became close friends, and Good Kid told him how lucky he was to have missed sailing with Commander Summers. McGuire also made friends with Johnson, and the two of them were forever goofing off. Once, outside the wardroom where the officers sat eating a meal, Johnson sneaked up behind McGuire, grabbed him, whipped out a knife, and held it against his throat.

"White boy, pass your money back!" Johnson growled. The officers froze in mid-chew, but Johnson and McGuire both laughed and headed down the passageway.

"We'd always play like that," McGuire said. "I always felt mentally like I was seventeen years old."

Johnson soon found a girlfriend who worked in a house of ill repute. He wanted to show her off, so he got McGuire to accompany him one evening. After the initial pleasantries, Red and Johnson shacked up in adjoining rooms. In the middle of the night, Charlie awoke to the sound of a woman's voice sounding through the paper-thin walls, melodiously calling the name of John Lewis Johnson.

In a few seconds, Johnson crept up to McGuire and told him to be quiet and get dressed; they had to get out fast. "Like hell," said McGuire. He had paid his money, and he was staying the night. Then they heard the plaintive call again: "John Lewis, darling, where are you?" Apparently Johnson had more than one girlfriend hunting for him, and McGuire called out, "He's in here, Miss!" Johnson took off for the adjoining room, and McGuire was able to get back to bed.

The next morning the two sailors had buttoned up their bell-bottomed trousers and had headed back through the sleepy streets of Perth when they were stopped at a checkpoint. Aussie MPs headed them into a clinic.

"What for?" the sailors protested. They hadn't done anything.

"All you damn Yanks say the same thing, now get in there!" one MP threatened. The sailors received injections—McGuire called it the most painful shot he ever got—directly into the penis. "Boy, that put me out of commission," McGuire said. "I pissed fire for three days." He vowed never to go out with John Lewis Johnson anymore.

On yet another escapade, the sailors decided they would have to take out "one of our young guys" and fix him up with a "date." Fireman First

Class Kenneth J. Jansen had enlisted in June 1943 in Saint Louis, Missouri, and had come aboard *Pampanito* in Pearl Harbor before the second patrol. Said Spence Stimler: "He was a typical baby-faced innocent young guy. Some reports had his age at fifteen, and he certainly looked no older . . . and from his remarks he must have led a very sheltered life."

The crew decided that it was time Jansen lost his virginity. They took him to a place called "Rose's," then "explained their mission to Rose herself, and paid her in advance for her services if she would take his virginity away." Apparently Rose made Jansen comfortable and was about to take care of him when he looked up to see several mates peeking through the door. Said Stimler, "That was the end of everything. Rose wouldn't give them their money back or let someone else take his place."[4]

Most of the crew avoided the red-light district and simply celebrated the New Year of 1945 by tipping a few drinks. Ona Hawkins and his buddy Fireman First Class Johnny Goodson, a slow-talking, easy-going fellow from North Carolina, went on liberty together. They went into restaurants and "ordered meals like kings," said Hawkins. "It was fantastic." New Year's Eve, they "decided to raise a little heck." After eating to their fill, Goodson bought a bottle of liquor from a cab driver, and they retired to their room on the second floor of the Ocean Beach Hotel. The liquid was definitely not like the milk that Ona usually preferred. "I was stewed to the gills," he said. He wanted to leave the room to have a little more fun, but Goodson tried to hold him back. Hawkins got as far as the stairwell before tumbling down and breaking his nose. He spent New Year's Day in the hospital.

In January, several sailors, including Paul Pappas, Jim Behney, and Clod Hopper, took a train to Harry Pickett's place. Harry had a special feeling in his heart for Jim Behney, the sailor who had lifted him off the raft and carried him below. His family hugged and kissed Behney. They ate, drank, and spent the evening telling tales, learning the details of Harry's life in Japanese prison camps. To conclude the evening, Harry played them several excellent pieces on the piano, which changed their image of him as an untutored Digger. They carried quarts of Aussie beer with them for the train ride back to Perth. No sooner had they returned to the Ocean Beach when they were visited by Alf Winter. The submariners threw another party and listened to Alf's war stories. Pappas succinctly scribed: "A good time was had by all. Nothing broke, and no fights."

After recuperating from his accident, Ona Hawkins joined about one dozen submariners on a kangaroo hunt. They rode outback in a large panel truck and stayed in what he thought was a Catholic boys camp. Early the next morning they were paired up, given rifles, and dropped off along a dirt road. Their instructions were to walk east toward the sun until noon, then turn around and walk back west toward the road. Hawkins and Goodson dutifully followed the route, but returned empty-handed. Van Atta said, "We went into the bush and blasted away all day, but never got a kangaroo." Someone made a kill however, for back at the camp that night they had great-tasting kangaroo steaks. They had brought enough iced beer along to keep everyone satisfied. The second day, however, after returning from another hunt, the ice was long gone. "We were thirsty as thunder," said Ona, and the hot beer with 12 percent alcohol "really wasted us."

As he had promised when first rescued, Jack Cocking invited a number of sailors to his ranch. After a great breakfast of fried steak topped with fried eggs, Cocking took them to the racetrack. One of his own horses, Gay Parade, was running in the Perth Handicap but was considered a long shot at ten-to-one odds. Cocking suggested to Bill Yagemann that he find a bookie and place ten on his horse. Yagemann did so, but wondered why the bookie looked so flustered when he accepted the bet. To everyone's surprise, Gay Parade won the race. When a smiling Yagemann showed the winning ticket to Cocking, he exclaimed, "My God! Ten pounds! I meant for you to bet ten shillings." Cocking figured the payout almost broke the poor bookie.

George Moffett supplied his carefully considered opinion of Australia: The beer was good, and it came in thirty-two-ounce cans instead of the usual twelve-ouncers; the bread was heavier and firmer than the American style; the butter was good and came packed in tins; the mutton was too plain-tasting; and he didn't care for the flies. Some flora that he thought had an odd, dark foliage proved to be entirely covered with black flies.[5]

Liberty in Australia never lasted long enough for most submariners, yet for the officers it may have lasted too long. Men wanted to get off the boats for shore duty in Perth. On *Crevalle*, Lieutenant Ruhe threatened that if being such great lovers of Aussie women affected even one man's on-board performance, he would have him shipped to the Aleutians. The officers were afraid that the men would get too accustomed to a soft life and would lose their enthusiasm to face the rigors of a war patrol. Relief crew on Midway was no prize; Perth was another story.

Some *Pampanito* men requested to get off the boat; others rotated off by luck of the draw. Thirteen men went to the relief crew, but if any of them thought they were going to win a long stay in Perth, they were sadly mistaken. The disappearing Japanese merchant marine was making southern Australian bases superfluous. Plans were being made to move north, and in a short time Submarine Division 121 was sent packing. Clyde Markham lamented: "We thought we'd get to spend some time in Australia, but in a little while, we all got shipped back to the States."

While packing to leave, Hubie Brown saw Wally Winters hanging around with the crew at the Ocean Beach. Someone loaned him a sailor suit. It was Winter's plan to steal aboard *Pampanito* and go on the next patrol. "He thought that the submarines saved Australia," Brown said. Before the boat left, Winter was discovered on the dock in sailor whites. He and a few other Diggers were allowed to remain nearby, but under close surveillance. It was ironic that Americans were trying to get off the boat while Aussies were trying to get on it.[6]

It was time, also, for Lieutenant Commander Landon Davis, Jr., to move on. After nine patrols on *Growler* and *Pampanito*, Davis was given command of the old *Seadragon*. The crew would miss him; his empathy and understanding were appreciated. Before letting his men go on liberty, Davis generally gave them a gentle admonishment: "Don't get into any trouble that I can't get you out of."

Coming aboard as the new exec was Lieutenant Commander Lynn S. Orser (USN). Lieutenant Sherlock's first impression was that Orser was "a buffoon," but it just took some time to realize his competence. Commander Earl Hydeman was detached to take command of USS *Sea Dog* (SS 401), where he eventually made a name for himself as commander of the nine-boat wolf pack "Hydeman's Hellcats" when they invaded the Sea of Japan in June 1945. Replacing him as PCO was Lieutenant Commander William J. Bush (USN). Also leaving after three patrols was the quiet and reserved Lieutenant Howard Fulton. The newest and greenest officer coming aboard was Ensign Edward E. DePaul (USNR).

Perth, Australia, January 1945. Left to right: Isaac Robinson, Donald Ferguson, Al Van Atta, and Clyde Markham. (Photo courtesy of Clyde Markham.)

After Charlie McGuire recovered from his escapade with Johnson, he was standing on the pier, jawing with a buddy from USS *Cobia* (SS 245). Charlie was showing off his new uniform. Captain Fenno had made him chief. Fenno recognized talent, Charlie bragged. Pete Summers would never have promoted him. Charlie preened, making sure his new outfit had been properly ironed and creased. Then, out of the corner of his eye, he saw a familiar face strolling up the pier. Could it be? It looked like Pete Summers!

It took McGuire a couple of seconds to clear his throat and respond to Pete's greeting. After a minute of small talk, Summers said: "McGuire, you've done a good job. I've decided to make you chief." Was Summers playing a game? Certainly he could see he wore a chief's outfit. Was he trying to get him mad and make him snap out a retort that would give Summers an excuse to bust him back down? McGuire maintained his cool. "Gosh, thanks Captain," he said. "I'd appreciate you making me chief."

Pete smiled and walked up the gangway. My God! McGuire thought. Summers is back.

For the past few months, Paul Summers had been resting in the States. He had gained back his appetite and put on several pounds. He returned to help run a relief crew in Pearl Harbor, flew to Melbourne for Christmas, then caught a plane to Perth. Captain Fenno, in the meantime, with one more Bronze Star to his credit, made the trip back to Pearl to resume his job as ComSubDiv 201.

Back on board, Summers wasted little time in tightening the screws. George Ingram got another tongue-lashing, as did John Johnson when he apparently couldn't remember that Summers was the new skipper and that he was supposed to get his meals served first. Both stewards threatened to jump ship.[7]

Although it had been a happy interlude in Australia, all the news was not good. *Sealion II* made one more patrol and had sunk a destroyer and a battleship, but Eli Reich was through. He returned to Guam and received a third Navy Cross, but he was burned out and asked to be relieved of command. Lockwood was naturally disappointed to lose such a fine skipper. A worse loss occurred when *Growler* failed to return from her eleventh war patrol. Maurice Demers had tried communicating with his friend Thompson, much as they had done on the previous patrol, by clicking signals to each other on the SJ. *Growler,* still under Ben Oakley, had left Fremantle on 20 October in command of another wolf pack with USS *Hardhead* (SS 365) and USS *Hake* (SS 256). In the South China Sea near Luzon on 8 November, *Growler* attacked a small convoy, then disappeared. When *Pampanito* got to the area in mid-November, Demers clicked the SJ a few times a day, several days in a row, but never received an answer. *Growler* was already gone.

Summers would be taking *Pampanito* out for her fifth patrol. He would also lead his first wolf pack, albeit a small one, consisting of his boat and USS *Guavina* (SS 362). As sailing time approached, the stewards decided they would make good on their threats to jump ship. Johnson disappeared on 18 January while the boat went out for exercises. He was later found and convinced to return. For punishment he was reduced in rank to a steward second class and given extra kitchen duties for one week. Ingram, who had been transferred briefly to *Fulton* at Saipan, got into trouble and was busted two steps. He came back to *Pampanito* as a lowly steward third class. He made the best of it, but now that Summers had returned, Ingram disappeared. The men learned he was hiding in the segregated black barracks near the sub base, but they declined to go in after him. Dick Sherlock got the job. About an hour before they were scheduled to leave, Sherlock made his way ashore.

"I had to talk my way into a hostile black barracks," he said, "talk Ingram into coming back, and make it back on time. I think that was my worst half-hour in the service." Nevertheless, Sherlock did convince Ingram to come back aboard. McGuire tried to console him. "Don't worry, Iggy, Pete won't bother you." But, of course, the minute Ingram got back, McGuire said, "Pete jumped all over him."

What seemed strange to Sherlock was that Ingram was not given any further punishment. It may have been that, as a steward third class, there were not many lower ranks to which they could break him. What was more probable to Sherlock was that Ingram was saved by the machinations of his friend the yeoman. McGuire often bragged that he could get Summers to sign anything he wanted, simply by placing a stack of "routine" papers in front of him when he had more pressing things to do. Pete would usually scribble his signature without reading what he was signing. Said

Sherlock: "The bust in rate and the AWOL report on Johnson instead of Ingram sounds like McGuire was involved in a switch."

"I could get Pete to sign things if he was very busy," said McGuire. "But it wasn't good to do it often, because he watched me like a hawk." As to whether he pulled a switch, McGuire only commented: "Well, John Lewis [Johnson] was never AWOL as far as I remember." Ingram, meanwhile, resumed spitting in the captain's coffee with a vengeance.[8]

The Thompson-Pappas feud also warmed up again. During the past two weeks, Andy Currier, Wally Cordon, and Bob DePray had been at a place called "Sawyer's Valley" about twenty miles out of town and had all returned much the worse for wear. Currier had caught some unknown bug and was laid low for a couple of days with a high fever and flulike symptoms. He tried to work until he could barely stand up. Pappas told him to hit the sack. When Chief Electrician's Mate Thompson found out, he raged at Pappas and put him on report for causing another man to "shirk his duty in the face of the enemy." The new exec, Lieutenant Commander Orser, checked Currier and thought that maybe the man should go to sick bay. Currier ended up in the hospital with the comment that he should have been admitted three days earlier.

Pappas's troubles continued. One afternoon, an old, grain-loaded Panamanian cargo ship caught fire. Mike Carmody got out his sketch pad to draw the scene: *Guavina* to port and inboard of *Pampanito*, both bows pointed to the smoking freighter tied up against the pier, perhaps one hundred yards away.

When the dock burst into flames, word was given to clear the harbor. However, few boats could move, because they had been blocked in by a British freighter. According to Gordon Hopper, the freighter wouldn't move because its captain wasn't aboard to give the order to cast off, and the crew refused to throw off the mooring lines without proper authority. "The fire was so close," said Hopper, "that paint on the bow of the British ship started to burn." Finally, one of the other sub skippers "ran up the ship's gangplank, took over command and backed it off, tearing out 20 or 30 feet of flaming dock . . . to the cheers of all the topside submariners."

Bennett and Yagemann were going on liberty when they saw the fire. They heard the alarms and knew the boats would pull out. Instead of returning, they ran to the gate and barely got away. Pappas was in town at the supply depot drawing stores. When he returned to the dock, he saw men putting out a fire, and *Pampanito* was gone. Paul slept on the dock that night. On board the boat, Punchy Thompson noticed that Pappas was missing.

"He ratted on me to the Captain," Paul said, "and accused me of being AWOL." Pappas was on official business, but there were other sailors in their blues, in town, who were not supposed to be there. They found Pappas on the pier in the morning and pleaded with him to tell the officers that they had all been caught in the same predicament and had slept on the dock. Pappas did so, but he was the only one placed on report. Thompson declared that it was Pappas's duty to make every effort to get back to his ship. Pappas asked how he was supposed get back to a submarine at sea. Regardless, Paul was restricted to the boat for thirty days, a punishment that meant little however, for *Pampanito* was almost ready to sail.

The dock fire made a shambles of the supply situation. Woody Weaver was loading torpedoes when the fire broke out. West Australia is very dry, and the wooden pier was in flames within minutes. Boxes of food and canned goods were hastily moved out of harm's way, and the subs pulled out. When the fire died down, the supplies were brought out on deck. The fire flared up again, and there was a second rush to clear the deck. When the goods were finally aboard, they were badly disorganized, with too much of one food and not enough of another, and the cooks had a hard time finding an appropriate selection of meals.

The fire may have caused a foul-up in the laundry situation, too. Clean clothes were important on a patrol that might last two months. Ona Hawkins never could keep clothing in good shape. No matter how careful he was, battery acid would always eat holes in his shirts and dungarees. Roger Walters got four weeks out of each mattress cover by flipping it over every week, then turning it inside out and flipping it again for two more weeks. He gave up trying to keep laundered white socks. He'd buy a dozen or more pairs at ten or fifteen cents per pair, wear them two or three days, and throw them away. It was cheaper to buy new ones than to have them cleaned.

Before the fifth patrol, it was Bob Bennett's turn to be "laundry queen." He was to oversee the collection, washing, and return of the crew's clothing. Everything had been routine until shortly before sailing. Bennett checked the laundry in, but it seemed to be a very large load. In any event, *Pampanito* and *Guavina* sailed on 23 January. When Bennett finished unpacking all the laundry, he found that they had two loads of clothes; "ours and a duplicate set of shirts, pants, and skivvies from another submarine crew." They never knew which sub was shorted, but thought it was very funny that another crew might be sailing with only the one set of clothes on its back.

Leaving North Wharf, Fremantle, *Pampanito* conducted sound tests and night approaches with *Guavina* and minelayer HMAS *Warnambool* in Cockburn Sound. On the evening of the first day out, the escort departed, and the subs headed north. Their patrol area was to be off the Indo-China coast. Japanese convoy routes had been steadily shrinking. In 1944, submarines had destroyed over six hundred merchant ships, one battleship, seven carriers, nine cruisers, and thirty destroyers. Imports of Japanese industrial commodities had declined by 40 percent. Oil stocks had collapsed, and most of the remaining Japanese warships were hiding in the Inland Sea or would soon be sent there. Convoy routes were now confined to the Asian coast, from Singapore in the south to Paramushiro off the Kamchatka Peninsula in the north, and there were 156 submarines competing for the remaining prizes.

The run to Exmouth Gulf had taken two days, and on 26 January the boats made a ten-hour fueling stop. *Pampanito* received a small amount of mail and two pouches to deliver to *Hake* and USS *Pargo* (SS 264). Exmouth Gulf was still a wild, desolate place. On 3 February, one week after *Pampanito* left, the place was completely destroyed by a cyclone.

During the three-day run to Lombok Strait, they conducted training exercises, drills, and dives. In Fremantle, *Pampanito* got a new 40-mm gun in place of one of the 20-mms, but it was found inoperable as assembled; the feed pawls and the stop pawls were reversed. The gun crew broke it down and reassembled it correctly, and now *Pampanito* had a more powerful punch with both fore and aft 40-mms.

Gordon Hopper had recently been rated quartermaster third class. One of his first duties, however, was to climb the shears with a bucket of blue paint, because Summers was dissatisfied with *Pampanito*'s periscope camouflage. Said Hopper: "Holding onto the greasy scopes and paint bucket with one hand while painting with the other was touch and go until a larger than usual swell rolled the boat, causing me to grab tighter and, in the process, drop the paint. When the bucket of paint hit the Conning Tower deck it splashed mightily, covering the captain who was supervising the job."

Summers was furious and called for a .45, pronto. When the order was acknowledged, Summers had second thoughts. "Belay that," he called down. "If you send up a .45 there'll be a dead quartermaster up here." Another sailor came up to finish the paint job.

On the afternoon of 29 January, SJ radar contact was made on the high, volcanic mountains of Lombok at eighty thousand yards. Summers made a submerged approach until sunset. At 1930 he surfaced, flooded low to minimize the silhouette, and began the two-and-one-half-hour transit of the strait. The trip was uneventful, and Summers recorded: "The Nips must be very reluctant tonight. Nothing sighted."

On the northern exit, *Pampanito* exchanged recognition signals with *Bergall*, back on patrol after having her shell damage repaired. Just before midnight, they sighted a few small vessels about eight thousand yards off the port bow, and Summers steered to avoid them.

Heading west through the calm Java Sea, *Pampanito* passed Masalembo Island about midway between Borneo and Java and avoided another vessel fishing nearby. They were not far from the spot where three years before, in the February 1942 Battle of the Java Sea, Rear Admiral Karel Doorman's fleet was nearly destroyed by the victorious Imperial Japanese Navy. Two cruisers, USS *Houston* and HMAS *Perth*, survived that debacle and made it as far west as the Sunda Strait. There, on the last night of February, they sailed into the middle of a Japanese landing force in Banten Bay on the northwest tip of Java. *Houston* and *Perth* were sunk. It was not until *Sealion II* and *Queenfish* rescued some of the same *Perth* survivors off *Rakuyo Maru* that Allied forces learned of the fate of those ships and crews.[9]

On 31 January *Pampanito* ran at three-engine speed to be in position for the transit of Karimata Strait during the evening. The strait lies between Karimata Island off the Borneo coast and Belitung Island and divides the South China Sea from the Java Sea. It is about sixty miles wide and one hundred miles long, making for about an eight-hour passage. On the morning of 1 February, *Pampanito* had passed safely through, and by noon she spotted USS *Bluegill* (SS 242) and USS *Bream* (SS 243). So far, she had sighted as many friendly craft as she had enemy.

That afternoon, east of the large Japanese harbor at Lingga Roads, currently home to the battleships *Ise* and *Hyuga*, *Pampanito* crossed the equator for the second time. Since the shellbacks now outnumbered the pollywogs by a considerable margin, the initiation ceremony for those entering the Realm of Neptunus Rex began in earnest.

One man who didn't count on the full initiation treatment was Lynn Orser. He had flown down to Australia and had never yet crossed the equator on a ship. When he first got on board, Orser seemed to go out of his way to be nice. Dick Sherlock described him as "a big lovable teddy-bear and combination cheer leader." He could be boisterous, yet had a buddy-buddy approach, which perhaps set him up for the initiation. He had to dress up in foul-weather gear and go below to get a sample of bilge water. Orser was then blindfolded and stripped down to his skivvies. The sailors hung a twenty-four-inch pipe wrench around his neck. He had to kneel down and, said Pappas, "kiss the Buddha's belly," which was in reality the sweaty gut of Punchy Thompson. Next, they gave him some foul-tasting potion to drink and shaved a shock of red hair from his head. On his bare skull they coated a layer of peanut butter. Last, Orser had to sit on the "hot seat," which shocked him to his feet. He grabbed the metal table and got shocked again, falling back in the seat for a third jolt. That was enough. Orser stormed off and complained to Summers, but his captain was not sympathetic. Instead, Summers gave him a lecture about comportment and an order to command proper respect in the future. From then on, Lieutenant Commander Orser was not so buddy-buddy with the crew.

Another haircut was administered to a crewman, but it was not part of the equator crossing ceremony. John Madaras was called "Foo Foo" for all the lotions and potions he used on his head. He was convinced he was going bald and tried every known remedy to save his hair. The men thought that Madaras, whose every other word was "F——ing this, or F——ing that," probably was losing his hair because of his diet. He used Tabasco sauce on everything, including scrambled eggs, mashed potatoes, pie, bread, ice cream, and coffee. They thought that if the cooks ever ran out of Tabasco sauce, Madaras would starve. Tired of John's bitching about his receding hairline, the men told him that by shaving his head, he could prevent baldness. It was a proven fact, they said, that if you shave off all your hair, it will grow back thicker and faster. Madaras fell for it and permitted his head to be shorn as smooth as a cue ball. The next night when he was sound asleep, a prankster broke in to Demers's locker and made off with a large bottle of merthiolate. As Madaras snored away, his head was painted bright red. Poor John never knew until he checked the mirror the next morning to see if any of his hair had begun to come in. Needless to say, he was hopping mad, and he sounded off with a new set of curses that would make a longshoreman blush. The merthiolate did not wash off; it had to wear off—and his hair did not grow back until the war was over.[10]

After the equator crossing ceremony, Summers rendezvoused with Ralph H. Lockwood, commander of *Guavina,* and passed him a grid chart of the area. On 2 February they made trim dives and tested Hopper's camouflage paint job by making practice approaches on *Guavina.* The gray-blue paint worked well, and *Pampanito* remained very hard to spot until the boats were quite close. That evening Summers received a message to change patrol stations. He notified Lockwood, and at 2300 the boats entered the area.

All day of 3 February they patrolled off the Malayan coast east of Pulau Redang. There, on 10 December 1941, Japanese aircraft had sunk the British battleship *Prince of Wales* and the battle cruiser *Repulse.* It marked the beginning of the end of the era of the great battlewagons and the rise to prominence of the airplane and submarine. However, by early 1945 the days of the great Japanese fleets were gone, and all *Pampanito* saw were six sailboats. On 5 February, *Pampanito's* lookouts sighted a floating mine. The gunners unleashed their 40-mms and scored numerous hits, but the mine would not sink. An hour later they came across about one dozen bales of floating crude rubber, and Summers was tempted to fill the superstructure with what he called "this priceless material."

Instead of wasting time scooping up rubber from the sea, however, Summers met with Lockwood and reconfigured the patrol assignments. *Guavina* would run east at latitude 6 degrees from the coast to longitude 104 degrees, 30 minutes east, and *Pampanito* would patrol eastward from there.

Payoff came on 6 February. Through the high periscope, *Pampanito* sighted smoke bearing 140. Summers notified Lockwood, and they began

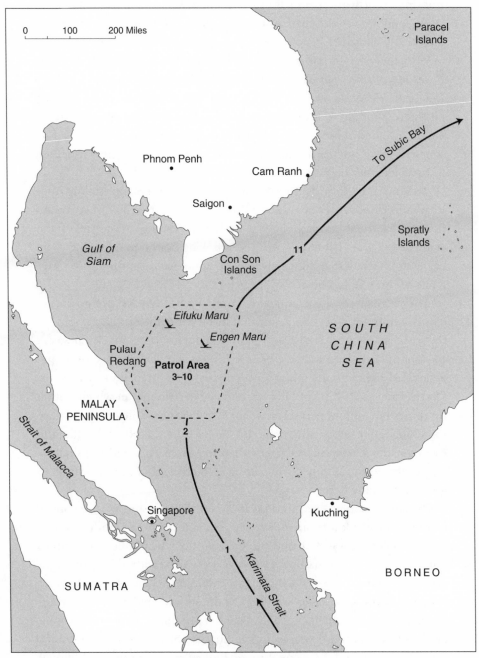

Detail of fifth patrol, 1–11 February 1945

tracking. Shortly thereafter they determined that the target course was north, and Summers began an end-around to set up for a night surface attack. He recorded: "Smoky Joe very helpful in tracking convoy."

They had crossed paths with HI 88D, a small convoy consisting of the *Engen Maru, Taigyo Maru,* and *Haruyasa Maru* and escorts *Yashiro* and *Coast Defense Vessels No. 13* and *No. 31.* They had left Singapore on 4 February and were heading to Moji, Japan. Early in the morning of 6 February, *Yashiro,* situated at the convoy's rear, discovered a trailing submarine. She sent a warning, and the convoy turned to port. The submarine appeared to have been left behind.

An hour after sighting the convoy, *Pampanito* saw a plane circling overhead and dived. After remaining down an hour, the crew were apprehensive that the ships might have pulled away. The convoy was still off the starboard quarter, however, with "Joe" smoking heavily and leading them to the doorstep. Radar contact was made at twenty-seven thousand yards: a line of three ships covered by three escorts.

They were faced with a familiar conundrum: Summers could go in very close at night for a periscope attack if there was sufficient moonlight for the scope to operate, or he could go in close for a surface attack if it wasn't too bright. Unfortunately, he believed it was too dark for a submerged attack and, although the moon wasn't up yet, too light for a surface attack. His decision probably would be second-guessed no matter which option he chose, but Summers resolved to go in as far as possible on the surface for a long-range shot. Influencing his choice were the possibility that the escorts had a slower surface speed than the submarine and the shallowness of the water; at only thirty fathoms (180 feet) there was no room to go deep to evade depth charges.

*Pampanito* maneuvered into position. Final setup showed the convoy running at eight knots on course 040, range forty-three hundred yards. The sub's course was 330, and the torpedo track would be 100 degrees starboard. At 2157 all six bow torpedoes were fired with a 7-degree right gyro angle at the nearest two ships. As the minutes ticked away on the long run, the third ship was seen overlapping the second, making a nice group and increasing the chances of a hit. After an interminable six-minute wait, two hits flashed on the nearest target. Success! Standing near Summers, Lynn Orser watched the scene through binoculars. He noticed additional flashes on the nearest escort, which he quickly identified as blinker signals. Even more quickly he was proven wrong, as shell splashes fountained up near the submarine. Summers made a sarcastic comment about Orser's visual acuity and ordered *Pampanito* to clear out.

The convoy veered away from the attack on course 350. On *Engen Maru,* torpedo tracks were first seen at five hundred yards and closing fast. She turned to port, but it was too late. A great explosion tore apart the engine room, and violent flooding commenced. Quickly, her bow went up at 60 degrees, and her stern settled to the bottom in the shallow water. *Pampanito*'s radar tracked the pip as it decreased in intensity while the escorts closed in, and Summers ordered flank speed to make another end-around on the convoy. As the escorts rushed east toward the suspected submarine, Summers looped around on the convoy's port quarter, heading northwest and leaving the escorts astern. He had sunk the civilian-controlled, 6,890-ton oiler *Engen Maru,* taking down forty-four passengers and crew, 7,110 tons of crude oil, 1,195 tons of rubber, and 217 tons of copper. So far, so good.[11]

*Pampanito* was on the convoy's port beam when at 0023 of 7 February, Summers discovered that the two escorts he had left astern were quickly gaining on him. Apparently they had tired of searching for the elusive submarine back at the scene of *Engen Maru*'s sinking and were rapidly returning to the convoy. Probably unbeknownst to them, they were getting very close to *Pampanito*'s starboard beam.

The range to the convoy was over five thousand yards, but the range to the trailing escorts was four thousand yards and closing. Summers recorded: "We were neatly boxed in and believed the escorts on starboard beam had seen us sometime before; so had to shoot and get out."

The men in the forward torpedo room had been sweating the past two hours, trying to reload all six fish. They had just finished when they got another call to ready all the torpedoes. Many skippers at this stage of the war preferred electric torpedoes, and Fenno had twenty-four electrics on the fourth patrol. In Fremantle, however, they were not available in sufficient quantity, and Summers had to settle for sixteen steam torpedoes in the forward room and eight electrics in the after room. In this case he was fortunate to have the steam torpedoes, for he could not have fired from so great a distance with the electrics. Even so, the range was probably too great. When Woody Weaver got the word to set the forward torpedoes at

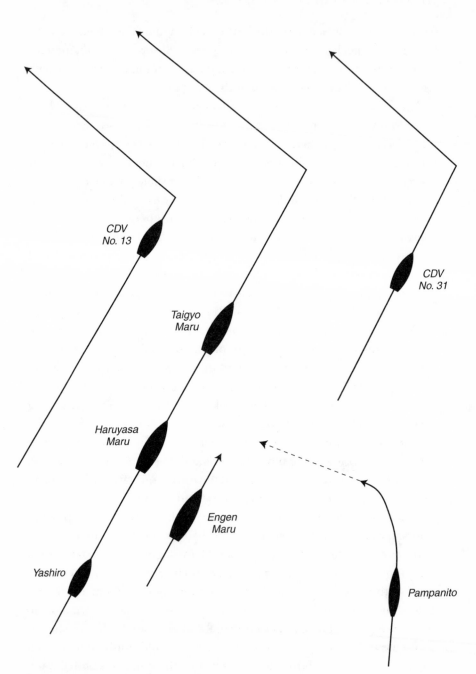

CDV
No. 13

CDV
No. 31

Taigyo
Maru

Haruyasa
Maru

Engen
Maru

Yashiro

Pampanito

Attack on Convoy HI 88D, 6 February 1945

low speed, he knew that Summers was again making a longshot at over five thousand yards. Nevertheless, concerned with being boxed in, Summers ordered all six bow tubes fired before the trailing escorts could get any closer. They went off with a 95-degree port track at fifty-three hundred yards' range.

As soon as the fish were fired, *Pampanito* reversed course and pulled clear. There were no hits, but Summers was more concerned about getting out of what he perceived as a dangerous predicament. The log read: "Escorts had us cornered but fortunately they didn't realize it—they certainly had no radar in this outfit." The officers may have wondered why Summers would not pull in closer to attack a radarless convoy.

By 0100 the convoy shifted course to the north, and *Pampanito* attempted an end-around on its port flank. The trailing escorts dropped back and disappeared from radar. The moon was due to rise in another hour, and Summers hoped to be ahead of the enemy track by then. Sixty more minutes at flank speed put the sub in position on the convoy's port beam, but now the moon was beginning to poke above the horizon. The first attack had been rushed because Summers was reluctant to get in too close, the second had been rushed because of the sudden appearance of two escorts, and now the third was being rushed because it was getting too light. At 0217 the last four fish left the forward torpedo tubes at 135 degrees port track and range of forty-one hundred yards. Again, no hits.

Summers fumed. He believed the setup checked perfectly and wanted an explanation why they missed. Woody Weaver was convinced that they were simply too far away to have a reasonable chance of hitting. In addition, the convoy had been alerted after the first attack, and the ships and escorts put on a sharp lookout for the tell-tale steam torpedo tracks. Said Weaver: "A submarine skipper hated to waste that many torpedoes, and ours was pretty unhappy." Summers, he said, "accused the torpedomen of improper maintenance of the torpedoes, which he blamed for his failure."

*Guavina* did not seem to be having the same troubles. At 0230, Lockwood radioed that he was attacking. Shortly after, *Guavina*'s SJ radar interference disappeared, which indicated that her skipper saw no trouble going in close for a submerged attack. One-half hour later, Summers radioed the convoy's position and attack results to ComTaskFor 71. At 0352, those on *Pampanito*'s bridge witnessed "two nice hits in the larger of the two remaining ships." The victim looked like an oiler, and the bridge watch saw it sink beneath the waves, while Moffett confirmed that the pip disappeared from radar. No depth charges were heard, and Summers suggested that to evade, *Guavina* must have gone down to hide under a blanket of mud at 160 feet. With two out of three torpedoes, Lockwood had sunk the *Taigyo Maru*, a 6,892-ton civilian-controlled cargo ship.

At sunup, *Pampanito*'s lookouts sighted two escorts milling around near the position of the first attack, about four miles away. Nothing else was in sight. Summers ordered the boat down for the day so that everyone could get some rest.

While most of the crew got some shuteye, the skipper rankled about the torpedo misses of the night before. He was certain the torpedomen were lax in their maintenance duties, and he felt very uncomfortable with no forward fish and a full load in the stern. Summers proposed that they transfer four electric torpedoes to the forward room. Almost to a man, the torpedomen considered the plan to be unworkable.

"It was a hare-brained scheme," said Woody Weaver. The plan was to rig the torpedo handling boom on deck, pull the torpedoes out through the after loading hatch, lower them into the rubber boat, float them forward, move the boom forward, pick up the torpedoes, and lower them through the forward hatch. It would have been a long, difficult, labor-intensive process, and it would have had to be done four times.

"No," Lieutenant Swain said to Summers. "I'm sorry, I can't. You're going to have to get someone else to do it." But Summers was insistent, and Swain could not refuse an order. At 1715 on 7 February, *Pampanito* surfaced. Many thoughts raced through Weaver's head. He was in charge of the forward torpedo room, and he had been told that he would be advanced to chief petty officer at the end of the fifth patrol. Since Weaver would be very much involved in the transfer, he could see his chances of making chief going down the drain should the operation prove disastrous. All they had to do was lose control of one of the torpedoes while trying to balance it on the rubber raft. Each electric torpedo weighed about as much as a small car. Woody worried that the torpedo and the rubber boat would head straight for the bottom. Said Bob Bennett: "The torpedo transfer scheme was the dumbest idea I ever heard," and Roger Walters added, "What a Rube Goldberg solution!"

As the transfer party went topside at 1755, it was interrupted by a radio message from *Guavina*. She saw smoke on the horizon. Summers rushed to the bridge, said Weaver, "and we were spared the torpedo transfer operation by the skin of our teeth." *Pampanito* set off on an interception course. Woody looked up at the sky and thanked the Lord.

At 1830, high periscope picked up smoke at 276 degrees: a convoy, apparently heading north. By 2015, SJ had a bearing on it at 300 degrees, range twenty-three thousand yards. Shortly after, the lookouts saw flashes near the convoy and assumed *Guavina* was working it over. In fact, Lockwood's attack had been unsuccessful, and it was *Guavina* that was being worked over. Summers maneuvered frantically to get in position ahead of the convoy for a stern shot, a formidable task while approaching from behind. When close in, the PPI showed that this was only a small convoy, with one medium-sized ship that appeared to be a tanker, covered by one escort astern and another escort now off to starboard chasing *Guavina*.

At 2132, Summers was far enough ahead to slow down, spin his stern around to the target, and wait. Twenty minutes later he let go all four aft torpedoes, set at six feet, with a 44-degree port track. The range was 4,370 yards, but because of the slow speed of the electrics and the converging course of the target, the torpedo run would be about 3,800 yards—still near the maximum range of an electric torpedo. The result: four more misses.

Summers tore off for another end-around, frustrated and cursing under his breath. Two hits out of twenty fired. It had to be somebody's fault. Damn the torpedomen. Weaver simply observed, "Our skipper was fit to be tied." However, since the electric torpedoes left no bubbling wake, the convoy did not even know it had been attacked and steamed on unconcernedly.

While Summers pulled ahead for yet another try with his last torpedoes, he thought of a ruse that might allow him to pull off a successful attack. *Guavina* was about ten thousand yards off the convoy's starboard beam. The escorts were now on either quarter of the target, but as far as they knew, the only threat to their safety was off to starboard, the direction where *Guavina* last appeared. The fact that another submarine was pulling ahead on their port bow was unknown to them. At 2300, Summers radioed to Lockwood and asked for a favor. Would *Guavina* please distract the attention of the escorts by firing a Very pistol so *Pampanito* could come in for an attack from the other side? Lockwood complied, and as the flare shot high in the sky, the starboard escort charged off after *Guavina.* She had done a good job, but now she had to shake off an angry escort.

While *Guavina* led one escort away on a merry chase, the remaining ship and escort zigged left, away from the flare, which threw *Pampanito* out of position again. While she worked ahead, the convoy made another radical shift, coming north to course 015. An hour of frantic maneuvering finally placed *Pampanito* ahead, but this time on the starboard bow of the convoy. *Guavina,* however, could only distract the enemy's attention for so long. Now the starboard escort was hurrying back to the position it had vacated before chasing off after the mysterious flare. Again, Pete Summers was being rushed.

At 0025, 8 February, with the starboard escort moving up on the convoy's beam, Summers was forced to shoot. *Pampanito* slowed to four knots on course 065 and pointed her stern toward the target, which maintained a speed of ten knots. After all the maneuvering, Summers could still get no closer than four thousand yards. It was another long shot at best. Saving only one torpedo for an emergency, Summers fired three fish on a 75-degree starboard track, spread from 1 degree left to 1 degree right and set at a depth of four feet.

*Pampanito* pulled away. Four minutes later there were still no explosions, and Summers might have blown up himself when suddenly a great flash lit the sky, followed by a roll of thunder. To Lieutenant Swain on the bridge, the target appeared to be a tanker. It was a tremendous explosion, he said. "The bow kept going forwards, the stern was going backwards, and the center went up in the air."

"Judging from the intense flames and explosions," Summers wrote, "the ship was evidently loaded with aviation gasoline." Topside, Hopper also thought that the ship must have been carrying gasoline. "The fire fueled by its cargo made it nearly as bright as day," he said.

One escort was so close to the detonation it appeared to be damaged by the blast. Just then a second torpedo rammed into the wreckage and exploded, but not nearly with the same ferocity as the first. Said Summers: "The whole area looked like a Fourth of July celebration and we felt slightly naked in all this gaslight." *Pampanito* had obliterated the 3,520-ton *Eifuku Maru,* a former merchant ship now armed and being used as a gunboat.

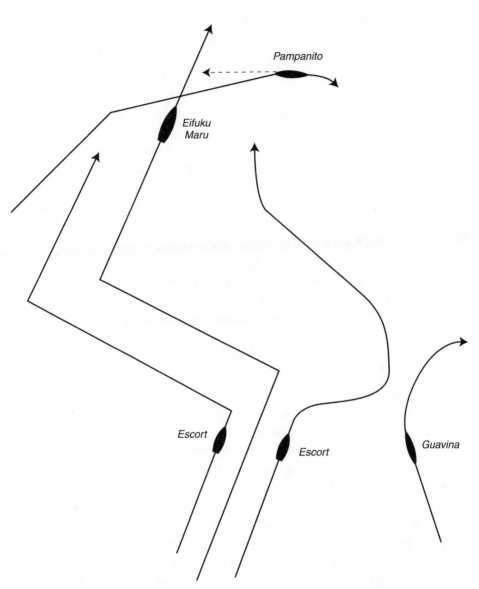

Convoy attack, 8 February 1945

The escort on the starboard quarter that had just returned from chasing *Guavina* evidently saw *Pampanito* in the light of the fires and peeled off after her. It commenced firing and placed several close rounds right over the bridge. "Maneuvering!" Pete slapped on the 7 MC, interior communications, and shouted, "Give me more speed!"

The topside lookouts watched in awe as one violent explosion after another tore the target to pieces. The stern sank, separated from the rest of the ship by about a thousand yards, while "the bow put on the finishing touch by exploding beautifully in technicolor." In a final explosion in the bow, flames, water, and parts of the ship went five hundred feet in the air and came down in a cascading "bluish green fountain" of water. Paul Pappas was topside with his ubiquitous camera. He tried to soak in the scenery but was concerned about the charging escort. He heard the roar of one shell as it flew over the conning tower and saw two more splash just wide. The "tanker," he said, "exploded and was burning. There's flames all over the horizon. I went on the bridge and made moving pictures of it. There was one more big explosion after I came below, and that was the end of it."

However, there was more to be concerned about than waxing poetic over the stunning, flaming explosions on the nighttime sea. *Pampanito* was conducting her own version of Mush Morton's famous description about his submarine in a running gun battle with a destroyer: "*Wahoo* running, destroyer gunning." Summers did not want to dive in such shallow water, and he hoped his speed would eventually outdistance his pursuer. Moffett had the SJ so finely tuned that he could track the incoming shells. Summers chased salvoes, heading directly for the spot of the last shell splash, under the assumption that the escort's gun crews would naturally adjust for their last miss. It would take a very well trained crew, or an extremely lucky shot, to hit the speeding, fishtailing submarine. Pete called for all excess lookouts to go below, and Spence Stimler heard McGuire sing out, "Gladly! Gladly!" as he dashed down the conning tower ladder. After several close misses, *Pampanito* hauled away into the blackness.[12]

Two hours into the mid watch, *Pampanito* sent out another message to ComTaskFor 71 with the results of the latest attack. She met *Guavina* and transferred to her the mail she had been carrying for *Pargo* and *Hake*. Upon parting, *Guavina* sent the message: "A beautiful job. Well done," which *Pampanito* answered, "Thanks for the flares. Take over." With only one torpedo left, Summers was anticipating an early end to the patrol, and he set his course south. It appeared that they would get another liberty in Australia.

It was not to be. Early on 9 February, a message brought the disappointing order to reverse course. Their new destination was north, up the Indo-China coast. Where could they be going? Most bets were on Saipan— a destination definitely lacking in Australian-type amenities.

The next two days were devoid of contacts as *Pampanito* sliced through the empty swells heading northeast into the South China Sea. For a few sailors, however, the ride was anything but routine. Some had been a little too free with the Australian women. One electrician was in serious pain and could not stand his watch, and the others had to cover for him. Ona Hawkins didn't mind at first. He was now the interior communications (IC) electrician. One of his jobs was to maintain the sound phones. His bunk was in the after torpedo room, where Jim Behney was in charge. Hawkins called Behney "a nice guy, but headstrong." Behney hated the sound phones and was unnecessarily rough on them, always throwing them off his head. Every day Hawkins had to repair them.

Hawkins was pleased to learn all the new tasks, but because of the electrician who "was kind of incapacitated," the extra work wore him down. Besides the IC job, Ona had to check the battery wells, the gauges, and the grounds. Even though Cordon had "adjusted" one meter to eliminate some of the problems, Punchy Thompson was always finding extra work for him. With one man not pulling his own weight, sympathy for his condition quickly evaporated. Unfortunately, Doc Demers couldn't help, for he had not yet been issued any of the "miracle drug," penicillin.

Another man having a tough time was Ensign Edmund DePaul. With DePaul's appearance, Sherlock and Bartholomew were no longer the lowest ranking officers. DePaul was now "George," low man, and "gopher." Unfortunately, the ensign was constantly seasick and rarely left his bunk. "He had the dry heaves so bad he could not stand," said Dick Sherlock. "The sea was relatively calm for most of the patrol, so some of it may have been from fright."

DePaul was a "good guy," said McGuire, "but he always got seasick, and Summers didn't like him because of it." Being rather naïve, and unable to perform many routine duties because of his sickness, DePaul was naturally the one selected to confront Summers with a concern of the officers. Before the patrol they had pitched in two or three dollars apiece to buy a dozen cans of mixed nuts, pecans, cashews, and almonds. Summers kept the nuts in his cabin and only doled them out when he felt like it, "as if he was their father," explained McGuire. Even more aggravating, Summers would take one can for himself and pass out only one can for nine officers. The large number of crewmen and poor food stocks kept Summers grumbling the entire patrol.

At least the peanut situation could be addressed, but this time Ensign DePaul would lead the nascent mutineers. With a calm sea, DePaul was able to rise up out his bunk. Like the other officers, he was angered by Pete's paternalistic and capricious treatment, and with the instigation of his cohorts, DePaul marched to the captain's cabin. Pete thumped his fingers on his desktop for a few moments while the ensign grieved. Then, in another Queeg-like reaction, he absolutely "blew up." He severely dressed down DePaul and told him that he had no business being on a submarine. As the ensign retreated, Summers stepped out of his cabin and added that he was the captain and could do as he damned well pleased. "RHIP!" (rank has its privileges), he called out to DePaul as he snapped his curtain shut. Another man was on Pete's "list."

On 10 February, *Pampanito* milled around awaiting orders. There was so little action that even the usually busy John Johnson was getting restive. While at periscope depth, the steward approached Lieutenant Sherlock and requested permission to go out on deck. Sherlock explained: "He said it was his second patrol and he had never been on deck and he felt the need of some fresh air. When I explained to him that we were submerged, he was amazed. I honestly believe that was his first comprehension that the boat could dive beneath the surface." Sherlock could only shake his head in disbelief.

On 11 February a message finally arrived: "Proceed to Subic Bay, Philippine Islands, for refit." Subic Bay? They wondered where it was and if it had any women or booze. *Pampanito* put on speed and continued across the China Sea. By 1300 on 12 February, she pulled into Subic Bay, Luzon, and the crew would soon discover the luxuries of a Philippine liberty.[13]

## CHAPTER TEN

# To the Gulf of Siam and
# Back to the States

As far as the crew was concerned, Subic Bay was not much different from Exmouth Gulf. In Fremantle on 30 December, Admiral Christie had been relieved by Admiral Fife. One of Fife's first jobs was to facilitate moving the Brisbane base in Queensland, Australia, to a forward location. Admirals Nimitz and Lockwood had just shifted their headquarters to Guam, and it was thought that Subic Bay would be a good location for the Brisbane unit.

Not everyone had the same opinion. Most of those who would have to occupy the base compared it to the ill-advised move to Exmouth Gulf in 1943; it was too far from any civilized amenities, too hot, too unhealthy, and too desolate—and the humidity was worse. Fife, however, went ahead with his plans.

Subic Bay is at the narrow neck of the Bataan Peninsula, only about fifteen miles from the head of Manila Bay to the east. The XI Army Corps had landed nearby on 29 January, and on the next day elements of the 38th Infantry Division marched to Olongapo while the Japanese retreated east into the hills. For the next several days they fought in Zigzag Pass in the Cabusilan Mountains. There was still fighting nearby on 11 February when sub base construction began. *Pampanito* waited in the China Sea because it was not known if a tender would get there in time to service her. When she sailed past Grande Island and into Subic

Bay on 12 February, she was the first submarine at the new base. Almost
nothing was ready.

Wanting to look professional at the new base, Lieutenant Commander
Orser had the crew assemble on deck. He requested that they wear their
uniforms, but the men mustered in all manner of dress: whites, blues,
dungarees, and T-shirts. Said Bob Bennett: "Orser thought he could get
us to line up like two rows of corn," but his plan came to naught.

"Right dress!" Orser commanded as the men stumbled about topside.
Few knew what he was talking about, for a submarine crew had little
parade ground training. Instead of looking smart, they looked foolish.
Above them, the crew of the tender *Griffin* (AS 13) lounged at the railings,
making catcalls. "The deck was so hot," said Bennett, "that it burned the
soles of my feet right through my shoes." He stood on the outside edges
of his shoes with his ankles bowed out. "We were trying to hide our heads,"
said Pappas, "while the other submariners were laughing at us."[1]

The boat was turned over to the Submarine Division 122 relief crew,
but because of the tender's unreadiness, *Pampanito*'s sailors did much of
their own repairs. Blow holes had developed in the number one engine's
cylinder liners, probably the result of the high-speed run from the escort.
They were filled with silver solder, but the liner had expanded from the
heat and had cracked the water jackets on three cylinders. Temporary
gaskets were fitted to prevent leaks. They tried to fix the cooling system for
the overheating number four engine, but it still ran hot at top speed. They
would need a full overhaul to replace all the water and oil lines.

Summers complained about the food situation in his patrol report. The
meat was below standard, and the selection was poor. The distillers could
not keep up with the demands of eighty-one men, and there was not
enough fresh water. If they thought they were going to make up for the
subpar food and drink situation by supplementing their rations in town,
they were sorely mistaken.

Japanese were still in the nearby hills, and liberty began at noon and
ended at nightfall. Subic City and Olongapo were two of the worst
places anyone could have imagined. It was said that officers were sent
there as a punishment. Olongapo was called the "most depraved village
in the world." Most of it was out of bounds for the military. The main
street was "a one-lane open sewer" overrun with dirty, naked children,

dogs, chickens, and pigs. The major entertainment was a cockfight in a chicken coop.

"There was not much of liberty because of the fighting," said Ona Hawkins. They went to the beach and set up a tent and a volleyball net. It was extremely hot and humid, Ona said, "so we all sat in the tent and drank beer. Not one person played volleyball." Bennett watched distant planes dogfighting and saw a smoking fighter go down over the mountains. While lazing around under the palms, Ervin McGehee saw one sailor get knocked in the head by a falling coconut.

Although the people were kind and received them as liberators, Moffett declared that he never saw one thing in the Philippines that would make him want to return. Even the local brew was nasty.

"The beer was green!" declared Walt Madison. It was a brand called Grayson Dock that the submariners immediately rechristened "Greasy Dick." For recreation, Madison tried swimming, but he stated, "Hell, there were dead Japs still floating in the bay." Peder Granum got dumped into the filthy water. He and Ervin McGehee had been drinking, and when Peder conked out, McGehee wheeled him back to the dock in a two-wheeled native cart. Ervin couldn't quite negotiate the incline, the cart got away, and Granum careened into the drink. The Filipino stevedores cursed McGehee for losing their cart.

At night there was a blackout, and no movies were shown topside. The sailors watched flashes from the gunfire winking on and off in the hills, accompanied by the occasional rumbling of distant artillery. While a new movie they received, a western, *The Ox-Bow Incident,* was playing in the forward torpedo room, no one noticed that a few of the crew were missing. Stockslader, Madison, and Fireman First Class Stanley F. Butler had missed the last boat. During the afternoon they had been drinking "Greasy Dick." Stockslader dozed off under a palm tree, and Madison and Butler had gone exploring. The launch left without them. When Stockslader awoke, everyone was gone and night was falling. He tried to get back to the boat, but the guards would not let him out of the perimeter. Ed scooped out a makeshift bed in the sand and spent the night being eaten alive by insects. Madison and Butler crawled under a bulldozer. The next morning they hopped the first navy launch back to the boat, and, Stockslader said, "We had a lot of explaining to do."[2]

A somewhat haggard *Pampanito* crew on liberty, Subic Bay, Philippines. (Photo courtesy of Robert Bennett.)

On an excursion to Subic City, Roger Walters and his shipmates were introduced to the mayor, who lived in a corrugated iron shack with a dirt floor. *Griffin* had sent a three-piece band over for a liberation dance. The mayor, said Walters, had the entire ship's party dance with all of his daughters and nieces. They had a pretty good time, even though the mayor's daughters were not all beauty queens. The sailors had only soft drinks, but during the celebration some soldiers brought in a home-made alcoholic concoction stored in open beer bottles. They passed around the brew for sample sips and asked the sailors if they would like to purchase any at ten bucks a bottle. "It wasn't very good," said Walters, "and no one wanted to buy any." The upshot of the story was that about ten days after *Pampanito* had pulled out, they received a radio message with a warning to destroy any bottles of a concoction that was being sold illicitly in Subic City. It turned out to be wood alcohol, and one man had died and a couple more had gone blind from drinking it.

*Pampanito* received three endorsements for the fifth patrol. One congratulation came from Charles W. Wilkins of Squadron 12; one from James Fife, who commented on the clever stratagem of firing a Very pistol and who awarded the crew another combat insignia; and the third from the Seventh Fleet commander, Admiral Thomas E. Kincaid. Even so, Summers was still in a bad mood because of all the wasted torpedoes. Woody Weaver was not advanced to chief petty officer as he had been led to believe he would be. He thought Lieutenant Swain's refusal to take part in the torpedo transfer scheme had made Summers angry, and the audacity of DePaul's asking for his fair share of peanuts had contributed to the captain's irascibility. In fact, Summers would not suffer any more of DePaul's brashness—nor his seasickness. He reported DePaul as unfit for submarine duty and booted him out of the service. The ensign asked McGuire for help, but pulling a switch in the forms would not work this time.

There were few other personnel changes. Lieutenant Commander Bush remained for another patrol as PCO. Only three sailors were detached. One new man coming aboard was Chief Gunner's Mate William I. Aiken, who had made five patrols on *S-28*. Summers named him the new chief of the boat. No one knew what Chief Smith had done to warrant the change. The crew was angered by the demotion and because none of the chief petty officers on board were selected. Picking a brand new man over those who had served their time was another strike against the captain.

Because the fifth patrol had been short, the subsequent leave was commensurate. However, there were not many sailors who longed to remain at Subic Bay. Besides, *Pampanito* was going out for her sixth patrol, and in past practice, submarines were sent to the States for an overhaul after six patrols. Meanwhile, Admiral Fife came to settle in at his new base in the Philippines. He promptly caught malaria.

In the South China Sea on 25 February, Summers opened up his orders and learned his patrol area would be at the Gulf of Siam again. The area had seen some action while he was gone. ULTRA intelligence had discovered that on 11 February the two Japanese hybrid carrier-battleships, *Ise* and *Hyuga,* had left Lingga Roads loaded with thousands of drums of oil and headed for the Japanese Empire. Accompanied by a heavy cruiser and three destroyers, they made a two-thousand-mile dash across the length of the South China Sea.

The British submarine *Tantalus* had first crack at them near Singapore, but missed. Farther north, Admiral Fife arranged his boats to intercept. The same day *Pampanito* pulled into Subic Bay, USS *Charr* (SS 328) picked up the Japanese battleships on radar but could not make an attack; the same was the case for USS *Blackfin* (SS 322). *Bergall* and USS *Blower* (SS 325) each fired six torpedoes at them but missed. *Bashaw* closed in but was sighted by one of the battleships and attracted a main-gun salvo for her effort. *Ise* and *Hyuga* eluded fourteen submarines in the South China Sea, and eleven more sent by Lockwood to intercept them in the East China Sea. Both Fife and Lockwood were disappointed at the poor showing. Once again, ULTRA could be a great advantage, but good seamanship and a little luck were still needed.

After parting with *Pampanito, Guavina* also missed a chance to catch the elusive battleships. However, on 20 February, Ralph Lockwood sank the 8,673-ton tanker *Eiyo Maru.* That tonnage, combined with the cargo ship sunk while in Summers's wolf pack, gave Lockwood 15,565 tons of shipping destroyed in February and the top individual score for the month. The rather meager total illustrated just how scarce Japanese shipping had become. Also on 20 February, near Cam Ranh Bay, Commander David B. Bell in *Pargo* sank *Nokaze,* the last Japanese destroyer sunk by submarines in the war. Japan had begun hostilities with 113 destroyers. By the end of February 1945, only 37 were left. Although some new ones were built during the war, 126 were lost, and submarines accounted for 39 of them.

In fact, there were probably more U.S. submarines along the convoy route from Singapore to Formosa than there were Japanese ships. A veritable traffic jam occurred off the Indo-Chinese coast. On 23 February near the present-day city of Qui-nhon, Commander Miles P. Refo III was running submerged in USS *Hoe* (SS 258) in a four-knot current when his boat bounced off what he thought was an underwater rock. It wasn't. Running just a little bit deeper on a perpendicular course was Commander James E. Stevens in USS *Flounder* (SS 251). *Flounder* received a great jolt and was sent angling toward the bottom. Stevens needed no additional information to know that he had just been run over by another submarine. Although *Hoe* had lost only some paint along her keel, *Flounder* had a twenty-five-foot gash in her superstructure between her forward four-inch gun and her conning tower. The deck around the forward 20-mm gun, the SJ mast, antennas, and a vent line to a fuel oil tank were damaged. *Flounder* had to break off the patrol and go to Subic Bay for repairs. There was sense in the orders for submarines diligently to remain in their assigned areas.[3]

As *Flounder* was nearing Subic Bay, *Pampanito* was leaving, conducting exercises with a navy search plane to establish procedures for coordinated submarine-aircraft operations. Throughout the daylight hours of 26 February, Mervin Hill and Radioman First Class Allan C. Elliot, and Commander Gordon Selby (USN) on the exercise plane, played hide-and-seek, testing their respective communications and detection equipment. The biggest problem was keeping both sets calibrated to the same frequency. The new VoyCall system did not work well, with twenty miles being the maximum range, while the VHF faded at fifteen miles. The plane's signals were best while overhead but weakened while at 0 degrees or 180 degrees (bow and stern) relative. The sub could communicate with the plane using the SD while submerged. When surfaced, the plane had no idea where the sub was until it turned on its SD and IFF. At that point the plane could easily home in on the submarine's signals—which only verified what the skippers had believed for years.

*Pampanito* bid adieu to Commander Selby and conducted more drills on her own. That evening, Summers received new orders to conduct a coordinated patrol with two other boats. Once again, Paul Summers was the commander of a wolf pack, this one consisting of his boat; *Sealion II,* on her fifth patrol, now under Charles F. Putman; and USS *Mingo* (SS 261), on her seventh patrol, under John R. Madison.

En route to the rendezvous on 27 February, *Pampanito*'s SD located six friendly planes during the day. None had any news for *Pampanito,* but Summers had one Catalina relay a message to Commander Selby that a change in the sub's orders would not allow them to conduct further exercises. At 1945, Summers entered his assigned area and sent a message to *Sealion II* and *Mingo* asking for their estimated times of arrival. Late that night *Pampanito* made SJ contact with USS *Hawkbill* (SS 366), which was finishing her third patrol and heading for Subic Bay.

Summers spent the next day in almost the same waters where he had sunk the *Engen Maru* less than one month earlier. On 1 March he moved closer to the Malay Peninsula near Kota Bharu, and the SJ picked up land from thirty-five miles away. High periscope watch found a floating mine, and the gun crews worked it over with 40-mm and .30-caliber fire but were unable to sink it.

Meanwhile, three other submarines were converging in the Gulf of Siam. *Sealion II* and *Mingo* were closing in for the rendezvous, while *Pintado* was coming up after performing lifeguard duty off Singapore. While *Pampanito* was dodging mines, *Pintado* spotted *Sealion* making several course changes. *Pintado*'s exec, Lieutenant Commander Corwin Mendenhall, guessed that she was after something. They sent an inquiry but got no response. However, smoke was soon reported in the north, and *Pintado* joined in the chase. The mysterious ship was on course 190, and *Pintado* worked into position directly ahead. Before she submerged, lookouts saw *Sealion* about eight miles to the west and closing in.

There would be no attack, however. As the vessel hove into view, they could plainly see it was a hospital ship. Mendenhall saw no air or surface escort, and it was on a steady course. From three thousand yards away he made a series of still and moving pictures as the liner steamed on past.

What ship was this? It could very well have been *Awa Maru,* an 11,600-ton passenger-cargo ship and one of Japan's last large, fast liners. *Awa Maru*

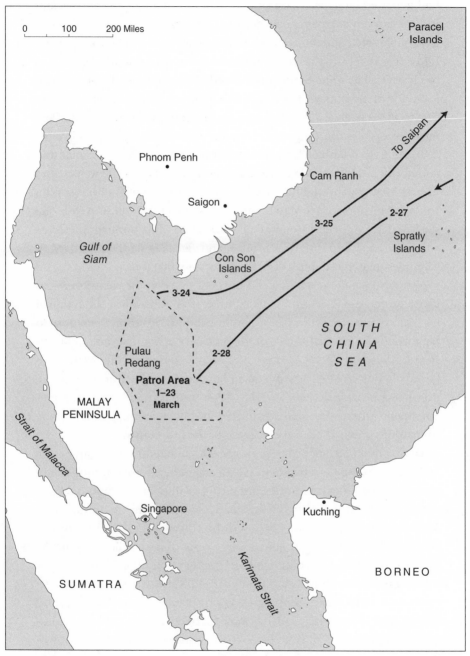

Detail of sixth patrol, 27 February–25 March 1945

had departed Moji, Japan, on 17 February to visit Singapore and various Indonesian ports. Japanese authorities had contacted the United States to arrange safe conduct, for *Awa Maru* was supposed to be transporting Red Cross relief supplies to prisoner-of-war camps. Its markings were to be clearly visible: white crosses on each side of the funnel, white crosses on each side of the ship, and all navigation lights on. Its sailing schedule was sent to all the submarines, along with an admonition to leave it alone. The message was broadcast three times on three successive nights in February.

Indeed, Mendenhall "concluded that our contact was a hospital ship about which we had been alerted in messages earlier in the week." *Awa Maru*'s itinerary showed her crossing the mouth of the Gulf of Siam en route to Singapore on 1 March, but she was an 11,600-ton ship with one stack and white crosses; Mendenhall's black-and-white photograph shows a two-funneled ship with dark crosses, and *Pintado*'s skipper, Bernard A. Clarey, estimated the ship's displacement was 4,000 tons.

Were the Japanese sending two hospital ships on the same course to take advantage of *Awa Maru*'s safe conduct pass? Regardless, it was one of the war's ironies that *Awa Maru*, on her previous trip from Singapore to Japan, had carried the balance of the prisoners of war that did not sail on *Rakuyo Maru* and *Kachidoki Maru*. *Awa Maru* had hugged the Asian coastline all the way to Moji, arriving on 15 January 1945. After depositing the prisoners, she was reloaded with Red Cross supplies and was returning to Singapore, where she narrowly missed an attack by some of the same submarines that had been the nemesis of the first convoy.[4]

During mid watch of 2 March, *Pampanito* made rendezvous with *Sealion* and *Mingo*. Summers gave them patrol assignments, establishing a line along latitude 6 degrees north and giving each boat a section of about seventy miles, with *Sealion* off the coast, *Pampanito* in the middle, and *Mingo* to the east. Summers believed the configuration would prevent anything from slipping by. His modus operandi had radically changed since the days in the Carolines and off Japan, when he spent entire days submerged. His experience and comfort with surface search tactics, plus the scarcity of Japanese shipping and poor plane coverage, dictated the change. Even when enemy planes were spotted, excellent radar warning gave the boat plenty of time to dive. By this stage of the war most sub skippers were following suit and remaining on the surface day and night.

On 3 March, SD contacts were made on three planes, but Summers never dove. Then, just when the radar seemed to be working perfectly, the "gremlins" reappeared. Early the next morning the SJ indicated pips at nine hundred and fifteen hundred yards, well within eyesight range. Nothing was there.

With no ship contacts since they assembled, Summers changed the pack's alignment, with *Pampanito* moving close to shore, *Mingo* in the middle, and *Sealion* farthest out to sea. The shift did not cause any change in luck. The next three days brought only sightings of sailing vessels or floating mines. Finally, at 1630 on 7 March, *Pampanito* got a message from *Sealion* reporting that she had sighted a ship on a northerly course, speed about thirteen knots. The tracking party plotted an interception course, and the boat was off on what would be a seven-hour end-around. "It will be a long haul," Summers recorded, "but if there's more than one we'll get in on the killing."

Unfortunately, when just beginning the chase, a close SD contact drove *Pampanito* down for half an hour, but other boats were barreling in. For the past few days, *Pintado* had worked in a coordinated attack group with USS *Caiman* (SS 323). They patrolled the area along the Malay coast south of Summers's pack. On 7 March, *Pintado* spotted smoke, sent a message, and began tracking. *Sealion* also picked up the contact, but *Pintado* got the first visual. It looked like the same hospital ship they had seen traveling south a week earlier, and *Pintado* duly notified *Caiman* and *Pampanito* of her discovery. To Lieutenant Commander Mendenhall on *Pintado,* the South China Sea "was becoming like Grand Central Station, what with so many U.S. submarines hanging around and no Jap ships to sink."

Although Summers broke off the chase, he was still suspicious. He was driven down by planes prior to *Pintado*'s message, and he wondered, if the target was a hospital ship, why were there aircraft in such proximity. He asked Clarey if *Pintado* planned to observe the ship after dark to see if it would be illuminated with its proper running lights. Negative, Clarey answered. Shortly thereafter, *Sealion* chimed in with its contact report about spotting a hospital ship, and Summers finally ordered the pack to end the chase.

This time the hospital ship was not *Awa Maru,* for she had continued south to Jakarta, Java, and would not leave Singapore on the return leg to

Japan until 28 March. *Awa Maru* had dodged a few more bullets, but her charmed life was almost over. Due at Tsuruga, Honshu, on 5 April, she got as far as the Formosa Straits on 1 April when she was spotted by *Queenfish*. *Queenfish*'s commander, Elliot Loughlin, had received an encoded message about a hospital ship, but the message gave no details about course, speed, or routing. The communications officer had not bothered to show Loughlin the many plain-language messages received beforehand. *Queenfish* made radar contact at seventeen thousand yards on a dark, foggy night. The target was traveling at seventeen knots and seemed to have too small a pip for a large liner. Loughlin closed to twelve hundred yards and fired four stern torpedoes, and four explosions flashed through the fog. *Awa Maru* went down in two hundred feet of water about ten miles off the China coast, killing over two thousand people, more than died on the *Titanic* or the *Lusitania.*

The target disappeared from radar, and Loughlin headed in. He picked up one survivor and only then learned what he had done. Loughlin reported his error to Lockwood and was immediately ordered back to ComSubPac at Guam. Before leaving, Loughlin searched the area for evidence of what type of cargo the ship had been carrying. He managed to pick up some crude rubber and tins of an unidentified black substance, hopefully to help in his defense that the ship was carrying contraband.

Regardless, Loughlin faced a court-martial. U.S. submarines could not go around sinking ships that the government had guaranteed safe conduct to, no matter what they were carrying. In fact, ULTRA already knew that on the outward passage, *Awa Maru* carried five hundred tons of ammunition, two 155-mm cannons, about two thousand bombs, and twenty crated planes. On the return she carried a cargo of rubber, lead, tin, tungsten, and sugar and nearly two thousand passengers. Admiral Lockwood had even requested to be allowed to sink *Awa Maru* because of this breach of agreement. Nimitz had refused. Of course the U.S. could not deny safe passage to the *maru* because it was carrying war material without also giving away the secret that the Japanese codes had been cracked. Loughlin's defense would have to rest on what he could fish out of the sea. Nevertheless, the court ruled that he could not have known of the cargo before the sinking, and he received a letter of admonition from the secretary of the navy.[5] Even though he was a courageous skipper with a fine record,

Loughlin became an indirect sacrifice to maintaining the secret of ULTRA.

Since the patrol lines established by Summers had resulted in few sightings and no sinkings, he decided to rearrange the setup. He guessed that the Japanese had spotted them and were rerouting traffic close along the Malay coast and into the Gulf of Siam. Instead of an east-west scouting line extending out from Kota Bharu, the wolf pack reconfigured on a southeast-northwest line running into the gulf. *Pampanito* took position at the mouth, with *Sealion* and *Mingo* extending into the gulf at seventy-mile intervals. Summers sent the new instructions on 8 March; nevertheless, over the next three days they sighted no ships, and only a few plane contacts broke up the monotony.

Just after midnight on 11 March, *Pampanito*'s crew received a very pleasant surprise. They established VHF communications with *Sea Robin* (SS 407), which was having a fine second patrol under Paul C. Stimson. Early in March, Stimson had sunk three freighters and a converted gunboat near the Borneo coast. It was a great accomplishment for this stage of the war. No other sub would sink four ships on a patrol until "Hydeman's Hellcats" invaded the Sea of Japan in June.

Stimson informed Summers that he had a delivery to make. The boats pulled as close together as possible in seas that had become inopportunely rough. *Sea Robin*'s gift was dozens of mail sacks. It had been a long time since *Pampanito* had received any. When Fenno took the boat to Australia, mail that was being forwarded to Saipan had to be shifted to Fremantle. *Pampanito* missed it there, then missed it again when she went to Subic Bay. *Sea Robin*, leaving Fremantle, was finally given the mail and told to find *Pampanito*.

The transfer however, was not simple. Bob Bennett said, "Submariners were not all good boatswain's mates when it came to tying lines," and the bobbing subs and heavy waves meant that almost every bag got dunked. Summers said that they received thirty-four bags, but Pappas thought it was between forty and fifty. At one-half sack per trip, the transfer took over four hours to complete, and dawn was breaking when they finally finished. Nevertheless, the crew was truly grateful, and Summers thought it was certainly worth the trouble. "Christmas finally caught up with us," he recorded in the log. Gordon Hopper had similar thoughts, but the age of some of the packages and the dunking they had received did not enhance their condition. "It was Christmas in March in the Gulf of Siam," he said, "albeit a pretty mouldy one."

Paul Pappas happily recorded in his diary: "Got quite a few packages from home and they were a sight for sore eyes. Fruit cakes lasted around two days. Darn good." Woody Weaver's sister Josephine had actually sent fried chicken; it had been mailed in October. Fortunately, she had had the foresight to seal it in cans, and it arrived in very good condition. Many sailors received the ubiquitous fruit cakes, but apparently they did not know just how long these stout items would stay fresh. Weaver learned that many cakes were trashed, and he sent some of the torpedomen to the crew's mess to salvage as much as they could. Said Woody: "We soon had a two-foot-high mound of fruit cake in the Forward Room which we enjoyed for the remainder of the patrol."

Of course the food was secondary to news from home. Maurice Demers had been married in January 1944, shortly before being sent to Midway. His wife had a baby boy on 25 October, the day *Pampanito* pulled out for her fourth patrol. Demers had received the news two days later over the nightly Fox sked, but had heard nothing since. Several subsequent letters from his wife finally caught up with him, and he read them in amazement. His baby was already eating beef, lamb, chicken, and vegetables. He proudly announced this to the crew, adding that, with such a diet, his boy was sure to grow into a big, strapping bruiser. Doc didn't realize until later that his wife was writing about pureed baby food.[6]

Sailors congregated around Ona Hawkins. If his girlfriend had been sending her usual one or two letters per week, Ona should have about thirty envelopes, each with a colorful drawing of a pretty girl. The men loved the drawings. Many of them kept their own favorite pin-ups folded in their wallet or taped on a bulkhead. Perhaps the undisputed leader in the wartime pin-up parade was Betty Grable. She exemplified the sex appeal of the all-American girl next door. The fact that women liked her, too, suggested that her appeal was less erotic than as a symbol of American womanhood. Her "hominess," plus her much-photographed "million dollar legs," made her the queen of the pin-ups, and twenty thousand requests were made each week for photos of her in her famous bathing suit pose.

Runner-up to Betty Grable in the wartime pin-up parade was Rita Hayworth, a sultry brunette who exuded the sex appeal of a mature woman. Other favorites were Dorothy Lamour, famous for her low-cut sarong; Carole Landis, known as "The Ping Girl"; Marlene Dietrich, an exotic femme fatale; Ann Sheridan, known as "The Oomph Girl," with her hard-boiled sex appeal; Esther Williams, Olympic swimmer; and Veronica Lake, "The Peekaboo Girl," who hid her wistful face behind her flowing hair.

The prize for the sexiest pin-up however, went to Jane Russell, whose thirty-eight-inch bust was shamelessly exploited by Howard Hughes in his movie *The Outlaw,* and a photo of Jane seductively sprawled in a haystack was released in the June 1942 *Esquire* magazine. Female "cheesecake" became a wartime staple for America's soldiers and sailors. Morality complaints were usually met with indignity. Said one sailor: "Don't slam our pin-ups. If I had a wife I would make sure her picture was up. . . . Maybe if some of those 'panty-waists' had to be stuck some place where there are no white women and few native women for a year and a half, as we were, they would appreciate even a picture of our gals back home."

Ona Hawkins was lucky to get his letters before the crew did, but he was a good sport. "I would get the letters to read," he said, "and the envelopes would make the rounds on the boat, and finally get back to me." Lacking the real thing, there was not much else to raise the morale of lonely sailors than pictures of pretty girls.[7]

The sudden appearance of the mail unfortunately did not portend the sudden appearance of shipping. Summers kept the pack pointed like an arrow into the Gulf of Siam until 12 March, when he rearranged the positions, with *Sealion* farthest northwest, *Pampanito* in the middle, and *Mingo* near the mouth. *Pintado*'s recent departure for Fremantle left *Caiman* as a lone wolf, and that boat, on her second patrol, under William L. Fey, Jr., was ordered to join up with Summers. On the night of 14 March, all four boats rendezvoused and were given new instructions. They would patrol south in two staggered lines extending eastward from the Malay coast between 5 degrees and 6 degrees north latitude. Summers ordered the two boats closest to the coast to patrol submerged during daylight hours.

The realignment brought no change in luck. *Pampanito* sighted a mine, but again failed to sink it. Sailors hauled aboard a red life raft, but found no identifying markings, so they threw it back. On 16 March, Summers called for a surprise emergency dive to test and train the new chief of the boat, William Aiken, who, like McGuire, was also nicknamed "Red" because of his bright pate. The dive was satisfactory, yet crewmen still grumbled about Aiken's elevation to chief. He did not have the easygoing personality of Smitty, the previous chief.

Pappas, who had had enough trouble with Thompson, put them both in a class with a few officers he didn't care for. In order for them to qualify, said Paul, "They ran the sub in circles, went to Maneuvering and killed the engines, leaving us dead in the water, then they blew the heads all over the bulkheads—but they all passed the tests." According to Pappas, it was best to avoid all the chiefs and officers: "They were like the police, and they would get you in trouble for nothing."

Red Aiken, like Punchy Thompson, also had the annoying habit of running to an officer, usually Lieutenant Commander Orser, whenever things did not go as planned. Said Moffett: "Aiken and Orser hit it off well and had two things in common—red hair and being generally disliked by most of the crew." Aiken had a propensity for cleanliness, certainly not a bad trait, but the crew considered that his continued calling for field days was excessive. Trouble began when Aiken decided he wanted all the men in the after battery, even those not on watch, to be out of their bunks to clean the compartment.

Moffett had recently changed bunks to a new location near Demers's medicine locker, but it was under the aft battery blower. The exhaust contained small amounts of sulfuric acid, which could condense and drip down. Said Moffett: "I had mattress covers and T-shirts that looked quite moth-eaten for a couple of years after this." There were simply no first-class beds on a submarine. Moffett's new bunk also had a light bulb hanging close to his face, but this was no real problem. As did almost every other man who wished to get some shut-eye, Molly simply reached up and unscrewed the bulb.

Unscrewed bulbs, however, did not facilitate matters when Aiken called for a field day. He would barge in, announce that everyone must get out of his bunk, and proceed to screw in the bulbs. When he moved on to the next compartment, the men would simply unscrew the bulbs and go back to sleep. Of course, after a few rounds of this, Aiken would run to Orser, and the men would finally, grudgingly, comply.

Having successfully survived Aiken's first test dive, the crew relapsed into its daily routine. On 18 March a spark of excitement was provided when the SJ picked up a fast-moving contact at thirteen thousand yards. The target was zigzagging wildly but still managing to make twenty-two knots. On the enemy's quarter and without much hope of overhauling him, *Pampanito* sent a contact report and continued her high-speed chase. Within an hour the target had moved north, beyond seventeen thousand yards' range, and disappeared. None of the boats could catch it. Late that evening, Summers again changed the pack's disposition, this time shifting east into the South China Sea. The only good news came from *Sealion II;* the day before, she had sunk an unescorted Siamese Navy oiler, the 1,458-ton *Samui,* off the Malay coast near Pulau Tenggol. It was the wolf pack's only success.

On 19 March, Summers again passed on new area assignments in a futile attempt to find enemy shipping. Late that evening *Pampanito* rendezvoused with *Mingo* and *Sealion,* but no one had any news. The next day, *Pampanito* lost the use of all her gyro repeaters because of an overheated motor and had to dive for six hours to make repairs. On 21 March, Summers maneuvered close to talk with Putman on *Sealion* about further patrol options. He sent messages instructing *Caiman* and *Mingo* to head further into the Gulf of Siam, while *Pampanito* and *Sealion* stalked the waters close to the Malay coast. *Pampanito*'s gyro repeaters conked out again, and soon after, the crew sighted wreckage in the water: remnants of a wing and landing gear from a Japanese plane. At 1818, lookouts sighted a large explosion in the water ahead of *Sealion,* and Summers headed in at full speed to investigate. He approached with some apprehension, when Putman sent a message that his gun crew had merely exploded a mine. Summers resumed course "with a little more peace of mind" but probably could not help but wonder why his crew had not yet succeeded in detonating a mine.

The long, fruitless patrol was wearing on everyone's nerves. Summers ordered *Sealion II* and *Mingo* to conduct a submerged patrol off Pulau Redang, while *Pampanito* teamed up with *Caiman.* That night, Summers sent his third message to ComTaskFor 71, with little positive news to pass on. The following night, after receiving instructions, Summers met up with *Caiman.* While the two subs bobbed in the waves as close together as possible, *Pampanito*'s PCO, William Bush, was rowed across in a rubber raft to finish the patrol aboard Bill Fey's boat. On 25 March, Summers turned the command of the pack over to *Caiman* and headed north. *Pampanito*'s assignment to the Southwest Pacific was over.[8]

Although the patrol was winding down, it was a long way to Pearl Harbor. The men had mixed emotions; some were sad that they wouldn't be returning to Australia, and others were disappointed that they had sunk no ships, but most were simply tired after another long, fruitless patrol and were glad to head to any port. The food supplies were low again, for improper refrigeration had resulted in the tossing of 354 pounds of spoiled meat overboard.

Late on 25 March, *Pampanito* exchanged recognition signals with USS *Boarfish* (SS 327). It was true that by this stage of the war U.S. submarines were spotting more friendly subs than enemy ships. Still, the days were not without highlights. Halfway through the patrol, Ed Stockslader came down with a high fever and chills, but Demers had trouble diagnosing his illness. It looked like malaria, but Doc couldn't believe it. He didn't think the short time they had spent on the beach at Subic Bay would have exposed Stockslader to infected mosquitoes. "He was only on shore for about an hour," Demers declared. Ed didn't want to tell Demers that he had missed the launch and had spent the night on the beach. He was afraid Summers would find out. Stockslader suffered in silence for days before seeking treatment. It was only after the war when the two met again at the Brooklyn Naval Hospital that Demers learned the whole story.

Demers was kept busy. One man developed a toothache, and Demers searched his locker in vain for a pair of pliers. Apparently the navy didn't expect pharmacist's mates to extract teeth. Demers improvised. He drilled the sailor's filling out with a 35,000-rpm hand-held power carving tool. He successfully removed the old filling and repacked the tooth with a softer filling, which relieved the man's pain until he could get to Pearl and visit a dentist.

Another potentially serious situation occurred when Torpedoman's Mate Third Class George Strother, wearing the usual sandals, dropped a hatch cover on his toe. "He almost cut it off," said Demers. When Demers got to him, Strother was holding the toe on with one hand. Demers pressed it back and bandaged it tightly. In a couple of days the toe was discolored, and both men were concerned about gangrene. Yet Demers persevered. He cleaned and bandaged it a few times a day. Then he tried one of his "magic bullets"—penicillin. Demers had finally received a supply of the new drug, but only two doses, and Strother was his first test case. Whether it was the drug or the care or a combination of both, in about ten days the toe was almost healed. Strother got to a doctor at Pearl Harbor. There he found that the nerves were severed and that the toe might wriggle uncontrollably at times, but otherwise it was in as good shape as could be expected.

The men unwound as the boat left the Japanese shipping routes, and they fell into a relaxed banter, talking and joking even while on duty. One evening in the conning tower, Moffett was engaged in a three-way conversation with the helmsman and the quartermaster, Johnny Greene. Lieutenant Commander Orser, however, was not in a jovial mood, and he ordered the three men to shut up. There would be no talking in the conning tower while on duty. Molly Moffett bided his time until he had an SJ contact at six thousand yards. Then, following orders, he calmly wrote out a note about the contact and had it passed to the bridge. Of course he knew the idiosyncrasies of his radar screen and could tell the difference between a plane and a flight of birds. These were birds. He was in the process of writing out a second note to those on the bridge to inform them of the fact, when "unfortunately, the OOD sounded the diving alarm and we were on the way to periscope depth before I could pass the second note." Moffett thought it was pretty funny; regrettably, the skipper didn't think so. "Captain Summers failed to see my point when I had to explain to him what happened," he said. "He told me that he had been considering recommending me for a commission, but perhaps he should be thinking of a court-martial instead." No more notes were passed, but talking resumed in the conning tower.

The next day, *Pampanito* crossed the border into ComSubPac's operational zone, and on 28 March she received orders to stop at Saipan for fuel. South of Formosa the next day, the IFF went on the blink, making plane identification difficult. The SD made one contact at ten miles. Two hours later, it picked up a flight at eight miles, seemingly friendly and heading toward Formosa. Charlie McGuire was topside. The way he figured, *Pampanito* was leaving the war zone, and if the sub was really heading back to the States for an overhaul, this might be the last chance Charlie would get to spot a Japanese plane.

"I had been up on lookout a thousand times," he said, "but I had never spotted a plane. They'd always come in another sector. If I was port, they'd come from starboard, and if I was starboard, they'd come from port." At 1147, a close contact at four miles sent the boat heading down with the alarm blaring. Not this time, Charlie thought. He was going to spot the plane. He delayed about ten seconds, fruitlessly scanning the horizon. "What I saw instead," he said, "was the hatch closing!"

McGuire ran for the hatch, yelling his loudest. As he dove headfirst for the opening, the OOD heard his cry and popped the lid back up. Charlie's face and the hatch cover reached the same point at the same time. Wham! Out went his front tooth. He clambered down the ladder, cupping his mouth with one hand. Those in the conning tower thought it was the funniest thing they had ever seen.

"Here I am bleeding like a stuck pig," Charlie said, "and all the guys are laughing at me! The 'Old Man' made some kind of a joke. 'Yeah, yeah,' I said. 'Real funny. Twenty-four years old and I got no front teeth!'" Charlie glumly finished off his watch while Doc packed his bleeding gums.

*Pampanito* left Formosa behind, coursing through the narrow channel between Itbayat and Batan Islands that evening. It was a cloudy night, with Force 4 winds from the northeast. The China Sea was giving *Pampanito* its farewell blow. She would never again cut its glassy surface or beat her bow into the monsoon. The only sea where every one of her triumphs had taken place was rapidly falling astern. *Pampanito* entered the deep Philippine Sea, nose pointed toward Saipan.

Through the final days of March, *Pampanito* headed east, still buffeted by storms, heavy seas, and high winds. On the last day of the month she passed *Snook*, headed on an opposite course. A Portsmouth boat commissioned in October 1942, *Snook* had a fine record, having sunk seventeen ships by the time of this, her ninth patrol. Summers exchanged signals with Commander John F. Walling, who was heading *Snook* to the waters east of Formosa. *Snook*, in company with USS *Tigrone* (SS 419), was assigned to lifeguard duties covering a British carrier strike. A Royal Navy Grumman Avenger was forced down in Walling's area on 20 April. Messages were sent requesting *Snook* to proceed to the crash site, but no response was ever received. No Japanese attacks were recorded in the vicinity. The submarine that had made the first lifeguard mission also ended its career on a lifeguard mission. The waters quietly closed over *Snook*, and she was never heard from again.[9]

The incident, and many similar episodes, would cause George Moffett to wax philosophical:

> The populace has little or no concept of the major foe of all sailors: the power of the ocean. The ocean is relentless, without compassion or remorse; it does not forgive mistakes and it takes no prisoners. This is a fact of life for every vessel that sails upon it and is especially true for submarines. War simply increases the hazards that a submarine and her crew face on a daily basis. We lost submarines prior to the war, and I suspect during the war, not from enemy action, but due to the power of the ocean and mistakes made by unknown crew members.

Whether due to enemy action, human error, or the power of the seas, *Snook* was gone. Even though Japan's defeat now appeared certain, vigilance could never be relaxed aboard a submarine. Unaware of *Snook*'s impending doom, the men aboard *Pampanito* turned to more pleasant thoughts. Paul Pappas concisely recorded in his diary: "Are heading home. No luck this trip. If everything goes well, hope to be home soon." The boat pounded through the vast empty stretches of the Philippine Sea while the bad weather remained. On 1 April the winds shifted around to the east, and the skies remained completely overcast. *Pampanito* contacted two ships at twenty-one thousand yards, and although the APR showed them to be friendly, Summers swung wide and clear. Over the next four days the winds shifted out of the southeast, but the heavy seas and gray skies remained.

Below decks, the crew engaged in its usual activities to fight monotony. The ongoing card games were in evidence: poker, acey-deucey, cribbage, and gin. In the wardroom, almost all of Lieutenant Sherlock's and Lieutenant Bartholomew's off-duty hours were spent in a marathon gin rummy game. Even though the stakes were not high, only a tenth of a cent per point, the hours spent flipping cards eventually resulted in a considerable amount of money.

Summers had made a firm rule against gambling among the officers, so the two lieutenants had to keep score on the sly. Sherlock was losing badly, being down about $650, and Summers was becoming suspicious. Bartholomew, of course, wanted to end the game while he was ahead, but Sherlock wanted to recoup his losses. When they all sat down to dinner one day, "Black Bart" began complaining that he owed Sherlock $1,400. "The Captain," said Sherlock, "immediately ordered us to stop gambling and I was ordered to forgive the debt."

No way would Bart get away with that, Sherlock vowed. He cajoled him into continuing the game, but Sherlock only succeeded in going down to $750 in the hole. Bartholomew had him in a corner, and the next day he moaned to Pete that he owed Sherlock $2,000. That was that. Summers threatened Sherlock with a court-martial if he continued gambling and ordered an immediate end to the game and the debt. Bartholomew chuckled at his stratagem, but Sherlock refused to pay the $750. They did not settle accounts until after the war was over.

On the morning of 5 April, under warmer weather and clearing skies, *Pampanito* pulled into Saipan. A quick restocking of food supplies and fuel left little time for play. Mail was available, and good news was received by Doc Demers. He had been promoted to warrant officer back in January. He was ecstatic, as he believed that going from enlisted man to warrant officer in three and one-half years was pretty darn good. His mates were happy for him, too, and they showed their usual appreciation of good fortune by grabbing him and throwing him overboard. They tossed him into the water next to *Fulton*, said Demers, "right in the middle of the crap from the freshly blown sanitary tanks."

*Pampanito* had a one-day layover, and on 6 April she was off for Pearl Harbor. Most of the Pacific had been swept clean, and from 7 to 11 April no entries were logged in the record. The great majority of Japanese naval and merchant shipping had been reduced to sneaking from harbor to harbor along the Asian coast. Any activities in the greater Pacific Ocean area were confined to submarine supply runs to starving, by-passed island garrisons.

ULTRA had discovered one of these operations, and *Pampanito* was diverted from her trip home and ordered to join another wolf pack. "Bennett's Blazers," under Commander Carter L. Bennett in *Sea Owl* (SS

405), with *Piranha* (SS 389) and *Puffer*, were waiting off Wake Island in the hopes of catching a Japanese supply submarine. The "Blazers" had just finished a fruitless patrol in Convoy College and had pulled out of Saipan three days before *Pampanito*.[10]

The "Blazers" were headed for refit at Midway when Bennett got the ULTRA message to detour to Wake. All Bennett had seen around the island was a sampan-type patrol craft. On 11 April, *Pampanito* joined the crowd, then *Thresher*, and five American subs skulked around Wake Island, hoping to score one kill. Truly, there were slim pickings of Japanese ships.

On 13 April, a Friday, while lying in wait, the sailors were shocked to learn of the death of their President. Just after dawn a message was relayed to the fleet that the commander-in-chief had died of a cerebral hemorrhage at his vacation home in Warm Springs, Georgia. "President Roosevelt is dead," blared the loudspeakers on almost two thousand navy ships, from the smallest LCI to the biggest battleship. On *Pampanito* the word was passed while the men lapsed into an unfamiliar silence, and knots tightened in many a man's stomach. Roosevelt had been first elected in 1932. "It was sobering news," said Woody Weaver. "Most of the young sailors aboard had never known of another President in the White House." They were deeply moved by the loss of a leader who had come to personify the cause they had been fighting for.

The news made the men more than willing to take out their hurt on the enemy. The radiomen manned their sets assiduously, listening for news that would give them a clue as to what course of action to take. One evening, Roger Walters was relieved by Radioman Third Class Leonard Wanerman. At designated hours, all the subs were to change their wolf pack radio frequencies in an ongoing attempt to confuse any listening Japanese and to keep abreast of current orders. Wanerman forgot to change the frequency, and for two hours *Pampanito*'s radio crackled with nothing but static. The mistake was discovered.

"Pete was absolutely furious," said Walters. "He brought the entire radio crew to the wardroom and chewed us out for an hour. I mean, heads would fall if something happened and we were not there to take advantage of it."

Something did happen, and *Pampanito* was not involved. On 16 April, about six miles northwest of Wake, *Sea Owl* was tracking what she thought was a patrol craft when it suddenly dived. Bennett called the pack with the information that a sub was in the vicinity and positioned the boats around the island to block all possible retirement routes. On the next day, the elusive Japanese boat was seen rounding Peacock Point on Wake's south-east shore, heading for the anchorage. Finally, before dawn of 18 April, *Sea Owl* approached to within five hundred yards of the boat landing. Bennett let go three fish in an underwater periscope attack, claiming one solid hit in the stern of a large Japanese I-class submarine. Scuttlebutt aboard *Pampanito* had it that a Japanese cargo sub had gotten by four of the American boats, but that *Sea Owl*, a newer and quieter boat, was able to sneak right into Wake's lagoon and torpedo the Japanese boat while it was being unloaded. With that news the wolf pack broke up, and *Pampanito* was once more free to head east for Pearl Harbor.[11]

During the days they played hide and seek at Wake Island, Paul Pappas, Wally Cordon, and Walt Madison remembered a strange event. They were all in the maneuvering room early one morning. The boat was on the surface, so although the diesels were running in the forward engine room, it was relatively quiet in their compartment. Suddenly the calm was interrupted by a loud clang. All three men were startled.

"We heard something whack into the side of the hull," said Pappas. "We thought it was a torpedo."

"Goddamn, something hit us," exclaimed Walt Madison, "and I about fell off my stool."

They hurried forward and met Mike Carmody in the after engine room. Yes, he had heard it too. Carmody remembered it was early in the morning when he suddenly got the start-up bell. "I got numbers three and four engines on line in about seven seconds," he said. "And about two seconds later I felt a heavy thud that echoed throughout the ship." Most of those who had heard and felt the impact were in the after compartments. In the after torpedo room, Peder Granum heard the whack into the side of the boat and guessed it must have been a torpedo. It hit hard enough that he thought the ballast tanks might have been dented.

Topside, at least one sailor saw what had happened. Signalman Second Class Herman Bixler was on the bridge scanning his sector when out of nowhere he saw a torpedo rushing in from only yards away. Before he could open his mouth, the torpedo, coming in at a small angle, glanced off the hull near the stern. Bixler readied himself to go flying sky high, but nothing happened. The torpedo porpoised up for a second and then sank in the submarine's wash. He finally called to the OOD and the other lookouts, frantically waving at the spot, trying to verbalize what he had seen. The rudder was thrown hard over, and the course change was felt by Carmody in the engine room, but Bixler's story was viewed with skepticism. Only later, when Bixler talked with the men below decks, did they confirm that their hearing and his sight were not playing tricks on them.

The incident never entered the patrol log. Were they hit by a dud, or by a glancing blow that did not have enough force to detonate? Was it a wakeless Japanese oxygen torpedo fired by the boat that *Sea Owl* later destroyed? *Pampanito* had nearly been hit by a U-boat torpedo in the Caribbean. She had been narrowly missed by three torpedoes in two incidents off the coast of Japan. Now she had been struck by a dud. Perhaps they were all living on borrowed time.

From 19 to 23 April the days blended into one seamless blur. Routine might be dull for landlubbers, but for sailors it was a blessing. The boat became a home. Lieutenant William Ruhe, on the *S-37*, said that most sailors felt snug and secure while aboard a submarine, almost "like a child in a mother's womb that is safely protected from the outside world." The men felt a sense of well-being while on submerged patrol and more comfortable and free of concerns than while on a surface ship. To many civilians it was a mystery how a man could like being on a submarine, but liking it, feeling comfortable, and having the camaraderie of shipmates was taken for granted by almost every submariner.[12]

The ride back to Pearl was a time of endless days fusing into one another. Few incidents stood out, but the few were memorable. Looking forward to cutting loose in Hawaii, the men began their gilly-cooking ritual. The torpedomen had constructed a still in the after head, figuring no officer would bother inspecting that commode. Unfortunately, they plugged the hot plate into the circuit for the radio and record player and blew the fuse. Moffett had to track down the problem and put them on a different circuit.

The cooks tried their hand. They made some "raisin jack" with water, raisins, sugar, and yeast. Said Gordon Hopper: "They fermented it in the warmth under the radio equipment, next door to the galley. It was foul stuff."

The motor macs also built their usual contraption in the engine room. But this time the still overheated or was knocked over. The heat ignited the oil-soaked decks and bulkheads, and pretty soon a small fire was crackling in the engine room bilges. Even a small fire on a ship has the potential for disaster. The motor macs scrambled to seal off the compartment and douse the flames. That night they cleaned and repainted the entire area. The next day Lieutenant Fives inspected the compartment. He was pleasantly surprised at its spotless condition and lauded the initiative the men had shown in sprucing up their area. Fives, however, familiar with the mischief the men usually got into, privately remained skeptical. "But," said Moffett, "he never did know why they did this."

As *Pampanito* neared Pearl Harbor, the quiet days enabled the men to ruminate about their fate. They received word that they would be sent to the West Coast for a navy yard overhaul. Woody Weaver was elated at the prospect of being in the States. "I do not know of anyone in the navy who enjoyed fighting the war," he said, "but those who drew the duty of serving on the ships faced up to the job and did the best they could."

Sub sailors had the opportunity to serve for a couple of patrols and then transfer back to the States to put a new submarine into commission. Said Weaver: "I was no Gung Ho hero and would like to have played that game myself, but the CO would not approve my transfer. Maybe that was a compliment to me." Weaver did know that in the long run his staying on board for all six patrols worked out for the best.

Before the war, advancement was determined by examinations and limited by a quota. That all changed, however, when the war began and commanding officers could advance men without an exam. The chief petty officers (CPOs) advanced under this system were called "Tojo chiefs" by the lowly "white hat" sailors, their thinking being that many chiefs would not have made it without the extraordinary wartime conditions.

Regardless of whether he would be labeled a "Tojo chief," Weaver was thrilled when informed by Lieutenant Swain that he would be rated a CPO as soon as they arrived in San Francisco. He would be a chief after only four years and eight months of service. Before the war it was not uncommon to wait sixteen years before making chief. "I had the war and six straight war patrols to thank," said Woody, "as well as old Tojo, I suppose."

*Pampanito* arrived at Pearl Harbor at 1100, 24 April 1945, almost six months since she had pulled out for her fourth patrol under Captain Fenno. The men were ready to cut loose, but orders were to proceed to Hunter's Point, San Francisco, for a complete overhaul. This was terrific news, for the majority of the crew had not been in the States since the boat left New London over fifteen months before. In Pearl, they would only have time for a few quick errands.

Weaver made preparations for his advancement. He went into Honolulu and purchased a brand new chief's garrison cap at the naval tailor shop. He admired it and smiled. "I put the hat in my locker and looked at it every day. I could not put it on until we got to San Francisco," he said, "but I was enjoying the anticipation."

Charlie McGuire visited a dentist to have his lost tooth replaced. He was told that the procedure back in the States would have cost a civilian about a thousand dollars. "However," said Charlie, "it didn't cost me anything. I couldn't eat caramels and such, but oh well, at least it was something the Navy did for me."

Once more Paul Pappas concisely recorded in his diary: "Pulled into Pearl Harbor. Took on fuel. Stocked up on cigarets. Tomorrow we are leaving for good old U.S.A."

It was a week's run to San Francisco. The men were restive, and the days couldn't pass quickly enough. The officers worked out the upcoming leave procedures. Their plan was to have all the married officers and men who didn't live in California take first leave so they could get their families and bring them back. All married men who lived in California, plus all the bachelors, would have second leave. This seemed fair enough, and it divided up the crew about fifty-fifty. Lieutenant Commander Orser turned the plan over to Summers for approval, but, said Lieutenant Swain, "Pete tore it up." It was typical of Summers's cussedness. Whatever you might propose, Swain said, "you could be sure that Summers would do just the opposite." And so it was.

Swain was in a foul mood. He had been married in 1942 and was looking forward to seeing his wife. Now he would have to wait an extra month. He was glad the patrol was almost over. Even the food was getting on his nerves. It seemed the cooks had no imagination. Although Dan Hayes and Bill Morrow were both experienced, Swain was not satisfied

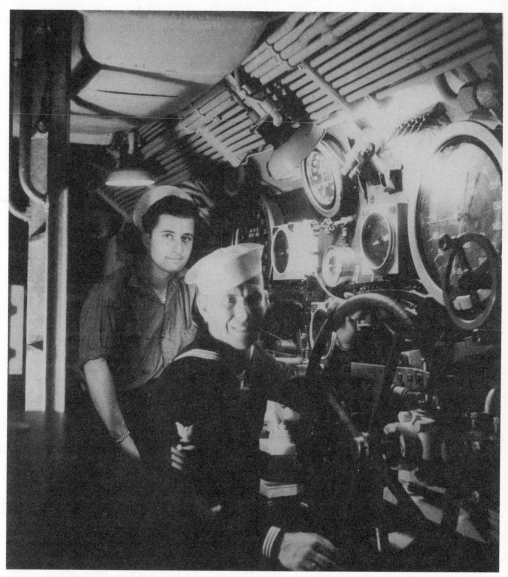
Paul Pappas and Bob Bennett in the Control Room. (Photo courtesy of Robert Bennett.)

with the cuisine, and he took over. He was once a mess trainer, and he believed the meals could be made more appetizing. "I wanted it right, and I'd tell them," Swain said. The first thing he chided them about was serving mashed potatoes every day. He found a cookbook and pointed out new recipes. "Here!" he said. "There are over 60 ways to make potatoes. Try one of them." The cooks were not pleased with Swain's bossing, and mashed potatoes were served again and again.

Hoping to impress the brass upon docking, Orser and Chief Aiken decided it would be a good idea to have field days to make the boat spic and span. They insisted that all lights be turned on in the crew's quarters and everyone be out of his bunk by 0800. Even the off-duty personnel were to assist in cleaning and repainting the boat. Of course, the men had different thoughts.

"Most of the crew considered this to be ridiculous," said Moffett, "since the boat would be cleaned and repainted after refit and overhaul by yard personnel." Bob Bennett remembered that the first thing they did was to unscrew all the bulbs so they would not come on when the switch was thrown. They were ordered to screw them back in.

Next, they hid all the light bulbs, but Aiken had them replaced. The following morning, Moffett got into the act and removed the circuit fuse so the lights couldn't come on at all. When that was remedied, he placed a thermal disc flasher in each socket, so when the lights were turned on they would start flashing on and off like a blinking Christmas tree. Late one night Moffett loosened all the bulbs in their sockets. On the one hanging closest to the main switch he wrapped tinfoil on each side, but added insulation to prevent the foil from touching. Pappas agreed to turn up the juice.

The next morning Chief Aiken entered the compartment to roust everyone out of his bunk and, Moffett said, "I suspect that more than one of the crew was awake, because by now the word had been passed around and they wanted to see what was next." Aiken flipped the switch and nothing happened. He was getting very pissed off at these games. "He then reached up," said Moffett, "and turned the doctored bulb in its socket, and received a 100 volt DC thrill."

While the men lay in their bunks, doubled up from laughing, Aiken stormed off again to complain to Orser. Someone in the crew was trying to electrocute him, he moaned. Orser confiscated the doctored light bulb for evidence. They had everything they needed for a captain's mast, Moffett conceded, but "they just did not have the culprit—their problem."

At any rate, Molly mused, it was no big deal. It did make for conversation and relieved some of the tension, besides giving the crew something to look forward to each morning.

Finally, at 0700 on 3 May, *Pampanito* passed under the Golden Gate Bridge and tied up at Hunter's Point Naval Drydock. The first men off the boat ran to the nearest phone booths. Paul Pappas jotted down the last script in his diary: "Called up home and it was sure good hearing Mom's voice again. The old *Pamp* is going into dry dock for overhaul and I'm heading home."

The first rush of sailors headed for the bus stations, train depots, and airports only to find long lines and longer waits. The war was winding down, and many servicemen were looking for transportation home. Gordon Hopper was lucky enough to catch a flight to Saint Louis. En route, he heard the news of Germany's surrender and knew it would hasten the end of the war with Japan. From Saint Louis, Hopper took a taxi to the Union Station, arriving just in time to dash aboard a train bound for his home town of Clinton, Illinois. Unfortunately, Hopper had no ticket. When the conductor reached him and Gordon came up empty-handed, the conductor just sighed and shook his head. "Obviously," Hopper said, "I wasn't the first homesick sailor to jump on his train without buying a ticket in advance."

Back home, Hopper visited his family, his friends, and, of course, his girlfriend, Dorothy McKee. Gordon was having a great time, and the thirty-day leave flew by. Yet there was something wrong, something hard to pinpoint. The town looked the same, but everything felt a little different. Most of the men Gordon had gone to high school and college with were gone—married, moved away, or off to war. Perhaps it was not the town, but he who had changed. "I felt a vague uneasiness," Gordon said, "away from the boat, the crew, and submarine life."

While half the crew went on leave, those remaining continued the endless job of repairing and refitting the boat. The supplies were removed, and Woody Weaver was in charge of unloading twenty-four unused torpedoes, proudly wearing his new chief's hat. As he worked on deck, a stiff breeze blew his hat off his head and into the dirty water.

9967-45-S8
VIEW FORWARD - SHOWI
HUNTERS POINT, CALIFORNIA

*Pampanito* undergoing alterations (in areas shown), Hunter's Point, July 1945. (U.S. Navy photo)

"I was devastated," he said. "I looked pretty silly trying to fish my hat out. It was embarrassing, but I survived. My shipmates had a good laugh at my expense." Woody was able to snag the soaked hat with a boat hook. Undaunted, the next day he went into San Francisco and bought his new uniform.

While Chief Aiken was given first leave, Weaver was appointed chief torpedoman and acting chief of the boat. He wanted to get home, but he realized that being the chief, even on a temporary basis, would give him valuable experience. While waiting his turn to visit his family, Woody met "a stunning redhead" named Eve who worked as a welder at the Kaiser shipyard in Richmond, California. Woody's brother, Horace, who was in the merchant marine, showed up, and the three of them spent many hours at the North Beach amusement park. At least two of them had a great time on the rides, but Woody couldn't help but feel a bit undignified taking part in such merriment while in the uniform of a chief petty officer.

As usual, Charlie McGuire got into trouble. He and Merv Hill were in a bar talking with two women. Apparently they were also friends of two coast guardsmen, and when the guardsmen entered, they wanted "their girls" back.

"Bug off," McGuire told the guardsmen, then he started to get up. Merv Hill, trying to restrain McGuire, got up faster. As he reached across the table, one of the guardsmen thought Hill was standing up to throw a punch, and he swung at Hill instead. As he punched Hill, Charlie got in a shot to the guardsman's jaw. Only two punches were thrown before the SPs broke it up. On their way back to the boat, Hill vowed to punch McGuire himself when his own jaw healed.

*Pampanito* would soon head back to Hawaii. She received a five-inch gun in place of the four-incher and a load of new acoustic torpedoes, which Bob Bennett called "tickle pickles." They were sound activated, and Bennett thought their sensitivity was amazing. In a test, the gyro and rudders would turn, energized by only the slight hum of an automobile driving down the street.

While high and dry in the dock, workmen and submariners inspected the outer hull. To everyone's surprise, except to those sailors who had experienced the incident, there was indeed a significant dent in the ballast tanks outboard of the maneuvering room. Something had crashed into

*Pampanito*, Summer 1945, with her new five-inch gun aft. (U.S. Navy photo)

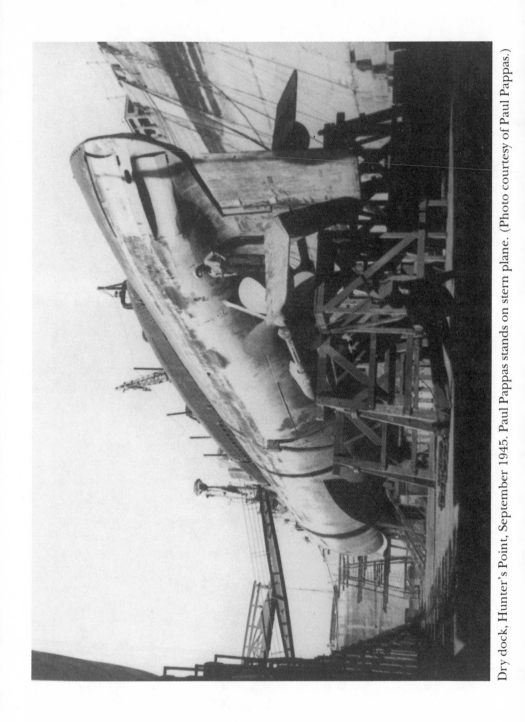

Dry dock, Hunter's Point, September 1945. Paul Pappas stands on stern plane. (Photo courtesy of Paul Pappas.)

the boat, and it was not a myopic dolphin mistaking *Pampanito* for its mother.

Transfers whittled down the remaining plank owners to a handful. Twelve more sailors were detached, including Charlie McGuire, Clarence Smith, and Merv Hill. Ed Stockslader, with his persistent malarial fever, went to a U.S. Naval Hospital in New York.

Mike Carmody, now a motor mac first class, went to advanced training with Relief Crew 3—an assignment that included an unspecified disciplinary action. Mike, however, didn't remember it that way.

"I wasn't kicked off the boat," he said. "I had already made ten war patrols and was given a Commendation before going to New York in June 1945, to get married." When he returned to California, he was assigned to *Hoe.*

Roger Walters was given the choice of going either to school-boat duty as an instructor or to new construction. He figured with new construction he might be sent back out to the war zone again, so he chose school-boat duty. In New London, Walters called his girlfriend Trudie, and they arranged to get married. The ceremony was set for August.

The time came for even Paul Summers to say good-bye. He was being assigned as CO of the new submarine USS *Cusk* (SS 348), built at the Electric Boat Company in New London and launched in July 1945. Ted Swain hoped to avoid a prolonged farewell. There had always been hard feelings between the two, and Swain did not feel like extending a warm handshake and a good luck wish. While Pete hoisted up his sea bags to make his exit, Swain ducked inside under the pretext of inspecting the ballast tanks. Summers, however, hunted Swain down. He went below and found him. For an awkward moment, nothing was said. The two adversaries simply looked at each other. Pete finally held out his hand and Ted grasped it. It was a submariner's bond that past animosity could not supplant.

"He actually came to find me to say good-bye," Swain said. "It was surprising and kind of complimentary." Then he added, "His thought processes were never easy to understand."[13]

*Pampanito* was in San Francisco for over two months, and it was time to hit the war trail again. On 20 July her new skipper conned her beneath the Golden Gate and out into the Pacific. Commander Donald A. Scherer had served on USS *Pike* (SS 173) and *Lapon.* He had first commanded the

*Pampanito*'s Battle Flag with the "73" indicating the number of POWs she rescued. Celebrating in San Francisco at war's end. (Photo courtesy of Robert Bennett.)

old USS *Permit* (SS 178) on that boat's twelfth patrol, acting as a lifeguard off Truk while *Pampanito* was on her first patrol lifeguarding off Yap. Scherer claimed sinking a twenty-two-hundred-ton submarine, but postwar assessments discredited the claim.

Scherer took *Permit* out again for her thirteenth patrol. This time he claimed sinking an eight-hundred-ton vessel but was again denied. In September 1944, Brisbane's hospitality warmed the hearts of *Permit*'s crew, but it brought no change in fortune. On the fourteenth patrol they only managed to sink a small fishing boat. Old *Permit* was retired from combat duty, and Don Scherer looked for a new command.

It had taken time, but now he was heading to Pearl with a veteran boat and crew. Perhaps Scherer could win them a few more laurels. The men were certain they would be involved in a Japanese invasion, and after they pulled into the sub base, their speculation appeared correct. Said Woody Weaver: "One thing did not look good; we were being equipped with mine detecting devices. In addition, devices to deflect the cables of moored mines were attached to our bow and stern planes." Scuttlebutt was that they would be going to the Sea of Japan, where *Wahoo* had been lost. "I certainly did not look forward to the prospects of such operations," Weaver said.

Many submariners shared these concerns. Frank Michno, who had been "marooned" on Midway until January 1945, was now at Pearl Harbor, preparing his boat for the upcoming campaign. He had finally gotten off the island when *Grouper* came in and had a spot for a motor mac. That boat's twelfth patrol in the East China Sea and Yellow Sea was character- ized by the usual late-war lack of enemy ship contacts. *Grouper* spent time lifeguarding, dodging fishing vessels, and damaging a 50-ton sampan with gunfire—before discovering the occupants were Chinese. On 27 March, *Grouper*'s skipper, Commander Frederick H. Wahlig, had a chance for a big kill when he discovered the 9,347-ton liner, *Takasago Maru,* on a course between Shanghai and Nagasaki. However, the vessel was properly marked and lighted as a hospital ship, and Wahlig let it go by.

For Michno, there were two patrol highlights. On 5 March, in the middle of the Philippine Sea, the sleeve of the lower bushing support on the number one lubricating oil purifier snapped off. Michno was able to fashion a replacement on the lathe, and the purifier was back in operation. On 16 March, in the East China Sea about eighty miles south of Quelpart

Island, the fourth-stage piston of the number one high-pressure air compressor froze in the cylinder and was broken upon removal. Once again, Michno got on the lathe and shaped a new piston from a length of steel stock. After rethreadings and additional dowels were added, the air compressor was back in working order.

At Pearl Harbor, Michno was surprised to be mentioned in the patrol report as "a very expert lathe operator" who was invaluable to *Grouper*. Shortly thereafter, he was advanced to CPO. Frank was given the usual courtesy. His buddies swiped his new cap, urinated in it, set it back on his head, and tossed him overboard.

Now, as chief, Michno was concerned about the latest scuttlebutt. They were to be painted bright yellow, along with a dozen other boats, and would be sent to the Empire's shores to attract kamikazes. By drawing off the Japanese suicide pilots from the carriers and landing craft, they would facilitate the upcoming invasion of the Japanese homelands. Needless to say, there was much grumbling about this tactic, although it proved more fancy than fact.[14]

*Pampanito* received her new equipment and Commander Scherer was readying them for a training run when word reached them that a terrifying new kind of bomb had been dropped on Japan. Three days later a second bomb was dropped. The sailors knew little about it, but almost to a man they were glad the bombs were used. Ona Hawkins heard about the weapon and thought its power was being exaggerated. "It was unbelievable," he said, "but I was just tickled to death." Now maybe the war would end sooner.

"In my mind," said Weaver, "Truman did the right thing." He felt that without the bomb, an invasion of Japan was inevitable and would have cost thousands of American lives. "His decision had personal significance for me," Woody said, "as it kept us out of those mine fields for which our sub was being prepared."

Charlie McGuire left *Pampanito* in June and was on his way to Portsmouth to fit out USS *Spinax* (SS 489). He was in Philadelphia, visiting old friends, when news of the A-bomb was announced. Years later, in his usual succinct way, McGuire commented: "Anyone who finds fault with Hiroshima should have his head examined."

Throughout the Pacific, the sailors welcomed the news. Hubert Brown left Australia after the fourth patrol, went to the States for a time, but was back on Midway in August 1945. The atomic bomb was a surprise, but, he said, "I hope they sunk the whole damn island. I didn't care what they did to them." He and his buddies felt no pity for the Japanese. In fact, Brown said that they celebrated "by drinking up all the hot beer on the island."

Al Van Atta also left Australia and returned to San Francisco. After a thirty-day leave, he went back out to Midway, assigned to the tender *Proteus.* He was about to be sent to new construction when word came that a new, powerful bomb had been dropped on Japan. Somehow they all knew that this portended the end. "I was standing in the chow line on the tender when the A-bomb announcement was made," Van Atta said. "We knew it was a big thing, because they started to ship guys home right away. I was one of the first to go."

The reaction to the news of the atomic bomb was mild compared to the jubilation a week later. For many of the *Pampanito* crew, the evening of 14 August began as another routine night. Gordon Hopper remembered that the men were being seated at the outdoor sub base movie, waiting for the start of the show. "Suddenly," he said, "from the moored fleet, whistles screamed, flares burst in the night sky and we heard cheering that grew in volume. An announcement over the movie's P.A. system informed us of the Japanese surrender. It was a night of immense celebration and an immense relief."

Woody Weaver said the word of the surrender was quite a shock. Things started a bit slowly, but soon a full-fledged celebration began. "Ships sounded their whistles and sirens. Signal flares and Very star pyrotechnics filled the sky." Fireworks such as these had not been seen in the harbor and surrounding bases since 7 December 1941.

"Sailors at the barracks were raising Cain," said Weaver, "and the sub base commander drove up in his jeep to try and quell the noise. They picked him up and threw him in the swimming pool. He crawled out, got back in his jeep, and left them to their celebration." The noise and hoopla went on for hours, and, Weaver added, "It may have become quite serious if liquor had been available, but it was a rationed item in Pearl and not too much was available."

Paul Pappas realized the shortage would provide an opportunity to make a few dollars. When *Pampanito* was at Hunter's Point, he purchased twelve bottles of Four Roses. Much to his surprise, he met Tony Hauptman, who was at the navy yard on duty as the base mailman. Tony agreed to sneak aboard the bottles while making his regular deliveries. In Pearl Harbor the whiskey was gold. "On V-J Day," said Pappas, "guys from another crew bought nine bottles for 30 bucks apiece. I made 270 dollars!" Paul felt a little sheepish about accepting so much money, but, he said, "they really wanted to celebrate and I figured I could help them out." Paul gave two bottles to his brother, who was in the merchant marine and visited Paul in Hawaii. He gave the last bottle to Punchy Thompson "to keep him happy" and, he hoped, to keep him off Paul's back.

There was no trouble getting potent potables in the States after the news of Japan's surrender. Roger Walters was on a seven-day leave in New York City for his honeymoon. He and his new bride were in a downtown hotel eating a lobster dinner when the news was announced. "Pandemonium broke out," he said. Roger and Trudie ran out into Times Square. He found a liquor store and bought three bottles of Scotch. It was ecstasy. People were milling about, cheering, hugging, and kissing. Roger shared his largesse with everyone. This was too good, too wonderful to miss. He held his wife close and found it difficult to hold back a tear. He had made it.

There would be no last patrol to Japan. Commander Scherer did not get another chance to sink a ship, but none of the crew complained. They had had enough. Within three weeks *Pampanito* would reverse course and go back to San Francisco for decommissioning. The men had done their duty. Most of them had a hard time explaining why it was that they fought in the first place. Certainly they were patriotic, but they were not zealots. They were fighting for their country, true, but not for any idealistic reasons such as making the world safe for democracy. They fought for their families, girlfriends, wives, and buddies. As one man worded it, they fought "for the smell of fried chicken, or a stack of Dinah Shore records on the phonograph, or the right to throw pop bottles at the umpire at Ebbets Field." The war was an aberration—a disrupter of normality and an unpleasant task that had to be finished before they could get on with their lives. Not facetiously, they had to fight so they could quit fighting. The war was over—at least the combat part. Later would come the remembering.[15]

# *Exeunt Omnes*

With the war over and demobilization moving into high gear, *Pampanito*'s crew rapidly dispersed. Those who remained were busy getting the old boat ready for retirement—mothballing it—lubricating and preserving the machinery to withstand rust, weather, temperature, and time.

Paul Pappas stayed until November. At that time, Commander Scherer called him in for a talk. "The captain said he noticed that I had one year to go on my enlistment," Paul said. "He asked me where I wanted to go. 'New London,' I told him." Scherer had the orders written up. The next day, Pappas did little of his assigned work; instead, he made ready for the trip east. The new CEM found Pappas carrying his sea bags down the gangway. He complained about the unfinished work and asked him where he thought he was going.

"Don't tell me your troubles, chief," Paul snapped back. "I'm going home."

When Pappas was mustered out in New London, he decided to buy a motorcycle for the trip back home to West Virginia. Bob Bennett had always talked about cycles and had finally convinced Paul that they were the coming mode of transportation. He purchased a big bike for seven hundred dollars. The trouble was, he had never driven one before. Loading up his belongings, Paul headed west. He got as far as New York's

Holland Tunnel when the machine stalled out. He couldn't get it started, nor could he lift it. The police helped him push it out of the tunnel and get it started. In Wheeling, West Virginia, Paul lost control and swerved off the road—right into a chicken coop. After repairing the motorcycle, he drove it home and immediately sold it. Pappas went back to his father's photography shop, where he felt much more comfortable.

Ona Hawkins stayed behind; his new residence was a barge at Hunter's Point. In October he was transferred to the sub tender USS *Aegir* (AS 23) as an electrician second class in charge of a crew of four men. It seemed that all they did was repair electric motors. Finally, Hawkins was released in April 1946.

While attending the University of Missouri in 1948, Ona finally married his longtime sweetheart, Muriel. In 1951, Ona graduated with a degree in engineering. Muriel had a job with the University of Missouri's art department. Together, the first major item they ever purchased was a new 1951 Chevrolet. Ona worked for General Electric Company from 1951 until he retired in 1986.

When Woody Weaver left San Francisco in July, he thought he would never see his "stunning redhead" Eve again. However, said Woody, "Fate has a way of intervening in our lives." He ran into Eve again, and by December they were planning to get married. Woody thought it would be nice to be married on his parent's wedding anniversary. The arrangements were worked out, and he and Eve were married on Christmas Day.

Weaver had to remain in the area for *Pampanito*'s decommissioning. In charge were Lieutenants Sherlock and Bartholomew—still arguing about Sherlock's gambling debt. Lieutenant Swain was there. He had been working on the periscopes for the longest time. They never could be completely straightened out, he said, probably as a result of that depth charging on the first patrol.

*Pampanito* was the first of the *Balao*-class boats to be decommissioned, leaving service on 15 December. Lieutenant Sherlock transferred off the next day and went home to Ohio. The next year he was employed in Pittsburgh, Pennsylvania. On Christmas Eve of 1946, Sherlock was paid a surprise visit by Charlie Bartholomew, who was passing through Pittsburgh on his way home to Albany, New York. Bart's car had broken down, and he wondered if Dick could loan him his car to get home. Sherlock did.

One week later, Bartholomew dropped the car off with a burned out engine and transmission. It cost Sherlock about the same amount of money to get it repaired as the gambling debt he owed Bartholomew. Thus, Sherlock finally conceded, "things balanced out."

Dick Sherlock was discharged in June 1946. He held various high-level positions in the postwar years, including a stint as president of Teledyne Ohio Steel. Presently residing in Panama City, Florida, Sherlock has shared several letters telling of his war experiences. "I would classify my feelings as fond memories," he said. "I have fond memories of all 75 years of my life. I have been blessed to live through the most fantastic years in the history of mankind." Then, in closing, Sherlock thought about all the intimate stories he had related. "I know that if I take the time to read what I have written I will burn it," he concluded, "I suggest that you do it for me."

Bob Bennett returned to Mason City, Iowa, after a service stint of three and one-half years. He stayed in the Naval Reserve until 1980. Bob worked as a master plumber for a number of years and eventually acquired his own motorcycle agency. He raced cycles for many years and still owns, rides, and collects them. After his war travels, he had had enough roaming. Said Bob: "I've lived in the same house for over seventy-five years."

Bob tried his best to keep in touch with the POW survivors he had helped rescue. One of them, "Gunner" Bill Cray, wrote to him from Hull, England, about his journey back home. Admiral Nimitz visited with the English survivors at Pearl Harbor, and the navy treated them well, Cray said. When he went through Chicago, the train stopped and he got out and bought some popcorn. It was the first time he had ever tasted the treat, and he thought it was excellent. Back home, he wasted no time in finding his girlfriend and getting married. He wrote: "Thanks to you and all the crew for the great work you all did in saving our lives . . . however, I'll say 'Cheerio' now, and here's wishing you and your ship good luck and all the best."

Several of the Australian survivors kept in touch with Bennett. One, Frank Farmer, called him every year on 15 September, the anniversary of the day he was rescued. "Bob," Frank would tell Bennett, "Thank you for another year of my life."

Woodrow Weaver also had contact, although vicariously, with one of the survivors. He stayed in the navy, and in 1946 was assigned to USS *Carp*

(SS 338), whose exec was Lieutenant Commander Lynn Orser. Weaver was offered a commission and became a lieutenant junior grade in 1961 and a lieutenant in 1963. In 1968 he was serving with the Pacific Coast Section of the Naval Board of Inspection and Survey, which conducted trial inspections of all newly constructed ships. That summer, Weaver was involved in testing HMAS *Brisbane*, an Australian destroyer built in a U.S. shipyard. While on board, Woody heard a Lieutenant Cocking's name called over the ship's intercom. Upon further inquiry, he met the young lieutenant, Ron Cocking, and discovered that he was, indeed, the son of the same Jack Cocking that Woody had helped rescue twenty-four years earlier.

"My father seldom talks about those days," said Ron Cocking. "But he kept a little black notebook, rather tattered now, with the names of the *Pampanito* crewmen. And he asked me to look up any I could find." Jack, then fifty-seven, had rejoined the Australian army and was stationed near his home in Perth. He was still robust and doing fine.

The black book was the same one Weaver had given to Jack on the submarine. He had asked his son to try to find the crew, but none of the addresses were current enough for Ron to track anyone down. Now, by chance, Weaver had found him. However, after *Brisbane* sailed away, Weaver lost contact with both father and son.

After leaving *Pampanito* after her third patrol, Bill Grady got on *Shad* for two more patrols. On *Plunger, Pampanito,* and *Shad* he had made eleven war patrols, more than enough for any submariner. Grady was discharged in September 1945, then went into the Naval Reserve for four more years.

Grady operated a mechanical contracting firm from 1947 until 1989. He attended night classes at the Universities of Massachusetts and Connecticut that prepared him to successfully pass the state professional engineer's examination.

Grady couldn't tolerate retirement, so he worked for Pitney-Bowes Corporation for two years and as a field consulting engineer for a mechanical-electrical firm until the present. Bill was bored to death with retirement. "I am very happy with my work," he said, "and will remain until I die or am physically unable to continue my duties."

A member of the SubVets of WW II, Grady attended eight commissionings and launchings of both fast attack and boomer boats and was on the commissioning committee for USS *Springfield* (SSN 761). He made two cruises on her, as well as on USS *Corpus Christi* (SSN 705) and USS *San Juan* (SSN 751). Grady lives in Massachusetts and has four grandchildren and six great-grandchildren.

Joe Eichner left *Pampanito* after her third patrol. He thought he was going to be sent to the States for new construction, but he, Wendell Smith, and John Schilling stayed out a little too late one evening and were not able to make the morning muster. Their promise of new construction was off, and, said Joe, "we found ourselves on a tender headed for Guam."

All three men were transferred to *Balao*. Eichner made two more patrols on that boat and then was assigned to USS *Diablo* (SS 479) until his discharge in 1948 after six years of service.

Eichner remained in New York City most of his life. In 1986 he attended a *Pampanito* reunion. While talking to another shipmate, the subject of the POWs came up, and Joe related the story of the inscribed water heater plate he had given to a POW forty-one years earlier. When asked what had happened to the plate, Joe could never really answer.

During the reunion's closing ceremony, Joe was sitting on a chair on the pier listening to the speakers, who included Captain Summers. Then one of the POW survivors got up to the podium. He put his hand in his pocket, pulled out an oblong plate for all to see, and said, "One of you fellows gave this to me." It was Frank Farmer.

Joe shot up out of his seat "with goose bumps all over my arms." He called out, "I gave it to you." Farmer addressed the veterans and thanked them for saving his life. However, he said, even if he had perished in the water after the sinking, he would have died a free man, for freedom had meant more to him than anything else. After the speeches, Joe and Frank met with a handshake and an embrace.

"Since that day," Joe said, "Frank and I wrote letters to each other, he called me now and then, and we really had a good friendship going."

The first man picked up by *Pampanito*, Frank Farmer was discharged in June 1945 and went back to his teaching job at a Melbourne high school. He became principal at two high schools before his retirement in 1974. Frank made several visits to the United States and England. He stayed at the Eichners' in New York and kept up a correspondence with several former submariners. Over the years, however, prostate cancer

*Pampanito* tied up at Fisherman's Wharf, November 1996. (Photo by author.)

finally got the best of Frank Farmer. He last called Bennett in September 1995, and before Christmas of that year Frank Farmer had passed away. He was cremated, and his ashes were sown upon the ocean.

After their rescue, the Australians returned home in mid-October 1944—about one month after they had been picked up. Debriefings over, they were given three months' leave, and the Australian government made their epic story public.

Alf Winter returned to his teaching job. Don McArdle became a barber. Harry Pickett taught and played music. Bill Cuneen bought a five-hundred-acre sheep ranch.

Bob Farrands was discharged from the army in May 1945. He married in 1946 and had three daughters. He joined the New South Wales Fire Brigade (Sydney) and served for thirty-seven years, retiring in 1982. His hobby is gardening. In early 1997, Bob went into the hospital for a second knee replacement, but other complications laid him low for a month. He is recuperating, and, said Bob, "I cannot get well quick enough to get back into my garden."

Cliff Farlow returned to Hay, Australia, where he was given a warm, civic welcome at the railroad station. During his leave, Cliff went to Melbourne to talk to the Intelligence Bureau about the POWs and the prison camps. Cliff was surprised that they knew almost everything that he knew—and many things he didn't.

Farlow continued the family dairy-farming business, breeding pure Guernsey cattle and supplying milk for the local population for over thirty years. The vision he had in the South China Sea had come true. He was back milking cows again, and, said Cliff, "It was wonderful."

The war was the prime experience of Farlow's life, although he said he'd never become a prisoner of the Japanese again. "I would stand up and shoot or be shot," he declared. "Personally, I don't want to have anything to do with them." As for the United States, Farlow believed that Australia might not be here today if it had not been for American involvement in the war. He thought America's participation "was the salvation of the Western World." Farlow concluded: "God bless America."

Roy Cornford, who was too sick to leave Saipan with the others, was later flown to Brisbane. When discharged, he weighed less than 120 pounds. Roy got a 10-percent war pension, but he had to work to take care of his wife and family. Because he was working, he said, "after three or four years they took it away from me." He did not get his pension back until he was fifty-six years old.

Roy worked as a house painter and wallpaper hanger. He began his own business and was very successful with it, his son taking over when he retired. Roy moved to a waterfront home on Jervis Bay, about a hundred miles south of Sydney. He enjoys deep sea fishing, even after his experience on the open ocean. His wife, he said, will fish from the beach, "but she won't come to sea with me."

Roy Cornford and Bill McKittrick both traveled to the United States to attend *Pampanito*'s fiftieth reunion in San Francisco in 1993. McKittrick died the next year. "Of the six of us who flew home from Saipan," Roy said, "only two are alive today. Of the 92 Aussie survivors rescued by the four subs, 28 of us are still alive."

The second man rescued by *Pampanito*, Curly Martin, thought that all would be fine when he returned home. He stated: "We were treated good in Australia—at first. But it has been 55 years and governments change. A lot of promises have been conveniently forgotten." Martin celebrated his eightieth birthday on 1 January 1997. "I am still in good shape and I hope to have many more," he said.

Yet there were a number of men who would have no more birthday celebrations. Thirteen of them came back to Western Australia, Martin believed, but only about five were left. "I keep in touch with a few," he said, "but some, their memories are gone completely."

The third man rescued, Ken Williams, spent most of his working years as a foreman in a soft drink company. He retired in 1967 at the age of sixty-two and took a service pension. His wife had severe arthritis, and Ken looked after her until she passed away in 1992 after sixty-four years of marriage. He has two daughters, five grandchildren, and seven great-grand-children. As of this writing, Ken is ninety-one years old and still going strong.

"I have lived on my own since I lost my wife," he said, "and will continue to do so while my health lasts. I still play golf in the winter and on cool days in the summer. I also play pennant bowls. That keeps me in good trim."

When Lieutenant Junior Grade William Bruckart left *Pampanito* after her second patrol, he was ordered to the SubDiv 201 relief crew to await further orders. Bruckart reported aboard *Kingfish* in September 1944 and made her tenth and eleventh war patrols, both to Empire waters, where they sank three small cargo ships for about five thousand tons. He was promoted to lieutenant on 1 December 1944.

In April 1945, Bruckart went to Portsmouth for the commissioning of USS *Odax* (SS 484), after which he served as electronics officer, damage control officer, and first lieutenant. He was detached in September and ordered to *Plunger* as executive officer. In November, Bruckart was ordered to inactive duty. He remained in the U.S. Naval Reserve and was promoted to lieutenant commander in 1951. He obtained a master's degree in engineering at Ohio State University while working and being active in the reserve. In 1956 he was promoted to commander.

After several years with Universal-Cyclops Steel Company, Bruckart set up as an independent technical and marketing consultant. He moved to California in 1963 and became affiliated with Aerojet-General Corporation as manager of the Metals and Refractories Department. After thirty years in the service, Bruckart retired, only to accept an appointment as assistant professor in the School of Engineering at California Polytechnic. He was promoted to associate professor and then to professor. After sixteen years, Bruckart "retired" again in 1984.

When Al Van Atta got back to the States, he took a train to Great Lakes Training Center, where he was discharged in October 1945. He was in the "20-50 Club," in which former servicemen got twenty dollars a week for fifty weeks. Al married his girlfriend, Dorothy, in 1949. One of the best things that happened to him was getting his college education at the University of Dayton with the help of the GI Bill. He graduated in 1951, worked for the phone company, for the City of Dayton, and then at Wright-Patterson Air Force Base until he retired in 1985. Al has three sons and sixteen grandchildren.

In a 1996 interview, Van Atta said that the war experience was good for him. He believes he owes the government respect and thanks for training him, educating him, and giving him a life's worth of experiences in a few short years. Sure, he put in his time and paid his dues, he said, "but the Government has re-paid me many times over." As he thought about his experiences of fifty years ago, he concluded: "I have no regrets about going into the submarine service. Sometimes it was terrifying, but it was all worthwhile."

After leaving *Pampanito,* Earl Watkins made two runs on USS *Manta* (SS 299). They were off the coast of Japan when they received word of the war's end. *Manta* sailed back to Midway, and Watkins, because he had a wife and a child, was able to go home. He sailed on an old destroyer to Pearl Harbor and then back to the States. He was discharged in Toledo, Ohio, in October 1945.

Earl went back to Pennsylvania and used his motor mac experience to work for a General Motors dealership for forty years. He retired in 1983, and he has two sons, one daughter, and seven grandchildren.

Interviewed in April 1996, Earl thought about the people he had met a half-century ago. "Sub sailors were a dedicated bunch of guys that really stuck together," he said. "They were very close knit. Your lives depended upon one another. You really grew up on the subs, you really matured." Earl laughed when thinking back, about how a thirty-year-old skipper was considered an old man. He thought the Regular Navy was too formal, but he enjoyed the informal atmosphere of the boat. "I liked sub duty," he concluded. "If I had to do it all over again, I think I'd do exactly the same thing."

With the war over, Hubert Brown went from Midway to San Francisco, and he spent the next several months mothballing warships. He was discharged at Great Lakes Training Center on Christmas Day in 1945. When his time was up, he was asked if he wanted to reenlist.

"No," he said. "I wasn't going to get into anything else. I figured I had about used up my luck."

Hubert moved to Ohio and spent seven years as a Ford mechanic and then owned and operated his own service station for thirty years. After retiring, he turned to farming as a hobby.

In a 1996 interview, Hubert said that he liked the navy. He had made up his mind to do the best job he could, which was what any person ought to do. At first, he thought it would be a rousing good time, but he found out "that I had a lot of maturing to do." He was satisfied with the service, with what he had seen and accomplished, but it also gave him some of the "most scary" experiences in his life. "I thought it would be exciting," he said, "but I guess being 19 years-old had to help." Although he doubted he'd do it again, Hubert said, "I never was sorry I did it. It was a good experience. As a matter of fact, it was probably the highlight of my life."

Clarence Carmody brought his wife, Doris, back to California with him. Still a very close friend of Maurice Demers, the two of them moved in with Doc while Demers had a small apartment in San Francisco. Demers had no furniture, and Mike and Doris slept on the floor. But there was beer in the refrigerator, and that tided them over.

Carmody always had been in good physical shape, excelling at swimming and athletics. He stayed in the navy twenty-two years, twenty-one of them on submarines. For two of those years Mike was a diving and escape instructor at the escape tank at the sub school in New London. After retiring from the navy in 1963, Carmody found another career in the New York City Fire Department, where he became chief engineer on the city fire boats, a job he held for another twenty-two years before retiring again.

After the war, Charlie McGuire was assigned to *Spinax*. Even so, it seemed he couldn't get out from under the shadow of Pete Summers. Summers had been on *Cusk* for the past year, but his boat pulled in to Portsmouth, and sailors from both subs congregated in the same nightclub. When Charlie learned that *Cusk* sailors were there, he started telling his *Spinax* mates about the lousy commander that ran *Cusk*.

"Summers is not an enlisted man's captain," he said. "He looked down his nose at anyone he didn't consider in the same class with him. He treated you like a dog. Others might like him," McGuire said, loud enough for the other crewmen to hear him, "but only if they never got to know him. When you work with him, you won't like him." McGuire warmed up, droning on and on about Pete.

Finally, a few *Cusk* men strolled over to McGuire's table. They politely told McGuire that they liked their captain, and if he didn't stop bad-mouthing him, they would settle it with fists. McGuire knew he was feeling his liquor a little and thought it best not to take them up on their challenge.

"So I shut-up," he said. But after they went away, McGuire couldn't help but add: "At least on the *Pampanito* he was a miserable S-O-B."

McGuire sailed on *Spinax* to Washington, D.C., where President Truman came aboard for an inspection. Charlie got to shake his hand, and the President asked him if it was true that the chiefs ran the navy.

"They think they do, Sir," McGuire answered.

While on recruiting duty in Boston, McGuire also met and went to lunch several times with a former PT-boat man, then a congressman from Massachusetts, John F. Kennedy.

After spending so many years in the service, McGuire decided to make a career of it. He was assigned to the new USS *Tang* (SS 563) and traveled to Japan, Singapore, and, once more, Australia. After Charlie left the navy, he got a job with Lockheed Corporation working on Polaris missiles. There, he said, "I made more in a week than I did in a month in the Navy."

Charlie and his wife once traveled to Scotland. In a chapel in Edinburgh was a listing of all the Scotsmen killed in World War II. Charlie looked but could not find reference to John Campbell. He informed them about the Gordon Highlander, his POW experience, and how he had come to be committed to the deep in the South China Sea. Campbell's name was added to the list.

In later years McGuire still remembered going through the depth charging on the first patrol. He always admitted he was frightened, unlike some of the others, who he thought put up a false bravado. "It was only in old age, when they didn't care so much what people thought, that they finally admitted they were frightened." The experience was indelible. "You change when you go through a depth charging. No doubt about it."

As for his years in the navy, Charlie had dichotomous, but concise thoughts: "I dislike the Government; but I wouldn't hesitate to give my life for my country. I was glad I was in the submarine service; but I'd never do it again."

Paul Summers made twelve war patrols—never, as he had hoped, having to make a thirteenth. The war ended before he had to take *Cusk* into battle, but he did make peacetime test runs to the Arctic Ocean.

In 1947, *Cusk* was operating in conjunction with the Naval Air Missile Test Center at Point Mugu, California. *Cusk* and USS *Carbonero* (SS 337) had been modified at Mare Island to fire the Loon missile, an experimental guided rocket based on the idea of the German V-1. The Loon carried a beacon operating on the submarine's radar frequency, enabling mid-air course modifications. During the first test, *Cusk* lost control of the missile because of poor radar reception, and the Loon crashed into the Pacific. One month and six Loons later, Summers and *Cusk* finally controlled the missile out to seventy-five miles. Successful tests led to the development of the operational Regulus I missile.

In 1948, Summers left *Cusk* to become exec at the Naval ROTC unit at the Alabama Polytechnic Institute in Auburn, Alabama. In 1951 and 1952 he was operations officer with SubRon 5 and division commander with SubDiv 51. The next two years, Summers was exec at the U.S. Naval Powder Factory at Indian Head, Maryland, and in 1955 he was promoted to captain. In 1957 he was involved with missiles once more, as officer in charge of Guided Missle Evaluation Unit One. Summers retired in October 1957. He joined Lockheed in the Polaris missile program until his second retirement in 1978.

Summers had a fleeting television appearance on the weekly 1950s NBC program, *The Silent Service,* as a guest of Thomas M. Dykers. The show highlighted his rescue of the seventy-three POWs.

Summers attended a few reunions, but he never could make friends with McGuire. "I gave him a hard time," Charlie admitted.

"Why are you always jumping on me?" Summers asked McGuire at a 1986 get-together.

"Because you were always so damn tough on me during the war," Charlie snapped back.

Pete excused himself, telling Charlie that he was under a lot of pressure. Charlie's mates admonished him, asking Red to ease up on the old man. He might have been a bad egg, they said, "but at least he brought us back." It was more than could be said for some of the other poor sailors. Later, Charlie admitted that he had done a lot to deserve an occasional reprimand. "I guess I deserved to get kicked in the butt a few times," he said.

It was quite an accomplishment to get Summers to attend the reunions. He moved to Oklahoma and spent his later years quietly, out of the spotlight as much as possible. "I never kept much in touch with the *Pampanito* crew," he said. "I was never a very good correspondent."

Paul E. Summers died at his home in Oklahoma City on 28 August 1993. He was interred at Arlington National Cemetery.

When *Pampanito* returned to San Francisco after the war, Gordon Hopper was transferred to Mare Island and discharged in January 1946. Hopper rode a bus to Chicago, where he ditched his sailor's dungarees and bought new clothes to wear home. However, when he stepped off the train in Clinton, Illinois, wearing slacks and a sport jacket instead of navy blues, ribbons, and dolphins, his parents and girlfriend were disappointed. "They didn't understand my strong desire to get into civilian clothes again," Hopper said.

Hopper had a visit from a shipmate one day when Tony Hauptman showed up in Clinton with his girlfriend. Tony remembered that Gordon's father was a minister, and he decided it would be nice if the Reverend Lewis Hopper would marry the two of them. The ceremony was performed to the satisfaction of all, although Hopper was quite amused when Tony kept calling him Clod—he had never learned Gordon's real name.

Hopper had two overlapping careers—one in association management and the other in public relations. For over forty years he had deliberately put World War II behind him, concentrating on helping his wife raise five daughters and one son.

When thinking back, Gordon remembered how enthusiastic he had been to get into combat, and, as is true of most young men, how he had believed in his invincibility. However, that only lasted, he said, "until the beating we took during our first encounter with the enemy. From that time on I was more realistic about the war, submarine combat and our vulnerability." Gordon had mixed feelings. He was proud of his accomplishments. He had the unique experience of helping to rescue seventy-three men, he made it home alive, and he received many plaudits for the accomplishments of the U.S. submarines in general and for *Pampanito*'s exploits specifically.

On the other hand, Gordon said, "I was repulsed by the dehumanizing nature of armed combat as I gradually accepted the reality that what we euphemistically called 'targets' were ships and people. When we cheered a sinking we were also cheering the killing of people as well as celebrating destruction of ships and essential materials." Gordon described himself as "close to being a conscientious objector," a rather mixed-up man with conflicting feelings of pride and revulsion. He refused to join any veterans' organizations, because he was aware that his pacifist leanings and his tendency to speak his mind would only lead to trouble.

With reluctance, Hopper attended *Pampanito*'s fiftieth reunion "prepared to be bored out of my mind." However, he said, "Reuniting with shipmates of a half-century ago on the boat that was our surrogate mother was an unexpectedly emotional experience." After all those years, Gordon said, "I realized for the first time the extent to which going to war on the *Pampanito* influenced my life." He concluded: "Although I spent only a few months more than two years aboard the *Pampanito*, lifelong friendships with shipmates resulted. We shared, in the closest of quarters, life and death experiences, had known the terror of combat, had survived the boredom of day after uneventful day at sea, had laughed at so many funny incidents, and had gotten drunk and disorderly together. Ours was, and still is, a lasting fraternity of unmatched closeness. In great measure, this compensates for the negative sentiments that have plagued me so many years."

Paul Pappas agreed to be interviewed in April 1996. Still in his home town of Parkersburg, he related his war experiences and concluded with some words of wisdom:

> If you missed the war, don't regret it. It was a good experience. I wouldn't trade the experience, but if I missed it, and know what I know now, I'd say, 'Paul, use your head, you didn't miss anything.' You got boredom. You got heartache. The biggest thing you looked forward to was getting home. You planned, waited, and hoped to get home. The war came third; home and family were on top. If you missed the war—no matter how they talk at the reunions—you didn't miss anything. I made terrific friends, it educated me, but don't regret having missed it. Then again, I wouldn't take any amount of money for my memories.

Frank Michno finished the war on *Grouper* and wanted to make a career of the navy, but his wife had different ideas. Marian was tired of living in a quonset hut at Mare Island, and in 1947 Michno was discharged and made his way back to Detroit.

Like his father and brothers, he went into the bar business, then owned a hardware store and ended up working at P&M Tool and Die Company for many years. He would often tell his only son about his war experiences—stories that grew in number and drama with every shot and beer that he drank. For somehow the mundane necessity of punching a time-clock in a factory and making lifelong mortgage payments did not measure up to the indelible experience of war. It was almost as if he had reached the epitome of his life as a young man; there was no climax left for the final chapters.

Marian Michno always believed it was her Easter prayers that saved *Pampanito*. Perhaps. But Frank Michno died of heart failure, after his usual morning brace of brandy, on 7 April 1988. It was exactly forty-four years to the day of that Good Friday depth charge attack in 1944.

I became acquainted with about fifty *Pampanito* men during the course of almost two years of letter writing, taping, and personal interviews. Some men could not recall my father at all, but they explained that most of the rates associated with their own kind—for example, electricians with electricians and torpedomen with torpedomen. Some recalled him after having his photograph pointed out. Others knew the man upon first mention of his name.

A man's memory was pretty selective, said Mike Carmody. He thought it was strange how one person would remember things a certain way when the fellow who had been standing next to him would have a completely different recollection. Paul Pappas thought it was weird how something could happen on such a small boat and some men never knew about it. For example, he knew they were hit by a dud torpedo, but the first time he heard about the torpedoes paralleling them off Japan was at a reunion almost forty years later.

Some men were hesitant to contribute information. George Moffett wrote: "Personally, I find it difficult to talk to non-submariners about war patrols, life aboard the boat and the day-to-day routine that was a mandatory part of every submariner's life." The general populace, he said, had no concept of war, submarines, or submariners, "and probably never will." In his estimation, movies and television had substituted a poor ersatz, celluloid corruption of reality. It was only with reluctance that he agreed to write. But then he provided a treasure trove of information.

Charles McGuire said that he knew who my introductory letter to him was from as soon as he saw the name on the envelope. He provided about three hours of oral recollections on cassette tapes. During one taping poor McGuire again got into hot water. While talking about his experiences in the red light district of Perth-Fremantle, the tape suddenly went dead, with a muffled, "Oh, hell," then silence. When the voice finally returned,

McGuire explained that his wife had been in the next room, listening to him tell his story. He had told her that he never did any of that sort of thing. "Damn it Greg," he said, "you got me in trouble."

Sorry Charlie.

Paul Pappas asked me to come down to Parkersburg, West Virginia, to talk to him. He provided a few hours of stories, many photographs, and the use of a very detailed dairy. Paul was still active, now working in his son Toli's photography shop. At one point we talked under the red lights in the studio's darkroom, which, with a little stretch of the imagination, was not unlike sitting in the red glow of *Pampanito*'s control room. Paul had to finish up a last-minute job. We made the delivery and then went out to dine at the local McDonald's restaurant.

"Oh yeah," Paul said after we ate, "When you talk or write to the other guys, don't forget to tell them that Pappas actually took you out and bought you dinner. They ought to get a kick out of that."

I told them, Paul.

Pappas was tickled that someone was writing about the old boat. He wanted to go to the latest reunion in November 1996, and he made me promise to go to San Francisco to meet the guys. I did, but Paul got sick and couldn't make it. I talked to him in December 1996. He was really sorry he couldn't attend, but he explained that he was feeling much better. Unfortunately, time finally caught up with him. Paul died in his sleep, Sunday morning, 26 January 1997.

The fifty-third reunion was held 4–6 November 1996. There were fewer men in attendance than in past years. Time is telling. Those that made it were Norm Arcement, Roger Walters, Bob Bennett, Ona Hawkins, Earl Watkins, Gordon Hopper, Spence Stimler, George Moffett, Walt Cordon, Walt Richter, Woody Weaver, Bill Bruckart, and Dick Sherlock. Charlie McGuire was able to drop by one afternoon, and Janet Granum was there with her two sons, representing her husband, Peder, who passed away in the summer of 1996. I suppose I was representing my father.

The men renewed acquaintances, explored the boat, and retold sea stories. The men of the Maritime Museum Association cooked in the galley and made a great on-board breakfast. The two forward engines were started up. Even the TDC, restored by Terry Lindell, was operational—the only working instrument of its kind in the country. Weaver demonstrated how

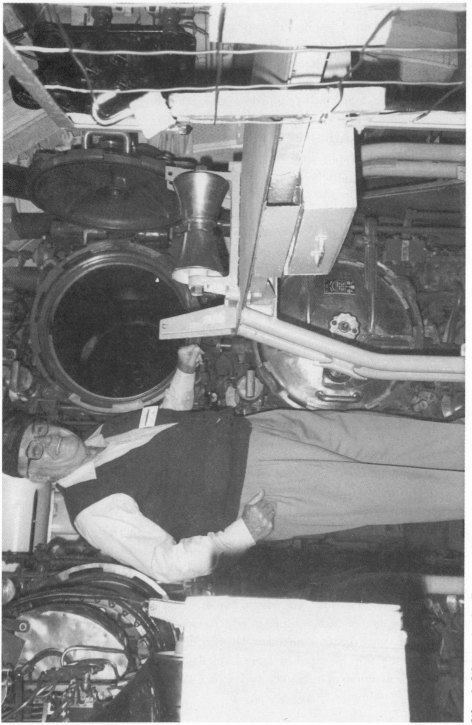

Woody Weaver in the Forward Torpedo Room, 1996. (Photo by author.)

George Moffett shows how the radar was operated in the Conning Tower, 1996. (Photo by author.)

the torpedoes operated, Walters explained how he worked the sound equipment, Bruckart and Sherlock told stories up in the conning tower, and Moffett demonstrated how he operated the radar. As an added attraction, Molly showed how he "hot-wired" the light bulb to shock Chief Aiken fifty-one years earlier. Gordon Hopper wrote a poem for the occasion which commented on the propensity of "Old Salts" to recall and sometimes exaggerate their stories over the years. The culminating ceremony took place on the pier. Norm Arcement solemnly read the names of the boats lost during the war, followed by Earl Watkins's tolling of the ship's bell. At each name and ring the submariners' wives, standing alongside the pier, would throw one rose into the gently undulating waters of the bay; fifty-two rings and fifty-two roses, one for every boat that never returned. It was a moving experience.

Sitting in the hotel room the last evening, the storytellers gathered, and parting thoughts were given about war and life in general. Norm Arcement said he really couldn't remember much about the war. It all blended in after a time. "I just kind of forgot about it," he said. "But at the reunions, when I get with the guys, I can remember some of it."

He went to Australia in 1988 to visit some of the Aussies they had rescued. There weren't many left, he thought. It seemed that they were passing away faster than the submariners. He still keeps in touch with them, passing cards and letters during the Christmas season. When asked for a final summation, Norm thought for a minute and said: "I wouldn't take a million bucks for the experience I had in World War Two, but I wouldn't give you a dime to go through it again." Then, after another few seconds of silence, he added, "At least I'll keep the memories of it."

Ona Hawkins had no regrets about going into the service. "I certainly have fond memories of submarine duty and not too much of the hardships," he said. Ona realized that most memories seem to acquire a golden haze. "The bad parts are just not uppermost in my mind. It was a maturing experience," Ona said. "Also, I was very grateful for the GI Bill. I don't think I could have gone to school without it. I really feel that I was pretty well-paid, in essence, for the time I was in the service. It was funny. I went for years without thinking about the subs at all. I was in the SubVets organization for a little bit in the 1950s, but I dropped out. It was no fun. After I retired in 1986, I got back into it." It seemed to him that the memories became more important as the years went by.

Earl Watkins tolls the ship's bell, 1996. (Photo by author.)

Bob Bennett finished up his tape with some sobering thoughts. "Being on the *Pampanito* and in the sub service was probably the most memorable time of my life. The shipmates that you live with under those conditions are your buddies forever." Here, Bob's voice broke a bit, and it took a few seconds for him to compose himself. He continued: "That's about all I can say right now. The more I look at these pictures, the more I remember your dad, and the more things come back to me about the crew all the time." Bob couldn't continue.

I met Roger Walters at a party store across the street from the San Francisco hotel hosting the 1996 reunion. He had finished his enlistment as an instructor on the school boat *R-9* and never returned to Mason City, Iowa. Roger was in the retail business for three years and then went on the road in the Pacific Northwest for thirty-six years, selling housewares wholesale and retail. He retired in 1985 and celebrated his fiftieth wedding anniversary in 1995. He has seven children and thirteen grandchildren.

Roger and I were both stocking up for the coming festivities and storytelling. I had jokingly made several of the old sailors promise that there would be no gilly cooking in my hotel room. Later, Roger brought a bottle of Jack Daniels upstairs. As was customary, his largesse was shared, passed around in a paper cup. Feeling comfortable, Walters related a few stories, then continued:

> I sowed my wild oats as infrequently as I had the opportunity when I was in the service. I did what I wanted to do, but when it was all done, it was behind me. Here's what I wanted to do: I wanted to get married, have a family, and settle down and make a living. But when I think back on it, it was probably the most exciting time of my life. I would never have done anything differently. I don't have any regrets about it at all. It was the most exciting, greatest experience of my life, bar none. I will never forget it. I will never regret it. War is hell, and when I hear threats of war and think of all the young men who might have to go to war to defend their country it just brings me to tears.

There was silence for awhile. It was getting late, and the others had gone back to their rooms to find their wives or prepare for the final reunion

Aboard *Pampanito* at the November 1996 reunion. Left to right: William Bruckart, Norm Arcement, Walt Cordon, Woody Weaver, Janet (Peder) Granum, George Moffett, Roger Walters, Ona Hawkins. (Photo by author.)

dinner ceremony. Roger concluded: "With all the horror and all the glory, and everything that went with it, it was something that made an impression on us that would last a lifetime. Yet, we don't consider ourselves as heroes at all. We just did our job. But I would not have missed it for the world."

After the war the navy immediately scrapped 20 fleet submarines, placed 106 in reserve, and kept 19 as trainers. Creating a reserve fleet took a great deal of time and resources. The boats received overhauls and treatments with chemicals and paint. In addition, ballast tanks were coated with preservatives and sealed. Dehumidifiers were installed, and an inventory was taken.

*Pampanito,* following her decommissioning, was placed in the Pacific Reserve Fleet until April 1960, when she was placed back in service as a pierside trainer for reservists at the Mare Island Naval Shipyard in Vallejo. In 1962 she was reclassified as the AGSS 383, an auxiliary submarine.

In June 1971, *Pampanito* was classified IXSS 383, a miscellaneous designation, but in December of that year she was stricken from the rolls a second time. *Pampanito* languished in the Bay Area for another few years, with the scrap heap her most likely fate. The idea to save the boat for a WW II display got off to a rocky start. It was opposed by members of the International Longshoremen's and Warehousemen's Union, who called the sub a "disgraceful symbol of war" because it took part in sinking ships carrying English and Australian prisoners. In 1975, however, the boat was acquired by the National Maritime Museum Association, and restoration began in 1981. It was moved to Pier 45 at San Francisco's Fisherman's Wharf and opened to the public in 1982.

From then on, *Pampanito*'s fortunes waxed. In 1986 she was selected by the U.S. Department of the Interior to become a National Historic Landmark. Attending the reunion that year were Rear Admiral Richard O'Kane and Captain Edward Beach, as well as Rear Admiral Paul Summers. In 1989 the government of Australia awarded the boat with an Australian Defence Force Plaque for its role in rescuing the Australian POWs. During the succeeding years she received updates to restore her old WW II features, including a four-inch deck gun, a JP-1 hydrophone, the medical locker and thirty-six bunks, a working ventilation system, refrigerator, stove, and crew's head. Lube and fuel pumps were restored, and two main engines, "Beast" and "Scupper," were brought back on line.

Last lookout. Bob Bennett at top. Left to right: Gordon Hopper, Spence Stimler, and Earl Watkins. (Photo by author.)

In 1993, *Pampanito* was towed to San Francisco Drydock Company to repair storm damage she had suffered during a massive windstorm that struck the area in December 1988. She had six damaged sections of hull plating replaced and welded. The outer hull was blasted with high-pressure water to remove old paint and marine growth, and the chain locker was cleaned and recoated. In November 1993 a recommissioning ceremony was held for the boat's fiftieth anniversary, which was attended by thirty-three crew members.

Because she was one of the few seaworthy World War II submarines remaining, *Pampanito* became a movie star. In 1996 she was a top attraction for 20th Century Fox's, *Down Periscope*, a comedy starring Kelsey Grammar, Rip Torn, Bruce Dern, Harry Dean Stanton, and Lauren Holley. *Pampanito* played an old World War II boat brought out of mothballs to go up against a force of nuclear boats. In the movie she was named the *Stingray*, which was, ironically, the boat in which Pete Summers had made his first war patrols. Grammar felt as if he was in a costume drama. He changed his hair, trimmed down, and put on a uniform. "But you get on to that boat," he said, "and you start to walk a little differently."

Today, *Pampanito* is visited by over three hundred thousand people every year. That she wasn't sold, scrapped, or sunk like hundreds of her sister boats was simply a matter of fortune.

*Pampanito*'s battle flag is on display at the wharf where the boat still rides on the gentle swells of the bay. Unlike other submarine battle flags that were commonly emblazoned with miniature emblems representing all the Japanese ships they had sunk, the focus of *Pampanito*'s flag is a red cross with a white 73 over it, symbolizing the number of men she had rescued. "It is staggering," said Gordon Hopper, to think that some men might have known that there were POWs aboard that convoy. "Unquestionably," he said, "war is a brutal exercise in self-interest and survival at any cost. I've understood that for years, but had until now, believed that in the rescue we had accomplished an exception."

It was an exception. The officers and men aboard the submarine performed an act of mercy that required no orders. Even in the midst of war, men will still find humanity and compassion and act to save lives rather than take them. In the final chapter, *Pampanito* has become more remembered not as a killer, but as an angel.

# *Appendix A*

PERSONNEL SERVING ON THE *PAMPANITO* FROM
COMMISSIONING, 6 NOVEMBER 1943, TO 1 MAY 1945

| *Name* | *Patrols* (*=Plankowner. Lack of a number designates assignment, but made no patrols.) |
|---|---|
| Agnello, Lewis Jerry | *1 |
| Aiken, William Ives | 6 |
| Aimone, Otto Peter, Jr. | *1 |
| Arcement, Norman J. | *1, 2, 3, 4, 5, 6 |
| Attaway, Ralph Winston | *1, 2 |
| Austin, Joseph Charles Cave | 1, 2, 3, 4, 5, 6 |
| Bacskay, Albert Joseph | *1, 2 , 3, 4, 5, 6 |
| Bain, Cole Edward | 2, 3 |
| Baron, Leonard | *1, 2, 3 |
| Bartholomew, Charles K. | 3, 4, 5, 6 |
| Beaulieu, Laurent | 1, 2, 3, 4, 5, 6 |
| Behney, James Harris | 1, 2, 3, 4, 5, 6 |
| Bennett, Robert | *1, 2, 3, 4, 5, 6 |
| Berganio, Fermin Roquero | 5, 6 |

| | |
|---|---|
| Bergfeld, Patrick Henry | 4, 5, 6 |
| Bienkowski, Chester Charles | * |
| Bixler, Herbert James | 3, 4, 5, 6 |
| Bobb, Louis Edward | *1 |
| Boozer, James Steadman | * |
| Bouchard, Jacques Florian | *1, 2 |
| Bourgeois, Roger Norman | 1, 2, 3, 4, 5, 6 |
| Bowring, Harry Samuel | 2, 3, 4, 5, 6 |
| Branch, Lamont | *1, 2 |
| Brown, Duncan | 1 |
| Brown, George Valentine | * |
| Brown, Hubert Nelson | *1, 2, 3, 4 |
| Brown, Kenneth Lee | |
| Bruckart, William Lee | 1, 2 |
| Bulceco, Rufino | 4 |
| Bush, William J. | 5, 6 |
| Butler, Stanley Freemont | 4, 5, 6 |
| Byrd, Robert | 2, 3 |
| Canty, William Stephen | 1, 2 |
| Carmody, Clarence George | 1, 2, 3, 4, 5, 6 |
| Chapman, Henry Roy | 2, 3 |
| Chichak, Andrew Frank | 3, 4, 5, 6 |
| Chinn, Harold | 1, 2, 3, 4 |
| Connelly, William Guy | * |
| Cordon, Walter Harold | *1, 2, 3, 4, 5, 6 |
| Costello, Irving Francis | *1, 2, 3, 4 |
| Cox, James Elton | * |
| Crane, Travis Lee | 4, 5, 6 |
| Currier, Andrew Louis | *1, 2, 3, 4, 5, 6 |
| Davenport, Bartlett Nathaniel | *1, 2, 3, 4, 5, 6 |
| Davis, Landon Leslie, Jr. | *1, 2, 3, 4 |
| DeBuono, Jaguindo | * |
| DeLorme, Murray Neil | 5, 6 |
| Demers, Maurice Lawrence | 3, 4, 5, 6 |
| DePaul, Edward E. | 5 |
| DePray, Robert Francis | 2, 3, 4 |

| | |
|---|---|
| Dondzillo, Walter John | |
| Eberhard, Robert Earl | 1, 2 |
| Eichner, Joseph Frederick | *1, 2, 3 |
| Elkins, Kelly | 3, 4, 5, 6 |
| Elliot, Allan Charles | 3, 4, 5, 6 |
| Elliott, Richard Eugene | 3, 4, 5, 6 |
| Evans, Jack Jay | 2, 3 |
| Evans, Robert Edward | 3, 4, 5, 6 |
| Fenno, Frank Wesley, Jr. | 4 |
| Ferguson, Donald Innes | *1, 2, 3, 4 |
| Fisk, William Arthur | 3, 4, 5, 6 |
| Fulton, Howard Thomas | 2, 3, 4 |
| Fives, Francis Michael | *1, 2, 3, 4, 5, 6 |
| George, Howard Edwin | *1, 2, 3 |
| Gladfelter, Lewis Howard | |
| Glazik, Henry John | *1 |
| Goldfarb, Adolph | |
| Goodson, John Evans | 4, 5, 6 |
| Grady, William Christopher | *1, 2, 3 |
| Granum, Peder Anton | 3, 4, 5, 6 |
| Greene, John Herman | 3, 4, 5, 6 |
| Grommet, Clifford Charles | *1, 2, 3 |
| Hannon, Edward Joseph, Jr. | 1 |
| Harley, Glen Albert | |
| Hauptman, Anthony Carl | *1, 2, 3, 4 |
| Hawkins, Ona Denham | 4, 5, 6 |
| Hayes, Daniel Edward | 3, 4, 5, 6 |
| Heist, James Samuel | *1 |
| Herber, Ralph Monroe | *1, 2, 3 |
| Hill, Mervin | *1, 2, 3, 4, 5, 6 |
| Hill, Samuel Richard | * |
| Higgins, Joseph John | 4, 5, 6 |
| Hopper, Gordon Lewis | *1, 2, 3, 4, 5, 6 |
| Hydeman, Earl T. | 4 |
| Ingram, George | 1, 2, 3, 4, 5, 6 |
| Jackson, Charles B., Jr. | * |

| | |
|---|---|
| Jansen, Kenneth James | 2, 3, 4, 5, 6 |
| Johnson, John Lewis | 4, 5, 6 |
| Johnson, McMillan Houston | 2, 3, 4, 5, 6 |
| Kapustynski, John | 5, 6 |
| Kaup, Norbert Anthony | *1, 2, 3, 4 |
| King, Theodas Cowan, Jr. | *1 |
| Keady, Walter Emmet | |
| Kordich, Nickolas | *1, 2, 3, 4, 5, 6 |
| Kubacki, Edward | *1 |
| Langin, Lawrence Harold | *1, 2 |
| Large, Bonham Davis | 1, 2 |
| Lederer, Frank Joseph | *1, 2 |
| LeFevre, Ellsworth Thomas | |
| Lombardi, Renard Joseph | *1 |
| Lynch, Harry Steven | 3 |
| MacVane, Lloyd Vivian | *1, 2, 3 |
| Madaras, John George | *1, 2, 3, 4, 5, 6 |
| Madison, Walter Robert | 4, 5, 6 |
| Markham, Clyde Boyd | 2, 3, 4 |
| Martin, Lynn Leonard | 1, 2, 3, 4, 5, 6 |
| Matheny, Robert Joseph | *1 |
| McClaskey, William Harrison, Jr. | *1 |
| McCollum, William Henry | 1, 2 |
| McCurry, William Hamilton | |
| McGehee, Ervin Omer | 4, 5, 6 |
| McGrath, James Walter | 5, 6 |
| McGuire, Charles Albert, Jr. | *1, 2, 3, 4, 5, 6 |
| Mendez, Manuel Alfred | 3, 4, 5, 6 |
| Merryman, William Walter | *1, 2, 3, 4, 5, 6 |
| Meyers, Milton Alfred | *1, 2 |
| Michno, Frank Ben | *1, 2 |
| Moffett, George Edward | *1, 2, 3, 4, 5, 6 |
| Moore, Melvin Henry | *1 |
| Morrow, William Franklin, Jr. | *1, 2, 3, 4, 5, 6 |
| Mosey, Ray George | *1 |
| Mountain, Andrew Wray | 6 |

| | |
|---|---|
| Noker, Lawrence Edward | 4, 5, 6 |
| Olive, Richard Hugh | 2, 3, 4 |
| O'Neill, John Bernard | *1, 2 |
| Orser, Lynn S. | 5, 6 |
| Ossiander, Glenn | 5, 6 |
| Pace, Charles Anthony | 4, 5, 6 |
| Pappas, Paul, Jr. | *1, 2, 3, 4, 5, 6 |
| Parris, Kyle Stanley | 2, 3, 4, 5 |
| Partridge, Leland Root | * |
| Payton, Albert, Jr. | 1, 2, 3 |
| Penn, Leonard Thomas | * |
| Pennell, James Thomas, Jr. | 4, 5, 6 |
| Pike, Percy Bryan | 1, 2 |
| Price, William Francis | 3 |
| Rahner, Harold Joseph | *1 |
| Rechner, George Martin | 4, 5, 6 |
| Red, John West, Jr. | 1, 2, 3, 4, 5, 6 |
| Redfield, Richard Wentworth | 4, 5, 6 |
| Rice, Charles McClellan | 5, 6 |
| Richter, Walter Herman | 1, 2 |
| Robinson, Issac Frederick | *1, 2, 3, 4 |
| Russell, Theodore Kenneth | 4, 5, 6 |
| Schilling, John Beveridge | *1, 2, 3 |
| Schwartz, Ernest Edward | 5, 6 |
| Scionti, Santo Sebastian | 2 |
| Sheehan, Thomas Francis | 6 |
| Shepard, Calvin Kay | 5, 6 |
| Sherlock, Richard James | 3, 4, 5, 6 |
| Smith, Addison Russell | 5, 6 |
| Smith, Clarence Harrold | 1, 2, 3, 4, 5, 6 |
| Smith, Elmer William | 3, 4, 5, 6 |
| Smith, Jess D., Jr. | 5, 6 |
| Smith, John, Jr. | |
| Smith, John Franklin | * |
| Smith, Wendell Tyng, Jr. | *1, 2, 3 |
| Smith, William Clyde | 2, 3, 4, 5, 6 |

| | |
|---|---|
| Stimler, Spencer Hunt | 2, 3, 4, 5, 6 |
| Stinson, Harry | * |
| Stockslader, Edmund William | 1, 2, 3, 4, 5, 6 |
| Stoll, Robert, Jr. | 6 |
| Strother, George William, Jr. | 3, 4, 5, 6 |
| Summers, Paul Edward | *1, 2, 3, 5, 6 |
| Swain, Ted Nier | 2, 3, 4, 5, 6 |
| Tansil, Jack Spencer | 5, 6 |
| Thaxton, O'Neal | * |
| Thompson, Donald Elwood | |
| Thompson, Herbert Earl | 3, 4, 5, 6 |
| Tonkin, Edward Martin | *1, 2, 3, 4, 5, 6 |
| Van Atta, Albert Dillon, Jr. | *1, 2, 3, 4 |
| Van Housen, LeRoy Ellsworth | 3, 4, 5, 6 |
| Vaughn, Ishmael Worth | * |
| Vitello, Donato | 4, 5, 6 |
| Wagner, Edmond Follmer | 5, 6 |
| Walters, Roger Marcellus | 1, 2, 3, 5, 6 |
| Wanerman, Leonard | 3, 4, 5, 6 |
| Watkins, Earl Finley | *1, 2 |
| Weaver, Woodrow Wilson | *1, 2, 3, 4, 5, 6 |
| Whitt, Lloyd Arthur | 5 |
| Wilkerson, Jack Roslyn | *1, 2, 3 |
| Williams, Clarence | 3, 4, 5, 6 |
| Wilson, John Edward | *1, 2, 3, 4, 5, 6 |
| Withers, William Lee | |
| Wood, Paul Jackson | 4 |
| Yagemann, William Ferdinand | 1, 2, 3, 4, 5, 6 |
| Ylinen, Arthur | 2, 3 |
| Zalusky, Bernard | *1, 2 |

# *Appendix B*

ENGLISH PRISONERS OF WAR
RESCUED BY *PAMPANITO*

C. "Andy" Anderson
G. Baldwin
H. J. Barker
Thomas B. Brierly
John Campbell
Stanley Costello
William Cray
Douglass A. Cresswell
W. Everitt
Ernest Fieldhouse
Jesse Harrison
Ernest Hughes
C. Jay
Harry Jones
W. Kidman
William A. Mandley
A. Nobbs
Alfred Ogden

Charles A. Perry
Harry Smethurst
Denny Smith
Thomas Smith
Thomas Taylor
George K. "Dagger" Ward
Samuel T. Whiley
F. E. "Curly" Wiles

# *Appendix C*

## AUSTRALIAN PRISONERS OF WAR RESCUED BY *PAMPANITO*

James L. Boulter
J. F .M. Browne
Reginald C. Bullock
H. C. Chivars
A. John Cocking
Frank J. Coombes
Roydon C. Cornford
D. William Cuneen
Maxwell W. Curran
Cliff L. Farlow
Frank E. Farmer
M. Robert Farrands
D. A. Flynn
R. J. Gainger
R. Glen Gollin
Reginald J. Harris
Reginald H. Hart
John R. Hocking

Frank Holcroft
Frank W. Jesse
Harry L. Kinleyside
James H. Lansdowne
C. T. S. Latham
Claude Longley
Darcy F. Lynch
Charles W. Madden
Harold D. "Curly" Martin
R. H. Mawby
Donald F. McArdle
Charles B. McKechnie
William H. "Mac" McKittrick
Ronald C. Miscamble
T. A. Pascoe
Harry Pickett
K. C. Renton
C. F. Smith
C. G. Smith
Pat Smith
Reginald S. Stewart
John W. Turner
J. A. Vickers
Herbert J. Wall
Hilton G. "Harry" Weigand
Strachan M. White
Ken Williams
Alfred D. Winter
Walter V. "Wally" Winter

# Notes

CHAPTER 1

1. Paul R. Schratz, *Submarine Commander: A Story of World War II and Korea,* 302.

2. Ibid., 48; Charles A. Lockwood, *Down to the Sea in Subs,* 32, 161; Samuel Eliot Morison, *John Paul Jones: A Sailor's Biography,* 103.

3. Gary E. Weir, *Forged in War: The Naval-Industrial Complex and American Submarine Construction, 1940–1961,* 3, 13, 16; John D. Alden, *The Fleet Submarine in the U.S. Navy: A Design and Construction History,* 38, 45–47.

4. Charles A. Lockwood and Hans Christian Adamson, *Through Hell and Deep Water,* 92–93.

5. Carl LaVO, *Back from the Deep: The Strange Story of the Sister Subs* Squalus *and* Sculpin, 19–22.

6. Paul E. Summers, interview with Clay Blair, Jr., 1977.

7. Clay Blair, Jr., *Silent Victory: The U.S. Submarine War against Japan,* 122–23; Summers-Blair interview.

8. Blair, *Silent Victory,* 306; Summers-Blair interview; John D. Alden, letters, 8 July 1997, 18 February 1998. Moore sank *Harbin Maru* in January 1942 and *Saikyo Maru* in June. The attack on 21 November 1942 heavily damaged the 8,360-ton converted seaplane tender *Sanyo Maru,* but the ship did not sink.

9. Blair, *Silent Victory,* 449; Summers-Blair interview; Alden, letters, 8 July 1997, 18 February 1998. *Stingray* sank the 8,156-ton *Tamon Maru* and lightly damaged the 6,385-ton *Ussuri Maru.*

10. Schratz, *Submarine Commander,* 34.

11. Edward L. Beach, *Submarine!* 4; Lockwood and Adamson, *Hell and Deep Water,* 79.

12. Studs Terkel, *The Good War: An Oral History of World War Two.*

13. Norman Friedman, *U.S. Submarines through 1945: An Illustrated Design History,* 208, 310–11, 351; Corwin Mendenhall, *Submarine Diary: The Silent Stalking of Japan,* x.

14. Friedman, *U.S. Submarines,* 200, 350.

15. Mark P. Parillo, *The Japanese Merchant Marine in World War II,* 159; James F. Dunnigan and Albert A. Nofi, *Dirty Little Secrets of World War II,* 154, 313; Alden, *Fleet Submarine,* 45–47.

16. Lockwood, *Down to the Sea,* 158; Weir, *Forged in War,* 15.

17. Friedman, *U.S. Submarines,* 206; Alden, *Fleet Submarine,* 225.

18. Theodore Roscoe, *United States Submarine Operations in World War II,* 273.

## CHAPTER 2

1. LaVO, *Back from the Deep,* 36–39, 72–73; Alden, *Fleet Submarine,* 56. William L. Bruckart, radar officer on *Squalus* after it was renamed *Sailfish,* states that quick-closing, spring-driven shutoff valves may have been installed on other boats, but not on *Sailfish.* Even after the disaster, hers were still hand-operated, requiring a sailor standing at the forward end of the compartment to rotate a long reach rod. "This 'improvement,'" said Bruckart, "was made so that the crewman would not be forced to stand immediately under the inboard valve while screwing it down!"

2. Lockwood, *Down to the Sea,* 70, 116, 125–26, 170; LaVO, *Back from the Deep,* 8; James F. Calvert, *Silent Running: My Years on a World War II Attack Submarine,* 7–8.

3. Schratz, *Submarine Commander,* 302; LaVO, *Back from the Deep,* 32.

4. David O. Woodbury, *What the Citizen Should Know about Submarine Warfare,* 90; Lockwood and Adamson, *Hell and Deep Water,* 111–12. The authors incorrectly claim that fresh water is heavier than salt water. Harder probably had taken on more salt water than usual, not fresh water.

5. Blair, *Silent Victory,* 520, 789; Summers-Blair interview.

6. Lockwood and Adamson, *Hell and Deep Water,* 113; Calvert, *Silent Running,* 3.

7. *Pampanito* Muster Roll, 9 January, 13 January 1944.

8. Summers-Blair interview.

9. *Pampanito* Muster Roll, 15 January 1944; Blair, *Silent Victory,* 429.

10. Jon Erickson, *Violent Storms,* 108–109.

11. Harry Holmes, *The Last Patrol,* 73–74; Calvert, Silent Running, 23.

12. Alastair Couper, ed., *The Times Atlas of the Oceans,* 152; USS *Pampanito* War Patrol Report, First War Patrol.

13. Summers-Blair interview; Blair, *Silent Victory,* 640.

14. Couper, *Atlas of the Oceans,* 60–61.

15. Ibid., 66.

16. Eugene B. Fluckey, *Thunder Below! The USS* Barb *Revolutionizes Submarine Warfare in World War II*, 100–101; Schratz, *Submarine Commander*, 28–29.

17. Herbert S. Zim, *Submarines: The Story of Undersea Boats*, 112–17; Alden, letter, 8 July 1997.

18. Mendenhall, *Submarine Diary*, 2–3. Mendenhall states that enlisted men got silver dolphins, but this was not until after the war.


CHAPTER 3

1. Richard H. O'Kane, Wahoo*: The Patrols of America's Most Famous World War II Submarine*, 302–303.

2. Roscoe, *Submarine Operations*, 251–63; Friedman, *U.S. Submarines*, 243; Robert Gannon, *Hellions of the Deep: The Development of American Torpedoes in World War II*, 80, 84, 137; Clay Blair, Jr., *Hitler's U-Boat War: The Hunters, 1939–1942*, 150, 159–60, 426. Blair makes it clear that Germany also experienced scandalous torpedo failures.

3. Admiral I. J. Galantin, *Take Her Deep! A Submarine against Japan in World War II*, 103; O'Kane, Wahoo, 307; Gannon, *Hellions*, 183.

4. Blair, *Silent Victory*, 132–37, 176–78; Galantin, *Take Her Deep*, xv.

5. Blair, *Silent Victory*, 419; Lockwood and Adamson, *Hell and Deep Water*, 130.

6. Summers-Blair interview.

7. Thomas F. Walkowiak, *Fleet Submarines of World War Two*, 12; Roscoe, *Submarine Operations*, 70–71; First Patrol Report.

8. Lockwood and Adamson, *Hell and Deep Water*, 230–31.

9. *Pampanito*, First Patrol Report; Captain William J. Ruhe, *War in the Boats: My World War II Submarine Battles*, 4; James F. Dunnigan and Albert A. Nofi, *Victory at Sea: World War II in the Pacific*, 206, 226. The Japanese "Lily" was a Ki-48 light, one-engine, two-man bomber built by Kawasaki. If lookouts spotted a two-engine plane, it probably was not a "Lily."

10. Samuel Eliot Morison, *History of United States Naval Operations in World War II*, vol. 8, *New Guinea and the Marianas, March 1944–August 1944*, 29–31; Blair, *Silent Victory*, 547–49; Lockwood and Adamson, *Hell and Deep Water*, 230; Donald M. Goldstein and Katherine V. Dillon, eds., *Fading Victory: The Diary of Admiral Matome Ugaki, 1941–1945*, 344.

11. Beach, *Submarine*, 262.

12. Lockwood, *Down to the Sea*, 314–15.

13. Morison, *New Guinea and the Marianas*, 33; Edward P. Stafford, *The Big E: The Story of the USS* Enterprise, 329–30; *Pampanito*, First Patrol Report.

14. Joel Whitburn, *Top Pop Singles, 1940–1955*, 17, 20, 26, 28, 33, 41, 43.

15. Zim, *Undersea Boats*, 123–36; Friedman, *U.S. Submarines*, 259–60.

16. Weir, *Forged in War,* 41–48, Friedman, *U.S. Submarines,* 261–63; Calvert, *Silent Running,* 16, 188; Alden, letter, 8 July 1997.

17. *Pampanito,* First Patrol Report; Goldstein and Dillon, *Fading Victory,* 346.

18. A typical slow-sinking charge at 8–10 feet per second had a 5 percent chance of sinking a submarine 150 feet down. That figure fell to 1.1 percent at 400 feet and to 0.3 percent at 600 feet. Friedman, *U.S. Submarines,* 161, 205, 355; O'Kane, Wahoo, 165–66.

19. Parillo, *Merchant Marine,* 108–10.

20. Roscoe, *Submarine Operations,* 212–13; Parillo, *Merchant Marine,* 110; John Dower, *War Without Mercy: Race and Power in the Pacific War,* 260; Carl Boyd and Akihiko Yoshida, *The Japanese Submarine Force and World War II,* xiii, 26–34; Lockwood and Adamson, *Hell and Deep Water,* 129, 302; Fluckey, *Thunder Below,* 275, 306; Friedman, *U.S. Submarines,* 248, 355. In the last book, Friedman discounts the contention that the American secret of deep diving was given away. He shows that test depth was the one technical secret the Japanese failed to obtain. The U.S. Navy discovered this very fact when it captured the April 1944 Japanese antisubmarine warfare summary put out by the Japanese Battle Lessons Investigation Committee. The Japanese never discovered U.S. diving depths.

21. John Prados, *Combined Fleet Decoded: The Secret History of American Intelligence and the Japanese Navy in World War II,* 626–27; Goldstein and Dillon, *Fading Victory,* 61, 388, 400.

22. Holmes, *Last Patrol,* 189. The *Tullibee* was the twenty-ninth submarine lost up to this point, and the men lost on all of them totaled 1,637.

23. Friedman, *U.S. Submarines,* 234, 247; Wier, *Forged in War,* 49–56; Peter T. Sasgen, *Red Scorpion: The War Patrols of the* USS Rasher, 61.

24. Galantin, *Take Her Deep,* 19; Summers-Blair interview; videotape of *Pampanito* reunion, 1985.

25. Hansgeorg Jentschura, Dieter Jung, and Peter Mickel, *Warships of the Imperial Japanese Navy, 1869–1945,* 275, 278; National Archives and Records Administration (NARA), RG 457, Japanese Navy Message Translations (SRN), 23045; Japanese Naval Radio Intelligence Summaries (SRNS) 1480, Box 13. The actual *Hokuyo Maru,* a 4,216-ton transport, was already sunk by American carrier aircraft in a 17 February 1944 attack on Truk. The main ship of this convoy was probably the *Nissho Maru No. 18,* a 1,990-ton transport. It had left Guam early on 7 February and was en route to Woleai.

26. Many submarine skippers identified small escorts as a *"Chidori."* In fact, the *Chidori* ("plover") was a single boat in the four-boat class of *Tomozuru* ("flight of cranes") torpedo boats. It displaced about seven hundred tons, was 260 feet long, had a 24-foot beam and 8-foot draught, and was capable of thirty knots. Standard weapons were two 4.7-inch guns, ten 25-mm antiaircraft guns, two torpedo tubes, and forty-eight depth charges. These boats could easily be confused with the very similar *Otori* ("stork") class, a slightly improved version

of eight units. The similar high, raked bows of most Japanese escorts made identification difficult. See Jentschura, Jung, and Mickel, *Warships of the Imperial Japanese Navy,* 128–29.

27. The telltale click that precedes the explosion of a depth charge has been commented upon by many. Admiral Galantin, *Take Her Deep,* 128, said the click can be discerned only when far away. When too close, only the explosion is heard. Commander Beach, *Submarine,* 15, claimed the click is from the concussion wave preceding the explosion. The time between the click and the explosion is a measure of the distance of the depth charge. When very close, the click-wham is almost simultaneous. Vice Admiral Calvert, *Silent Running,* 85, said some sailors believed the click came from a detonator pistol inside the depth charge, but he believed it was a preliminary shock wave. He said a click always preceded a wham, but the time interval had nothing to do with the distance of the depth charge.

28. *Pampanito,* First Patrol Report; Summers-Blair interview. The thought that the Japanese had weapons that could be thrown ahead—the Y-gun projector or "hedgehog" or "mousetrap" depth charges—was apparently widespread. Yet in October 1944, after being attacked by a U.S. destroyer escort, *I-56* surfaced with an unexploded hedgehog charge sitting on its deck. It was a piece of ordnance that aroused intense interest in Japan, for they had never seen such a weapon. W. J. Holmes, *Underseas Victory II, 1943–1945: The Tide Turns,* 7; Boyd and Yoshida, *Japanese Submarine Force,* 157.

29. Summers, reunion tape; Ruhe, *War in the Boats,* 224, 260.

30. The *Fubuki* ("blizzard") class of destroyers consisted of twenty ships. Displacement was about two thousand tons, length was 370 feet, beam was 34 feet, and draught was about 11 feet. Top speed was about thirty-four knots. In 1944 they were armed with four 5-inch, 50-caliber guns, fourteen 25-mm antiaircraft guns, four 13-mm guns, nine torpedo tubes, and thirty-six depth charges. By April 1944, fourteen of the class had been sunk. See Jentschura, Jung, and Mickel, *Warships of the Imperial Japanese Navy,* 144–45.

31. Jentschura, Jung, and Mickel, *Warships of the Imperial Japanese Navy,* 143–44, 216, 226; John D. Alden, *U.S. Submarine Attacks during World War II,* 92, 94; SRN, 23045, 23204, 23447, 23448, SRNS 1480, Box 13, RG 457, NARA. Interestingly, the *Sanyo Maru* was the same ship that Summers thought he had sunk while on *Stingray. Minazuki* ("June") and *Yuzuki* ("evening moon") were built in the late 1920s as 1,770-ton destroyers, 338 feet in length, 30 feet in beam, and with a draught of just under 10 feet and a speed of thirty-seven knots. Upgrades in 1941–42 gave them two 4.7-inch guns, ten 25-mm antiaircraft guns, six torpedo tubes, and thirty-six depth charges.

32. *Pampanito,* First Patrol Report.

33. *San Francisco Progress,* 16 November 1986; Summers-Blair tape; Schratz, *Submarine Commander,* 87–88.

34. William J. Broad, *The Universe Below: Discovering the Secrets of the Deep Sea*, 18–19.

35. Gannon, *Hellions*, 118–19; Beach, *Submarine*, 33, 71; Mendenhall, *Submarine Diary*, 10.

36. Friedman, *U.S. Submarines*, 205, 210; O'Kane, Wahoo, 89–90.

37. Zim, *Undersea Boats*, 146; Woodbury, *About Submarine Warfare*, 90; Sasgen, *Red Scorpion*, 23; Alden, letter, 18 February 1998. The danger of blowing high-pressure air into ballast tanks at extreme depth has no greater illustration than in the loss of the nuclear submarine USS *Thresher* on 10 April 1963. In that case the pressure differential was probably too small to expel air fast enough at test depth of thirteen hundred feet, and expansion probably caused ice to form in the blow valves. See Robert D. Ballard, *Explorations: My Quest for Adventure under the Sea*, 5–6; Broad, *Universe Below*, 56–58.

38. Summers-Blair interview; Reunion videotape; O'Kane, Wahoo, 90; Galantin, *Take Her Deep*, 169.

39. Lockwood and Adamson, *Hell and Deep Water*, 245–52; Roscoe, *Submarine Operations*, 374; Alden, *Submarine Attacks*, 93; Dave Bouslog, *Maru Killer: The War Patrols of the USS* Seahorse, 93; SRN, 23277, 23293, 23300, RG 457, NARA. *Harder* exacted more revenge on 17 April when it sank *Matsue Maru*, albeit after that ship had unloaded its supplies and was returning to Guam. It is not known which ship, if any, *Pampanito* had hit.

40. The A6M Zero, or "Zeke," was a one-engine, one-man fighter. It had a top speed of 307 mph and a range of 850 miles. It was fast, nimble, and a most formidable adversary early in the war. Over ten thousand were built by Mitsubishi. See Dunnigan and Nofi, *Victory at Sea*, 204, 209.

41. Summers-Blair interview.

42. The crew seemed to have trouble identifying planes. If they saw a two-engine bomber, it was not a "Kate." The B5N "Kate" was a single-engine, carrier-based torpedo bomber built by Nakajima. It had an air speed of 205 mph, a range of 530 miles, and a crew of two. About eleven hundred were built, but few were still in service by 1944. See Dunnigan and Nofi, *Victory at Sea*, 204, 214.

43. *Pampanito*, First Patrol Report; Sasgen, *Red Scorpion*, 18.

44. Lockwood, *Down to the Sea*, 21; Dunnigan and Nofi, *Dirty Little Secrets*, 324; James Pack, *Nelson's Blood: The Story of Naval Rum*, 123–27.

45. Dunnigan and Nofi, *Victory at Sea*, 181–82; Calvert, *Silent Running*, 211–12.


CHAPTER 4

1. Lockwood, *Down to the Sea*, 279; Calvert, *Silent Running*, 88.

2. Galantin, *Take Her Deep*, 100–101; Lockwood, *Down to the Sea*, 269; Schratz, *Submarine Commander*, 79–80; Fluckey, *Thunder Below*, 63; John Costello, *Virtue under Fire: How World War II Changed our Social and Sexual Attitudes*, 216–18.

3. Richard H. O'Kane, *Clear the Bridge! The War Patrols of the U.S.S.* Tang, 94, 198–200.

4. Summers-Blair interview; O'Kane, *Clear the Bridge*, 141; Peter Padfield, *War beneath the Sea: Submarine Conflict during World War II*, 239, 246; Roscoe, *Submarine Operations*, 474.

5. Parillo, *Merchant Marine*, 136–39, 243; Padfield, *War beneath the Sea*, 400, 402.

6. Morison, *New Guinea and the Marianas*, 19–20; Roscoe, *Submarine Operations*, 324, 388.

7. Lockwood and Adamson, *Hell and Deep Water*, 165; Sasgen, *Red Scorpion*, 94; Schratz, *Submarine Commander*, 32, 82, 137–38

8. Padfield, *War beneath the Sea*, 353–54; Roscoe, *Submarine Operations*, 275–78.

9. Summers-Blair interview.

10. *Pampanito*, Second Patrol Report; Galantin, *Take Her Deep*, 151–52.

11. *Pampanito*, Second Patrol Report; *San Francisco Progress*, 16 November 1986; Ted Nier Swain, interview with Clay Blair, Jr.

12. Lockwood and Adamson, *Hell and Deep Water*, 137.

13. *Pampanito*, Second Patrol Report; Erickson, *Violent Storms*, 24, 47.

14. Friedman, *U.S. Submarines*, 235–36; Galantin, *Take Her Deep*, 107.

15. Galantin, *Take Her Deep*, 106; O'Kane, *Clear the Bridge*, 211; Boyd and Yoshida, *Japanese Submarine Force*, 46; Goldstein and Dillon, *Fading Victory*, 54, 59, 169.

16. *Pampanito*, Second Patrol Report; Summers-Blair tape.

17. Paul S. Dull, *A Battle History of the Imperial Japanese Navy, 1941–1945*, 320–21; Padfield, *War beneath the Sea*, 420; Blair, *Silent Victory*, 632–33, 635.

18. Goldstein and Dillon, *Fading Victory*, 415–17; Morison, *New Guinea and the Marianas*, 309.

19. *Pampanito*, Second Patrol Report; William T. Y'Blood, *Red Sun Setting: The Battle of the Philippine Sea*, 231–32; Goldstein and Dillon, *Fading Victory*, 423.

20. Beach, *Submarine*, 71; Lockwood, *Down to the Sea*, 172; Ruhe, *War in the Boats*, 116–18; Zim, *Undersea Boats*, 193–96.

21. Schratz, *Submarine Commander*, 131; O'Kane, *Clear the Bridge*, 216.

22. Couper, *Atlas of the Oceans*, 46, 50; Lyall Watson, *Heaven's Breath: A Natural History of the Wind*, 28–29.

23. *Pampanito*, Second Patrol Report. Actually, the area near the mouth of Bungo Suido was relatively unproductive for American submarines, which sank only seven ships there during the course of the entire war. One of them, the Japanese submarine *I-371*, was sunk by USS *Lagarto* (SS 371) on 24 February 1945 right off Okino Shima.

24. There are several islands named O Shima along the Japanese coast, including one off Kyushu, one off Honshu east of Kii Suido, and one south of the entrance to Tokyo Bay.

25. *Pampanito*, Second Patrol Report; Galantin, *Take Her Deep*, 45–46.

26. Zim, *Undersea Boats*, 141–45; Friedman, *U.S. Submarines*, 264; O'Kane, *Clear the Bridge*, 82; Lockwood, *Down to the Sea*, 70–71.

27. Maurice L. Demers, interview with Clay Blair, Jr.; Swain-Blair interview; William R. Wolfe, "Radio Transmitting Facility Closes," Polaris 40, no. 2 (April 1996): 10; Prados, *Combined Fleet Decoded*, 703; Galantin, *Take Her Deep*, 43–44.

28. *Pampanito*, Second Patrol Report; O'Kane, Wahoo, 192; Friedman, *U.S. Submarines*, 282–83; Calvert, *Silent Running*, 60–61.

29. Joseph F. Enright, Shinano: *The Sinking of Japan's Supership*, 34, 71. During the war, American submarines in this sector sank fifty ships, about one ship for every four miles between Shiono Misaki and Iro Zaki.

30. The eight-unit *Otori* class was improved *Tomozuru*-class (*Chidori*) torpedo boats. They were stronger-hulled, longer, and heavier, with a 9-foot draught, length of about 290 feet, and displacement of 1,040 tons. There were six *Otoris* left in July 1944. See Jentschura, Jung, and Mickel, *Warships of the Imperial Japanese Navy*, 129–30. The real *Chidori* was sunk by USS *Tilefish* (SS 307) on 22 December 1944 only about ten miles east of *Pampanito's* attack site.

31. *Pampanito*, Second Patrol Report; Weir, *Forged in War*, 62.

32. Goldstein and Dillon, *Fading Victory*, 430.

33. *Pampanito*, Second Patrol Report. Although the patrol report indicates that this torpedo incident occurred in the early morning, Brown remembered it as being bright daylight, perhaps 1600 hours, not 0400.

34. Gannon, *Hellions*, 47–48; Boyd and Yoshida, *Japanese Submarine Force*, 37.

35. Enright, *Shinano*, 29. Coming through this same area in November 1944, Captain Toshio Abe of the supercarrier *Shinano* picked up a quick radar pulse from *Archerfish*. He thought the Americans were stupid if they believed their short bursts of radar could not be detected by the Japanese.

36. *Pampanito*, Second Patrol Report; Summers-Blair interview.

37. Charles McGuire, interview with Clay Blair, Jr.

## CHAPTER 5

1. Samuel Eliot Morison, *History of United States Naval Operations in World War II*, vol. 4, *Coral Sea, Midway, and Submarine Actions, May 1942–August 1942*, 71–72; Lockwood, *Down to the Sea*, 289; Schratz, *Submarine Commander*, 97; Beach, *Submarine*, 8; Blair, *Silent Victory*, 564.

2. Howard A. Thompson, "A Special *Scabbardfish* Drink at Midway," *Polaris* 40, no. 4 (August 1996): 20; O'Kane, *Clear the Bridge*, 129; Galantin, *Take Her Deep*, 56; Fluckey, *Thunder Below*, 213, 216; Mendenhall, *Submarine Diary*, 139–40; Watson, *Heaven's Breath*, 186; Schratz, *Submarine Commander*, 91–92.

3. Robert C. Bornmann and Jan K. Herman, "Operating under Pressure," *Naval History* 10, no. 4 (July–August 1996): 27–30; Demers-Blair interview.

4. Demers-Blair interview.

5. Lockwood and Adamson, *Hell and Deep Water,* 246; Fluckey, *Thunder Below,* 30–31; Galantin, *Take Her Deep,* 195–96; O'Kane, Wahoo, 192; Russell W. Howe, *The Hunt for Tokyo Rose,* 5, 23, 49, 65, 113, 199.

6. Blair, *Silent Victory,* 178; Joan Blair and Clay Blair, Jr., *Return from the River Kwai,* 88; Alden, *Submarine Attacks,* 236–43. The last compilation indicates that at least twenty-seven submarines made between two and eight patrols without hitting a Japanese ship.

7. O'Kane, *Clear the Bridge,* 301, 364; Alden, *Submarine Attacks,* 122, 123, 125–27.

8. *Pampanito,* Third Patrol Report; Blair, *Silent Victory,* 680–81; Blair, *River Kwai,* 84–85; Summers-Blair interview.

9. Fluckey, *Thunder Below,* 81–86; Blair, *Silent Victory,* 681; Alden, *Submarine Attacks,* 128–29; Alden, letter, 18 February 1998. In the letter, Alden indicates that the Joint Army-Navy Assessment Committee (JANAC) interpreted the ship's name as *Okuni Maru.* His sources identify it as *Taikoku Maru.*

10. *Pampanito,* Third Patrol Report; T. B. Oakley, Jr., Task Group 17.17 Patrol Report; Swain-Blair interview.

11. *Pampanito,* Third Patrol Report; Blair, *River Kwai,* 88–89.

12. *Pampanito,* Third Patrol Report; TG 17.17 Report; Fluckey, *Thunder Below,* 106.

13. *Pampanito,* Third Patrol Report; TG 17.17 Report; Blair, *River Kwai,* 89–90.

14. *Pampanito,* Third Patrol Report; Blair, *River Kwai,* 94–99; Blair, *Silent Victory,* 682; Richard J. Sherlock, interview with Clay Blair, Jr.; Padfield, *War Beneath the Sea,* 413–14; Roscoe, *Submarine Operations,* 205, 376–77; Office of the Chief of Naval Operations, Operational Records Series (ONS), Box 195, RG38, NARA. In Blair's *Silent Victory* (1975) he correctly listed the first ship *Growler* sank in this attack as *Hirado.* In Blair's *River Kwai* (1979), he incorrectly reconstructed the attack as being against the destroyer *Shikinami* and stated that this was a down-the-throat, bow-to-bow, surface shot at a Japanese destroyer, a feat never done before or since. The first part is true, but the attack was not against a destroyer. *Growler* first sank *Hirado,* a patrol craft about half the weight and half the speed of a fleet destroyer. *Hirado* was one of fourteen units in the *Etorofu* class. It weighed about 870 tons and had a speed of nineteen knots. It carried three 4.7-inch guns, fifteen 25-mm antiaircraft guns, and sixty depth charges. See Jentschura, Jung, and Mickel, *Warships of the Imperial Japanese Navy,* 187.

15. Summers-Blair interview; *Pampanito,* Third Patrol Report; Swain-Blair interview; O'Kane, *Clear the Bridge,* 42; Demers-Blair interview; Sherlock-Blair interview.

16. *Pampanito,* Third Patrol Report; William F. Yagemann, interview with Clay Blair, Jr.; Alden, *Submarine Attacks,* 132–33.

17. Blair, *River Kwai*, 106, 114, 132–33, 135, 143–44, 168; Fluckey, *Thunder Below*, 107, 114, 121; TG 17.17 Report. Blair's description of *Growler*'s attacks are excellent except for confusing *Shikinami* with *Hirado*. Oakley did correctly identify his target as a *Fubuki*-class destroyer.

18. *Pampanito*, Third Patrol Report; O'Kane, *Clear the Bridge*, 100; Swain-Blair interview.

19. Blair, *River Kwai*, 157; Swain-Blair interview. Blair states that the convoy was still on a westerly course heading for Hainan, and Summers "stumbled" across its track by "sheer luck." Studying intercepted Japanese radio messages, plotting the convoy's course, and noting how *Pampanito* finally relocated the convoy tells a different story. The convoy's announced positions and rendezvous point at 19 degrees north, 112 degrees east shows it had been heading toward Hainan, with a stated destination of Yulin, on Hainan's south coast. When the rendezvous point was reached at dusk, it made a radical change to the north, probably with the intention of dodging pursuing submarines. It was on a northerly course when *Pampanito* found it, and not until the attack did it zig west again toward Hainan. Far from stumbling into luck, *Pampanito*'s tracking party made an excellent decision.

20. Blair, *River Kwai*, 88; Sherlock-Blair interview.

21. Blair, *River Kwai*, 158; Swain-Blair interview. Swain's statements to Blair that he ran forward and directed Jim Behney to break the linkage in number four tube is disputed by Woodrow Weaver. Weaver insisted Swain was wrong on several accounts: Weaver was in charge of the forward room, not Behney; the bent gyro spindle in tube four had no bearing on the other five—they were set independently; Behney was not ordered by Swain to break a linkage, for if he had broken it, they would never have been able to open the outer door to eject the torpedo; and Swain would have had to get past Weaver to get to Behney, which he never did.

22. Demers-Blair interview.

23. *Pampanito*, Third Patrol Report; Blair, *River Kwai*, 159, 209; Summers-Blair interview; Swain-Blair interview; O'Kane, *Clear the Bridge*, 203; Alden, *Submarine Attacks*, 133. Summers claimed he sank four ships, including a "rubber ship" that burned for three days, but JANAC credited him only with the *Kachidoki Maru* and the 5,100-ton tanker *Zuiho Maru*.

24. SRN (Japanese Navy Message Translations), Entry 9014, Box 44, RG 457, NARA. Japanese radio intercepts indicate that there were no destroyer escorts with this convoy. Two of the remaining escorts at this time were *Coast Defense Vessel No. 11* and *Subchaser No. 19*.

25. *Pampanito*, Third Patrol Report; Blair, *River Kwai*, 167.

26. Calvert, *Silent Running*, 24.

27. McGuire-Blair interview; Swain-Blair interview; Sherlock-Blair interview; *Pampanito*, Third Patrol Report. The officers never could agree on torpedo firing

ranges for the attacks on 12–13 September, and references to distances were omitted from the patrol report.

28. Padfield, *War beneath the Sea*, 14–15; Sherlock-Blair interview; Swain-Blair interview.

29. Eric Bergerud, *Touched With Fire: The Land War in the South Pacific*, 100–101.

30. *Pampanito*, Third Patrol Report; Summers-Blair interview; Blair, *River Kwai*, 199. The smoldering wreckage was probably the remains of the tanker *Zuiho Maru*.

31. Blair, *River Kwai*, 209–10; Padfield, *War beneath the Sea*, 149, 381; John Bunker, "One Night of Hell," *Naval History* 9, no. 4 (July–August 1995): 9; Bernard Edwards, *Blood and Bushido: Japanese Atrocities at Sea 1941-1945*, 21, 57, 64, 73, 76, 95, 130, 213.

32. Mendenhall, *Submarine Diary*, 145; Ruhe, *War in the Boats*, 178; O'Kane, Wahoo, 153–54.

33. Blair, *River Kwai*, 210–11; Sherlock-Blair interview; Swain-Blair interview; Yagemann-Blair interview. More than thirty years after the incident, Dick Sherlock compared the plan to shoot the men in the water to a 1968 Vietnam massacre. "It was a My Lai type of approach," he said. "But you would have gotten a medal for it back in 1944."

## CHAPTER 6

1. John Costello, *The Pacific War*, 216–17, 232–33; John Toland, *The Rising Sun: The Decline and Fall of the Japanese Empire, 1936–1945*, 345; Gavan Daws, *Prisoners of the Japanese: POWs of World War II in the Pacific*, 96–98.

2. Costello, *Pacific War*, 427–29; Ernest Gordon, *Through the Valley of the Kwai*, 67–69, 188, 217; Meirion Harries and Susie Harries, *Soldiers of the Sun: The Rise and Fall of the Imperial Japanese Army*, 309–10, 476; Gavan McCormack and Hank Nelson, eds., *The Burma–Thailand Railway: Memory and History*, 61–62; Eric Lomax, *The Railway Man: A True Story of War, Remembrance, and Forgiveness*, 268; Blair, *River Kwai*, 40.

3. Annex to Patrol Report, "Rescue of British and Australian Prisoner-of-War Survivors," 28 September 1944, Story of C. Anderson; Blair, *River Kwai*, 36, 39–40, 44.

4. Letter from K. C. Renton, in "Life Story of Woodrow Weaver," typed manuscript, 1995, 44A–44E.

5. Ken Williams, letter, February 1997; Leslie Hall, *The Blue Haze: POWs on the Burma Railway*, 18–20, 105.

6. Cliff L. Farlow, taped interview, March 1997; Harold D. Martin, taped interview, February 1997; Harold D. Martin, letter, 10 February 1997; Hall, *Blue Haze*, 139, 143.

7. Blair, *River Kwai*, 19, 22, 27–29; Hall, *Blue Haze*, 73; Roydon C. Cornford, letter, January 1997; M. R. Farrands, letters, 20 February and 14 March 1997.

8. Blair, *River Kwai*, 29, 32–34, 47, 54–58, 60, 236; R. Cornford, letter, January 1997; K. Williams, letter, February 1997; R. Farrands, letter, 20 February 1997.

9. The *Shincho Maru* may be a garbled radio translation of the *Shinshu Maru*, a 4,182-ton oiler that was later sunk by the USS *Bergall* (SS 320), 13 October 1944.

10. SRN, Entry 9014, Box 44, RG 457, NARA; Kyle Thompson, *A Thousand Cups of Rice: Surviving the Death Railway*, iii. Although the great majority of POWs who worked the Burma–Siam Railway were Australian and British, a small portion were Americans, mostly from the 2nd Battalion, 131st Field Artillery Regiment, and the survivors from the cruiser USS *Houston*, slightly more than nine hundred men.

11. SRN, Entry 9014, Box 44, RG 457, NARA; David H. Grover, "The Turncoat Transport: President Harrison," *Sea Classics* 21, no. 3 (March 1988): 19–24. Four other "presidents" became the hospital ships *Bountiful, Refuge, Rescue*, and *Samaritan*.

12. Shinchichiro Komamiya, *Senji Yuso Sendan Shi* [Wartime Transportation Convoys' History], 246–49; SRN, Entry 9014, Box 44, RG 457, NARA. The *Mikura* class of patrol vessels displaced 1,020 tons, were 258 feet long, and had a draught of 10 feet. Their top speed was about twenty knots, and they carried three 4.7-inch antiaircraft guns, fourteen 25-mm antiaircraft guns, and up to 120 depth charges. See Jentschura, Jung, and Mickel, *Warships of the Imperial Japanese Navy*, 187–88.

13. SRN, Entry 9014, RG 457, NARA; Blair, *River Kwai*, 61, 66, 68–69, 71; R. Farrands, letter, 20 February 1997; R. Cornford, letter, January 1997; Gordon, *Valley of the Kwai*, 190–91.

14. Komamiya, *Senji Yuso*, 246–49; SRN, Entry 9014, Box 44, RG 457, NARA. *Coastal Defense Vessels No. 10* and *No. 20* were Type D patrol boats. Most were built late in the war with prefabricated parts in a program to increase the dwindling escort fleet. They displaced about 940 tons, were 228 feet long, and had a 10-foot draught. Top speed was just seventeen knots, but they could carry 120 depth charges. See Jentschura, Jung, and Mickel, *Warships of the Imperial Japanese Navy*, 190–91.

15. Blair, *River Kwai*, 73–75, 100–103; H. Martin tape; George K. Ward, letter to Hubert Brown.

16. Blair, *River Kwai*, 111–13; Komamiya, *Senji Yuso*, 246–49; R. Farrands, letter, 20 February 1997; John R. Hocking, letter, 22 May 1997.

17. Blair, *River Kwai*, 116–17, 119, 122, 126–28; C. Farlow tape; R. Farrands, letter, 20 February 1997.

18. Blair, *River Kwai*, 25, 32, 133–34; R. Cornford, letter, January 1997.

19. SRN, Entry 9014, Box 44, RG 457; ONS, Box 195, RG 38, NARA; Patrol Report Annex, story of C. Anderson; K. Williams, letter, February 1997; Blair, *River Kwai*, 118, 139, 150–54.

20. SRN, Entry 9014, Box 44, RG 457, NARA; Blair, *River Kwai*, 160–63, 166; Komamiya, *Senji Yuso*, 246–49. Japanese sources say that *Kachidoki Maru* took about fifty minutes to sink. Blair claims she took two hits, stood on end, and sank in fifteen minutes, taking seven hundred people down with her.

21. H. Martin tape; K. Williams, letter, February 1997; R. Cornford, letter, January 1997; Blair, *River Kwai*, 141, 180–87, 202–207.

22. ONS, Box 195, RG 38; SRN, Box 45, RG 457, NARA; Blair, *River Kwai*, 192–93; Linda Goetz Holmes, *Four Thousand Bowls of Rice: A Prisoner of War Comes Home*, 76–77.

23. Edwin T. Layton, *"And I Was There": Pearl Harbor and Midway Breaking the Secrets*, 298, 430; John Winton, *Ultra in the Pacific: How Breaking Japanese Codes and Cyphers Affected Naval Operation against Japan, 1941–1945*, 97–100.

24. Layton, *I Was There*, 81, 471; Alan Stripp, *Codebreaker in the Far East: How Britain Cracked Japan's Top Secret Military Codes*, 65, 67–79.

25. Stripp, *Codebreaker in the Far East*, 70–71; Edward J. Drea, *MacArthur's ULTRA: Codebreaking and the War against Japan, 1942–1945*, 74–76; Layton, *I Was There*, 472–73; W. J. Holmes, *Double-Edged Secrets: U.S. Naval Intelligence Operations in the Pacific during World War II*, 117.

26. Prados, *Combined Fleet Decoded*, 405–407; Layton, *I Was There*, 471.

27. Haruko T. Cook and Theodore F. Cook, *Japan at War: An Oral History*, 88; Costello, *Pacific War*, 515, 600.

28. Padfield, *War Beneath the Sea*, 196, 239, 246, 249; Parillo, *Merchant Marine*, 97–99, 134, 137–38; Holmes, *Underseas Victory*, 42. In Sasgen, *Red Scorpion*, 147, the author claims that small convoys were easier to protect. This does not appear to be the case.

29. Parillo, *Merchant Marine*, 139–42. The *Take* Convoy was escorted by the number six escort commander, Rear Admiral Kajioka, who rode in the coal-burning minelayer *Shirataka*. He later lost his life and his flagship, *Hirado*, to the torpedoes of *Growler*.

30. Fluckey, *Thunder Below*, 107; Drea, *MacArthur's Ultra*, 61, 64–66, 71; Lex McAulay, *Battle of the Bismarck Sea*, 19, 36–38.

31. Drea, *MacArthur's Ultra*, 93, 100, 106, 156, 176–77; Roscoe, *Submarine Operations*, 331–34, 343–45; Calvert, *Silent Running*, 129; Boyd and Yoshida, *Japanese Submarine Force*, 129–30; Stripp, *Codebreaker in the Far East*, 47, 66; Bruce Lee, *Marching Orders: The Untold Story of World War II*, 246.

32. ONS, Box 195, RG 38, NARA; Lee, *Marching Orders*, 234–35.

33. Van Waterford, *Prisoners of the Japanese in World War II*, 356; Roger Dingman, *Ghost of War: The Sinking of the Awa Maru and Japanese-American Relations, 1945–1995*, 73; Don Wall, *Heroes at Sea*, 19; Don Wall, letter, 13 March 1997.

34. SRNS, Entry 1485, Box 15; SRN, Entry 9014, Boxes 44, 45, RG 457, NARA; Stripp, Codebreaker in the Far East, x; Lee, *Marching Orders*, vii, ix, 16. Don Wall, in *Heroes at Sea*, p. 19, believes that if the Americans knew the ships were carrying

bauxite, they also knew about the POWs. It was their job to sink ships, and the POWs were expendable.

35. Yuki Tanaka, *Hidden Horrors: Japanese War Crimes in World War II*, 2, 13, 15; Wall, *Heroes at Sea*, 4–5, 12, 134, 138; O'Kane, *Clear the Bridge*, 217; Thompson, *Thousand Cups of Rice*, 173–76.

36. Daws, *Prisoners of the Japanese*, 285–87, 292–95; Donald Knox, *Death March: The Survivors of Bataan*, 344, 349, 356–57; William B. Breuer, *The Great Raid on Cabanatuan: Rescuing the Doomed Ghosts of Bataan and Corregidor*, 121–22, 139; Alden, *Submarine Attacks*, 12, 18, 130, 146.

37. Pence Collection, University of California, San Diego Library, Box 2, Folder 3; Daws, *Prisoners of the Japanese*, 295–97; Breuer, *Great Raid*, 100–101, 152, 200. Lockwood is cited in Winton, *ULTRA in the Pacific*, 193. My unfinished manuscript, "Death on the Hellships," thus far documents the stories of over one hundred POW transports.

38. Tanaka, *Horrors of War*, 75–76; John Dower, *War Without Mercy*, 11.

39. Patrol Report Annex: Names of British and Australian Survivors; Blair, *River Kwai*, 211–12; H. Martin tape; K. Williams, letter, February 1997; Renton to Weaver, in Weaver, "Life Story," 44F.

## CHAPTER 7

1. Blair, *River Kwai*, 211–15; K. Williams, letter, February 1997; Summers-Blair interview; Yagemann-Blair interview; C. Farlow tape; Wall, *Heroes at Sea*, 44, 61; R. Farrands, letter, 20 February 1997; R. Cornford, letter, January 1997; Patrol Report Annex, "Rescue of Survivors."

2. Peder A. Granum, interview with Clay Blair, Jr.

3. Blair, *River Kwai*, 215–18, 235–36; Swain-Blair interview; R. Farrands, letter, 20 February 1997; Renton to Weaver, in Weaver, "Life Story," 44F–44G; Demers-Blair interview.

4. Blair, *River Kwai*, 220–21; Blair, *Silent Victory*, 683–85; Fluckey, *Thunder Below*, 121–22, 136–37.

5. Blair, *Silent Victory*, 685; Fluckey, *Thunder Below*, 138–47.

6. Demers-Blair interview; McGuire-Blair interview; Blair, *River Kwai*, 237; Reunion videotape; Fluckey, *Thunder Below*, 147.

7. Roy Cornford, letter, 11 August 1997; McGuire-Blair interview; G. Ward letter; Blair, *River Kwai*, 236.

8. Blair, *River Kwai*, 238, 256–59, 266–67; H. Martin tape; R. Cornford, letter, January 1997; Demers-Blair interview; Swain-Blair interview; Patrol Report Annex: "Rescue of Survivors."

9. Demers-Blair interview; Morison, *New Guinea and the Marianas*, 338–40; Schratz, *Submarine Commander*, 163–64, 166–67; William Manchester, *Goodbye Darkness: A Memoir of the Pacific War*, 363.

CHAPTER 8

1. Landon L. Davis, Jr., Officer Biography Sheet, 26 August 1949; Blair, *Silent Victory*, 347–48; Roscoe, *Submarine Operations*, 207–208; Demers-Blair interview; Arnold W. Schade, letter 6 March 1997. In the letter, Schade said he could not fully trust his memory after fifty years and did not know exactly what happened up on the bridge. However, he did concur that Davis, as the diving officer, was the one who told the quartermaster to sound the diving alarm "and instructed the planesmen to take her down."

2. *Pampanito* Muster Roll, 28 October 1944; Demers-Blair interview.

3. Paul F. Boller, Jr., *Presidential Campaigns*, 261–66; Sidney Lens, *Radicalism in America*, 330, 332, 334–35; Ronald Lewin, *The American Magic: Codes, Ciphers, and the Defeat of Japan*, 8–11; Padfield, *War Beneath the Sea*, 277–78; Breuer, *Great Raid*, 75–76; Howe, *Tokyo Rose*, 188.

4. Padfield, *War Beneath the Sea*, 270; Fluckey, *Thunder Below*, 219.

5. Summers-Blair interview; Frank W. Fenno, Jr., Officer Biography Sheet; Roscoe, *Submarine Operations*, 79–80; Blair, *Silent Victory*, 432, 572–73.

6. *Pampanito*, Fourth Patrol Report; Rob Roy McGregor, letter, January 1997; Blair, *Silent Victory*, 150, 353, 619, 640, 834; Holmes, *Last Patrol*, 111, 146.

7. Group Commander's (F. W. Fenno's) Report of War Patrol, 28 October to 18 December 1944; Martin Caidin, *A Torch to the Enemy: The Fire Raid on Tokyo*, 52; Howe, *Tokyo Rose*, 305.

8. Galantin, *Take Her Deep*, 261, 269, 277, 281, 288; Parillo, *Merchant Marine*, 243, 243.

9. Goldstein and Dillon, *Fading Victory*, 518–20. The Japanese luck did not last. Having passed safely through Convoy College and Formosa Strait, they ran into *Sealion II* sixty miles north of Keelung. In the early hours of 21 November, Eli Reich torpedoed the destroyer *Urakaze* and the battleship *Kongo*, the first and only battleship to be sunk by an American submarine during the war.

10. Lewin, *American Magic*, 220. In May 1943, Admiral King expressly banned mention of ULTRA in submarine "war diaries." In July, ComSubPac reiterated the warning: "Neither actually nor by implication should reference be made to ULTRA messages sent by this command x same rule applies for writing up patrol reports."

11. *Pampanito*, Fourth Patrol Report; Group Commander's Report; SRN, Entry 9014, Box 52, RG 457, NARA; Alden, *Submarine Attacks*, xv, xvi, 157; Jentschura, Jung, and Mickel, *Warships of the Imperial Japanese Navy*, 274; Roscoe, *Submarine Operations*, 543. JANAC listed only Japanese sinkings of over 500 tons, and thus Roscoe's compilation does not list the 459-ton *Banshu Maru No. 17* as *Pampanito*'s victim. Jentschura, Jung, and Mickel credit USS *Gunnell* (SS 253) with sinking *Banshu Maru No. 17*, but *Gunnell*'s attack was against a seven-ship convoy, and it occurred ten hours earlier and one hundred miles southwest of *Pampanito*'s attack. The message sent by *Banshu Maru No. 17* definitely places it at the scene of *Pampanito*'s attack.

12. *Pampanito,* Fourth Patrol Report; Couper, *Atlas of the Oceans,* 49; Watson, *Heaven's Breath,* 55; Erikson, *Violent Storms,* 139, 145, 185–86; Dunnigan and Nofi, *Victory at Sea,* 193. A great typhoon hit U.S. Task Force 38 on 17 December 1944 in the Philippine Sea. Three destroyers were sunk, twenty ships were damaged, and over eight hundred sailors were killed.

13. *Pampanito,* Fourth Patrol Report; Group Commander's Report; Alden, *Submarine Attacks,* 161–62.

14. *Pampanito,* Fourth Patrol Report; Group Commander's Report; R. McGregor, letter, January 1997; Alden, *Submarine Attacks,* 161–62; J. Alden, letter, 8 July 1997. During Alden's research after the publication of his book, he found that the only ship sunk was *Coast Defense Vessel No. 64* by *Pipefish. Seishin Maru* was damaged by *Searaven,* and *Harima Maru* was probably hit once by *Searaven* and twice by *Sea Cat* but still did not sink.

15. The Central Philippines were declared Air-Surface Zones in November and December 1944, excluding U.S. submarines. Landings were made on Mindoro in mid-December, and the Third Fleet's aircraft rampaged throughout the islands. After USS *Robalo* (SS 273) was lost in the Balabac Strait minefield between Palawan and Borneo in July, that route was closed to submarines. Passage between Australia and the South China Sea was through Karimata Strait. *Pampanito* only used the Sulu Sea–Makassar Strait because of her dwindling fuel situation. See Holmes, *Underseas Victory,* 115, 164, 184, 186.

16. Reunion videotape; Beach, *Submarine,* 121–22; Lockwood and Adamson, *Hell and Deep Water,* 166; Dunnigan and Nofi, *Dirty Little Secrets,* 273; O'Kane, *Clear the Bridge,* 188; Schratz, *Submarine Commander,* 261. William Bruckart claimed that "no one was qualified in subs unless he had blown an inboard slug into his face. I am qualified from an experience aboard the *Plunger.*"

17. Couper, *Atlas of the Oceans,* 151; Blair, *Silent Victory,* 772–73.

18. Blair, *Silent Victory,* 260, 362–63; Prados, *Combined Fleet Decoded,* 421; Mendenhall, *Submarine Diary,* 46; Richard R. Lingeman, *Don't You Know There's a War On? The American Home Front,* 1941–1945, 223.


CHAPTER 9

1. Lockwood, *Down to the Sea,* 272; Calvert, *Silent Running,* 136–37; Demers-Blair interview.

2. Costello, *Virtue Under Fire,* 1, 17, 123, 239; Manchester, *Goodbye Darkness,* 88–90, 400; Peter Richmond, *My Father's War: A Son's Journey,* 93.

3. McGuire-Blair interview.

4. Costello, *Virtue Under Fire,* 86, 88, 96–97; O'Kane, *Wahoo,* 304.

5. Calvert, *Silent Running,* 139; Ruhe, *War in the Boats,* 233; Yagemann-Blair interview; Blair, *River Kwai,* 285.

6. Ruhe, *War in the Boats,* 242; Calvert, *Silent Running,* 142–43; *Pampanito,* Sailing list of 23 January 1945.

7. *Pampanito,* Fifth Patrol Report; Summers-Blair interview; F. Fenno, Officer Biography Sheet.

8. Blair, *River Kwai,* 285; Demers-Blair interview; Holmes, *Last Patrol,* 149–50; *Pampanito,* Fifth Patrol Report; *Pampanito,* Muster Rolls, 23 January 1945.

9. *Pampanito,* Fifth Patrol Report; Larry Kimmett and Margaret Regis, *U.S. Submarines in World War II: An Illustrated History,* 124, 125; Prados, *Combined Fleet Decoded,* 421; Samuel Eliot Morison, *History of United States Naval Operations in World War II,* Vol 3, *The Rising Sun in the Pacific,* 358, 368.

10. Samuel Eliot Morison, *History of United States Naval Operations in World War II,* Vol. 13, *The Liberation of the Philippines Luzon, Mindanao, the Visayas, 1944–1945,* 176; Demers-Blair interview.

11. *Pampanito,* Fifth Patrol Report; Morison, *Rising Sun in the Pacific,* 189–90; Alden, *Submarine Attacks,* 176; Komamiya, *Senji Yuso,* 375.

12. *Pampanito,* Fifth Patrol Report; Alden, *Submarine Attacks,* 176, 177; Swain-Blair interview; O'Kane, Wahoo, 168.

13. *Pampanito,* Fifth Patrol Report; Swain-Blair interview; Demers-Blair interview.


CHAPTER 10


1. Blair, *Silent Victory,* 789–90, 820–21; Morison, *Liberation of the Philippines,* 198–99.

2. *Pampanito,* Sixth Patrol report; Schratz, *Submarine Commander,* 320; Morison, *Liberation of the Philippines,* 200–202; Demers-Blair interview.

3. Blair, *Silent Victory,* 821–24; Morison, *Liberation of the Philippines,* 284; Roscoe, *Submarine Operations,* 452–53.

4. *Pampanito,* Sixth Patrol Report; Roscoe, *Submarine Operations,* 459; Mendenhall, *Submarine Diary,* 262–63; Wall, *Heroes at Sea,* 115; Dingman, *Ghost of War,* 39, 41–43.

5. *Pampanito,* Sixth Patrol Report; Mendenhall, *Submarine Diary,* 263–64; Blair, *Silent Victory,* 811–13; Roscoe, *Submarine Operations,* 459–60; Dingman, *Ghost of War,* 7, 50–51, 73, 91, 95, 157, 236.

6. *Pampanito,* Sixth Patrol Report; Demers-Blair interview.

7. Lingeman, *There's a War On,* 182–83; Costello, *Virtue under Fire,* 149–51, 153; Mark Gabor, *The Pin-Up: A Modest History,* 13, 122–126; Russell Booth, "Letters from Home," *The National Maritime Museum Association Sea Letter* 49 (Fall/Winter 1994).

8. *Pampanito,* Sixth Patrol Report; Alden, *Submarine Attacks,* 186.

9. Holmes, *Last Patrol,* 173-75.

10. C. L. Bennett, Report of Coordinated Attack Group 17.14. In an interesting note, on 2 March near Pratas Island, *Sea Owl* recovered a life ring that appeared to bear the inscription, "*Ryuko Maru*—Dairen." Since the *Ryuko Maru* was sunk by carrier aircraft near Palau on 30 March 1944, and *Sea Owl* found the life ring only about two hundred miles northeast of where the *Rakuyo Maru* went down, this may have been a lifesaver used by one of the rescued POWs.

11. Report of Attack Group 17.14; Demers-Blair interview; Costello, *Pacific War,* 606. Although Bennett claimed he sank a 2,800-ton boat, *Sea Owl* was credited by JANAC with sinking the small, 889-ton submarine, *RO-56.* However, Japanese sources show the *RO-56* was sunk on 9 April by American destroyers off Okinodaito-Jima, southeast of Okinawa and over two thousand miles away from Wake Island. Another possible victim of *Sea Owl*'s attack might have been the *RO-46.* Japanese sources show that it was last heard from on 17 April but was probably lost in an attack by U.S. aircraft, also off Okinodaito-Jima. See Roscoe, *Submarine Operations,* 551; Alden, *Submarine Attacks,* 193; Boyd and Yoshida, *Japanese Submarine Force,* 216.

12. Ruhe, *War in the Boats,* 17.

13. *Pampanito* Muster Rolls, 31 May, 30 June 1945; Paul E. Summers, Officer Biography Sheet, Naval Historical Center, Washington, D.C.; Swain-Blair interview.

14. Blair, *Silent Victory,* 582, 925, 935; USS *Grouper,* Report of Twelfth War Patrol.

15. Dunnigan and Nofi, *Dirty Little Secrets,* 367; John Ray Skates, *The Invasion of Japan: Alternative to the Bomb,* 63–66; Lingeman, *There's a War On,* 217, 264.

# Bibliography

PUBLISHED SOURCES

Alden, John D. *The Fleet Submarine in the U.S. Navy: A Design and Construction History.* Annapolis: Naval Institute Press, 1979.

———. *U.S. Submarine Attacks during World War II.* Annapolis: Naval Institute Press, 1989.

Ballard, Robert D. *Explorations: My Quest for Adventure under the Sea.* New York: Hyperion, 1995.

Beach, Commander Edward L. *Submarine!* New York: Holt, Rinehart and Winston, 1952.

Bergerud, Eric. *Touched with Fire: The Land War in the South Pacific.* New York: Viking Penguin, 1996.

Blair, Clay, Jr. *Hitler's U-Boat War: The Hunters, 1939–1942.* New York: Random House, 1996.

———. *Silent Victory: The U.S. Submarine War against Japan.* Book Club ed. New York: J. B. Lippincott Company, 1975.

Blair, Joan, and Clay Blair, Jr. *Return from the River Kwai.* New York: Simon & Schuster, 1979.

Boller, Paul F., Jr. *Presidential Campaigns.* New York: Oxford University Press, 1984.

Booth, Russell. "Letters from Home." *The National Maritime Museum Association Sea Letter* 49 (Fall–Winter 1994).

———. "Frank Farmer: A Life Remembered." *The National Maritime Museum Association Sea Letter* 51 (Spring 1996): 23–26.

Bouslog, Dave. *Maru Killer: The War Patrols of the USS* Seahorse. Sarasota, Fla.: Seahorse Books, 1996.

Bornmann, Robert C., and Jan K. Herman. "Operating under Pressure." *Naval History* 10, no. 4 (July–August 1996): 27–30.

Boyd, Carl, and Akihiko Yoshida. *The Japanese Submarine Force and World War II.* Annapolis: Naval Institute Press, 1995.

Breuer, William B. *The Great Raid on Cabanatuan: Rescuing the Doomed Ghosts of Bataan and Corregidor.* New York; John Wiley & Sons, 1994.

Broad, William J. *The Universe Below: Discovering the Secrets of the Deep Sea.* New York: Simon & Schuster, 1997.

Bunker, John. "One Night of Hell." *Naval History* 9, no. 4 (July–August 1995): 6–11.

Caidin, Martin. *A Torch to the Enemy: The Fire Raid on Tokyo.* New York: Ballantine Books, 1960.

Calvert, James F. *Silent Running: My Years on a World War II Attack Submarine.* New York: John Wiley & Sons, 1995.

Cook, Haruko T., and Theodore F. Cook. *Japan at War: An Oral History.* New York: The New Press, 1992.

Cooper, Kip. "Dramatic WWII Sub Action Recalled in Meeting Here." *San Diego Union,* 20 May 1968.

Costello, John. *The Pacific War.* New York: Rawson, Wade Publishers, 1981.

———. *Virtue under Fire: How World War II Changed our Social and Sexual Attitudes.* Boston: Little, Brown and Company, 1985.

Couper, Alastair, ed. *The Times Atlas of the Oceans.* New York: Van Nostrand Reinhold Company, 1983.

Daws, Gavan. *Prisoners of the Japanese: POWs of World War II in the Pacific.* New York: William Morrow and Company, 1994.

Dingman, Roger. *Ghost of War: The Sinking of the Awa Maru and Japanese-American Relations, 1945–1995.* Annapolis, Md.: Naval Institute Press, 1997.

Dower, John. *War without Mercy: Race and Power in the Pacific War.* New York: Pantheon Books, 1986.

Drea, Edward J. *MacArthur's ULTRA: Codebreaking and the War against Japan, 1942–1945.* Lawrence: University of Kansas Press, 1992.

Dull, Paul S. *A Battle History of the Imperial Japanese Navy (1941–1945).* Annapolis: Naval Institute Press, 1978.

Dunnigan, James F., and Albert A. Nofi. *Dirty Little Secrets of World War II.* New York: William Morrow and Company, 1994.

———. *Victory at Sea: World War II in the Pacific.* New York: William Morrow and Company, 1995.

Edwards, Bernard. *Blood and Bushido: Japanese Atrocities at Sea, 1941–1945.* New York: Brick Tower Press, 1997.

Enright, Joseph F. Shinano: *The Sinking of Japan's Supership.* New York: St. Martin's Press, 1987.

Erickson, Jon. *Violent Storms.* Blue Ridge Summit, Pa.: Tab Books, 1988.

Fluckey, Eugene B. *Thunder Below! The USS Barb Revolutionizes Submarine Warfare in World War II.* Urbana: University of Illinois Press, 1992.

Frank, Richard B. *Guadalcanal: The Definitive Account of the Landmark Battle.* New York: Penguin Books, 1990.

Friedman, Norman. *U.S. Submarines through 1945: An Illustrated Design History.* Annapolis: Naval Institute Press, 1995.

Gabor, Mark. *The Pin-Up: A Modest History.* New York: Universe Books, 1973.

Galantin, Admiral I. J. *Take Her Deep! A Submarine against Japan in World War II.* New York: Pocket Books, 1988.

Gannon, Robert. *Hellions of the Deep: The Development of American Torpedoes in World War II.* University Park, Pa.: Penn State University Press, 1996.

Goldstein, Donald M., and Katherine V. Dillon, eds. *Fading Victory: The Diary of Admiral Matome Ugaki, 1941–1945.* Pittsburgh, Pa.: University of Pittsburgh Press, 1991.

Gordon, Ernest. *Through the Valley of the Kwai.* New York: Harper & Brothers, 1962.

Grover, David H. "The Turncoat Transport: President Harrison," *Sea Classics* 21, no. 3 (March 1988): 18–26, 61.

Hall, Leslie. *The Blue Haze: POWs on the Burma Railway.* Kenthurst, New South Wales: Kangaroo Press, 1996.

Harries, Meirion, and Susie Harries. *Soldiers of the Sun: The Rise and Fall of the Imperial Japanese Army.* New York: Random House, 1991.

Holmes, Harry. *The Last Patrol.* Shrewsbury, England: Airlife Publishing Ltd., 1994.

Holmes, Linda Goetz. *Four Thousand Bowls of Rice: A Prisoner of War Comes Home.* Saint Leonards, New South Wales: Allen & Unwin, 1993.

Holmes, W. J. *Double-Edged Secrets: U.S. Naval Intelligence Operations in the Pacific during World War II.* New York: Berkley Books, 1981.

———. *Underseas Victory II, 1943–1945: The Tide Turns.* New York: Zebra Books, 1979.

Howe, Russell W. *The Hunt for Tokyo Rose.* Lanham, Md.: Madison Books, 1990.

Jentschura, Hansgeorg; Dieter Jung; and Peter Mickel. *Warships of the Imperial Japanese Navy, 1869–1945.* Annapolis: Naval Institute Press, 1986.

Kelly, Jim. "Old Crew Recalls Best, Worst of Times on Vintage Submarine." *San Francisco Progress,* 16 November 1986.

Kimmett, Larry, and Margaret Regis. *U.S. Submarines in World War II: An Illustrated History.* Seattle: Navigator Publishing, 1996.

Knox, Donald. *Death March: The Survivors of Bataan.* San Diego: Harcourt Brace & Company, 1981.

Komamiya, Shinchichiro. *Senji Yuso Sendan Shi* [Wartime Transportation Convoys' History]. Tokyo: Shuppan Kyodosha, 1987. (Title translated by William G. Somerville.)

LaVO, Carl. *Back from the Deep: The Strange Story of the Sister Subs* Squalus *and* Sculpin. Annapolis: Naval Institute Press, 1994.

Layton, Rear Admiral Edwin T. *"And I Was There:" Pearl Harbor and Midway—Breaking the Secrets.* New York: William Morrow and Company, 1985.

Lee, Bruce. *Marching Orders: The Untold Story of World War II.* New York: Crown Publishers, 1995.

Lens, Sidney. *Radicalism in America.* New York: Thomas Y. Crowell Company, 1969.

Lewin, Ronald. *The American Magic: Codes, Ciphers and the Defeat of Japan.* New York: Farrar Straus Giroux, 1982.

Lingeman, Richard R. *Don't You Know There's a War On? The American Home Front, 1941–1945.* New York: G. P. Putnam's Sons, 1970.

Lockwood, Charles A. *Down to the Sea in Subs.* New York: W. W. Norton & Company, 1967.

Lockwood, Charles A., and Hans Christian Adamson. *Through Hell and Deep Water.* New York: Greenberg Publisher, 1956.

Lomax, Eric. *The Railway Man: A True Story of War, Remembrance, and Forgiveness.* New York: Ballantine Books, 1996.

Manchester, William. *Goodbye Darkness: A Memoir of the Pacific War.* New York: Dell, 1979.

McAulay, Lex. *Battle of the Bismarck Sea.* New York: St. Martin's Press, 1991.

McCormack, Gavan, and Hank Nelson, eds. *The Burma-Thailand Railway: Memory and History.* Saint Leonards, New South Wales: Allen & Unwyn, 1993.

Mendenhall, Rear Admiral Corwin. *Submarine Diary: The Silent Stalking of Japan.* Annapolis: Naval Institute Press, 1991.

Morison, Samuel Eliot. *John Paul Jones: A Sailor's Biography.* Boston: Atlantic, Little, Brown & Company, 1959.

———. *History of United States Naval Operations in World War II,* vol. 3, *The Rising Sun in the Pacific.* Boston: Little, Brown and Company, 1948.

———. *History of United States Naval Operations in World War II,* vol. 4, *Coral Sea, Midway and Submarine Actions, May 1942–August 1942.* Boston: Little, Brown and Company, 1962.

———. *History of United States Naval Operations in World War II,* vol. 8, *New Guinea and the Marianas, March 1944–August 1944.* Boston: Little, Brown and Company, 1964.

———. *History of United States Naval Operations in World War II,* vol. 13, *The Liberation of the Philippines: Luzon, Mindanao, the Viscayas, 1944–1945.* Boston: Little, Brown and Company, 1963.

O'Kane, Richard H. *Clear the Bridge! The War Patrols of the U.S.S.* Tang. Novato, Calif.: Presidio Press, 1989.

———. Wahoo: *The Patrols of America's Most Famous World War II Submarine.* Novato, Calif.: Presidio Press, 1987.

Pack, Captain James. *Nelson's Blood: The Story of Naval Rum*. Annapolis: Naval Institute Press, 1995.

Padfield, Peter. *War beneath the Sea: Submarine Conflict during World War II*. New York: John Wiley & Sons, 1995.

Parillo, Mark P. *The Japanese Merchant Marine in World War II*. Annapolis: Naval Institute Press, 1993.

Prados, John. *Combined Fleet Decoded: The Secret History of American Intelligence and the Japanese Navy in World War II*. New York: Random House, 1995.

Richmond, Peter. *My Father's War: A Son's Journey*. New York: Simon & Schuster, 1996.

Roscoe, Theodore. *United States Submarine Operations in World War II*. Annapolis: United States Naval Institute, 1949.

Ruhe, Captain William J. *War in the Boats: My World War II Submarine Battles*. Washington: Brassey's, 1994.

Sasgen, Peter T. *Red Scorpion: The War Patrols of the USS Rasher*. Annapolis: Naval Institute Press, 1995.

Schratz, Paul R. *Submarine Commander: A Story of World War II and Korea*. New York: Pocket Books, 1990.

Skates, John Ray. *The Invasion of Japan: Alternative to the Bomb*. Columbia: University of South Carolina Press, 1994.

Stafford, Commander Edward P. *The Big E: The Story of the USS Enterprise*. New York: Dell Publishing Co., 1964.

Stripp, Alan. *Codebreaker in the Far East: How Britain Cracked Japan's Top Secret Military Codes*. New York: Oxford University Press, 1995.

Tanaka, Yuki. *Hidden Horrors: Japanese War Crimes in World War II*. Boulder, Colo.: Westview Press, 1996.

Terkel, Studs. *The Good War: An Oral History of World War Two*. New York: Pantheon Books, 1984.

Thompson, Captain Howard A. "A Special *Scabbardfish* Drink at Midway." *Polaris* 40, no. 4 (August 1996): 20.

Thompson, Kyle. *A Thousand Cups of Rice: Surviving the Death Railway*. Austin, Texas: Eakin Press, 1994.

Toland, John. *The Rising Sun: The Decline and Fall of the Japanese Empire, 1936–1945*. New York: Random House, 1970.

Walkowiak, Thomas F. *Fleet Submarines of World War Two*. Missoula, Mont.: Pictorial Histories Publishing Company, 1988.

Wall, Don. *Heroes at Sea*. Adelaide, South Australia: Griffin Press, 1991.

Waterford, Van. *Prisoners of the Japanese in World War II*. Jefferson, N.Car.: McFarland & Company, 1994.

Watson, Lyall. *Heaven's Breath: A Natural History of the Wind*. New York: William Morrow and Company, 1984.

Weir, Gary E. *Forged in War: The Naval-Industrial Complex and American Submarine Construction, 1940–1961*. Washington, D.C.: Department of the Navy, 1993.

Whitburn, Joel. *Top Pop Singles, 1940–1955*. Menominee Falls, Wisc.: Record Research, 1973.

Winslow, W. G. *The Ghost That Died in Sunda Strait*. Annapolis: Naval Institute Press, 1984.

Winton, John. *ULTRA in the Pacific: How Breaking Japanese Codes and Cyphers Affected Naval Operations against Japan, 1941–1945*. London: Leo Cooper, 1993.

Wolfe, William R. "Radio Transmitting Facility Closes," *Polaris* 40, no. 2 (April 1996): 10–11.

Woodbury, David O. *What the Citizen Should Know about Submarine Warfare*. New York: W. W. Norton & Company, 1942.

Y'Blood, William T. *Red Sun Setting: The Battle of the Philippine Sea*. Annapolis: Naval Institute Press, 1981.

Zim, Herbert S. *Submarines: The Story of Undersea Boats*. New York: Harcourt, Brace & Company, 1942.

## UNPUBLISHED SOURCES

National Archives and Records Administration (NARA)
  Records Group 38, Office of the Chief of Naval Operations, Operational Records Series (ONS).
  Records Group 457, Records of the National Security Agency/Central Security Service (SRNS), Japanese Navy Message Translations (SRN).
  USS *Pampanito*, War Patrol Reports, 1–6.
  USS *Grouper* (SS 214), Report of Twelfth War Patrol.
  Muster Roll of the Crew of the U.S.S. *Pampanito* (SS 383), 30 November 1943 to 1 October 1945.
  Annex to Patrol Report, "Rescue of British and Australian Prisoner-of-War Survivors," 28 September 1944.
  Patrol Report Annex: Names of British and Australian Survivors.
  Group Commander's (F. W. Fenno) Report of War Patrol, 28 October to 18 December 1944.
  Thomas. B. Oakley, Jr., Task Group 17.17 Patrol Report.
  Carter L. Bennett, Report of Coordinated Attack Group 17.14.
Naval Historical Center, Washington, D.C.
  Officer Biography Sheets
    William J. Bush
    Landon L. Davis, Jr.
    Frank W. Fenno, Jr.

     Francis M. Fives
     Howard T. Fulton
     Earl T. Hydeman
     Paul E. Summers
     Ted Neir Swain
Videotape: 1985 *Pampanito* Reunion, San Francisco.
University of Wyoming American Heritage Center. Clay Blair, Jr., Papers.
    Audiotape Interviews with Clay Blair:
     Maurice L. Demers
     Peder A. Granum
     Anthony C. Hauptman
     Charles A. McGuire, Jr.
     Richard J. Sherlock
     Paul E. Summers
     Ted Nier Swain
     William F. Yagemann
Audiotape Interviews with Author:
    Robert Bennett, March 1996
    Cliff L. Farlow, March 1997
    Harold D. Martin, February 1997
    Charles A. McGuire, Jr., March 1996, May 1997
In-Person Interviews with Author:
    Norman J. Arcement, 3 November 1996, 6 November 1996
    Robert Bennett, 4 November 1996
    Hubert Brown, 13 April 1996
    Walter H. Cordon, 4 November 1996
    Ona D. Hawkins, 4 November 1996
    Gordon Hopper, 3 November 1996
    Walter R. Madison, 21 July 1997
    Frank B. Michno
    Paul Pappas, 12 April 1996
    Spencer Stimler, 3 November 1996
    Albert Van Atta, Jr., 19 April 1996
    Roger Walters, 4 November 1996
    Earl Watkins, 13 April 1996
    Woodrow Weaver, 4 November 1996, 6 November 1996
Phone Interviews with Author:
    Daniel M. Bialko, 25 July 1996
    Walter H. Cordon, 3 January 1996
    George Debo, 21 February 1996
    Joseph Eichner, 11 February 1996
    Clyde B. Markham, 7 March 1996

William McClaskey, 10 March 1996
Tony McGehee, 21 December 1997
Paul Pappas, 27 February 1996, 18 June 1996
Clarence Williams, 18 January 1997
John E. Wilson, Jr., 29 January 1996
Correspondence with Author:
  John D. Alden, 8 July 1997, 18 February 1998
  Ralph W. Attaway, 6 May 1996
  Robert Bennett, 6 May 1996
  Jacques Bouchard, January 1996
  William L. Bruckart, 28 April 1996, 6 July 1996, 21 July 1996, 2 February 1997
  Clarence Carmody, 6 May 1996, 16 May 1996, 3 June 1996
  Harold L. Chinn, January 1996
  Fredric B. Clarke, 17 August 1996
  Roydon C. Cornford, January 1997
  Mrs. Andrew L. Currier, 9 January 1996
  Joseph Eichner, 5 July 1996
  Cliff L. Farlow, 17 March 1997
  M. R. Farrands, 20 February 1997, 14 March 1997
  Donald I. Ferguson, 14 February 1996
  William C. Grady, 1 August 1996, 22 August 1996, 11 September 1996
  Ona D. Hawkins, 19 February 1996
  Mrs. James S. Heist, 26 February 1996
  John R. Hocking, 22 May 1997
  Gordon Hopper, 23 January 1996, 20 May 1996, 20 June 1996, 3 March 1997
  Frank J. Lederer, 4 February 1996
  Renard J. Lombardi, March 1996
  Lloyd MacVane, January 1996
  Walter R. Madison, 15 April 1996, 21 May 1996
  Harold D. Martin, 10 February 1997
  William H. McCollum, 22 February 1996, 6 April 1996
  Tony McGehee, January 1997
  Rob Roy McGregor, January 1997
  Charles A. McGuire, Jr., 23 December 1995
  George E. Moffett, February 1996, March 1996, May 1996
  Lawrence E. Noker, 24 March 1996
  Walter H. Richter, 22 June 1996, 10 October 1996
  Arnold W. Schade, 6 March 1997
  Richard J. Sherlock, 10 February 1996, 18 February 1996, 17 May, 1996
  Wendell T. Smith, Jr., 19 April 1996
  Spencer Stimler, 12 July 1996, 22 July 1996, 3 August 1996, 15 August 1996, 11
      September 1996, 20 September 1996, 24 September 1996, 8 October 1996

Edmund Stockslader, 8 September 1996

Ted Swain, 1 May 1996

Albert Van Atta, Jr., 1 March 1996, 20 October 1996

Don Wall, 13 March 1997

Roger M. Walters, 7 February 1996, 23 February 1996, 4 March 1996, 29 March 1996, 13 May 1996, 18 June 1996

Earl Watkins, 21 January 1996

Ken Williams, February 1997, 25 February 1997, 19 March 1997

Woodrow Weaver, 2 February 1996, 29 February 1996, 17 March 1996, 1 April 1996, 1 June 1996, 18 June 1996, 2 July 1996, 24 July 1996, 12 September 1996, 1 October 1996, 28 December 1996, 7 February 1997

Personal Papers:

Gordon Hopper, "*Pampanito* Recollections—the Boat, the Crew, the Experiences, 1993." Typed manuscript (photocopy).

Paul Pappas, "Diary," 2 September 1943 to 3 May 1945.

Woodrow Weaver, "Life Story of Woodrow W. Weaver, 1995." Typed manuscript (photocopy).

Capt. Harry L. Pence, USN. Mandeville Special Collections Department, University of California San Diego Library, La Jolla, California.

# Index